ELECTRONIC DATA REFERENCE MANUAL

ELECTRONIC DATA REFERENCE MANUAL

Matthew Mandl

Reston Publishing Company, Inc., Reston, Virginia
A Prentice-Hall Company

Library of Congress Cataloging in Publication Data

Mandl, Matthew.
Electronic data reference manual.

Includes index.
1. Electronics–Handbooks, manuals, etc. I. Title.
TK7825.M25 621.381 79-12681
ISBN 0-8359-1641-3

A Prentice-Hall Company
Reston, Virginia 22090

10 9 8 7 6 5 4 3 2 1

Printed in the United States of America

To my niece
DORIS E. NICHOLSON
who has earned my
gratitude for being an
excellent typist, a good
speller, and a hard, yet
congenial, worker.

Contents

Preface, ix

Chapter 1. Signals, Phase, and Distortion, 1

Chapter 2. Electronic Symbols and Color Codes, 11

Chapter 3. Electronic Units, Terms, and Applications, 25

Chapter 4. Basic Component Combinations and Equations, 69

Chapter 5. Transistors, Bias, and Circuit Formations, 104

Chapter 6. Basic Linear Circuitry, 130

Chapter 7. AM, FM, TV, and CB Listings, 145

Chapter 8. Digital Data, 156

Chapter 9. Digital Circuits, 163

Chapter 10. Integrated Circuits, 172

Chapter 11. Power Supplies and Oscillators, 184

Chapter 12. RF Transmission Lines and Antennas, 196

Chapter 13. Vectors and Phase Relationships, 229

Chapter 14. Miscellaneous Tables and Related Information, 247

Chapter 15. Miscellaneous Information and Data, 274

Chapter 16. Modulation Data, 304

Index, 319

Preface

This manual contains a wide variety of data often needed by electronic or electric engineers, technicians, and students. It contains numerous basic equations, circuit explanations, tables, graphs, solid-state theory, design factors, as well as data on lasers, holograms, integrated circuitry, digital circuits and techniques, modulation types, antennas, symbols, color codes, and other related explanations and illustrations of electronic components and systems.

In a theory textbook the subject matter is usually arranged in a sequential manner in order of difficulty. For a reference manual such as this, however, topic groupings are chosen for the reader's convenience in referencing a primary topic as well as related material of a secondary nature. Thus, the first chapter contains information on signal types, phase relationships, and distortion data. The next two chapters cover symbols, color codes, units, terms, and applications. The basic aspects of component combinations and related equations are given in Chapter 4.

The fundamental nature of transistors, bias, and circuit formations are covered in Chapter 5. In Chapter 6 the operational attributes and applications of linear circuits are discussed. Chapter 7 contains listings of public entertainment frequency assignments, as well as CB and amateur information. Digital data and circuitry are found in Chapters 9 and 10, while power supplies and oscillators are explained in Chapter 11. Coverage of transmission-line factors and antenna theory and design are in Chapter 12.

The remaining chapters cover a significant range of topics including vectors and phase relationships in Chapter 13, miscellaneous tables and related facts in Chapter 14, and high fidelity terms in Chapter 15. Chapter 16 covers such items as AM, FM, telemetry, and pulse-code modulation.

There are numerous cross-references throughout the text to enable the reader to inspect associated topics while consulting a section of this book, but the greatest benefit will be obtained by referring to the Index in order to locate particular data.

MATTHEW MANDL

1

Signals, Phase, and Distortion

1-1. SINEWAVES AND *E-I* PHASE

The type signal produced by alternating-current (ac) generators and supplied to homes and factories is the *sinewave*, illustrated in Fig. 1-1A. When unadulterated by other signals or waveforms, the pure sinewave has some specific characteristics. The voltage (or current) rises to a positive-polarity peak with a gradual unbroken incline and drops to zero with a gradual decline. Next the sinewave repeats the process for a negative-polarity signal as shown. Each positive or negative change (from zero to peak to zero) is termed an *alternation*, and two alternations form a complete *cycle*. The number of times a cycle is repeated per second is termed the *hertz* (Hz). Thus, if a cycle repeats itself 60 times per second it is designated as a 60-Hz signal. When such a signal is generated by an electronic test instrument, it may range into the thousands of cycles (kHz), or millions (MHz).

The pure sinewave has a positive peak amplitude with the same value as the negative peak amplitude, and each alternation has the same duration as the other. The equivalent voltage (or current) of ac that does the same amount of work as direct current (dc) is referred to as the effective value or root-mean-square value (rms). The effective value is found by multiplying the peak value by 0.707. Knowing effective value, the peak can be found by multiplying the rms value by 1.41.

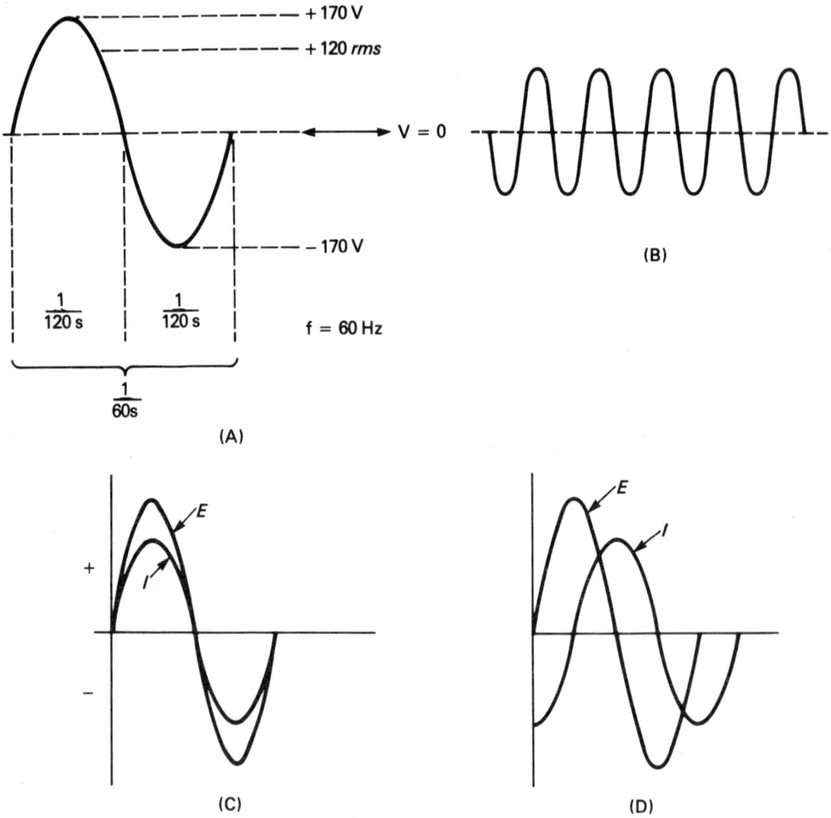

FIGURE 1-1. Sinewaves and phase.

A train of successive sinewaves is depicted in Fig. 1-1B, and a comparison between the voltage and current amplitudes of ac is shown in Fig. 1-1C. If no inductances or capacitances are in the circuit to create reactances or impedances, the voltage and current peaks would coincide for both alternations as shown, with both the voltage and current reaching zero levels simultaneously. For a given voltage the amplitude may remain fixed, though the current depends on the amount of resistance in the circuit. Though the current amplitude in Fig. 1-1C is shown at a lower peak level than the voltage, there are numerous occasions where the current levels are higher than voltage. For the waveforms in Fig. 1-1C, the *E* and *I* are *in phase*.

When reactive components are in ac circuits the phase between voltage and current will change from zero to some value depending on the amount of either inductive or capacitive reactance present. Thus, an *out-of-phase* condition occurs, as shown in Fig. 1-1D. Here the positive voltage peak precedes the positive current peak; hence the voltage *leads* the current. This phase difference could also be expressed as the current *lagging* the voltage. When inductive reactance predominates in a circuit, voltage leads. With a predominating capacitive reactance, current would lead and voltage lag. When there is a phase difference between E and I the power equation $P = EI$ is termed the *apparent* power, and the true power is found by multiplying the apparent power by the cosine of the angle between current and voltage. Thus if voltage is 30 and current .02 amperes, with a phase difference of 36.87°, the true power is: $P_t = EI\cos\theta = 30 \times .02 \times 0.8 = 0.48$ W.

1-2. SIGNAL-VOLTAGE PHASE FACTORS

In addition to the phase relationships discussed in Section 1-1 for voltage and current, similar conditions occur between signal voltages as shown in Fig. 1-2. (Similarly, signal-current phase differences can be illustrated without referencing voltages.) Voltages, when in phase in circuitry processing them, will be additive as shown at A for in-phase potentials. Here one signal has a potential of 12.5 V and the other 10 V. Because both signals are in phase, simple addition provides the total peak potential of 22.5 V.

Figure 1-1B shows two voltages having the same amplitude but out of phase. Here E_1 and E_2 are additive when both have a positive polarity at any instant in time, but subtractive when one is out of phase with the other at any instant. Thus, even though each potential has a 10-V amplitude, the total peak potential is only 14 V. As also shown in Fig. 1-1B, similar factors relate to the negative potentials. Also, for either Fig. 1-1A or B more than two voltages could be involved.

Two potentials having unequal values and also out of phase are shown in Fig. 1-1C. Here one waveform has a 15-V value and the other a 10-V value. Again, where positive conditions prevail for both voltages, addition occurs, and for dissimilar polarities subtraction occurs. The result, for the particular phases and potentials shown in Fig. 1-1C, is a 17.5-V total peak voltage. Again, more than two such voltages could be involved, and the same principles apply for finding the total voltage of the individual potentials.

For the three examples of phase relationship factors regarding signal voltages shown in parts A, B, and C of Fig. 1-2 the frequency of each signal voltage was identical, even though phase differences or voltage value differences prevailed. When voltages are of different frequencies the higher-frequency signals present a more rapid polarity change with respect to the lower-frequency signals, hence the total-voltage signal (sometimes

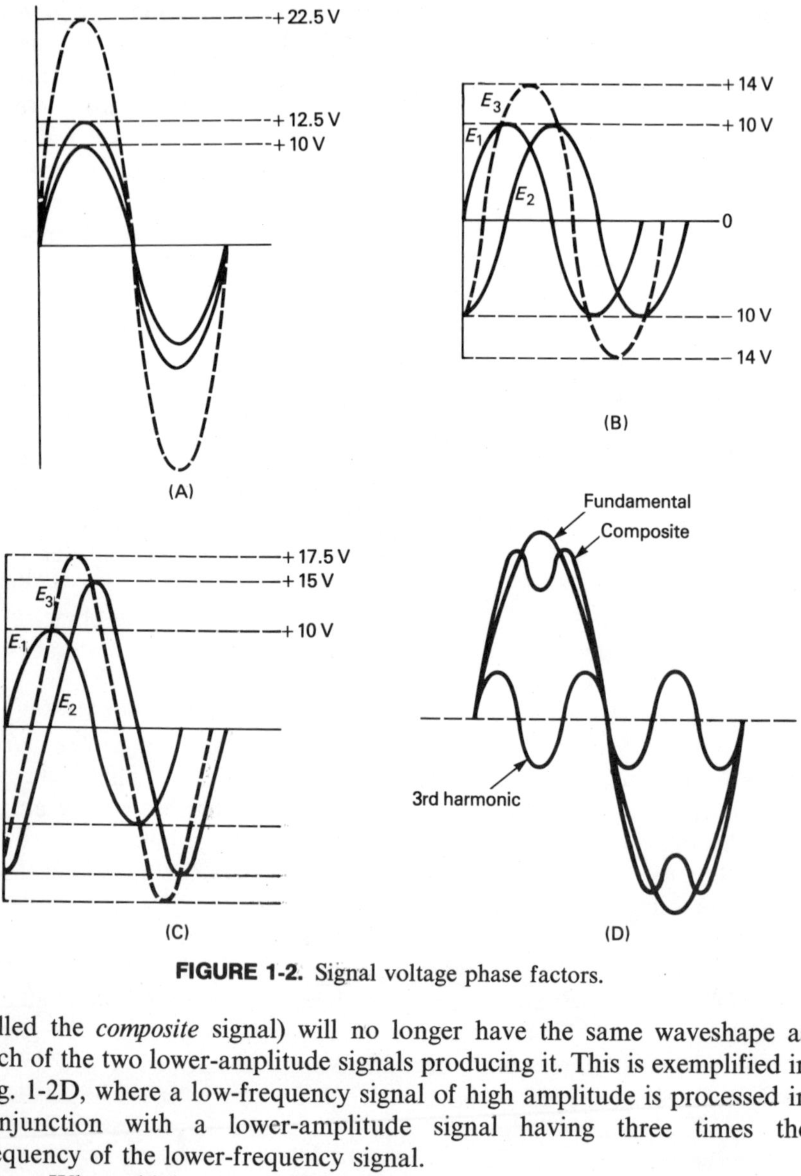

FIGURE 1-2. Signal voltage phase factors.

called the *composite* signal) will no longer have the same waveshape as each of the two lower-amplitude signals producing it. This is exemplified in Fig. 1-2D, where a low-frequency signal of high amplitude is processed in conjunction with a lower-amplitude signal having three times the frequency of the lower-frequency signal.

When higher-frequency signals are multiples of the lowest-frequency signal, they are termed *harmonics*. (In music they are called *overtones* in relation to the fundamental tone being generated by a musical instrument.) The lowest-frequency signal is termed the *fundamental*, as designated in Fig. 1-2D. Again, because of the additive function when of same polarity and the subtractive process when of different polarities, a resultant signal is produced. Now, however, the total amplitude does not exceed either of the two producing it. A dip occurs at the center of each alternation of the composite because the third-harmonic signal has a negative polarity at this time and opposes the peak of the fundamental signal. Thus, the resultant (composite) waveform somewhat resembles a sinewave except for the drop in amplitude at both the negative and positive peaks that produce the amplitude dips shown in Fig. 1-2D.

1-3. DISTORTION TYPES

Of significance with respect to the composite waveform shown in part D of Fig. 1-2 is the different terminology references for this particular signal for two different sets of conditions. Assume, for instance, that a pure sinewave is applied to an amplifier, but during the signal processing the amplifier generates another signal having a frequency three times that of the one being processed. Though such a generated signal may have a low amplitude, it can mix with the incoming signal. When this mixture of an unwanted third harmonic with the input signal occurs, the composite waveform shown in Fig. 1-2D would be obtained at the output. Now such a signal is referred to as a *distorted signal* because of the presence of the undesired third harmonic and its consequent modification of the input signal's waveshape.

Such distortion occurs in nonlinear amplification or during signal overload. If, on the other hand, the composite signal shown in Fig. 1-2D (with its positive and negative dips at the peaks) were applied to an amplifier and duly processed without any generation of additional signals, the output would be an amplified version of the composite signal. However, because the *same signal appeared at the output* as had been entered into the input, no distortion occurs, and the output signal is now termed an *undistorted signal*. Essentially, any signal deviating from a basic type could be considered a distorted signal, but the reference only applies if the signal being processed by an amplifier undergoes a waveshape change in addition to the normal amplitude change or the 180° phase reversal over a circuit such as the grounded emitter.

If the output signal from the amplifier is disturbed by the addition of any harmonic components, it is termed *harmonic distortion*. Other types of distortion include frequency and phase distortion as well as intermodulation distortion. Frequency distortion is the type that occurs when signals of some frequencies are not amplified to the same degree as others. A typical example is the attenuation of base-tone signals when a coupling capacitor is utilized, or a decrease in the amplitude of high-frequency signals because of distributed and shunt capacitances in the circuit.

Phase distortion occurs when a few signals of a group being amplified undergo a phase change. Thus, in video amplification (where signals may range up to 4 MHz) the higher-frequency signals will encounter a significant reactance in lead inductance, and a phase shift may occur. This could distort the fine details of the picture being displayed on a television screen. Similar phase shifting could occur for higher-frequency signals encountering distributed and shunt capacitances that have a negligible effect on lower-frequency signals.

Intermodulation distortion occurs when two RF carriers intermix and produce interfering signals. A typical example is a radio receiver tuned to a particular station but also picking up an unwanted station that is being received either because of poor receiver selectivity or because of excessive signal input from a nearby station. The two carriers can undergo a mixing process in the tuner and by heterodyning cause an interference signal output.

1-4. WAVEFORM VARIATIONS

Various other waveforms are illustrated in Fig. 1-3. A sawtooth train of signals is shown in part A. These are characterized by a gradual voltage or current incline to a predetermined peak followed by an abrupt decline. Successive waveforms in sequence resemble the teeth of a saw, hence the terminology. The sawtooth waves are extensively used in sweep applications in television, radar, and test-instrument oscilloscope usages. For electrostatic deflection, a sawtooth of voltage is impressed across deflecting plates, and as the sawtooth rises one plate becomes more positive than the other and attracts the electron beam. Thus the electron beam scans across the phosphor-coated inner surface of a picture tube and traces out an image. When the beam has swept across the tube, the decline of the sawtooth pulls the beam back to its starting position. For vertical deflection, a similar system is used for a pair of plates at right angles to the other. For magnetic deflection, as used in television receivers, current sawtooth waveforms are used. For the sawtooth waves shown at A, the amplitude is positive going from a zero reference level. Negative-going sawtooth waves, could, of course, also be utilized.

A train of squarewaves is shown in Fig. 1-3B, and here both positive and negative alternations occur as with a sinewave. Squarewaves of this type are composed of a fundamental-frequency signal plus a succession of diminishing amplitude odd harmonics. Thus, the third harmonic would have one-third the amplitude of the fundamental, the fifth harmonic would have one-fifth the amplitude, the seventh only one-seventh the amplitude, and so forth. The squarewaves shown could have higher positive and

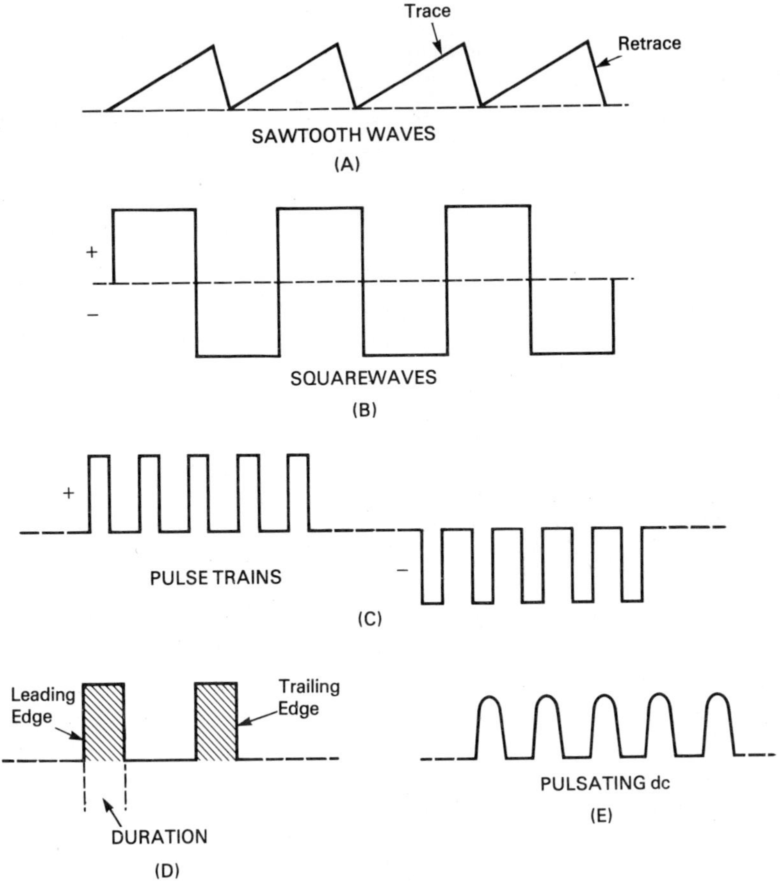

FIGURE 1-3. Various waveforms.

negative peaks, or the duration of each alternation could be changed from that shown. The duration of successive alternations, of course, depends on the frequency.

A train of pulses having a positive polarity is shown in Fig. 1-3C, as well as a negative pulse train for comparison purposes. Pulses are made up of a fundamental plus a series of both odd and even harmonics. Higher-frequency signal components contribute to the sharp leading and trailing edges as well as the sharp change of voltage as it rises to the flat top. Unlike squarewaves, the duration of pulses is not related to frequency. Thus, as shown in Fig. 1-3D, the duration of a pulse for a given number of pulses per second (pps) may be very short or may be long enough to almost close the gap between successive pulses. Pulses that have lost some of the high-frequency components have rounded areas at their peak amplitudes, as shown in Fig. 1-3E. Such a train of signals is also termed *pulsating dc*, as encountered in half-wave rectification. (Full-wave rectification patterns are shown in the next section.)

1-5. OSCILLOSCOPE PATTERNS

Waveshapes and signals of all types can be examined by utilizing an oscilloscope to display the signal pattern obtained at a specific point on the circuit. Oscilloscopes are also useful for observation of phase differences. For two signals having the same frequency, for instance, one can be applied to the vertical input and the other to the horizontal input. Hence if two sinewaves are utilized, the signal injected into the horizontal input serves as the sweep voltage for the signal applied to the vertical input. When the two signals are of the same frequency and are in phase, a slanting line appears as shown in Fig. 1-4. As the phase changes between the two signals, the slanting line will change into an oval, a circle for a 90° phase difference, and again an oval with a different tilt from that obtained for 45°, and finally a single line for 180°, as shown. When one signal has a frequency twice that of the other, a figure-eight pattern is obtained as

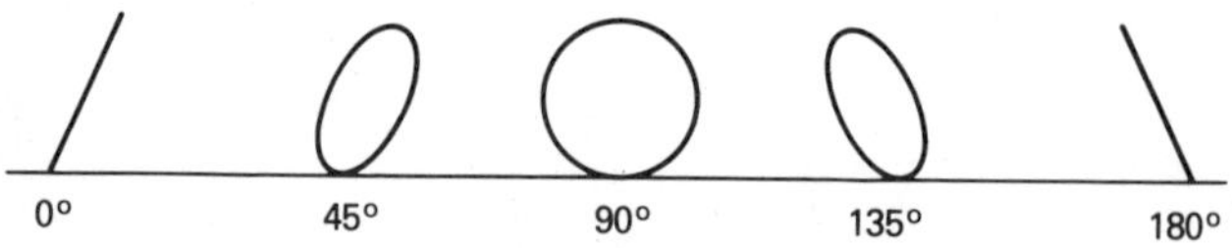

FIGURE 1-4. Phase patterns for two signals of the same frequency.

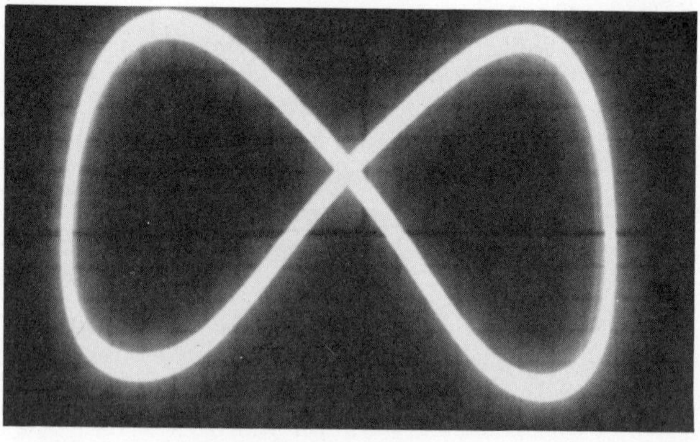

FIGURE 1-5. Lissajous pattern.

shown in Fig. 1-5. The display will be in a vertical position when the vertical input signal and the horizontal input signal are exchanged. Multiple loops appear for higher signal frequencies. For a frequency difference of three-to-one, three loops would be shown.

A representative display of a squarewave is shown in Fig. 1-6. Since the rise and fall of the waveform occurs at an extremely rapid rate, a fainter and more narrow image is obtained for the vertical scanning lines. For the low-frequency flat sections, a more visible waveform is obtained. Notice the slight imperfection visible at the trailing edge, where some curvature occurs. Such distortion denotes some high-frequency signal loss. Pulsating dc is shown in Fig. 1-7, and this is the type obtained from a full-wave rectifier in contrast to the half-wave pulsating dc shown earlier in Fig. 1-3E. Thus, for the full-wave type in Fig. 1-7, successive alternations of ac are converted to a unidirectional series of pulses as shown.

In oscilloscopes equipped to produce them, dual-trace displays are useful for signal-comparison purposes. A typical example is shown in Fig. 1-8, where two signal trains of different amplitudes are on display. Here, the frequency is identical for each but the amplitudes differ. Dual displays of this type are particularly useful in testing stereo amplifiers where the same amplitude pulse is inserted into each channel and the scope display is obtained from the output. Uneven amplification or distortion can thus be observed. With scope displays of this type it is difficult to judge whether or

FIGURE 1-6. Square waveform.

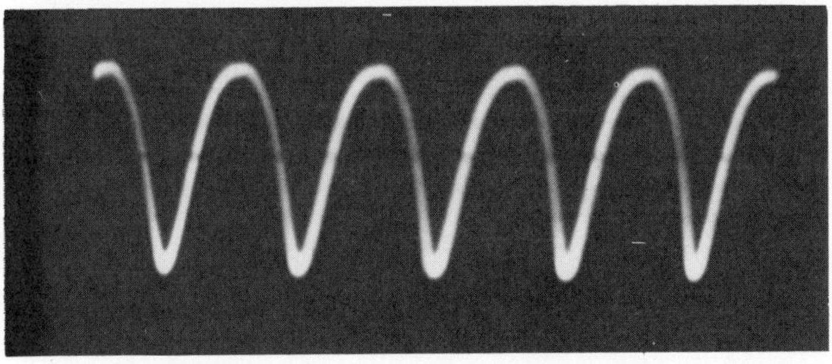

FIGURE 1-7. Pulsating dc (full wave).

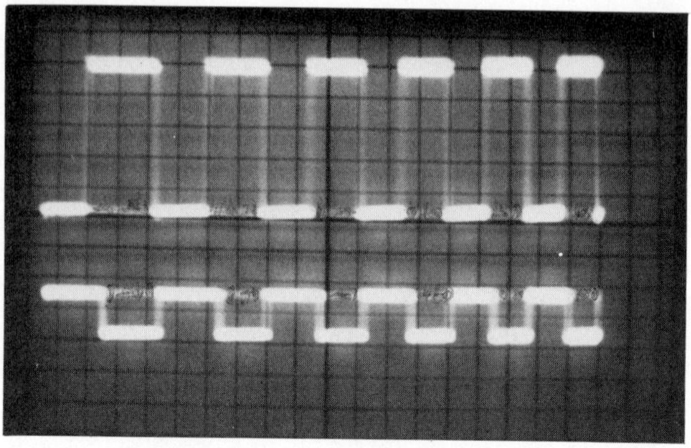

FIGURE 1-8. Dual-trace scope display.

not squarewaves or pulses are being displayed since no zero reference line is present. For pulse trains with short duration pulses and longer intervals between, identification is more readily accomplished. Generally, however, the nature of the injected signal is known and the primary purpose is for comparisons of amplitude and waveshape between the output signals processed by separate circuits.

2

Electronic Symbols and Color Codes

2-1. LETTER SYMBOLS

A wide variety of letter symbols are used in solid-state electronics as a convenience for indicating certain values, conditions, characteristics, or circuit parameter references. Table 2-1 is a general list of miscellaneous abbreviations and symbols, while Tables 2-2 and 2-3 relate primarily to junction transistors and FET units. The letter symbols, however, are not exclusive to a particular category, and hence various symbols in the following tables are often used in reference to either the junction transistor or the FET.

In Table 2-2, the subscript letters that are capitalized indicate dc or static conditions; for example, h_{FE} and h_{FB}. (On occasion, the first letter may appear as an uppercase one, as H_{FE}. Lower-case subscripts refer to ac signal-current ratios (h_{fe}, h_{fb}, etc.).)

TABLE 2-1. Miscellaneous Abbreviations and Symbols

α	(*alpha*) current gain in transistors
A	ampere, amplification
ac	alternating current
AF	audio frequency
AGC	automatic gain control
AVC	automatic volume control
B	bel (ratio of powers, voltages, currents), susceptance
β	(*beta*) feedback voltage, transistor current gain
BFO	beat-frequency oscillator
C	capacitance, capacitor
°C	degrees Celsius
cgs	centimeter-gram-second system
C_i	input capacitance
CW	continuous wave
dB	decibel (commonly used term; equal to one-tenth of a bel)
dc	direct current
dt	change in time
emf	electromotive force
ϵ	(*epsilon*) natural base log (2.7183)
ERP	effective radiated power
F	farad of capacitance
°F	degrees Fahrenheit
f_∞	frequency of infinite attenuation
f_c	cutoff frequency
FET	field-effect transistor
FM	frequency modulation
f_r	resonant frequency
G	conductance, giga as in gigahertz (GHz)
g_m	mutual conductance (transconductance) of tubes and field-effect transistors
H	henry (magnetizing flux)
Hz	hertz (frequency in cycles per *s*)
I	current
I_c	capacitive current
i_c	instantaneous capacitive current
ICW	interrupted continuous waves
IF	intermediate frequency
IGFET	Insulated-gate field-effect transistor
I_L	inductive current
i_L	instantaneous inductive current
I_m	maximum current

TABLE 2-1. (*Continued*)

I_p	plate current (primary I)
I_R	current through resistance
i_R	instantaneous resistive current
I_s	secondary current
I_T	total current
j	imaginary-number operator in rectangular notation
J	joule (work, energy, etc.)
JFET	Junction field-effect transistor
k	coefficient of coupling, dielectric constant
°K	degrees Kelvin
kHz	kilohertz (frequency in thousands of cycles per second)
λ	(*lambda*) wavelength
L	inductance, inductor
LC	inductance-capacitance
LCR	inductance-capacitance-resistance
LDR	light-dependent resistor
LED	light-emitting diode
LSI	large-scale integration (of circuitry)
L_T	total inductance
m	a constant used in filter design, also *milli*
M	mutual inductance
mH	millihenry
MHz	megahertz (frequency in millions of cycles per second)
mks	meter-kilogram-second system
MOSFET	metallic-oxide semiconductor field-effect transistor
μ	(*mu*) micro (as in μF), also amplification factor
N_p	number of turns in primary
N_s	number of turns in secondary
ω	(*omega*) angular velocity (6.28f)
Ω	(*omega*) ohms
π	(*pi*) 3.1416
p	pico, as in picofarads (pF)
P	power, watt
P_{ap}	apparent power
P_{av}	average power
P_{eff}	percentage of efficiency
P.E.P.	peak envelope power
Q	charge, quality, coulomb
R	resistor, resistance
RF	radio frequency

TABLE 2-1. (*Continued*)

R-F-C	radio-frequency choke
R_L	load resistance or load resistor
rms	root mean square
rpm	revolutions per minute
SCR	silicon-controlled rectifier
SHF	super-high frequency
SSB	single sideband
SW	short wave, switch
SWR	standing-wave ratio
VSWR	voltage standing-wave ratio
τ	(*tau*) time constant
t	time
TV	television
θ	(*theta*) phase angle
UHF	ultra high frequency
V	volt, voltage
VHF	very high frequency
V/m	volt per meter (field strength)
V_p	pinch-off voltage (or V_{po})
VU	volume unit
W	watt, power
X	reactance
X_C	capacitive reactance
X_L	inductive reactance
Y	admittance
Y_{11}	FET input impedance parameter
Y_{12}	FET reverse-transfer admittance
Y_{21}	FET forward-transfer admittance
Y_{22}	FET output admittance parameter
Z	impedance
Z_L	load impedance
Z_o	characteristic impedance (surge impedance)
Z_p	primary impedance
Z_s	secondary impedance
Z_T	total impedance

TABLE 2-2. Bipolar Parameter Symbols

h_{fe}	Common emitter	Small-signal forward current transfer ratio
h_{fb}	Common base	
h_{fc}	Common collector	
h_{FE}	Common emitter dc forward-current transfer ratio	
h_{FB}	Common base dc forward-current transfer ratio	
h_{ib}	Common base	Small-signal input impedance
h_{ic}	Common collector	
h_{ie}	Common emitter	
h_{oe}	Common emitter	Output admittance
h_{ob}	Common base	
h_{oc}	Common collector	
h_{re}	Common emitter	Small-signal reverse voltage transfer ratio
h_{rc}	Common collector	
h_{rb}	Common base	
I_c	Collector current (rms)	
i_c	Collector current (instantaneous)	
I_b	Base current (rms)	
i_b	Base current (instantaneous)	
I_e	Emitter current (rms)	
i_e	Emitter current (instantaneous)	
BV	Breakdown voltage	
V_{EB}	Emitter-base voltage	
V_{CE}	Collector-emitter voltage	
V_{CB}	Collector-base voltage	

TABLE 2-3. Miscellaneous FET Symbols

Symbol	Representation	Explanation
V_{DD}	Drain voltage (high)	Most positive voltage applied to unit, such as +9V
V_{SS}	Source voltage	Most negative supply potential applied and used as reference for other voltages (generally indicative of ground reference)
V_{IH}	Input voltage (high)	High-logic level range of input V
V_{IL}	Input voltage (low)	Low-logic level range of input V
V_{IH}(min)	Minimum input voltage (high)	Minimum permitted input high-logic level

TABLE 2-3. (*Continued*)

V_{IL}(max)	Maximum input voltage (low)	Maximum permitted input low-logic level
V_{OH}	Output voltage (high)	Range of voltages at output terminal with specified output load and given supply potential (Inputs conditioned for high-logic level at output)
V_{OL}	Output voltage (low)	Range of voltages at output terminal with specified output load and a given value of supply potential (Unit inputs are set for low-logic level at output)
I_{IN}	Input current	Current flow into unit at a given input voltage and V_{DD}
I_{OH}	Output current (high)	Drive flow out of unit at given output voltage (logic high) and V_{DD}
I_{OL}	Output current (low)	Drive current flow into unit at given output E (logic low) and V_{DD}
I_{DD}	Quiescent value of supply source I	Current flow into drain terminal at given input signal and established V_{DD} values
t_{TLH}	Transition time, low to high	Time between two specified reference points (usually given between 10 and 90 percent) on a waveform change from low to high
t_{THL}	Transition time, high to low	Time between two specified reference points (usually 90 and 10 percent) on a waveform changing from high to low

2-2. GRAPHIC SYMBOLS

Various symbols are used to designate components and transistors in electronics as shown in Figs. 2-1 through 2-7. Most of these have found general acceptance throughout the industry, though variations will be found among some manufacturers. Since characteristics for components and transistors vary considerably, the manufacturer's ratings, parameters, and characteristics should be consulted for data on particular types.

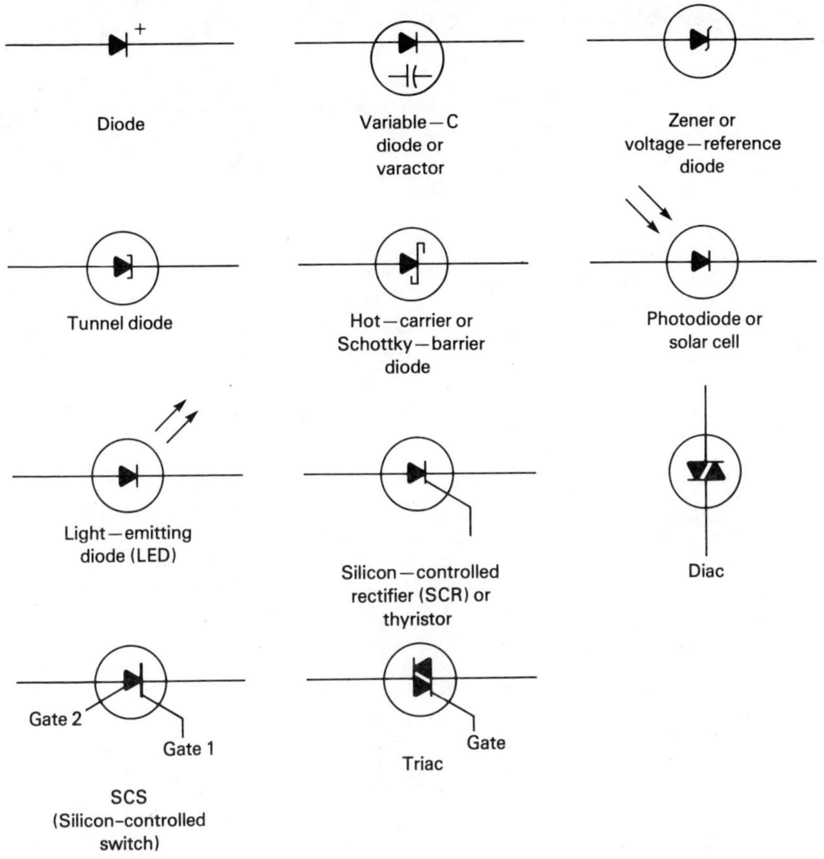

FIGURE 2-1. Diode symbols.

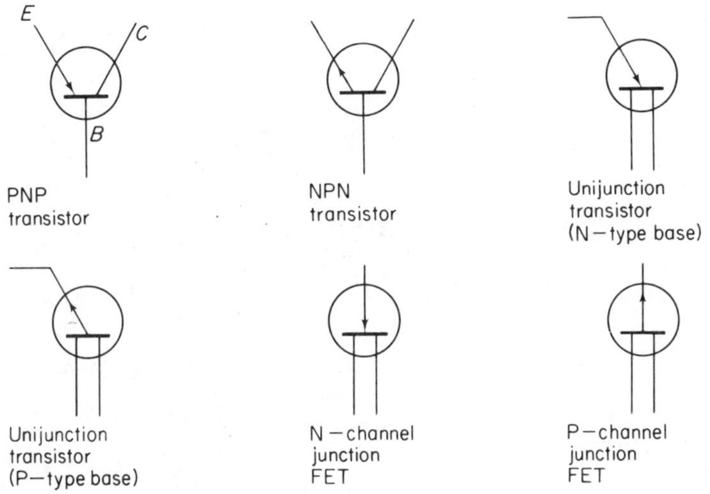

FIGURE 2-2. Basic transistor types.

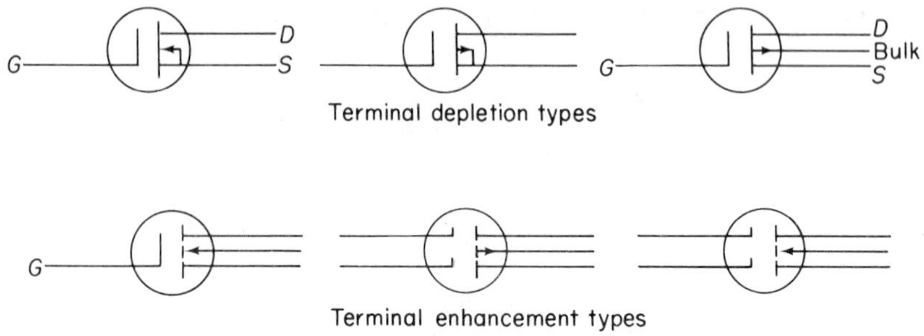

FIGURE 2-3. IGFETs (see also Fig. 5-5).

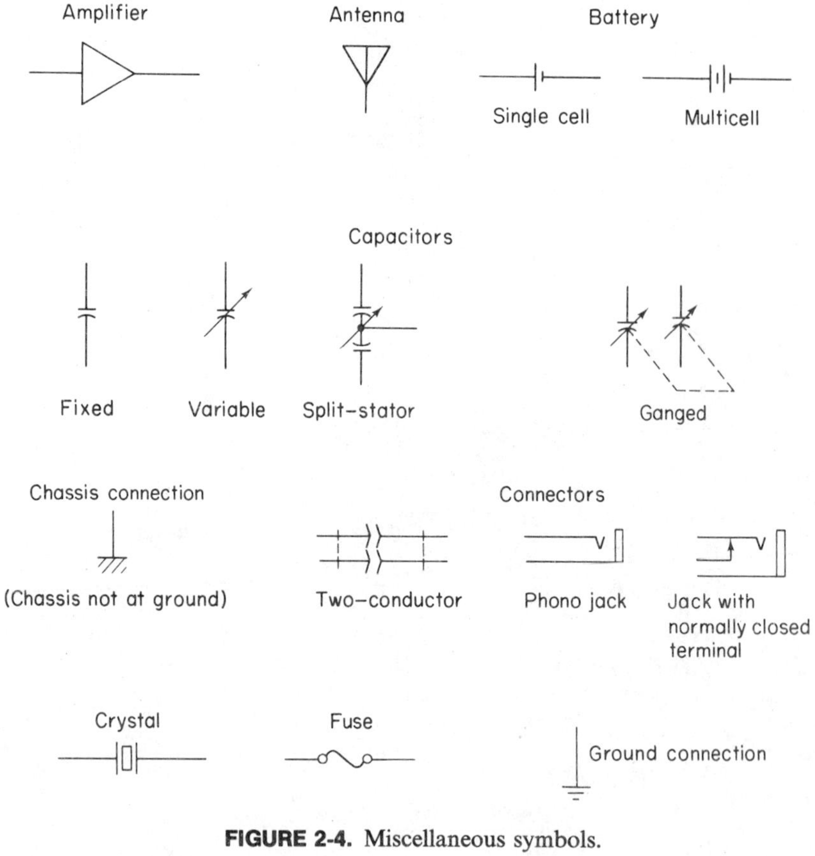

FIGURE 2-4. Miscellaneous symbols.

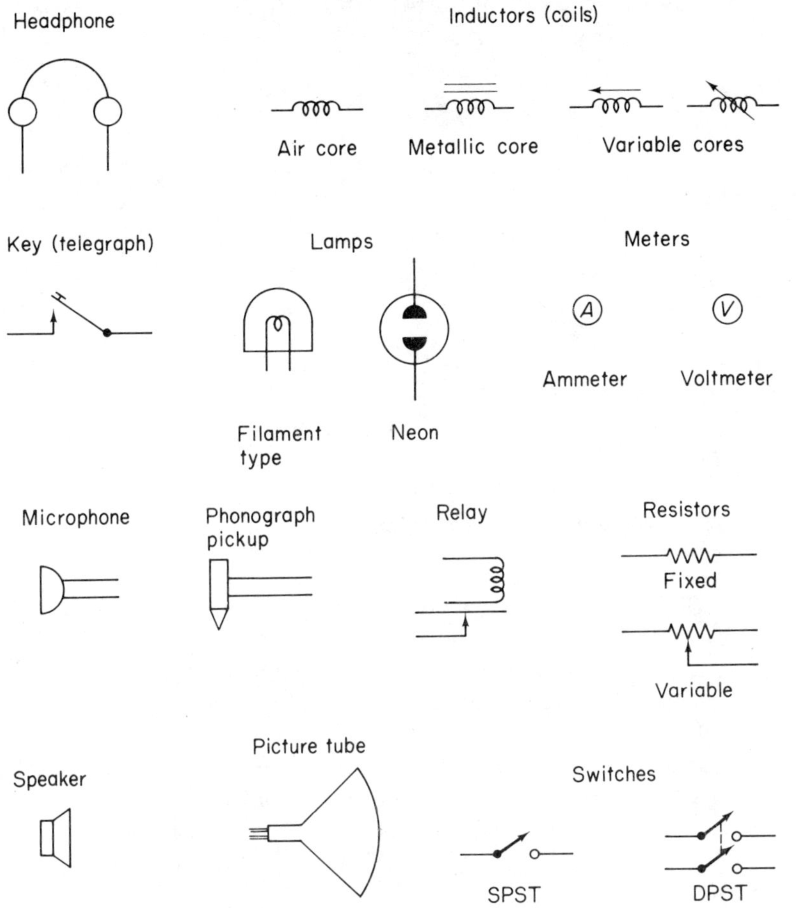

FIGURE 2-5. Miscellaneous symbols.

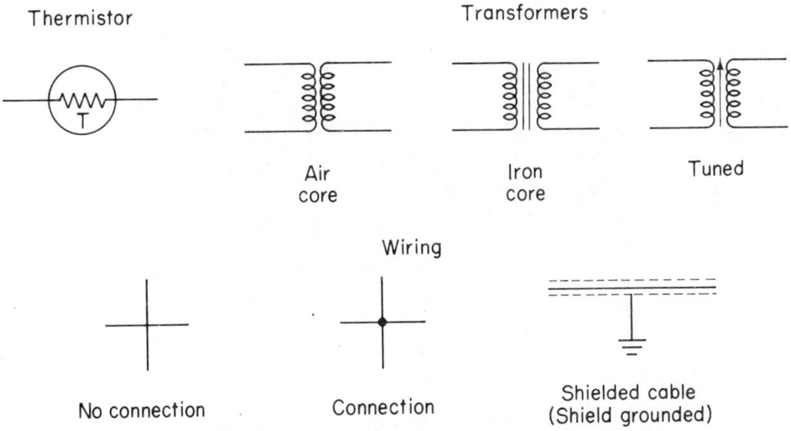

FIGURE 2-6. Miscellaneous symbols.

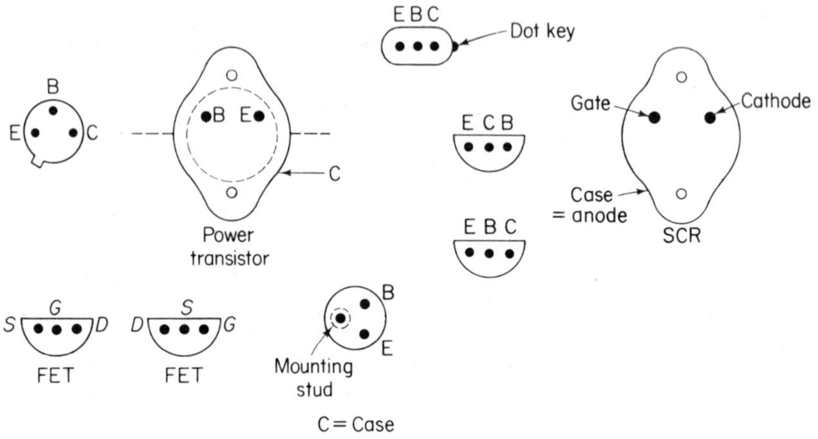

FIGURE 2-7. Typical solid-state leau identification.

2-3. RESISTOR COLOR CODING

Resistors of the molded composition type shown in Fig. 2-8 have colored encircling bands grouped at one end. The color coding for the resistors shown is read from left to right. Usually, four bands of color are present for the carbon composition type resistors, five bands for the film types. In either case, the last color denotes the *tolerance* that must be applied to the value obtained from reading the initial bands. Thus, if a rated 100-Ω resistor had a tolerance of 10 percent, its actual value could range from 90 to 110 Ω.

Table 2-4 indicates the color-code values and tolerances that apply to the carbon and film resistors shown in Fig. 2-8. The abbreviation GMV

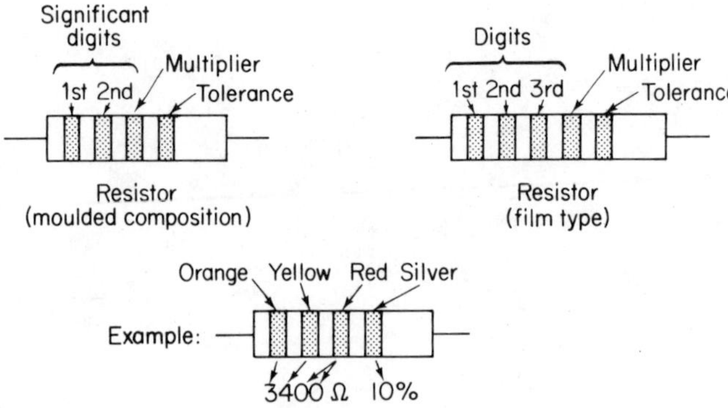

FIGURE 2-8. Resistor color coding.

TABLE 2-4. Resistance in Ohms (Ω)

Color	Digit	Multiplier	Carbon ± Tolerance	Film-type Tolerance
Black	0	1	20%	0
Brown	1	10	1%	1%
Red	2	100	2%	2%
Orange	3	1,000	3%	
Yellow	4	10,000	GMV	
Green	5	100,000	5% (*alt.*)	0.5%
Blue	6	1,000,000	6%	0.25%
Violet	7	10,000,000	12.5%	0.1%
Gray	8	0.01 (*alt.*)	30%	0.05%
White	9	0.1 (*alt.*)	10% (*alt.*)	
Silver		0.01 (*pref.*)	10% (*pref.*)	10%
Gold		0.1 (*pref.*)	5% (*pref.*)	5%
No color			20%	

indicates *guaranteed minimum value*. When a value is marked "alternate" (*alt.*), this indicates a coding that may have been used occasionally in the past, but is generally referred to in modern components by the "preferred" (*pref.*) coding designations.

2-4. CERAMIC CAPACITOR CODING

Various ceramic capacitors with color codings are shown in Figs. 2-9 and 2-10. As shown in Fig. 2-9, the tubular types may have *axial leads* (i.e., leads emanating from the ends) or *radial leads* (i.e., leads connected at right angles to the length of the capacitor). The values read from the digit color bands are in picofarads (pF). A *temperature-coefficient band* is also present, in addition to the tolerance color band and the digit bands.

The coefficient of the ceramic capacitors is given in parts per million per degree Celsius (ppm/°C). A letter N preceding this value denotes *negative-temperature coefficient* (capacity decrease with an increase in operating temperature). The P designation indicates a *positive-temperature coefficient*; NPO designates a *negative-positive-zero coefficient*. Thus, a designation of N220 indicates a capacitance decrease with a rise in temperature of 220 parts per million per °C and shows by how much the value changes during the warm-up time of the device in which the capacitor is used. The NPO types are stable units with negligible temperature effect on capacitance.

As shown in Fig. 2-9, five identification markings are used for these capacitors. For the axial-lead type, the identification starts at the end at

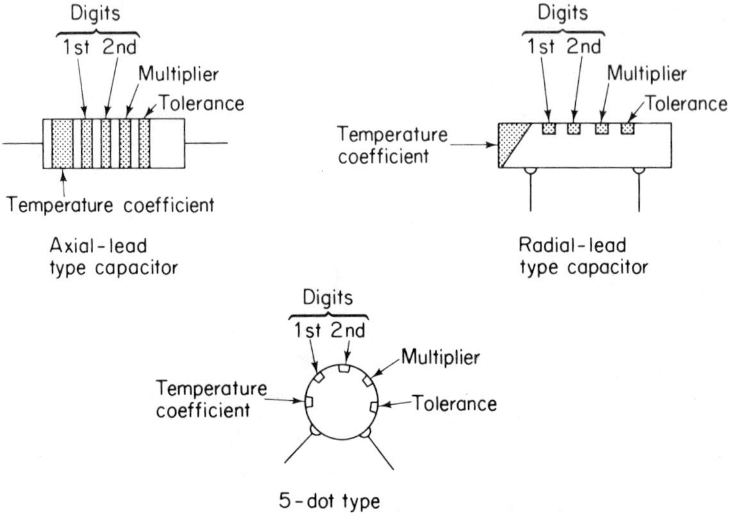

FIGURE 2-9. Ceramic capacitor color coding.

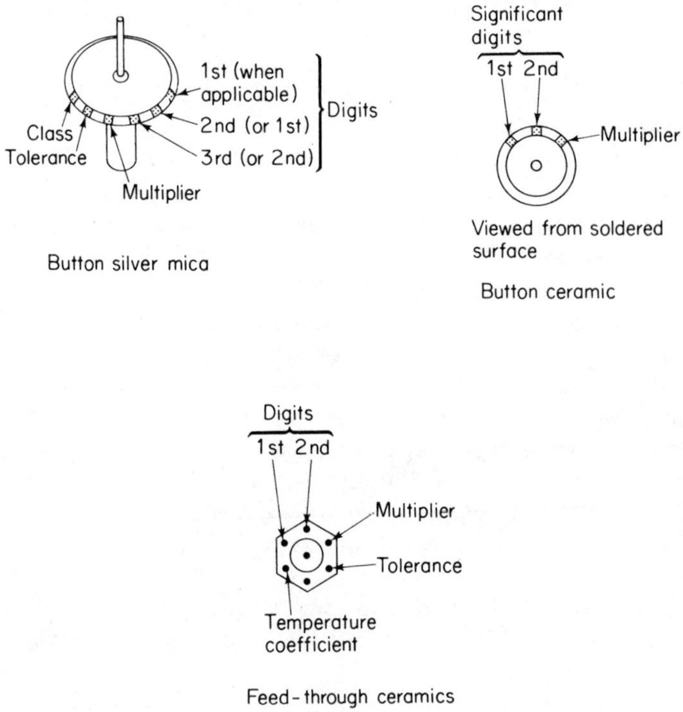

FIGURE 2-10. Button and feed-through capacitors.

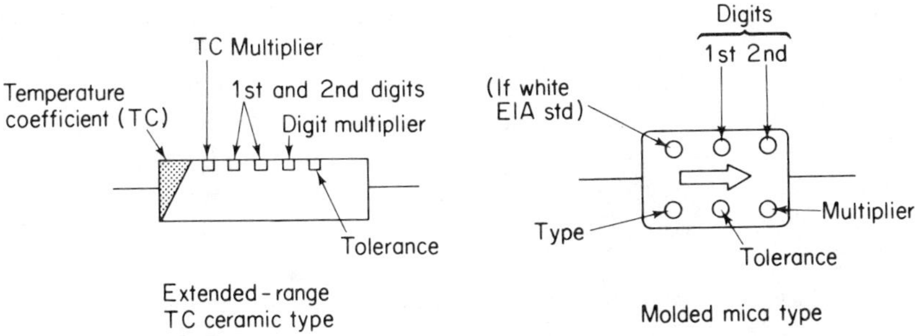

FIGURE 2-11. Extended TC and mica capacitor codings.

which the color bands are grouped; the first band being the temperature coefficient marking. The next two bands represent the significant digits.

Often, the axial-type ceramic capacitors have a wider first band for identification purposes. The radial types have an initial band of greater color area as shown. For the five-dot disc type shown in Fig. 2-9, the lower left color dot gives the temperature coefficient; the other dots in clockwise sequence have the same coding as do the axial or radial types. The button-silver mica, the button ceramic, and the feed-through ceramic types are shown in Fig. 2-10.

The extended-range temperature coefficient ceramic capacitor is shown in Fig. 2-11 with a molded mica type. For the extended-range type,

TABLE 2-5. Ceramic Types (Capacitance in Picofarads)

Color	Digit	Multiplier	10 pF or less	Over 10 pF	5-dot Temp. Coeff. TC	Extended Range Significant Digits	Extended Range Multiplier
Black	0	1	2.0 pF	20%	NPO	0.0	−1
Brown	1	10	0.1 pF	1%	N033		−10
Red	2	100		3%	N075	1.0	−100
Orange	3	1000		3%	N150	1.5	−1,000
Yellow	4	10,000			N220	2.2	−10,000
Green	5		0.5 pF	5%	N330	3.3	+1
Blue	6				N470	4.7	+10
Violet	7				N750	7.5	+100
Gray	8	0.01 (alt.)	0.25pF		*	†	+1000
White	9	0.1 (alt.)	1.0 pF	10%	**		+10,000
Silver		0.01 (pref.)					
Gold		0.1 (pref.)					

* General-purpose types with a TC ranging from P150 to N1500.
** Coupling, decoupling, and general bypass types with a TC ranging from P100 to N750.
† If the first band (TC) is black, the range is N1000 to N5000.

the first color sector indicates the temperature coefficient as is the case with the five-dot types, but the second color segment represents the temperature-coefficient multiplier. Table 2-5 applies to the five-dot and extended-range types, including the disc types. For those disc types that have only three color dots, the temperature coefficient and tolerance values are not given. In these, the first two dots (clockwise) are the significant digits and the last dot is the multiplier, as shown for the button ceramic in Fig. 2-10.

Table 2-6 applies to the flat, rectangular-shaped molded mica type capacitor shown in Fig. 2-11. An arrow, or an arrowhead, is imprinted on the capacitor face to indicate the direction of color-coding sequence. The lower left-hand color dot shows the type or classification of the particular capacitor according to the manufacturer's specifications regarding temperature coefficient, Q factor, and other related characteristics.

TABLE 2-6. Mica Types (Capacitance in Picofarads)

Color	Digit	Multiplier	Tolerance	Type Classification
Black	0	1	20% (±)	A
Brown	1	10	1%	B
Red	2	100	2%	C
Orange	3	1,000	3%	D
Yellow	4	10,000		E
Green	5		5%	
Blue	6			
Violet	7			
Gray	8			
White	9		10%	
Silver		0.01		
Gold		0.1		

3

Electronic Units, Terms, and Applications

3-1. INTERNATIONAL SYSTEM OF UNITS (SI)

The International System of Units (SI) was established in 1960 and is based on the meter. Thus, it represents a modernized version of the metric system. The official abbreviation is SI (derived from the French phrase *système internationale*) in all languages. Since this system has been adopted by international agreement, it is the basis of all national measurements throughout the world and it integrates such measurements for science, industry, and commerce. Thus, there is only one unit for a particular quantity, whether thermal, electrical, or mechanical.

The SI system can be considered to be an *absolute system*, using absolute units for simplification in engineering practices. Thus, the unit of force, for instance, is defined by acceleration of mass ($kg \cdot m/s^2$) and is unrelated to gravity. The SI system is formed on a foundation of six base units: *length*, *mass*, *time*, *temperature*, *electric current*, and *luminous intensity*. Four of these foundation units are independent: *length*, *mass*, *time*, and *temperature*; the other two basic units require use of other units for definition. Multiples and submultiples of all units are expressed in the decimal system. Two supplementary units are also used: the radian (for the measurement of plane angles) and the steradian (for the measurement of solid angles). These two units are termed *supplemental* because they are not based on physical standards, but rather on mathematical concepts.

The standards for the six base units are defined by international agreement. The prototype for mass is the only basic unit still defined by a

TABLE 3-1. SI Units and Symbols

Quantity	Symbol	SI Unit	Derivation
Base Units			
Length	m	meter	
Mass	kg	kilogram	
Time	s	second	
Temperature	°K	degree Kelvin	
Electric current	A	ampere	
Luminous intensity	cd	candela	
Supplementary Units			
Plane angle	rad	radian	
Solid angle	sr	steradian	
Derived Units			
Area	m^2	square meter	
Acceleration	m/s^2	meter per second squared	
Angular acceleration	rad/s^2	radian per second squared	
Angular velocity	rad/s	radian per second	
Conductance	S	siemens	A/V
Density	kg/m^3	kilogram per cubic meter	
Electric capacitance	F	farad	(A·s/V)
Electric charge	C	coulomb	(A·s)
Electric field strength	V/m	volt per meter	
Electric resistance	Ω	ohm	(V/A)
Energy, work, quantity of heat	J	joule	(N·m)
Flux of light	lm	lumen	(cd·sr)
Force	N	newton	$(kg \cdot m/s^2)$
Frequency	Hz	hertz	(s^{-1})
Illumination	lx	lux	(lm/m^2)
Inductance	H	henry	(V·s/A)
Luminance	cd/m^2	candela per square meter	
Magnetic field strength	A/m	ampere per meter	
Magnetic flux	Wb	weber	(V·s)
Magnetic flux density	T	tesla	(Wb/m^2)
Magnetomotive force	A	ampere	
Power	W	watt	(J/s)
Pressure	N/m^2	newton per square meter	
Velocity	m/s	meter per second	
Voltage, potential difference, electromotive force	V	volt	(W/A)
Volume	m^3	cubic meter	

rigid physical device. Thus, the kilogram is a cylinder of platinum-iridium alloy housed at the International Bureau of Weights and Measures in France. There is a duplicate at the National Bureau of Standards in the United States.

The *meter* (length) is defined as a specific wavelength in a vacuum of the orange-red line of the spectrum of krypton 86. The *second* (time) is defined as the duration of specific periods of radiation corresponding to the transition between two levels of cesium 133. The *degree kelvin* (temperature) is defined as 1/273.16 of the thermodynamic temperature of the triple point of water (the latter is approximately 32.02°F). The *ampere* (current) is defined as the current flowing in two infinitely long parallel wires in vacuum, separated by one meter, and producing a force of 2×10^{-7} newtons per meter of length between the two wires. The *candela* (luminous intensity) is the intensity of 1/600,000 square meter of a perfect radiator at the freezing temperature of platinum, 2024°K.

Table 3-1 includes the base units, the supplementary units, and the derived units. The derived units are produced without having to use conversion factors. Thus, a force of 1 N acting for a length of 1 m produces 1 J of energy. If this force is maintained for 1 s, the power is 1 W.

TABLE 3-2. Comparisons Between *mks* and *cgs*

Quantity	Symbol	*mks* Unit	*cgs* Unit
Capacitance	C	farad	farad
Conductance	G	mho	mho
Current	I	ampere	ampere
Electric charge	Q	coulomb	coulomb
Electric potential	$V(E)$	volt	volt
Flux density	B	weber/square meter	gauss
Force	F	newton	dyne
Inductance	L	henry	henry
Length	l	meter (m)	centimeter (cm)
Magnetic field intensity	H	ampere-turn/meter	oersted
Magnetic flux	ϕ	weber	maxwell
Magnetization	M	weber/square meter	
Magnetomotive force	mmf	ampere-turn	gilbert
Mass	m	kilogram	gram
Permeability	μ	henry/meter	gauss/oersted
Permeance	$\mathcal{P}$	weber/amp-turn	maxwell/gilbert
Power	P	watt	watt
Resistance	R	ohm	ohm
Reluctance	$\mathcal{R}$	amp-turn/weber	gilbert/maxwell
Time	t	second	second
Energy-work	$W(J)$	joule	joule

3-2. THE *mks* AND *cgs* SYSTEMS OF UNITS

The *mks* and *cgs* systems of units were the forerunners of standard units and symbols for the various quantities used in different branches of science. The *mks* designation refers to the meter-kilogram-second system of units, while *cgs* is the centimeter-gram-second system. The modern version is the International System of Units (SI), described in Sec. 3-1. The basic differences between the *mks* and *cgs* systems are shown in Table 3-2, which lists some of the common units.

3-3. DECIBELS AND NEPERS

The *decibel* system permits comparisons between power, voltage, or current levels in electric and electronic practices. The decibel is not a unit of measurement, but rather a unit of difference in levels.

The decibel (abbreviated dB) is based on the ways in which the human ear recognizes sounds at different intensities. The ear responds to a change in sound intensity in a fashion that is logarithmic. Hence, the ear is considerably more responsive to low-intensity sound level changes than to higher-intensity sound levels. One decibel indicates the change in volume, power level, or intensity that occurs when the *average ear* is barely able to recognize a difference in a gradually changing amplitude of sound.

The unit *bel* was named for Alexander Graham Bell (1847–1922), the noted American scientist and inventor. The unit value, however, is not used. Instead, one-tenth of a bel, the decibel, is the common term. Mathematically, the decibel for power has the relationship expressed by the following:

$$\mathrm{dB} = 10 \log_{10} \frac{P_1}{P_2} \tag{3-1}$$

In Eq. 3-1, the larger power value is divided by the smaller to obtain the ratio of the two, and the log of this ratio is multiplied by 10. Note that a doubling of power represents 3 dB:

$$10 \log \frac{2}{1} = 10 \times 0.301 = 3.01 \text{ dB}$$

Thus, if one amplifier has a rating of 20 W and another 40 W, there is a 3-dB difference between them. Similarly, there is only a 3-dB difference between a 40-W unit and one of 80 W. If the dB comparison relates to a higher value, the dB is usually expressed as a plus decibel; if a minus decibel is not indicated, it is assumed to have a plus value. Thus, if the power from a transmitting station were halved, it would mean a −3-dB decrease in power.

If the power were increased 10 times, the difference in dB would be 10:

$$10\log\frac{10}{1}=10\times 1.0=10\text{ dB}$$

The dB can also be used when referring to changes in current or voltage. When, however, we double current (or voltage), power does not double, but instead it quadruples:

$$P=I^2R=2^2\times 20=80\text{ W}$$

and

$$P=4^2\times 20=320\text{ W}.$$

Hence, the following equations apply:

$$\text{dB}=20\log_{10}\frac{E_1}{E_2} \tag{3-2}$$

$$\text{dB}=20\log_{10}\frac{I_1}{I_2} \tag{3-3}$$

Reference levels are often used to simplify analysis of power, voltage, and current changes. For example, one common reference is 0.006 W (6 mW) across 500 Ω.

Nepers use the natural base ϵ (2.7182....) to express the same factors as dB. The decibel is common in the United States, while the neper has been used extensively in Europe. There is a constant relationship between the two (1 dB=0.1151 neper, and 1 neper=8.686 dB).

$$n=\tfrac{1}{2}\log_{\epsilon}\frac{P_1}{P_2} \tag{3-4}$$

Table 3-3 lists some comparisons between power decibels and decibels of either voltage or current. Note that dB units are additive; that is, if amplifier X had a 3-dB difference in power output over amplifier Y, and X's power were doubled (adding 3 more dB), the gain of amplifier X over Y would then be 3 dB+3 dB=6 dB. Also note that a power increase of 10 times=10 dB, while a power increase of 100 times=20 dB. Thus, by increasing the power difference of 10 tenfold, we would obtain an additional 10-dB increase: 10 dB+10 dB=20 dB.

TABLE 3-3. Decibel Comparisons of E, I, and P Ratios

Decibel	Current or Voltage Ratio	Power Ratio
0.5	1.06	
1	1.12	1.26
1.5	1.19	
2	1.26	1.58
2.5	1.33	
3	1.41	2
3.5	1.49	
4	1.58	2.5
4.5	1.67	
5	1.78	3.16
5.5	1.89	
6	2	3.98
6.5	2.1	
7	2.24	5
7.5	2.35	
8	2.5	6.31
9	2.82	7.94
10	3.16	10
11	3.55	12.6
12	3.98	15.8
13	4.47	20
14	5	25
15	5.62	31.6
16	6.31	39.8
17	7.08	50.1
18	7.94	63.1
19	8.91	79.4
20	10	100
25	17.8	316
30	31.6	1,000

A typical example of the inclusion of a dB scale with a voltmeter is shown in Fig. 3-1. Here the 0 dB point is at 0.7746 V on the voltage scale. The dB scale may be read directly if the measurements are made across a 600-Ω load resistance. The dB scale indicates power ratios, and a number of such meters have for a reference 0 dB = 1 mW of power across a 600-Ω load. The dB scale in a combination meter is directly related to one of the ac scales (usually the lowest-value range). The abbreviation dBm designates dB based on 0 dB = 1 mW across 600 ohms.

Some manufacturers select a reference for their dB scale based on 0 dB = 6 mW at 500 Ω, where the 0 dB point is at 1.732 V on the voltage scale. Another reference that has been used is 0 dB = 6 mW at 600 Ω, when

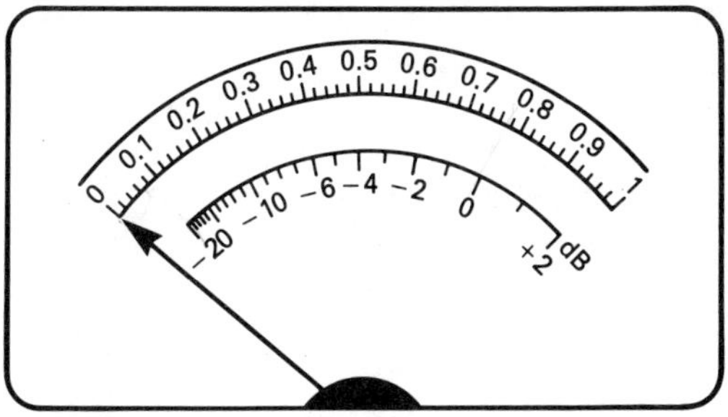

FIGURE 3-1. The dB scale on a voltmeter.

the 0 dB point is at the 1.897 point on the voltage scale. In all instances the dB readings can be made directly when taken across the load resistance designated.

3-4. THE DYNE AND VU

The *dyne* is the unit of force in the centimeter-grams-second (*cgs*) system (see Table 3-2). The dyne is the force required to produce, in a 1-gram weight mass, an acceleration of 1 centimeter per second for every second that the force is present. Thus, the dyne is the force that accelerates a one-gram body 1 centimeter per second per second (cm/s/s). The dyne unit is quite small, since only 980 equal a single gram of force. The dyne has been used to rate sensitivity of microphones and other audio devices.

The *volume unit* (VU) is often used in audio testing and describes a decibel-oriented unit wherein a reference level is indicated. With volume units the zero level is assumed to equal 0.001 W (1 mW) across 600 Ω of Z. The appropriate equations are:

$$\mathrm{VU} = 10\log\frac{P}{0.001} = 10\log\frac{P}{10^{-3}} \qquad (3\text{-}5)$$

$$= 10\log 10^3 P$$

Because the log 1000 is 3, Eq. 3-5 can be simplified to:

$$\mathrm{VU} = 30\log P \qquad (3\text{-}6)$$

Often, test instruments calibrate certain scales in dB where the indicated 0 is 0.001 W across 600 Ω. These dB indications are referred to as *decibel meters* (dBMs). Both the dBM and the VU have the identical

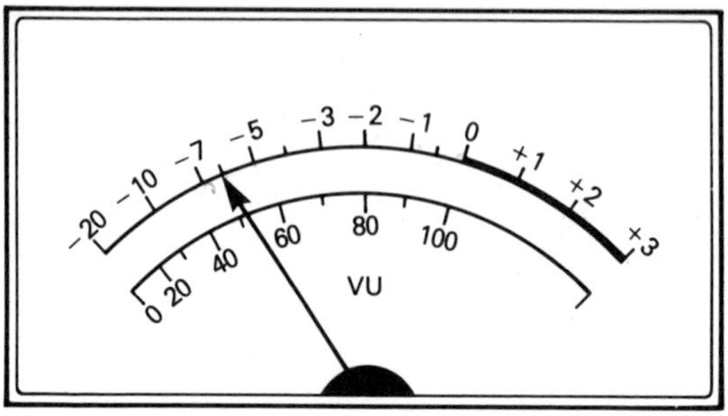

FIGURE 3-2. VU meter scale.

0-level base, with the dBM useful for sinewave signals and the VU for audio-type complex waveforms with multiple harmonic content.

A typical VU meter face is shown in Fig. 3-2. Note that the scale has a span of −20 to +3 VU on the upper-scale range. The lower scale is calibrated to indicate percentage of voltage, with 100 percent situated at the 0 VU point. For most meters, the numbers and scale markings to the left of 0 are in black print, while those to the right are in red. Normal volume level is considered to be at the 0 VU point (100 percent), which is positioned at about 70 percent of full-scale deflection. For audio measurements, the VU meter should be observed over a short time interval for adjustments to prevent overloading at peaks.

3-5. POWERS AND PREFIXES

It is common practice in electric-electronic references to use the power of ten to simplify lengthy quantities and values. Thus, the base number 10 is raised to some power, as identified by an exponent, to express large numbers without resorting to the unwieldy practice of writing a string of zeros. This process has been termed the *Standard System of Scientific Notation* (as well as *engineers' shorthand*). Thus, the expression 10^3 indicates the following multiplication process:

$$10 \times 10 \times 10 = 1{,}000$$

The basic number (here the 10 in 10^3) is called the *base* and the raised (or superior) number is called the *exponent*. Similarly, $6.28 \times 10^4 = 62{,}800$. For fractional values, a minus sign precedes the exponent, as:

$4.5 \times 10^{-8} = 0.000000045$. Representative values are:

$$10 = 10^1$$
$$100 = 10^2$$
$$1{,}000 = 10^3$$
$$10{,}000 = 10^4$$
$$100{,}000 = 10^5$$
$$1{,}000{,}000 = 10^6$$
$$0.1 = 10^{-1}$$
$$0.01 = 10^{-2}$$
$$0.001 = 10^{-3}$$
$$0.000001 = 10^{-6}$$
$$0.000000000001 = 10^{-12}$$

Prefixes relating to the powers of 10 have also been standardized and representative examples are given in Table 3-4. Relating these to electric quantities, current may be expressed as amperes (A), milliamperes (mA), or microamperes (μA). For voltage we commonly use kilovolts (kV), megavolts (MV), or the basic quantity volts (V). For capacitance we have microfarad (μF) and picofarads (pF). Such prefixes are widely used in all branches of electronics and are a convenience for expressing fractional or high values. In utilizing the prefix systems, we also avoid the confusion

TABLE 3-4. Standard Prefixes and Letter Symbols

Prefix	Symbol	Value	Submultiples and Multiples
atto	a		1×10^{-18}
femto	f		1×10^{-15}
pico	p	one-millionth millionth	1×10^{-12}
nano	n	1,000 of a millionth	1×10^{-9}
micro	μ	one-millionth	1×10^{-6}
milli	m	one-thousandth	1×10^{-3}
centi	c	one-hundredth	1×10^{-2}
deci	d	one-tenth	1×10^{-1}
deca	da	ten	1×10^{1}
hecto	h	one hundred	1×10^{2}
kilo	k	one thousand	1×10^{3}
mega	M	one million	1×10^{6}
giga	G	one-thousand million	1×10^{9}
tera	T	one-million million	1×10^{12}

resulting from the words trillion, billion, quadrillion, etc., which have different numerical values in various countries. A *billion*, for instance, represents a 1,000 *millions* in the United States and France, but in Britain or Germany it equals a *million millions*. A *giga*, however, equals a standard 1,000 millions (10^9) even though it may be referred to as a billion in France and the United States, but not in Germany or Britain. Similarly, *atto* (10^{-18}) would be referred to as a *quintillionth* in the U.S system, but under the British system it would be referred to as a *trillionth*. Table 3-5 shows the differences between the two systems.

TABLE 3-5. System Differences

Designation	U.S. and French	Power	British and German	Power
million	1,000 thousands	10^6	1,000 thousands	10^6
milliard	1,000 millions	10^9	1,000 millions	10^9
billion	1,000 millions	10^9	1 million millions	10^{12}
trillion	1,000 billions (a million millions)	10^{12}	1 million billions	10^{18}
quadrillion	1,000 trillions	10^{15}	1 million trillions	10^{24}
quintillion	1,000 quadrillions	10^{18}	A million quadrillions	10^{30}

3-6. FREQUENCY, VELOCITY, AND WAVELENGTH

The word *hertz* has been adopted internationally to designate the number of *cycles per second*. It was named for Heinrich R. Hertz (1857–1894), the German physicist. The abbreviation for hertz is Hz. One thousand cycles per second of ac is expressed as 1 kHz; three million cycles per second as 3 MHz, and 60 cycles per second as 60 Hz. This universal term eliminates the many different translations of the cycles-per-second expression in the various languages.

Sound waves, ac waves from power mains, or RF transmitted waves are all represented by the sinewave-type signal as shown in Fig. 3-3, where a positive and negative alternation make up a complete cycle. *Velocity* is the time rate of motional change of position in a specific direction. Thus, when radio-frequency (RF) waves are propagated, they span a given distance in a time interval dependent on velocity factors. The word *velocity* is often used loosely as a synonym for speed, though actually the latter is more accurately defined as the time rate of change of position in a given direction.

The velocity of sound is determined by the medium (air, water, etc.) through which sound travels. The velocity is dependent on temperature as

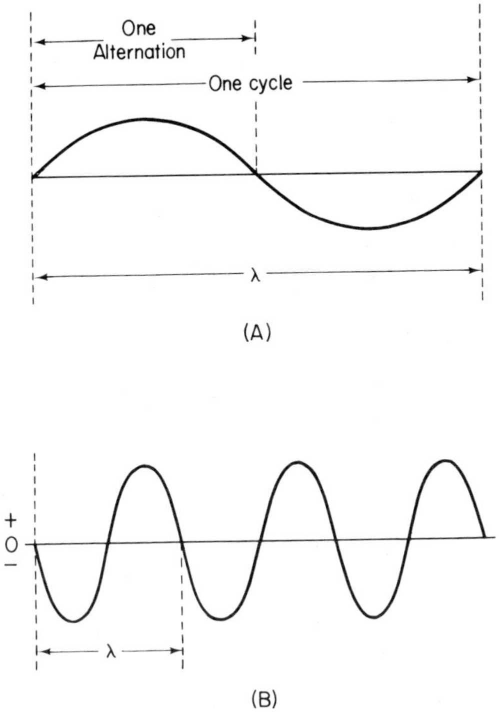

FIGURE 3-3. Wavelength of sinewave signal.

well. In air, the velocity of sound is approximately 1,100 feet per second (ft/s), or 750 miles per hour (mph). At 32°F, the velocity is 1,088 ft/s. In the metric system the velocity at 0°C is 349.8 meters per second (m/s).

Electromagnetic radio waves traveling through space have the same velocity as light—299,792.5 kilometers per second (km/s), or 186,282 miles per second in a vacuum. Most commonly used formulas for light waves and radio waves use a rounded-off velocity figure (300,000,000 m/s or 186,000 miles per second).

The distance spanned by one cycle of a propagated waveform in a given period is termed the *wavelength*. Hence, if a sound wave has a velocity of 331 meters per second, and one cycle is produced per second, the wavelength is 331 meters. Thus, for the single cycle shown in part A of Fig. 3-3, the wavelength, represented by the Greek *lambda* (λ), is the span between the beginning and end of the cycle and represents a distance of 331 meters. As the frequency (Hz) is increased, the wavelength shortens as shown in Fig. 3-3B. For a frequency of 3 Hz, the wavelength would be one-third of 331, or 110 meters. Wavelength (λ), velocity (v), and frequency (f) are related as follows:

$$v = f\lambda \tag{3-7}$$

$$f = \frac{v}{\lambda} \tag{3-8}$$

$$\lambda = \frac{v}{f} \tag{3-9}$$

3-7. UNITS OF CHARGE, CURRENT, AND VOLTAGE

The basic unit of electrostatic charge is termed the *coulomb*, named after Charles Coulomb (1736–1806), the French scientist. He defined the law of charged bodies, which may be stated as follows:

> The force between two electrically charged bodies is inversely proportional to the square of the distance between the two, and directly proportional to the product of the two charges.

The coulomb (Q) represents 6.28×10^{18} electrons, and the rate of flow of one coulomb per second is defined as one ampere of current:

$$I = \frac{Q}{t} \tag{3-10}$$

where I is the current in amperes
Q is the quantity of electrons in coulombs
t is the time in seconds.

By rearrangement of the symbols, we solve for Q:

$$Q = It \tag{3-11}$$

The ability of a substance to conduct electric current is known as its *conductivity*. The amount of current that flows is determined by the voltage (electric pressure) applied and the composition of the material (which also determines the amount of opposition to current flow). The unit of electric current is the *ampere* (A), named after André Ampere (1775–1836), the French scientist. The symbol for current is the capital letter I. Current-carrying materials are termed *conductors* and may be metal, liquids, gases, or plasma.

The electric pressure required to move electrons to establish current flow is known as *electromotive force* (emf). The unit of emf is the volt (V), named after Alessandro Volta (1745–1827), the Italian researcher who first built a cell that provided emf, the forerunner of our modern battery. A volt is the quantity of electromotive force that causes one ampere of current to flow through one ohm of resistance. (See Sec. 3-8.)

The source point of electrons (from a battery or other electric-generating unit) is known as the *negative terminal,* while the terminal toward which electrons flow is designated as the *positive terminal.*

3-8. UNITS OF RESISTANCE AND CONDUCTANCE

Opposition to current flow is known as *resistance*, and the symbol is the capital letter R. The unit of measurement for resistance is the *ohm*, named after Georg Ohm (1789–1854), the German professor who formulated the basic law relating to current and resistance which is covered in Sec. 3-9. The ohm has for its symbol the Greek letter omega (Ω). Subscripts with R identify a particular resistor; for example $R_1 = 2\ \Omega$; $R_5 = 25\ k\Omega$; $R_{10} = 3\ M\Omega$.

The standard value of one ohm is given by the resistance at 0°C that is produced by a column of mercury having a cross-sectional area of 1 square millimeter and a length of 106.3 centimeters. A unit specifically designed to offer a given amount of current opposition is known as a *resistor*.

The degree to which a substance permits current flow is known as its *conductance*. Because conductance (G) is basically the opposite of resistance, it is the reciprocal of resistance. In the SI system, the unit is *siemens* and the letter symbol is S. (See Table 3-1.) Thus, if a resistor has a value of 1,000 Ω (1 kΩ), its conductance is 1/1,000, or 0.001 S. Formerly, the unit for conductance was the *mho* (ohm spelled backwards). This unit reference will still be found in some of the literature. (See also Secs. 3-21 and 4-1.)

3-9. OHM'S LAW

The values of current, voltage, and resistance are all related because the amount of current flow is dependent on both the amount of electric pressure applied and the opposition encountered by the electron movement. These relationships were set down in equation form by the German physicist Georg Ohm. Ohm's equation lets us find one unknown quantity (either I, E, or R) by using known values of the other two. For ascertaining the amount of current given the resistance and voltage:

$$I = \frac{E}{R} \tag{3-12}$$

Thus if there is a 15-volt drop across a 2-kΩ resistor, current flow is $\frac{15}{2{,}000} = 0.0075$ A, or 7.5 mA.

By rearranging the terms of Eq. 3-12 we can solve for voltage when current and resistance values are known:

$$E = IR \tag{3-13}$$

If the values of voltage and current are known, resistance is found by:

$$R = \frac{E}{I} \tag{3-14}$$

Hence, if the voltage drop across a resistance is 80 V, and the current flow is 10 A, we obtain the result: $\frac{80}{10} = 8\ \Omega$.

The unit of electric power is the *watt*, named after the Scottish inventor, James Watt (1736–1819). One watt of power equals one ampere of current flow produced by one volt of electric pressure. The symbol for electric power is P and for the unit watt it is W. Thus, common expressions are: $P = 50$ W; $P = 25$ kW; $P = 10$ MW. Relating power to Ohm's law, we can express the equation for power as:

$$P = EI \tag{3-15}$$

When power is calculated in relation to time, the unit of energy is the *joule* (symbol J), also known as the *watt-second.* It is the amount of energy generated by one watt of power in one second. In measuring ordinary electric power consumed in homes, the kilowatt-hour (1,000 watts for one hour) is the reference used.

Other equations can be obtained by the rearrangement of the basic electric units in Ohm's law. The Ohm's law wheels shown in Fig. 3-4 are convenient for reference purposes. The one shown in part A is for dc and the one in part B is for ac. For the latter calculations, *impedance* (symbol Z) is used instead of R for resistance because the presence of inductors and/or capacitors changes the phase angle between voltage and current (unless the inductive and capacitive reactances are equal). Impedance is expressed in ohms, as is resistance. (See Secs. 3-14, 3-17, and 3-18.)

As shown on the Ohm's law wheel for ac, the power is calculated as:

$$P = EI\cos\theta \tag{3-16}$$

Equation 3-16 indicates the *true power* consumed in an electric circuit in contrast to the *apparent power*, expressed by $P = EI$. The ratio of the true power to the apparent power in *ac* is known as the *power factor*:

$$\text{Power factor} = \frac{\text{True power}}{\text{Apparent power}} \tag{3-17}$$

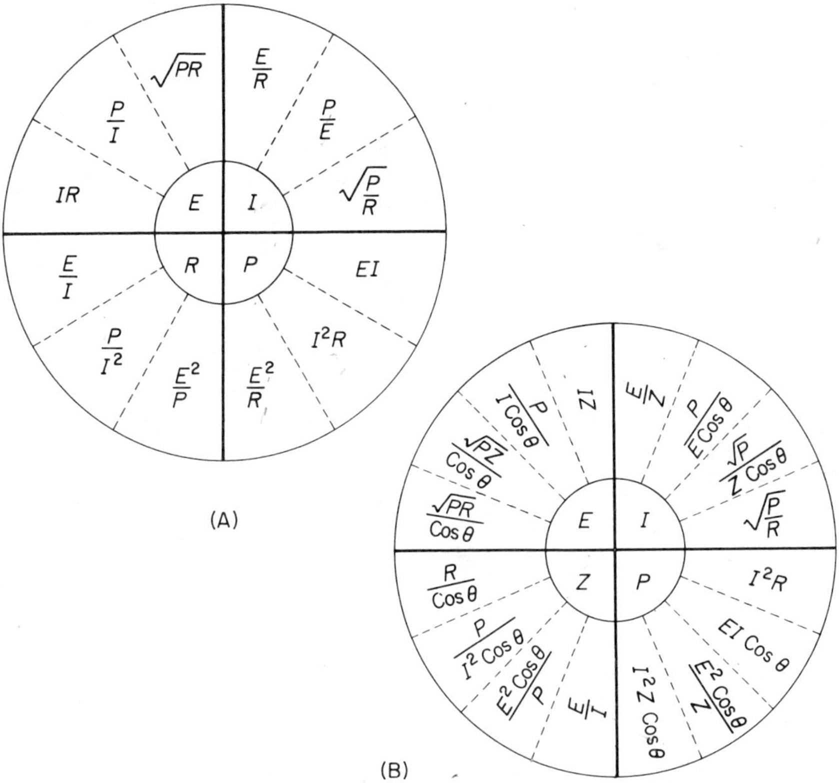

FIGURE 3-4. Ohm's law wheels for dc and ac.

The value of the cosine of the angle is equivalent to the power factor because the phase angle is zero when voltage and current are in phase, with the power factor equaling one (cosine of 0°). With a 90° phase difference between *I* and *E*, the power factor is the cosine of 90° and thus equals zero, indicating that no power is consumed, since the product of voltage and current multiplied by 0 equals 0.

3-10. UNITS OF MAGNETISM

Common terms, with definitions, for unit values relating to magnetism follow:

Magnetic flux. This term relates to the number of magnetic lines in a given area of magnetism. In the *cgs* system, the unit of magnetic flux is the *maxwell*. It represents one line of the magnetic flux and is symbolized by the Greek letter phi (ϕ). The maxwell is named after James Maxwell (1831–1879), the famed Scottish theoretical physicist. The unit of magnetic flux in the *mks* system is the *weber* (Wb). One maxwell $= 10^{-8}$ webers.

Flux density. Magnetic induction or flux density is defined by the number of magnetic lines that pass perpendicularly through a square centimeter. The capital letter B has been used as the symbol, and the unit is the *gauss*, named after the German mathematician Karl Gauss (1777–1855). A later designation is T for the unit called the *tesla* named after Nikola Tesla, American electrician and inventor (1856–1943).

Magnetic field intensity. Magnetic field intensity relates to the force (magnetic field strength) exerted by the field. Its unit is the *oersted* named after Hans Oersted (1777–1851), the Danish physicist. An oersted represents the intensity of the magnetic field at a one-centimeter distance from the unit magnetic pole (in air or vacuum). The symbol for the oersted is the capital letter H. When the magnetic field strength is related to the unit in terms of amperes per meter, the units are A/m. (Also see Secs. 3-19 and 12-18.)

Magnetic induction. Magnetic induction is the term applied to the magnetizing of a magnetic material by inducing into it the lines of force from a magnet. Thus, a bar of iron, when rubbed with a permanent magnet, can become magnetized through magnetic induction.

Permeability. Permeability is a measure of the conductivity of magnetic flux through a material. It is symbolized by the Greek letter mu (μ) and defined as the ratio of the flux that exists when a certain material is used to the flux present if air were used instead. The permeability of air is thus considered as unity (one), with all other materials having specific degrees of permeability above one. Soft iron, for instance, has better conductivity for magnetic lines than steel because of iron's greater permeability. Other materials with high permeability include ferrite, cobalt, and certain alloys.

Reluctance. Reluctance defines the opposition offered by a material to the magnetic flux. Reluctance (also termed reluctivity) corresponds to resistance to current flow in electric circuitry. The symbol is the script letter $\mathcal{R}$.

Permeance. Permeance is a designation seldom used and refers to the property that determines the magnitude of magnetic flux in a material. It is equal to the reciprocal of reluctance, and its symbol is the script letter $\mathcal{P}$.

Retentivity. Retentivity refers to the ability of a material to retain magnetism after the withdrawal of the magnetizing force. Steel, for example, has a higher retentivity than iron and thus retains more magnetism for a given applied force.

3-11. MAGNETIC PROPERTIES

Diamagnetic Materials. Diamagnetic materials are those which become only slightly magnetized, even when subjected to strong magnetic fields. When a diamagnetic material is magnetized, it is magnetized in a direction opposite to that of the external magnetizing force, as shown in Fig. 3-5A. Diamagnetic materials have a permeability of less than unity and include such metals as silver, gold, copper, and mercury.

Paramagnetic Materials. Paramagnetic materials become only slightly magnetized, even when they are subjected to strong magnetic fields, as with the diamagnetics. The difference between the two is that the paramagnetic materials become magnetized in the same direction as the external magnetizing field, as shown in Fig. 3-5B. The permeability of these materials is greater than unity, though low compared to the permeabilities of ferromagnetic materials (see below). Paramagnetic materials include chromium, aluminum, platinum, manganese, and also, air.

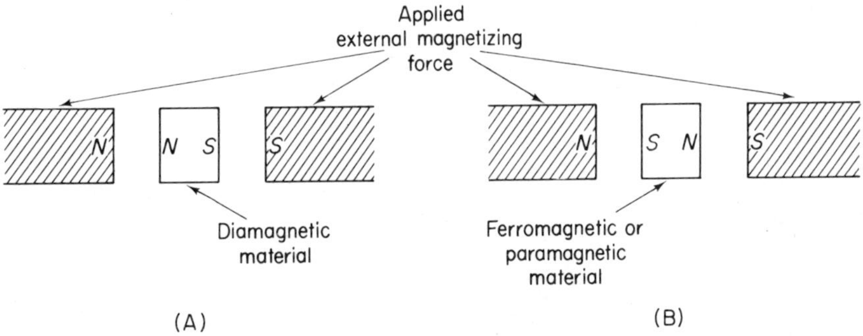

FIGURE 3-5. Pole directions of retained magnetism for various materials.

Ferromagnetic Materials. Ferromagnetic materials are characterized by high permeability and become very strongly magnetized by a field much weaker than that required to magnetize a diamagnetic or a paramagnetic material. The direction of the induced magnetism is identical to that of the magnetizing field, as shown in Fig. 3-5B.

The permeability of ferromagnetic materials varies with the strength of the magnetizing field. Among the ferromagnetic materials are iron, steel, cobalt, magnetite (lodestone), and alloys such as alnico and permalloy. Alnico derives its name from the metals used to form the alloy—aluminum, nickel, and cobalt (with some iron added). Permalloy (permanent-alloy) contains iron and nickel in a ratio of one to four. Such alloys form strong magnets and find extensive applications in various branches of electronics. Compared to soft iron, which has a permeability of about 2,000, these alloys achieve permeability ratings as high as 50,000 or more, depending on manufacturing practices and alloy types.

3-12. CAPACITANCE AND TIME CONSTANTS

Capacitance refers to the storage of electric energy. It occurs when two metals are brought into close proximity. The insulating material between the metallic electric conductors is called the *dielectric* and is typically composed of air, glass, plastic, paper, or other insulating materials. Units manufactured to provide capacitance are called *capacitors* and come in a variety of forms, voltage ratings, and units of capacitance ratings. Capacitors are available in both fixed or variable values in units

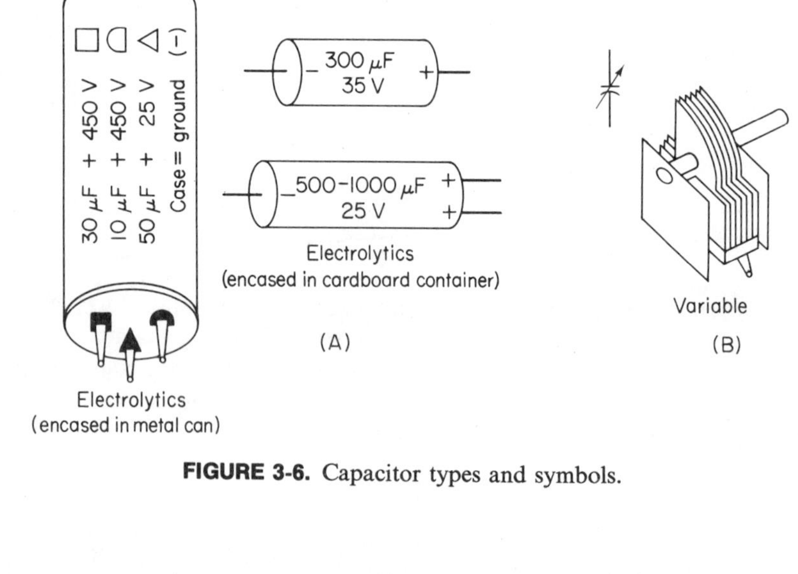

FIGURE 3-6. Capacitor types and symbols.

termed *fixed capacitors* and *variable capacitors*. (See Fig. 3-6.) Some capacitance always exists between chassis wiring (*stray* or *shunt capacitance*), as well as between turns of a coil or between coil layers (*distributed capacitance*).

The unit of capacity is the *farad*. It was named after the British scientist, Michael Faraday (1791–1867). The farad represents the amount of capacitance capable of storing 1 coulomb of charge Q at an applied electromotive force of 1 V. (See Sec. 3-7.) Since the farad is too large a quantity for virtually all electric-electronic applications, the more common terms in use are microfarad (μF) or picofarad (pF).

Applicable equations are:

$$C=\frac{Q}{E} \tag{3-18}$$

where C is the capacitance in farads
Q is the charge in coulombs
E is the applied voltage.

By rearrangement of Eq. 3-18 we obtain:

$$E=\frac{Q}{C} \tag{3-19}$$

$$Q=CE \tag{3-20}$$

When a capacitor holds a charge, stored energy is present. The amount of such energy which a capacitor can store is related to both the capacitance value and the voltage applied:

$$P(\text{energy})=\tfrac{1}{2}CE^2 \tag{3-21}$$

In Eq. 3-21 the capacitance C is in farads, and the unit of energy or work is the *joule* of the mks system. The joule is the amount of work required to force 1 coulomb of electricity through 1 Ω of resistance. Thus, if a 2-μF capacitor is charged to a voltage of 300 V, the energy is:

$$P=\tfrac{1}{2}\times 2\times 10^{-6}\times 300^2=0.09\text{ joule}$$

When a resistor is placed in series with a capacitor, and voltage is applied to the combination, virtually no electric pressure is initially needed to move electrons to one side of the capacitor and draw electrons away from the other side. Within a brief time interval, however, increased voltage (electric pressure) does become necessary to move electrons. Thus, as Fig. 3-7 shows, exponential curves are produced when the capacitor charge current and the capacitor charge voltage are plotted.

As the capacitor receives a charge, it acquires a voltage polarity that opposes that of the supply potential. The time required for the voltage across the capacitor to reach 63 percent of its maximum value is known as the *RC* time constant. The equation is:

$$\tau = RC \tag{3-22}$$

where C is the capacity in farads
τ is the time constant in seconds
R is the resistance value in ohms.

By rearrangement we also obtain:

$$C = \frac{\tau}{R} \quad \text{and} \quad R = \frac{\tau}{C} \tag{3-23}$$

Example

A 0.0025-μF capacitor is in series with a 3-kΩ resistor. The potential applied across the combination is 100 V. At what fractional part of a second after the voltage is applied will it reach 63 percent of full value?

Solution

$$\tau = RC = 0.0025 \times 10^{-6} \times 3000 = 7.5\ \mu\text{s}$$

Thus, since 1 τ is the time required for voltage to reach 63 percent of full value, the time is 7.5 μs. [Current flow to the capacitor ceases after approximately 5 time constants ($5 \times 7.5 = 37.5$ μs for the above example).]

Reference should be made to Table 3-6 for time-constant values. The following equations apply to the solution of instantaneous voltage values across a capacitor, or instantaneous currents, either during capacitor charge or discharge. For the following examples, it is also necessary to refer to the exponential functions given in Table 3-7 (or use a scientific calculator) for determining values of ϵ^{-x}, where ϵ is 2.718...(base of Napierian logs). For these equations involving *RC* circuits, the x value is always t/RC, where t is the time in seconds, R is the value of the resistance in ohms, and C is the capacitance in farads.

$$e_c = E(1 - \epsilon^{-t/RC}) \tag{3-24}$$

TABLE 3-6. Time Constants

Time Constant	Percentage of Capacitor Discharge Voltage or Charge Current, also Percentage of Inductor Charge Voltage or Discharge Current	Percentage of Capacitor Charge Voltage or Percentage of Inductor Charge Current
0.001	99.9	0.1
0.002	99.8	0.2
0.003	99.7	0.3
0.004	99.6	0.4
0.005	99.5	0.5
0.006	99.4	0.6
0.007	99.3	0.7
0.008	99.2	0.8
0.009	99.1	0.9
0.01	99	1
0.02	98	2
0.03	97	3
0.04	96	4
0.05	95	5
0.06	94	6
0.07	93	7
0.08	92	8
0.09	91	9
0.10	90	10
0.15	86	14
0.20	82	18
0.25	78	22
0.30	74	26
0.35	70	30
0.40	67	33
0.45	64	36
0.5	61	39
0.6	55	45
0.7	50	50
0.8	45	55
0.9	40	60
1	37	63
2	14	86
3	5	95
4	2	98
5	0.7	99.3

TABLE 3-7. Exponential Functions

x	ϵ^x	ϵ^{-x}	sinh x	cosh x	tanh x	coth x	$\sinh^{-1} x$	$\cosh^{-1} x$	$\tanh^{-1} x$	$\coth^{-1} x$
0.00	**1.000**	**1.000**	**0.000**	**1.000**	**0.000**	∞	**0.000**	......	**0.000**	
0.10	1.105	0.905	0.100	1.005	0.100	10.033	0.100	......	0.100	
0.20	1.221	0.819	0.201	1.020	0.197	5.066	0.199	......	0.203	
0.30	1.350	0.741	0.305	1.045	0.291	3.433	0.296	......	0.309	
0.40	1.492	0.670	0.411	1.081	0.380	2.632	0.390	......	0.424	
0.50	1.649	0.607	0.521	1.128	0.462	2.164	0.481	......	0.549	
0.60	1.822	0.549	0.637	1.185	0.537	1.862	0.569	......	0.693	
0.70	2.014	0.497	0.759	1.255	0.604	1.655	0.653	......	0.867	
0.80	2.226	0.449	0.888	1.337	0.664	1.506	0.733	......	1.099	
0.90	2.460	0.407	1.027	1.433	0.716	1.396	0.809	......	1.472	
1.00	**2.718**	**0.368**	**1.175**	**1.543**	**0.762**	**1.313**	**0.881**	**0.000**	∞	∞
1.10	3.004	0.333	1.336	1.669	0.800	1.249	0.950	0.444	......	1.522
1.20	3.320	0.301	1.509	1.811	0.834	1.200	1.016	0.622	......	1.199
1.30	3.669	0.273	1.698	1.971	0.862	1.160	1.079	0.756	......	1.018
1.40	4.055	0.247	1.904	2.151	0.885	1.129	1.138	0.867	......	0.896
1.50	4.482	0.223	2.129	2.352	0.905	1.105	1.195	0.962	......	0.805
1.60	4.953	0.202	2.376	2.577	0.922	1.085	1.249	1.047	......	0.733
1.70	5.474	0.183	2.646	2.828	0.934	1.069	1.301	1.123	......	0.675
1.80	6.050	0.165	2.942	3.107	0.947	1.056	1.350	1.193	......	0.626
1.90	6.686	0.150	3.268	3.418	0.956	1.046	1.398	1.257	......	0.585
2.00	**7.389**	**0.135**	**3.627**	**3.762**	**0.964**	**1.037**	**1.444**	**1.317**	......	**0.549**
2.10	8.166	0.122	4.022	4.144	0.970	1.030	1.487	1.373	......	0.518
2.20	9.025	0.111	4.457	4.568	0.976	1.025	1.530	1.425	......	0.490
2.30	9.974	0.100	4.937	5.037	0.980	1.020	1.570	1.475	......	0.466
2.40	11.02	0.091	5.466	5.557	0.984	1.017	1.609	1.522	......	0.444
2.50	12.18	0.082	6.050	6.132	0.987	1.014	1.647	1.567	......	0.424
2.60	13.46	0.074	6.695	6.769	0.989	1.011	1.684	1.609	......	0.405
2.70	14.88	0.067	7.406	7.473	0.991	1.009	1.719	1.650	......	0.389
2.80	16.44	0.061	8.192	8.253	0.993	1.007	1.753	1.689	......	0.374
2.90	18.17	0.055	9.060	9.115	0.994	1.006	1.786	1.727	......	0.360
3.00	**20.09**	**0.050**	**10.018**	**10.068**	**0.995**	**1.005**	**1.818**	**1.763**	......	**0.347**
3.10	22.20	0.045	11.08	11.12	0.996	1.004	1.850	1.798	......	0.335
3.20	24.53	0.041	12.25	12.29	0.997	1.003	1.880	1.831	......	0.323
3.30	27.11	0.037	13.54	13.57	0.997	1.003	1.909	1.863	......	0.313
3.40	29.96	0.033	14.97	15.00	0.998	1.002	1.938	1.895	......	0.303
3.50	33.12	0.030	16.54	16.57	0.998	1.002	1.966	1.925	......	0.294
4.00	54.60	0.018	27.29	27.31	0.999	1.001	2.095	2.063	......	0.255
4.50	90.02	0.0111	45.00	45.01	1.000	1.000	2.209	2.185	......	0.226
5.00	**148.4**	**0.0067**	**74.20**	**74.21**	**1.000**	**1.000**	**2.312**	**2.292**	......	**0.203**
5.50	244.7	0.0041	122.3	122.3	1.000	1.000	2.406	2.390	......	0.184
6.00	403.4	0.0025	201.7	201.7	1.000	1.000	2.492	2.478	......	0.168

Note: The symbol ϵ is 2.71828, the base of Napierian logs.

where e_c is the instantaneous voltage E across C
E is the maximum voltage applied

$$e_R = E\epsilon^{-t/RC} \tag{3-25}$$

$$i_R = \frac{E}{R}\epsilon^{-t/RC} \tag{3-26}$$

Example

A 200-kΩ resistor is in series with a 0.0005-μF capacitor and a 300-V battery. After 200 μs, what is the instantaneous voltage across the capacitor?

Solution

The 200 μs is divided by the product of 200 kΩ×0.0005×10^{-6} to obtain x:

$$\frac{0.0002}{0.0001} = 2$$

From Table 3-7, we can determine that the unit 2 for x gives a value for ϵ^{-x} of 0.135. Subtracting this from 1, and multiplying the result by 300, provides the answer:

$$300 \times (1 - 0.135) = 300 \times 0.865 = 259.5 \text{ V}$$

Equations 3-24, 3-25, and 3-26 are also used to find values during capacitor discharge in an RC circuit (resistor in series with capacitor).

3-13. CAPACITIVE REACTANCE

A capacitor opposes a change of voltage (in contrast to the inductor, which opposes a change of current). When ac is applied to a capacitor, there is a continual rise and fall of voltage and current at a periodic rate. Thus, while the opposition to a voltage change rises to an infinite value after five time constants with dc, when ac is used the changing reversal of the polarity of the applied voltage prevents the opposition from building up to an infinite value. Hence, a fixed unit value of capacitor opposition is created and is referred to as *reactance*. For the capacitor, the complete term is called the *capacitive reactance*, and it is symbolized by X_c.

The amount of capacitive reactance present for a given capacitance depends on the angular velocity of the ac as well as the unit value of the capacitance in farads. [Angular velocity is $2\pi f$ ($6.28f$) and is denoted by the symbol ω (lower-case Greek omega).] The complete expression for capacitive reactance is:

$$X_c = \frac{1}{2\pi fC} = \frac{1}{\omega C} = \frac{1}{6.28fC} \tag{3-27}$$

where X_c is the capacitor reactance in ohms
f is the frequency in Hz
C is the capacitance in farads.

By rearrangement of Eq. 3-27 we can solve for capacitance or frequency:

$$C = \frac{1}{6.28fX_c} \tag{3-28}$$

$$f = \frac{1}{6.28CX_c} \tag{3-29}$$

Capacitive reactance is also proportional to the voltage drop across the capacitor and the current flow *to* and *from* it (current does not flow through a capacitor unless it is imperfect and has current leakage). Thus, capactive reactance follows Ohm's law:

$$\begin{aligned} X_c &= E/I \\ I &= E/X_c \\ E &= IX_c \end{aligned} \tag{3-30}$$

3-14. *Z* IN *RC* CIRCUITS

With a perfect capacitor (no leakage current) the applied voltage initially causes high current flow as shown in Fig. 3-7. Thus, voltage lags current by 90° and no power is consumed, even with a high reactance. With a 90° phase difference, the cosine of the angle in Eq. 3-16 is zero, resulting in zero power consumption.

When a capacitor is in series with a resistor, the opposition to alternating current flow (ac) is no longer simple reactance or resistance, but rather an *impedance* (Z). Impedance is a function of the angle between 0° and 90°. Hence the following equation applies:

$$Z = \sqrt{R^2 + X_c^2} \tag{3-31}$$

The impedance-triangle relationships for R and X_c are shown in Fig. 3-8; the related circuit is shown in part A. Thus, if the resistance has a

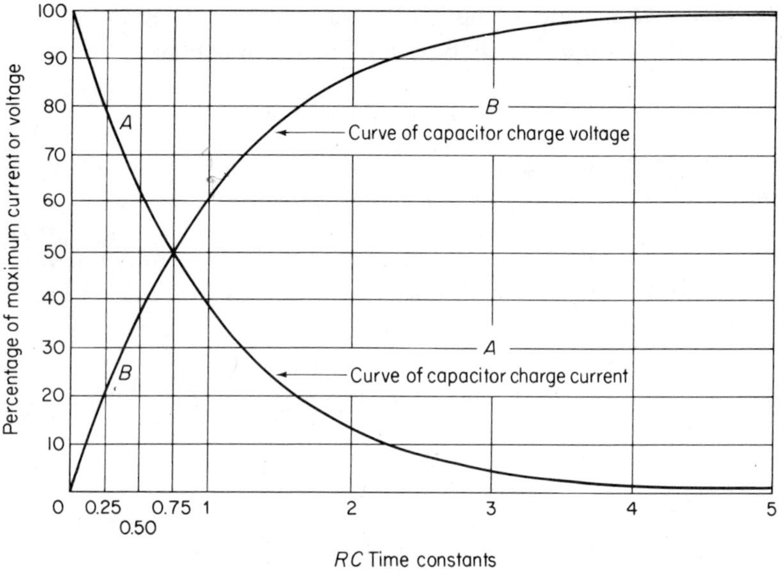

FIGURE 3-7. Universal time-constant chart for C and R.

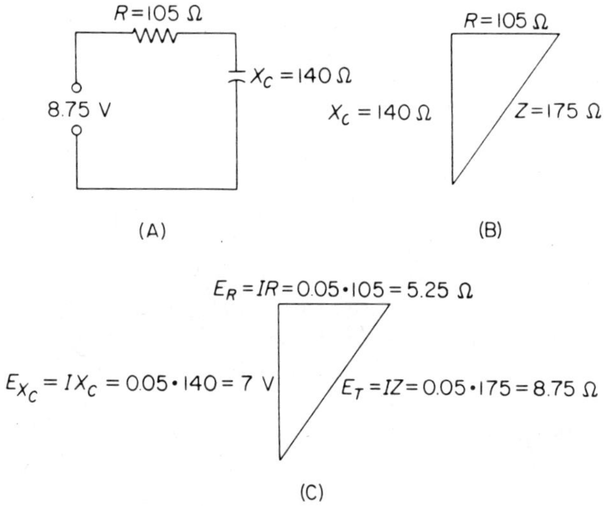

FIGURE 3-8. Z and V triangles (RC).

value of 105 Ω and the X_c has a value of 140 Ω, the right-angle relationships exist as shown in Fig. 3-8B. Using Eq. 3-31 we obtain:

$$\sqrt{27.5625+49} = \sqrt{76.5625} = 8.75 \text{ V}$$

As shown in Fig. 3-8C, voltage relationships also follow vector addition. $I = E/Z$; hence for the circuit shown in Fig. 3-8A, current is $8.75/175 = 0.05$ A. Thus, the voltage across the capacitor is $E_{Xc} = IX_c = 0.05 \cdot 140 = 7$ V, while $E_R = IR = 0.05 \cdot 105 = 5.25$ V. Therefore, Eq. 3-31 can be converted into an equation for ascertaining total voltage if we know the individual voltage drops across X_c and R:

$$E_T = \sqrt{E_R^2 + E_{X_c}^2} \qquad (3\text{-}32)$$

Thus, for the example of Fig. 3-8, we have:

$$\sqrt{27.5625+49} = \sqrt{76.5625} = 8.75 \text{ V}$$

Equations 3-31 and 3-32 apply to series combinations of reactance and resistance. For resistance in parallel to reactance, currents assume vector relationships:

$$I_T = \sqrt{I_R^2 + I_{X_c}^2} \qquad (3\text{-}33)$$

Solving for Z, the applied voltage E is divided by total current:

$$Z = E/I_T \qquad (3\text{-}34)$$

For additional data on impedance, see also Secs. 3-17 and 3-18.

3-15. INDUCTANCE AND TIME CONSTANTS

When voltage is applied to a circuit containing an inductor (coil), successive turns of the coil oppose a current change and must be overcome by applied electric force. As current builds up in each successive turn (in fractional time intervals), a *counter* voltage is induced, which sets up a counter current flow in the adjacent turn of the coil. The induced electromotive force (voltage) always opposes the applied voltage and hence is known as *back-electromotive force* (back emf) or *counter-electromotive force* (cemf). The coil characteristics relating to such counter emf determine the *inductance* of the coil, and it is from this circumstance that coils are also called *inductors*.

The unit for inductance is the *henry* (H) after the American scientist Joseph Henry (1797–1878). The henry is the amount of inductance in a coil when a current change of one ampere per second produces an induced voltage of one volt. The symbol for inductance is L. Usually the plural of henry is given as *henrys*, though on occasion the spelling *henries* may be found.

The opposition for the current change in an inductor causes a voltage lead and current lag (90°). The inductance involving mks units can be calculated by the equation:

$$L=\frac{\mu N^2 A}{l} \tag{3-35}$$

where L is the inductance in henrys
N is the number of turns of the coil
μ is the permeability of the magnetic
material in mks units ($\mu=4\pi 10^{-7}$ H/m)
A is the cross-sectional area in square meters
l is the length of the coil in meters.

Thus, the value of the inductance is proportional to the square of the number of turns of the coil. Consequently if the number of turns is doubled, the inductance will quadruple.

Since permeability varies with flux density, an inductor with a ferromagnetic core has different values of inductances for variations in flux densities. To solve for inductance, the effect of the operating current on permeability must be taken into consideration, hence the inclusion of μ in Eq. 3-35. For an air-core coil this variability is not a factor, since μ equals one.

When an inductor is placed in series with a resistor and voltage is applied to the combination, current flow starts at a low value and builds up rapidly as the back emf is overcome by the applied electric pressure. Thus, as shown in Fig. 3-9, exponential curves are produced when the inductor charge current and the charge voltage are plotted. The time required for the current through the inductor to reach 63 percent of its maximum value is known as the L/R time constant. The equation is:

$$\tau=\frac{L}{R} \tag{3-36}$$

where L is the inductance in henries
τ is the time constant in seconds
R is the resistance value in ohms.

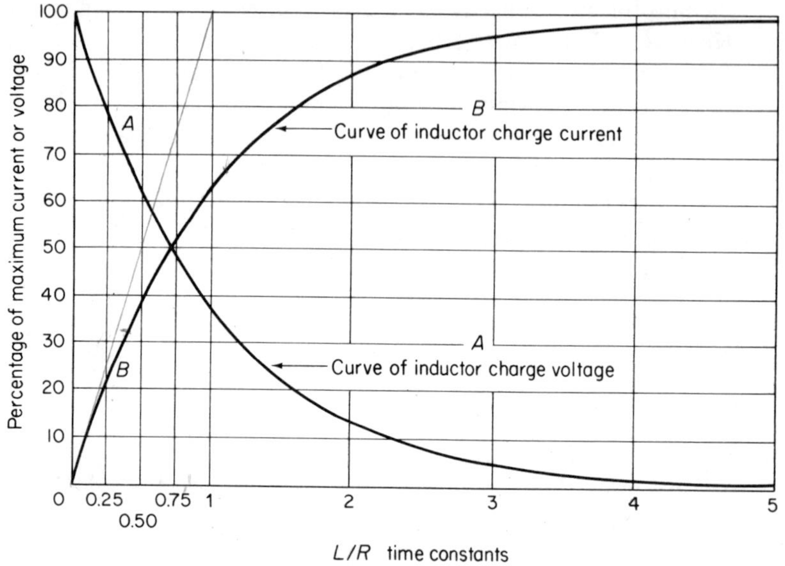

FIGURE 3-9. Universal time-constant chart for L and R.

By rearrangement we can also obtain:

$$L = \tau \times R \tag{3-37}$$

$$R = \frac{L}{\tau} \tag{3-38}$$

Example

A 15-mH coil is in series with a 150-Ω resistor. After voltage is applied, how long does it take for the current to reach 63 percent of its maximum value?

Solution

$$\tau = L/R = 0.015/150 = 0.1 \text{ ms } (100\ \mu\text{s})$$

Thus, 100 μs represents one time constant and is thus the time required for current to reach 63 percent of its maximum value. (After 5 τ the inductor voltage is considered to have reached the zero value, with current at a maximum.)

Reference should be made to Table 3-6 for time-constant values. The following equations based on exponential functions also apply for solving instantaneous values of current through the inductor or voltage across the resistor and inductor. These equations necessitate the use of tables of exponential functions for determining values of ϵ^{-x}. See Table 3-7, (or use a scientific calculator). For the equations involving L/R circuits, the x value is always tR/L, where t is the time in seconds, R the resistance in ohms, and L the inductance in henrys.

The instantaneous current (i_L) through the inductor is found by adapting the Ohm's law equation:

$$i_L = \frac{E}{R}(1 - \epsilon^{-tR/L}) \tag{3-39}$$

where i_L is the instantaneous current through the inductor
E is the maximum applied voltage
R is the ohmic value of the resistance.

By rearrangement we get:

$$e_L = E\epsilon^{-tR/L} \tag{3-40}$$

$$e_R = E(1 - \epsilon^{-tR/L}) \tag{3-41}$$

Example

A circuit with an inductor of 150 mH is in series with a 2.5-kΩ resistor. The applied voltage is 125 V. What is the instantaneous current value through the inductor at 15 μs after the voltage is applied?

Solution

Solving initially for tR/L:

$$0.000015 \times \frac{2500}{0.15} = \frac{0.0375}{0.15} = 0.25$$

The 0.25 value represents the x value in the ϵ^{-x} portion of the equation. Now reference is made to the exponential function tables (or a scientific calculator is used) for ascertaining the value of ϵ^{-x}. From the tables we find that for a value of 0.25 for x, the value of ϵ^{-x} is 0.7788. The equation now becomes:

$$\begin{aligned} i_L &= 0.05(1 - 0.7788) \\ &= 0.05 \cdot 0.2212 \\ &= 0.01106 \text{ A } (11.06 \text{ mA}) \end{aligned}$$

3-16. INDUCTIVE REACTANCE

An inductor opposes a change of current (in constrast to the capacitor, which opposes a change of voltage). The opposition in the inductor is the back emf generated during any voltage build-up or decline. With *ac* there is a continual rise and decline of potential at a periodic rate. Hence, while the opposition is overcome with dc (in a specific time interval), the changing *ac* maintains the opposition. As a result, a fixed unit value of inductor opposition is created for ac and is referred to as *reactance*, or more specifically as *inductive reactance*. The symbol is X_L.

The amount of inductive reactance present for a given inductance depends on the angular velocity of the ac as well as the unit value of the inductance in henrys. (As mentioned in Sec. 3-13, angular velocity is $6.28f$ and its symbol is ω.) The complete expression for inductive reactance is:

$$X_L = 2\pi fL = \omega L = 6.28fL \tag{3-42}$$

where X_L is the inductive reactance in ohms
f is the frequency in Hz
L is the inductance in H.

By rearrangement of Eq. 3-42 we can solve for inductance or frequency:

$$L = \frac{X_L}{\omega} \tag{3-43}$$

$$f = \frac{X_L}{6.28L} \tag{3-44}$$

Inductive reactance is also proportional to the voltage drop across the inductor and the alternating current through it. Thus, inductive reactance follows Ohm's law:

$$\begin{aligned} X_L &= E/I \\ I &= E/X_L \\ E &= IX_L \end{aligned} \tag{3-45}$$

3-17. *Z* IN *RL* CIRCUITRY

As shown for inductor time-constant curves in Fig. 3-9, when voltage is first applied across an inductor-resistor combination, the applied voltage across the inductor is initially high, while current values build from zero. Thus, in an inductor, current lags voltage by 90° and no power is consumed by an inductance unless some resistance is present. With some inductors that use large-diameter wire, the resistance may be so low in comparison to other circuit resistance that coil resistance may be considered negligible, and no significant power will be consumed. With a 90° phase difference between E and I, the cosine of the phase angle in Eq. 3-16 will be zero, resulting in zero power usage.

When an inductor is in series with a resistor, the opposition to alternating current flow (ac) is no longer simple reactance or resistance, but rather *impedance* (Z), as was the case with RC circuitry discussed in Sec. 3-14. Now the opposition is a function of the angles between 0° and 90°, and the following equation applies:

$$Z=\sqrt{R^2+X_L^2} \tag{3-46}$$

The impedance-triangle relationships for R and X_L are shown in Fig. 3-10, the related circuit being shown in part A. Thus, if the resistance has a value of 104 Ω and X_L has a value of 78 Ω, the right-angle relationships exist as shown in Fig. 3-10B. Using Eq. 3-46 we obtain:

$$Z=\sqrt{10{,}816+6084}=\sqrt{16{,}900}=130\ \Omega$$

As shown in Fig. 3-10C, voltage relationships also follow vector addition. As shown in Fig. 3-4B, $I=E/Z$, hence for the circuit shown in

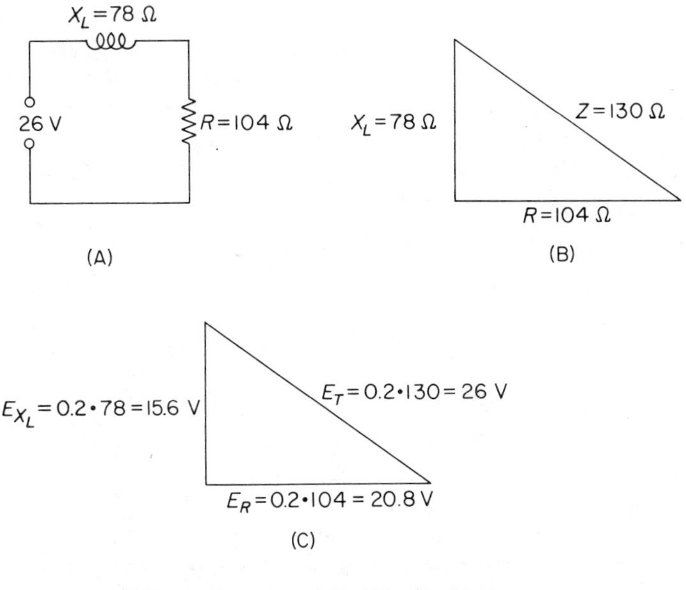

FIGURE 3-10. Z and V triangles (RL).

Fig. 3-10B current is 26/130=0.2 A. The voltage across the inductor is $E_{X_L} = IX_L = 0.2 \cdot 78 = 15.6$ V, while $E_R = IR = 0.2 \cdot 104 = 20.8$ V. Thus, Eq. 3-46 can be converted into an equation for finding total voltage if we know the individual voltages across X_L and R:

$$E_T = \sqrt{E_R^2 + E_{X_L}^2} \tag{3-47}$$

Thus, for the example of Fig. 3-10 we have:

$$\sqrt{432.64 + 243.36} = \sqrt{676} = 26 \text{ V}$$

Equations 3-46 and 3-47 apply to series combinations of reactance and resistance. For resistance in parallel to reactance, currents assume vector relationships:

$$I_T = \sqrt{I_R^2 + I_{X_L}^2} \tag{3-48}$$

Solving for Z, the applied voltage E is divided by total current:

$$Z = E/I_T \tag{3-49}$$

For additional data on impedance, see also Secs. 3-14 and 3-18.

3-18. *Z* IN *LCR* CIRCUITS

When both inductance and capacitance are present in either a series or parallel circuit, counter effects occur, and the tendency for inductance to oppose a current change is affected by capacitance's opposition to a voltage change. Thus, for a series circuit the following equations apply:

$$Z = \sqrt{R^2 + (X_L - X_C)^2} \tag{3-50}$$

$$E_T = \sqrt{E_R^2 + (E_{X_L} - E_{X_C})^2} \tag{3-51}$$

In Eq. 3-50, the ohmic value of X_C is subtracted from X_L, unless X_C is larger in value, in which case X_L is subtracted from X_C. Thus, the final result is the impedance triangle shown in Fig. 3-11, where the reactance (X) value represents the ohmic difference between X_L and X_C.

Currents in a parallel *LCR* circuit must also be reduced to resistive and reactive values as was done for Eq. 3-48. Thus, the equation for

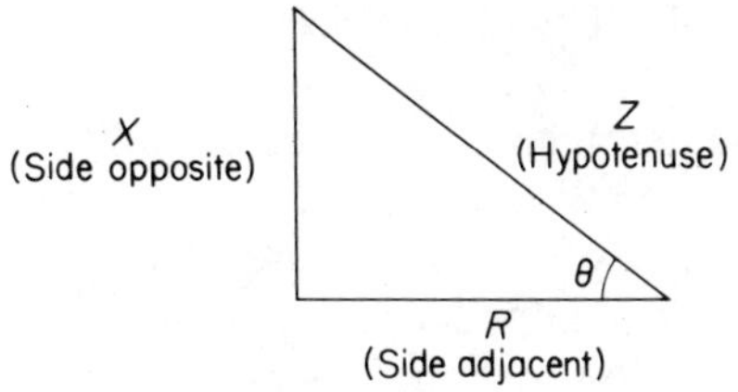

FIGURE 3-11. Z triangle.

finding total current in an *LCR* circuit is:

$$I_T=\sqrt{I_R^2+(I_{X_L}-I_{X_C})^2} \tag{3-52}$$

Thus, Z can now be calculated on the basis of E/I_T (Eq. 3-49).

Impedance, as well as other values, can be found by using such trigonometric techniques as measuring or solving for the angle θ in Fig. 3-11, or finding the tangent of the angle:

$$\tan\theta=\frac{\text{side opposite}}{\text{side adjacent}}=\frac{X}{R} \tag{3-53}$$

Once the tangent is known, the phase angle, the cosine, etc. can be obtained from trigonometric ratio, tables, or scientific calculators.

The impedance can also be found without the necessity for using Eq. 3-50. Since the cosine of an angle is the ratio of the side adjacent the angle to the hypotenuse, the value of the side adjacent (R) can be divided by the cosine to obtain the hypotenuse (Z). Thus, if $X=6\ \Omega$ and $R=8\ \Omega$, we have:

$$\tan\theta=6/8=0.75$$

$$\cos\theta=0.7986$$

$$\theta=37°$$

$$Z=8/0.7986=\sim 10\ \Omega$$

Other equations for finding Z are given in Fig. 3-4B, as well as in Sec. 3-21.

If, for Eq. 3-50 through 3-53, the inductive reactance should be equal to the capacitive reactance, the opposing factors would cancel all reactance, leaving only resistance. In such an instance the condition known as *resonance* has been produced. Resonance is discussed in detail in Sec. 3-22.

3-19. REACTORS AND TRANSFORMERS

Reactor is the term applied to a coil and is a synonym for an inductor. Another term applied to a coil is *solenoid*, particularly if the coil's length is greater than its radius. In industry, a variety of coils and transformers are used for impedance-matching purposes, for altering ac potentials, and for electric isolation of dc.

When current flows through a coil, the individual magnetic fields generated by the coil turns combine to form an electromagnet with characteristics similar to those of a bar magnet, with fields as shown in Fig. 3-12A. When a soft-iron core is inserted in the coil, the magnetic lines of the field are increased considerably, forming a more powerful electromagnet. Field intensity does not increase (unless current flow through the coil increases), but the increase in magnetic lines is caused by magnetization of the core material, which then produces fields of its own to reinforce those of the coil.

In a coil such as the one in Fig. 3-12A, magnetic fields occur only during current flow through the coil because of applied electric pressure (voltage). Thus, the fields are generated by *magnetomotive force* (mmf). In addition to applied voltage and current flow, magnetomotive force can also be applied by a magnetized external unit, such as a magnet or another electromagnet. In the cgs system the unit of magnetomotive force is the *gilbert*, after the English researcher in magnetism, William Gilbert (1540–1603).

Increasing the number of turns of a coil also increases magnetizing force over that obtained when current flow is increased:

$$\text{Magnetomotive force (F)} = 1.256NI \qquad (3\text{-}54)$$

where 1.256 is 0.4π
N is the number of turns of wire
I is the current in amperes.

A gilbert is defined as the magnetomotive force required to produce a flux of one maxwell in a magnetic circuit in which the reluctance is one. The product NI (number of turns times current) is also known as *ampere turns* in the mks system. As with Ohm's law, the relationships between flux (ϕ), reluctance ($\mathcal{R}$), and magnetomotive force (F) in magnetic circuits are expressed by the following equations. (See also Sec. 3-10, Units of Magnetism.)

$$\mathrm{F} = \phi\mathcal{R}, \quad \phi = \frac{\mathrm{F}}{\mathcal{R}}, \quad \mathcal{R} = \frac{\mathrm{F}}{\phi} \qquad (3\text{-}55)$$

When more than one winding is present on a core form, a transformer is the product, as is shown in Fig. 3-12B (step-down) and in Fig.

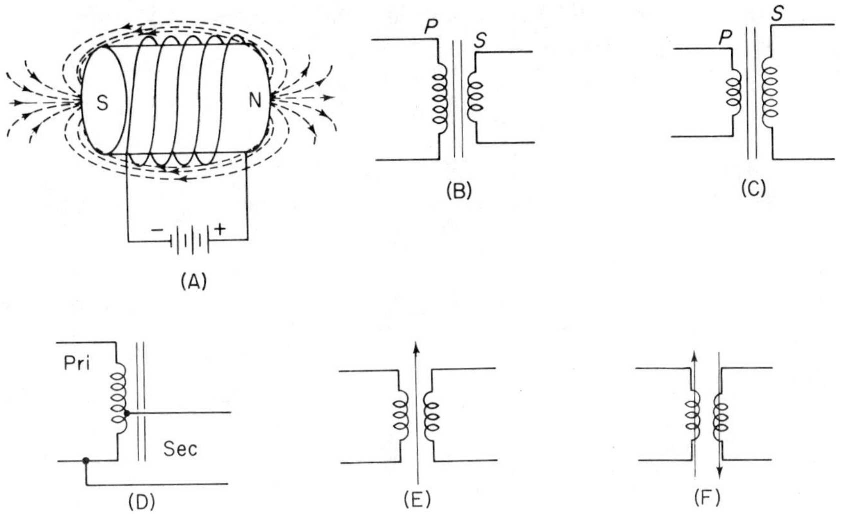

FIGURE 3-12. Inductors and transformers.

3-12C (step-up). A single tapped winding can be used as in Fig. 3-12D to form an autotransformer. In RF applications many transformers have *movable metallic cores*. The variable positioning is indicated by an arrow as in Fig. 3-12E, or by the two arrows in Fig. 3-12F, where both the primary and secondary have movable cores (also called *metal slugs* or *tuning slugs*).

The number of coil turns in the primary (P) winding and secondary (S) determines the voltage or impedance transfer ratio. The turns ratio relationships are expressed as:

$$\frac{E_{\text{sec}}}{E_{\text{pri}}} = \frac{N_{\text{sec}}}{N_{\text{pri}}} \tag{3-56}$$

where E_{sec} is the voltage across the secondary
E_{pri} is the voltage across the primary
N_{sec} is the number of coil turns in the secondary
N_{pri} is the number of coil turns in the primary.

By rearrangement of Eq. 3-56, the following equations are also produced:

$$E_p N_s = N_p E_s \tag{3-57}$$

$$E_p = \frac{N_p E_s}{N_s} \tag{3-58}$$

$$E_s = \frac{E_p N_s}{N_p} \tag{3-59}$$

If the turns ratio between primary and secondary is known, the following equation can be used:

$$E_s = \text{turns ratio} \times E_p \tag{3-60}$$

The inverse relationship of voltage and current in a transformer means that current step-down occurs just as voltage step-up does. Hence, the following equation applies:

$$\frac{I_p}{I_s} = \frac{N_s}{N_p} \tag{3-61}$$

Equations similar to Eq. 3-57 through 3-59 can also be derived:

$$I_p N_p = N_s I_s \tag{3-62}$$

$$I_p = \frac{N_s I_s}{N_p} \tag{3-63}$$

$$I_s = \frac{I_p N_p}{N_s} \tag{3-64}$$

The ratio of the secondary impedance (Z_s) to the primary impedance (Z_p) varies as the square of the turns ratio:

$$\frac{Z_s}{Z_p} = \frac{N_s^2}{N_p^2} \tag{3-65}$$

Thus, the turns ratio necessary to obtain an impedance match between two electronic circuits with a transformer is given by the following equation:

$$\text{Turns ratio} = \sqrt{\frac{Z_1}{Z_2}} \tag{3-66}$$

The impedance of one circuit can be stepped down to meet a lower circuit impedance, or stepped up as required to match a higher circuit impedance.

Transformer and reactor efficiencies depend on the type of core material, as well as other factors—using large-diameter wire decreases resistive losses, and using less winding turns minimizes capacitive losses. The core material can alter the speed by which voltages and magnetization fields change amplitude or polarity. Ferrite and other high-efficiency core material produce rectangular-type hysteresis curves as shown in Fig. 3-13. For soft-iron cores, the curves would slope more toward the horizontal.

Such curves are also called *hysteresis loops* and $B-H$ curves, since flux density B and the magnetizing force H are shown on the Y and X axis respectively. Such hysteresis graphs are obtained by applying voltage to the coil winding for creation of current flow and the production of a magnetizing force. As voltage is gradually raised, current increases as does the magnetizing force. Flux density rises at a rate dependent on core material. As current increases, a point is reached where the flux density levels off as core saturation is reached, as shown by the solid line in Fig. 3-13.

If the applied voltage is now lowered to decrease coil current, the flux density does not retrace in unison with the declining current. Instead, it follows a return path situated above the initial path as shown. Finally, when no voltage is being applied and current-flow ceases within the coil,

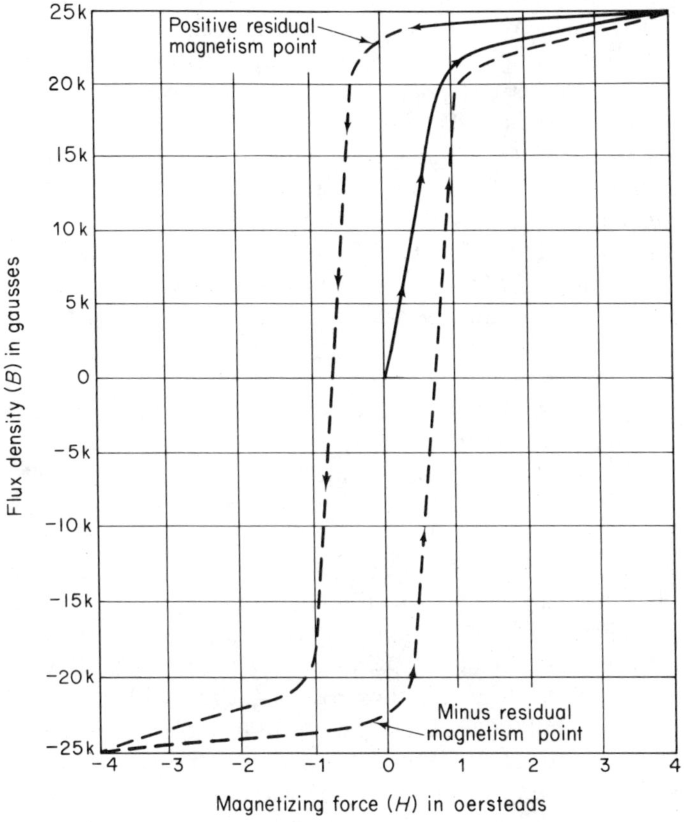

FIGURE 3-13. Hysteresis graph for ferromagnetic materials.

the magnetizing force no longer prevails. However, the flux density is not at zero, but is at the point on the graph marked *positive residual magnetism point*.

Thus, as the magnetizing force was lowered progressively, the flux density lagged behind the magnetizing force; it is because of this *lagging* characteristic that the word *hysteresis* originates, since it is derived from the Greek word *hysterein* meaning *to lag, to be behind*. The lower portion of the graph displays the curves obtained for application of voltage of opposite polarity to that applied initially.

3-20. *j* OPERATOR AND RECTANGULAR NOTATION

Rectangular notation is a system that employs both *real* and *imaginary* numbers for identifying units of resistance and reactance. It also has been termed *complex algebra* or *operator j algebra*. In this system a vector quantity is designated by an ordinate of real quantity and an ordinate of the *j* quantity, for example: $Z = 34 + j6\ \Omega$. This notation is in contrast to the *polar form* (also termed *polar notation*), which would lead to such expressions as: $Z = 50\underline{/36.8^\circ}\ \Omega$.

When two numbers with opposite signs are multiplied, the result is a negative number. Thus, if we multiply 30 by -1 we obtain -30. When, however, we multiply two numbers having negative signs, we obtain a positive number: $-1 \times -30 = 30$. In the foregoing examples, we could have considered the -1 as an *operator* which, during multiplication, would reverse the sign of the number by which it is multiplied *without changing its amplitude*.

This basic principle can be applied to the rotating vector arm of Fig. 3-14. There we use the sign-reversing characteristic of the operator -1 to indicate a counterclockwise rotation of 180 electric degrees. The vector arm, designated as A, has a fixed amplitude and angle with respect to the horizontal reference line X. Thus, if the vector arm had a magnitude of 50 units and were multiplied by -1, we would get a counterclockwise rotation, as shown by the broken circle, of 180° resulting in the representation of -50 units. This change constituted a complete reversal of polarity as shown by the vector arm position B. Now, if this -50 position is again multiplied by -1, the counterclockwise rotation for another 180° brings the vector arm back to its original position at A, again with a positive sign. If the vector-arm amplitude is multiplied *twice by the* -1 *operator*, a total rotation of 360° occurs (180 + 180).

For ac calculations the operator used causes a counterclockwise rotation of 90° instead of the 180° one produced by -1. This special operator must be one that produces -1 when multiplied by itself. It would

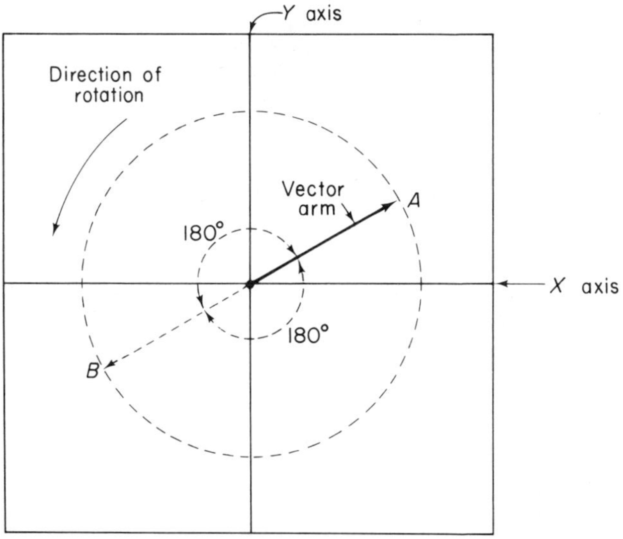

FIGURE 3-14. Vector factors of −1.

seem that the exact unit value of the required operator could be found by taking the square root of −1. However, this can't be done because a negative number has no real square root. (No negative or positive number, when multiplied by itself, produces a negative product. Multiplying either two negative numbers or two positive numbers produces a positive product.)

Since there is no real square root of −1, the number representing $\sqrt{-1}$ is designated an *imaginary number*. In mathematics the imaginary number $\sqrt{-1}$ is given the symbol *i*, but since *i* also indicates instantaneous current in electricity or electronics, the letter *j* is used to represent $\sqrt{-1}$

The signs of both the imaginary and real values are shown in Fig. 3-15, which illustrates the complete graph with its four quadrants. The *point of origin* is considered to be at the intersection of *X* and *Y* axes. Direction to the right of *Y* is positive, to the left is negative. A direction below the *X* axis is negative, above it is positive. One multiplication by operator *j* rotates the vector quantity 90°. The term j^2 indicates $\sqrt{-1} \times \sqrt{-1} = 90° + 90° = 180°$. For j^3 we obtain 270°, while for j^4 we have $(j^2)^2 = (-1)^2 = 1$; which brings the rotation back to the place of origin, i.e., a complete 360° rotation.

In rectangular notation we will consider resistance values as plotted along the *X* axis, and reactance values along the *Y* axis. An inductive reactance value is prefixed with a $+j$ and a capacitive reactance, with a

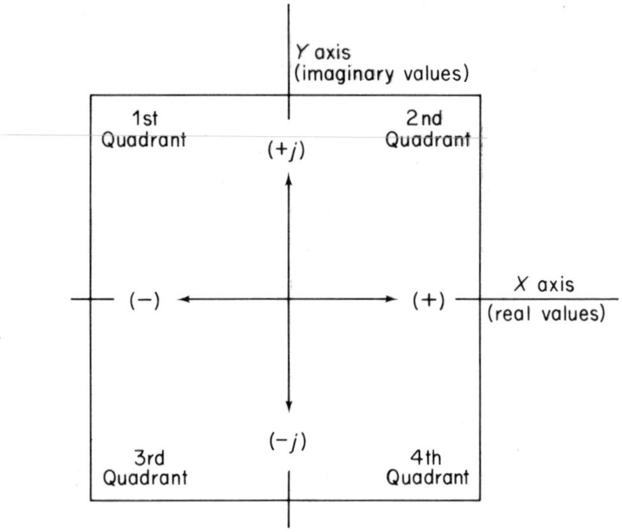

FIGURE 3-15. Graph quadrants and signs of values.

$-j$. Polar form can be converted to rectangular form by the following equation:

$$Z = Z\cos\theta + jZ\sin\theta \tag{3-67}$$

Thus, a polar form expression is converted to rectangular as follows:

$$Z = 5\underline{/36.8^\circ}\ \Omega$$
$$= 5 \times 0.8 + j5 \times 0.599$$
$$= 4 + j3\ \Omega$$

Equation 3-67 can also be utilized for total vector voltage (E_T) or total vector current (I_T) as shown below for E_T:

$$E_T = E_T\cos\theta + jE_T\sin\theta$$

Various *LCR* combinations are shown in Fig. 3-16. The impedance formula for each circuit is also shown, using rectangular notation. For other discussions on impedance, reference should be made to Secs. 3-14, 3-17, and 3-18.

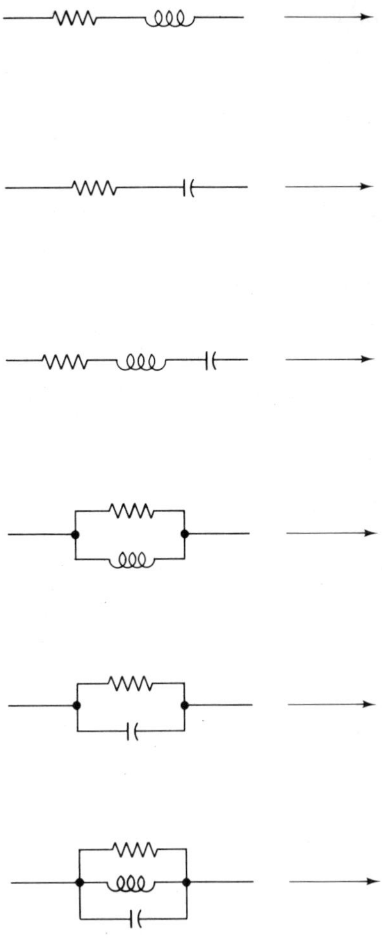

$$Z = R + j\omega L$$

$$Z = R - \frac{1}{j\omega C}$$

$$Z = R + j\left(\omega L - \frac{1}{\omega C}\right)$$

$$Z = \omega LR\left(\frac{\omega L + jR}{R^2 + \omega^2 L^2}\right)$$

$$Z = \frac{R(1 - j\omega CR)}{1 + \omega^2 C^2 R^2}$$

$$Z = \frac{\frac{1}{R} - j\left(\omega C - \frac{1}{\omega L}\right)}{\left(\frac{1}{R}\right)^2 + \left(\omega C - \frac{1}{\omega L}\right)^2}$$

FIGURE 3-16. Z in rectangular notation.

3-21. ADMITTANCE AND SUSCEPTANCE

As stated in Sec. 3-8, conductance (G) is the reciprocal of resistance. In addition to resistance, impedance and reactance also have reciprocal functions. The reciprocal of impedance is *admittance* for which the symbol is Y, with unit values in *mhos* as with conductance. Similarly, the reciprocal of reactance is *susceptance*, for which the symbol is B. On occasion, inductive susceptance may be expressed as B_L and capacitive susceptance as B_C. Again, unit values are in *siemens*. The following equations apply:

$$G = \frac{1}{R} \tag{3-68}$$

$$Y = \frac{1}{Z} \tag{3-69}$$

$$B = \frac{1}{X} \tag{3-70}$$

Admittance, susceptance, and conductance are functions useful in solving parallel circuits containing L, C, and R. The following equations are also useful:

$$Y = \frac{1}{R + jX} \tag{3-71}$$

$$Y = G - jB_L \tag{3-72}$$

$$Y = G + jB_C \tag{3-73}$$

$$B_L = \frac{X_L}{Z^2} \tag{3-74}$$

$$B_C = \frac{X_C}{Z^2} \tag{3-75}$$

3-22. RESONANCE

When the capacitive reactance is equal in ohmic value to inductive reactance, their opposing characteristics cause cancellation of reactance, leaving only resistance in the circuit. When this condition occurs, the circuit becomes *resonant*, and is thus useful for signal-frequency selection. A resonant circuit has the ability to discriminate against unwanted signals above and below the resonant frequency, while at the same time offering a highly selective circuit for the desired signal. Without these resonant-circuit characteristics, all types of radio, television, radar, and other familiar forms of communication as we know it would be impossible. Hence, the resonant circuit is one of the most vital and widely used devices ever discovered in electronics.

Because capacitive or inductive devices can be made variable, such components can be tuned to achieve resonance for a particular signal

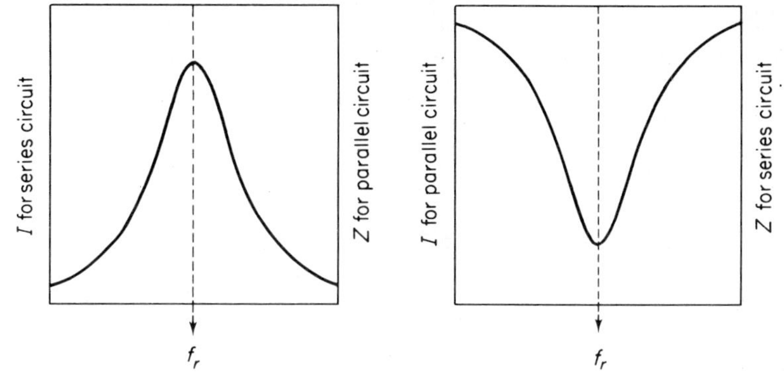

FIGURE 3-17. Resonant-circuit graphs.

frequency (or a cluster of signals having frequencies around the resonant frequency). At resonance, the circuit impedance becomes purely resistive. In a series resonant circuit, at resonance, current rises and impedance values drop. At parallel resonance, impedance rises, but currents drop. These characteristics are illustrated in Fig. 3-17. The degree of sharpness of the resonant curve determines selectivity. (See also Sec. 4-7.)

Because $X_L = X_C$ at resonance, $X_L - X_C = 0$. Expressed with the omega symbol (ω) for angular velocity, this becomes:

$$\omega L - \frac{1}{\omega C} = 0 \qquad (3\text{-}76)$$

From Eq. 3-76 we now obtain:

$$\omega^2 = \frac{1}{LC} \text{ or } (6.28f)^2 = \frac{1}{LC} \qquad (3\text{-}77)$$

hence,

$$LC = \frac{1}{\omega^2} \qquad (3\text{-}78)$$

From Eq. 3-77 we obtain:

$$f_r = \frac{1}{6.28\sqrt{LC}} \qquad (3\text{-}79)$$

where f_r is the resonant frequency in Hz
L is the inductance in H
C is the capacitance in F.

Example

An inductor with a value of 0.2 μH and a capacitor of 0.8 μF are in series. What is f_r?

Solution

$$f_r = \frac{1}{6.28\sqrt{0.2 \times 0.8 \times 10^{-12}}} = 398 \text{ kHz}$$

The radical signal in Eq. 3-79 can be removed by using the following equation:

$$f_r^2 = \frac{1}{4\pi^2 LC} \tag{3-80}$$

In Eq. 3-79 the determining factor for the resonant frequency is the product LC. Thus, there are any number of inductive-capacitive values that produce the same resonant frequency, as long as their product is the same. The LC product of 0.098, for instance, produces a frequency of 509 kHz, regardless of the values of L or C used to produce the 0.098 product. Circuit selectivity is determined by the specific values of L and C that are used. (See Table 14-4 as well as Sec. 4-7.)

Equation 3-79 can be converted to solve for the inductance in henrys if the frequency and capacitance value are known:

$$L = \frac{1}{4\pi^2 f^2 C} \tag{3-81}$$

Similarly, the capacitance value necessary with a given inductance for resonance can be found by:

$$C = \frac{1}{4\pi^2 f^2 L} \tag{3-82}$$

4

Basic Component Combinations and Equations

4-1. RESISTORS IN SERIES AND PARALLEL

A number of standard equations are available for calculating values of components in series or parallel. When resistors are connected in series, for instance, as in Fig. 4-1A, the total resistance of the individual resistances is equal to the sum of the ohmic values of the individual resistances:

$$R_T = R_1 + R_2 + R_3 + \cdots + R_N \tag{4-1}$$

Thus, if four resistors are in series, and their individual values are 60 Ω, 10 Ω, 15 Ω, and 5 Ω, their total resistance (R_T) is 90 Ω. Similarly, if two 25-kΩ resistors are in series, the total resistance is 50 kΩ.

If *two* resistors are in parallel, the following equation is used:

$$R_T = \frac{R_1 R_2}{R_1 + R_2} \tag{4-2}$$

Hence, if a 60-Ω resistor is in parallel with a 30-Ω resistor, total resistance is 20 Ω:

$$\frac{60 \times 30}{60 + 30} = \frac{1800}{90} = 20\ \Omega$$

For parallel resistor combinations, total resistance is always less than the ohmic value of the lowest-valued resistor of the combination.

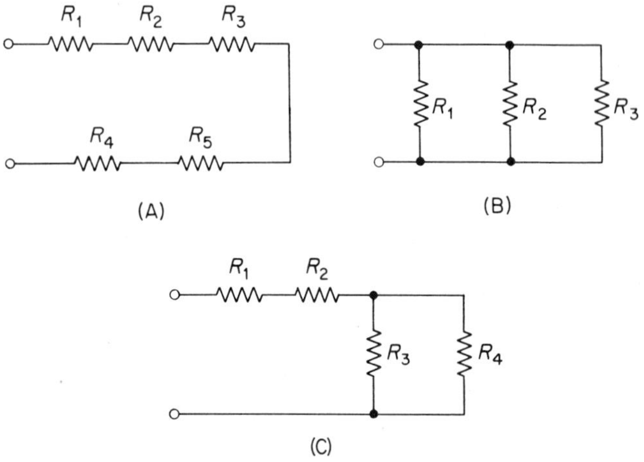

FIGURE 4-1. Series-parallel resistor circuits.

When three resistors are in parallel as shown in Fig. 4-1B, the following equation is useful. This formula can be expanded to solve for as many resistors in parallel as required.

$$R_T = \frac{1}{\frac{1}{R_1} + \frac{1}{R_2} + \frac{1}{R_3} + \cdots} \tag{4-3}$$

An alternate to Eq. 4-3 is the following:

$$\frac{1}{R_T} = \frac{1}{R_1} + \frac{1}{R_2} + \frac{1}{R_3} + \cdots \tag{4-4}$$

As discussed in Secs. 3-8 and 3-22, conductance (G) is the reciprocal of resistance, hence they are the inverse of each other:

$$G = \frac{1}{R} \tag{4-5}$$

$$R = \frac{1}{G} \tag{4-6}$$

For resistors in *parallel*, total conductance is the sum of the individual conductances:

$$G_T = G_1 + G_2 + G_3 + \cdots \tag{4-7}$$

When resistors are in series-parallel combinations, as shown in Fig. 4-1C, Eqs. 4-1 and 4-2 are combined:

$$R_T = R_1 + R_2 + \frac{R_3 R_4}{R_3 + R_4} \tag{4-8}$$

4-2. KIRCHHOFF'S LAWS

The German scientist Gustav Kirchhoff (1824-1887) formulated two basic laws concerning electric circuitry. Kirchhoff's laws may be stated as follows:

1. The current (or sum of currents) flowing into any junction of an electric circuit is equal to the current (or sum of currents) flowing out of that junction.
2. The source voltage (or sum of such voltages) around any closed circuit is equal to the sum of the voltage drops across the resistances around the same circuit.

The first law is illustrated in Fig. 4-2A. This law is also known as the *current law* and is often stated as: "the *algebraic* sum of all currents at any point in a circuit is *zero*." Thus, at a given point, the current flow toward that point has a direction opposite to that of the current flowing away from that point (one is positive, the other negative). Hence, the algebraic sum indicates zero from the standpoint of analysis, even though a definite amount of current flows.

Thus, for Fig. 4-2A we have:

$$I_T - I_1 - I_2 - I_3 = 0$$

$$20 - 10 - 6 - 4 = 0$$

NOTE: For Fig. 4-2, the direction of current flow has been taken as the direction of electron flow (from negative to positive). For conventional current flow theory (from positive to negative), Kirchhoff's laws still apply, and the final results are the same.

The second law (voltage law) can be stated as: "the algebraic sum of all the voltages around the circuit is zero." This law is illustrated in Fig. 4-2B, where individual meters show the voltage readings across the resistors. Starting at the plus side of the battery and going in the direction of electron flow (through the battery), we indicate the respective polarities

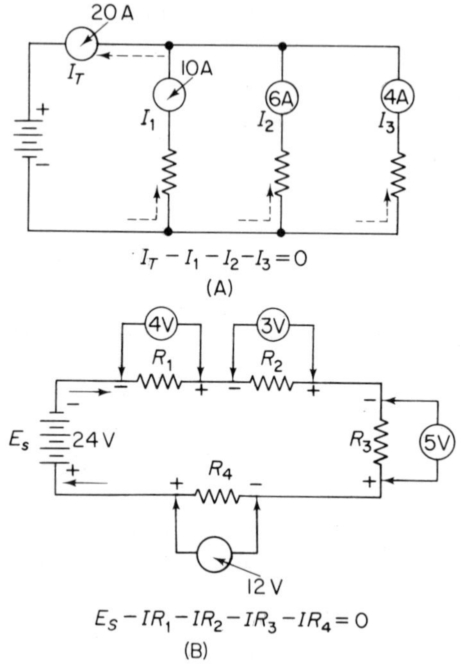

FIGURE 4-2. Kirchhoff's current and voltage laws.

and set down the values for voltage source (E_s) and IR drops across the resistors. Thus, we obtain:

$$E_s - IR_1 - IR_2 - IR_3 - IR_4 = 0$$
$$= 24 - 4 - 3 - 5 - 12 = 0$$

4-3. THÉVENIN'S THEOREM

When circuit components are not readily accessible for making measurements, circuit characteristics can be analyzed by the method referred to as *Thévenin's theorem.* Essentially, Thévenin's theorem states that a given network, with constant voltage and resistance, will produce current flow in the load resistor equal to that which would flow if the load resistor were applied across an equivalent circuit having: (a) an internal resistance measured at the terminals of the circuit, with the voltage source replaced by its equivalent internal resistance; and (b) a voltage at the terminals equal to that existing in the original circuit, after removal of the load resistor.

The load resistor mentioned in the theorem may be an actual resistor or some other network combination of components representative of a resistive load applied to the circuit under question. The theory is useful because if circuit components are not readily accessible for measurement or test, the components can be thought of as behaving as though the circuit were completely enclosed in a container (a box, for instance). Data can be gathered from the two or more terminals available. The box concept is often encountered in circuit design analysis and is usually referred to as a *black box* when this method of evaluating circuit characteristics comes under discussion.

4-4. NORTON'S THEOREM

Norton's theorem is based on a source voltage producing a *constant current* as opposed to the *constant voltage* theorem of Thévenin covered in Sec. 4-3. The impedance of the equivalent circuit is considered to be in parallel with the load resistance of the circuit in question.

Other than the difference noted above, Norton's theorem is similar to Thévenin's in that it also states that any resistive voltage network can be replaced by a single voltage and resistance as an equivalent.

4-5. CAPACITORS IN SERIES-PARALLEL

When capacitors are wired in series, as shown in Fig. 4-3A, total capacitance is less than the lowest-valued capacitor. Thus, the equations for finding total capacitance resemble the equations used for solving parallel resistance:

$$C_T = \frac{C_1 C_2}{C_1 + C_2} \tag{4-9}$$

$$C_T = \frac{1}{\dfrac{1}{C_1} + \dfrac{1}{C_2} + \dfrac{1}{C_3} + \dfrac{1}{C_4} + \cdots} \tag{4-10}$$

If a 5-μF capacitor is in series with a 15-μF unit, Eq. 4-9 yields the following:

$$C_T = \frac{5 \cdot 15}{5 + 15} = \frac{75}{20} = 3.75\ \mu\text{F}$$

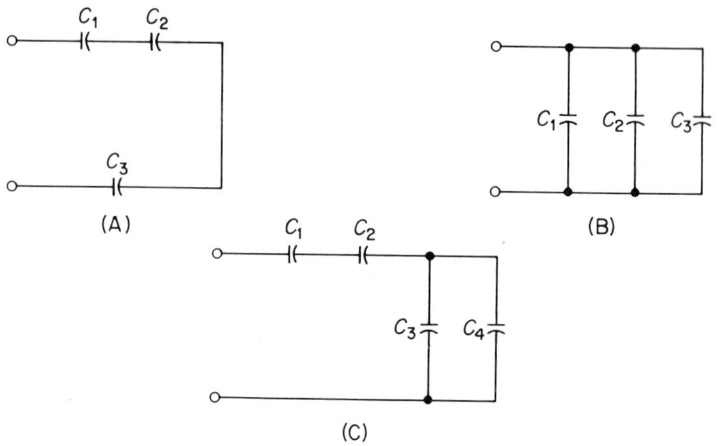

FIGURE 4-3. Series-parallel capacitor circuits.

For the parallel capacitors shown in Fig. 4-3B, the total capacitance equals the sum of the individual values:

$$C_T = C_1 + C_2 + C_3 + \cdots \tag{4-11}$$

For the series-parallel combination shown in Fig. 4-3C, we combine Eq. 4-9 and Eq. 4-11:

$$C_T = \frac{C_1 C_2}{C_1 + C_2} + C_3 + C_4 \tag{4-12}$$

If more than two capacitors are in series, Eq. 4-10 is used instead of Eq. 4-9 within Eq. 4-12. (For additional information on capacitance, see Secs. 3-12 and 3-13.)

4-6. INDUCTORS IN SERIES-PARALLEL

When two or more inductors are in series, as those in Fig. 4-4A, and are also spaced sufficiently far apart so that their fields do not interact, the total inductance is found by an equation similar to that for series resistors:

$$L_T = L_1 + L_2 + L_3 + \cdots \tag{4-13}$$

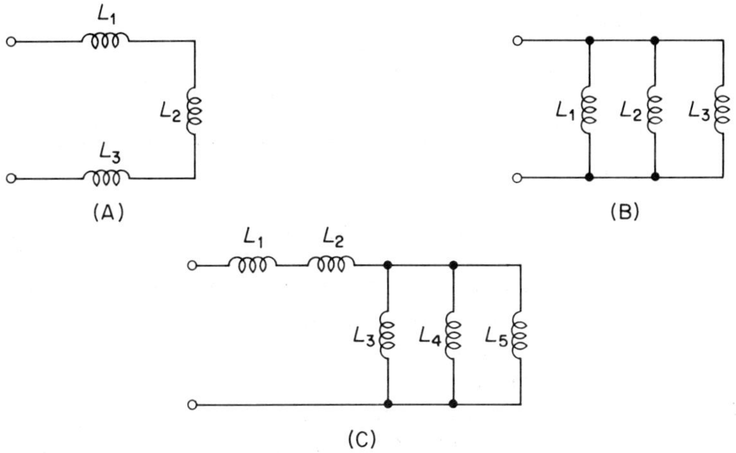

FIGURE 4-4. Series-parallel inductor circuits.

When inductors are in parallel as in Fig. 4-4B, (but again with no magnetic field interaction), the equation is:

$$L_T = \frac{L_1 L_2}{L_1 + L_2} \quad \text{(for two inductors)} \tag{4-14}$$

$$L_T = \frac{1}{\frac{1}{L_1} + \frac{1}{L_2} + \frac{1}{L_3} + \cdots} \tag{4-15}$$

For series-parallel combinations of inductors with no magnetic interaction between any of them, Eqs. 4-14 (or 4-15) and 4-13 are combined:

$$L_T = L_1 + L_2 + \frac{1}{\frac{1}{L_3} + \frac{1}{L_4} + \frac{1}{L_5}} \tag{4-16}$$

Additional information on inductance is found in Secs. 3-15 through 3-19.

When series inductors are sufficiently close for their magnetic fields to interact, the total inductance is affected by *mutual inductance*. If the coils are wound in the same direction, they are *series aiding*; but if one inductor is wound in a direction opposite to the other, they are *series opposing*. For series-aiding coils, the total inductance is found by the following equation:

$$L_T = L_1 + L_2 + 2M \tag{4-17}$$

For series-opposing coils, the total inductance is found by the following equation:

$$L_T = L_1 + L_2 - 2M \tag{4-18}$$

Mutual inductance is also a factor in transformers, since there is a mutual inductive interaction between the primary and secondary windings of the transformer. Mutual inductance may be defined as follows: When an ac of 1 A in the primary induces 1 V of ac in the secondary, the two inductances have a mutual inductance of 1 H. When all the magnetic lines of the primary cut the secondary winding (as in the case with ferromagnetic core transformers with overlapping windings), the equation for M is given as:

$$M = \sqrt{L_1 L_2} \tag{4-19}$$

With some RF coils, the coupling may not be as complete as with low-frequency transformers, hence all magnetic lines do not interact. In such instances the mutual inductance equation must be modified to compensate for the *coefficient of coupling* that exists. The latter is usually designated as k and Eq. 4-19 now becomes:

$$M = k\sqrt{L_1 L_2} \tag{4-20}$$

A coefficient of coupling (k) of 0.5 indicates that only one-half the magnetic lines of the primary winding intercept the secondary winding. Thus, the coefficient of coupling represents the percentage of coupling, which, in this case, is 50 percent.

If the mutual inductance (M) and the individual inductance are known, the coefficient of coupling (k) can be found by:

$$k = \frac{M}{\sqrt{L_1 L_2}} \tag{4-21}$$

When two inductors are in parallel with magnetic fields aiding, the following equation applies:

$$L_T = \frac{1}{\dfrac{1}{L_1 + M} + \dfrac{1}{L_2 + M}} \tag{4-22}$$

If the parallel inductors have opposing fields, the following equation applies:

$$L_T = \frac{1}{\dfrac{1}{L_1 - M} + \dfrac{1}{L_2 - M}} \tag{4-23}$$

4-7. Q (SELECTIVITY)

The *selectivity* of a resonant circuit is defined as its ability to reject signals having frequencies above and below the resonant frequency, while accepting signals at or around the resonant frequency. The symbol Q has been used as a figure of merit for the degree of selectivity. For the series resonant circuit shown in Fig. 4-5A, Q is altered by the amount of

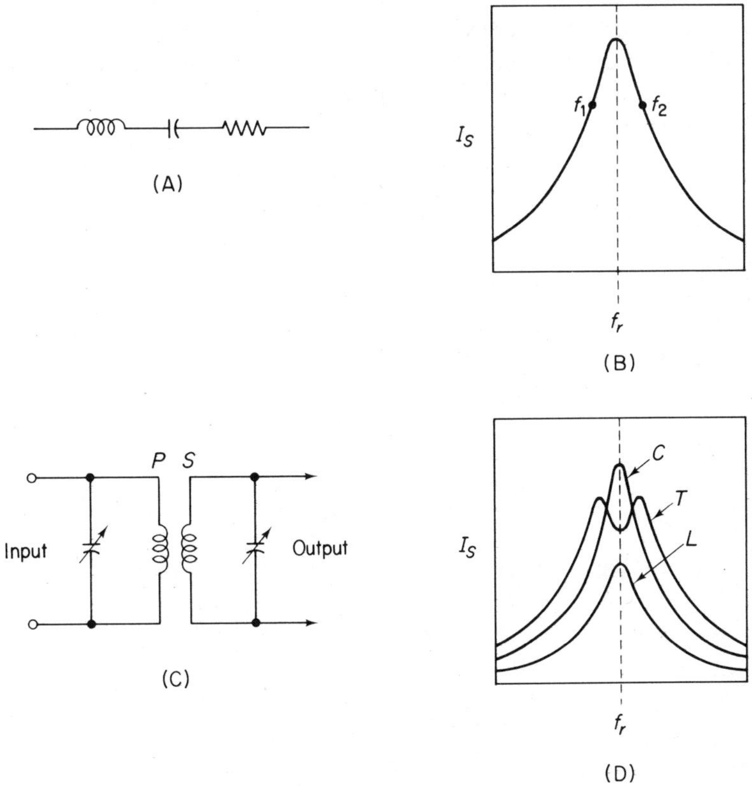

FIGURE 4-5. Resonant circuits and selectivity curves.

resistance present. When circuit current is plotted against frequency, we obtain a selectivity curve graph as shown in Fig. 4-5B. The sharpness of the resonance established is related to Q by the frequency points f_1 and f_2 as shown, with the resonant frequency (f_r) at the center.

The points, f_1 and f_2, are the frequencies at which the amplitude of the high- and low-frequency slopes are 0.707 of peak amplitude. These are known as *half-power frequencies*. The amplitude at these points, f_1 or f_2, is $1/\sqrt{2}$ of its value at f_r. The bandwidth of a particular circuit is the distance between the two points:

$$\text{bandwidth} = f_2 - f_1 \tag{4-24}$$

For the series circuit, the following equation applies:

$$Q = \frac{X_L}{R} \tag{4-25}$$

Thus, selectivity can be increased by increasing the X_L, decreasing R, or doing both in a series resonant circuit. (When L is increased to obtain a higher L/C ratio, however, the value of C must be decreased to maintain the same LC product.)

Additional related equations are:

$$f_2 = f_r + \frac{R}{4\pi L} \tag{4-26}$$

$$f_1 = f_r - \frac{R}{4\pi L} \tag{4-27}$$

$$f_2 - f_1 \text{ (bandwidth)} = \frac{R}{2\pi L} \tag{4-28}$$

$$Q = \frac{f_r}{f_2 - f_1} \tag{4-29}$$

$$f_r = Q(f_2 - f_1) \tag{4-30}$$

For parallel circuitry, the following equations apply:

$$Q = \frac{R}{X_L} \tag{4-31}$$

$$\text{bandwidth} = f_2 - f_1 = \frac{f_r}{Q} \tag{4-32}$$

When parallel circuits are coupled, as shown in Fig. 4-5C, the selectivity is altered by the degree of coupling since the load impedance connected to the secondary reflects some resistive characteristics to the primary, depending on the coefficient of coupling. For reference purposes, three degrees of coupling are identified: *loose coupling*, *critical coupling*, and *tight coupling*. The circuit characteristics of the three degrees of coupling are shown in Fig. 4-5D, where C identifies the critical coupling (with the highest peak). When the coefficient of coupling is increased to the point at which the reflected resistance equals that present in the primary, critical coupling occurs and secondary current is at a maximum.

With loose coupling (L), secondary current at resonance is lower than it is for other coupling methods, though a sharper response curve results. For increased coupling beyond critical, the term tight coupling (or *over-coupling*) (T), is used. Because of the increased reflected resistance added to that of the primary, the current curve at resonance undergoes a pronounced dip, providing for poor selectivity at the resonant frequency (thus widening the response curve).

At critical coupling the coefficient (k_c) is related to the individual circuit Q of the primary (Q_p) and the secondary (Q_s) by:

$$k_c = \frac{1}{\sqrt{Q_p Q_s}} \tag{4-33}$$

4-8. INTEGRATION CIRCUITRY

Simple component combinations are often used to modify signals to meet specific requirements. One such system is the *integrating circuit* used extensively in the vertical sweep systems of television receivers and in other applications where pulse modification is essential. The basic integrating circuit is shown in Fig. 4-6. It consists of a series resistor (R_1) and a shunt capacitor (C_1).

From the practical standpoint the integrator may be considered the equivalent of a low-pass filter network. This is because, for progressively higher-frequency sinusoidal signals, there will be an increasing attenuation

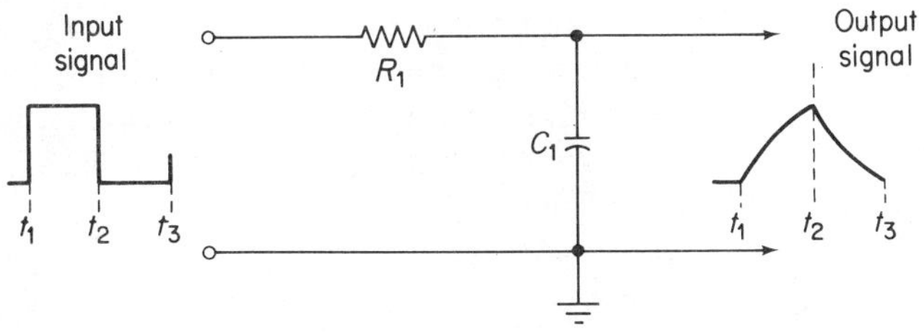

FIGURE 4-6. Integrating circuit.

since C_1 will have a decreasing reactance (hence, it behaves as a shunt). For square wave type signals and pulse waveforms, the output signal is an altered version of the input signal because of the filtering characteristic on the higher-frequency signal components that are contained in complex waveforms.

The charging rate (time constant) of the *RC* network determines the degree of modification that the input signal undergoes. From the calculus, the signal voltage applied to a capacitor (e_c) and the capacitor signal current (i_c) have the following relationship:

$$e_c = \frac{1}{C}\int i_c\,dt \tag{4-34}$$

where e_c is the signal voltage across the capacitor
C is the capacitance in farads
i_c is the capacitor signal current.

Equation 4-34 indicates that e_c, the signal voltage across the capacitor, is proportional to the time interval of i_c. For true integration, the time constant *RC* must be long compared to the input-signal (pulse) width. For the higher-order harmonic signal components of the pulse (for which the resistance value is much greater than that of the capacitive reactance of the capacitor), the following equation applies:

$$e_c = \frac{1}{RC}\int e\,dt \tag{4-35}$$

As shown by Eq. 4-35, the output signal voltage of an integrating circuit is proportional to the *integral* of the input-signal current. Thus, if a positive-going pulse is applied to the input as shown in Fig. 4-6, the steep leading edge applies a voltage across the circuit in a very short time interval. The flat top of the pulse then holds this voltage across the circuit for a time interval equal to the duration of the pulse, from time t_1 to time t_2 as shown. For a capacitor, the build-up of signal voltage lags that of the signal current, and voltage rises exponentially. During one time constant (*RC*), the capacitor reaches about 63 percent of the full charge. It takes approximately 5 *RC* to reach a full charge. Because of the long time constant of the integrator circuit, however, the voltage across C_1 is unable to attain the maximum amplitude where it would level off. Instead, there is a gradual incline as shown in Fig. 4-6.

At time t_2, when the input pulse amplitude decreases abruptly, the capacitor discharges through resistor R_1 and the impedance presented by the input circuit. Again, the long time constant prevents the output signal from making a sudden change, and a gradual decline occurs as shown. The gradual incline and decline of the output waveform produce the signal shown, wherein the higher-frequency harmonic components have been attenuated. The actual waveshape at the output depends on the relation of the time constant of the integrator circuit to the input pulse width.

4-9. DIFFERENTIATION CIRCUITRY

Like the integration circuitry discussed in Sec. 4-8, the *differentiator circuit* is another example of utilization of simple component combinations to modify signals to meet specific requirements. The basic circuit is shown in Fig. 4-7. In contrast to the integrator, it has a short time constant (RC) relative to the width of the input pulse signal. The differentiating circuit is useful for converting pulses of relatively long duration to sharp, narrow pulses useful for triggering purposes in computers, industrial control systems, radar, and other systems where rapid initiation of electronic processes is required.

The output waveform retains the leading edge of the input pulse (with identical polarity) and, in essence, behaves like a high-pass filter by attenuating the lower-frequency components of a pulse while retaining high-frequency harmonics.

From the calculus we find that the voltage applied to a capacitor produces a current flow in proportion to the time derivative of the voltage appearing across the capacitor. This is shown in the following equation:

$$i = C\frac{de_c}{dt} \tag{4-36}$$

For the short time constant (relative to input pulse width) of Fig. 4-7, certain signal components of the input pulse find that the resistor of the circuit has an ohmic value much lower than that of the reactance of C_1.

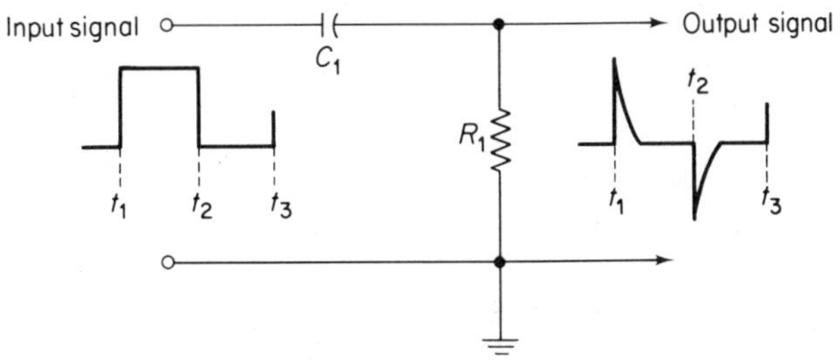

FIGURE 4-7. Differentiating circuit.

The voltage across the resistor is given by the following equation:

$$e_R = IR = RC\frac{de}{dt} \tag{4-37}$$

For the input pulse shown, at time t_1 the leading edge applies a steady-state voltage across the input for the duration of the pulse width. Since current leads voltage in a capacitor, the leading edge of the input pulse produces a high capacitor current, and a high current flows through R_1. Hence, a high-amplitude voltage suddenly appears across R_1, producing the rapidly rising leading edge of the spike-type output waveform shown in Fig. 4-7. During the time interval t_1 to t_2, the steady-state voltage applied to the circuit causes the capacitor to charge at a time rate dependent on the time constant of the circuit. As the capacitor charges, current declines, and with a short time constant, the capacitor charges rapidly and current drops to zero as shown in the output waveform prior to t_2.

When the trailing edge of the input pulse arrives (t_2), the voltage at the input suddenly drops to zero, and the capacitor then discharges. The discharge current-flow direction is opposite to that during charge; hence, current flow through the resistor is also opposite to that prevailing during the charging current interval. Consequently, a negative-spike waveform is produced at the output as shown.

When sinewaves are applied to a differentiating circuit, no waveshape change occurs between input and output signals, though attenuation occurs and varies inversely as the frequency (since C_1 offers an increasing capacitive reactance to signals of lower frequency).

In Fig. 4-7, C_1 can be replaced with a resistor and R_1 with an inductor. A short time constant again produces a differentiating circuit. However, inherent internal resistance of an inductor interferes with proper circuit function and makes design more difficult. Hence, the circuit shown in Fig. 4-7 is preferred.

4-10. PADS AND ATTENUATORS

When it is necessary to control signal levels in electric-electronic circuitry or match dissimilar impedances between interconnected units, *pads* and *attenuators* are utilized. These are resistive networks arranged to provide the desired results.

Tone and volume controls of the type shown in Fig. 4-8 are typical examples of attenuators (without impedance matching functions). Such tone controls are extensively employed in audio systems to alter the

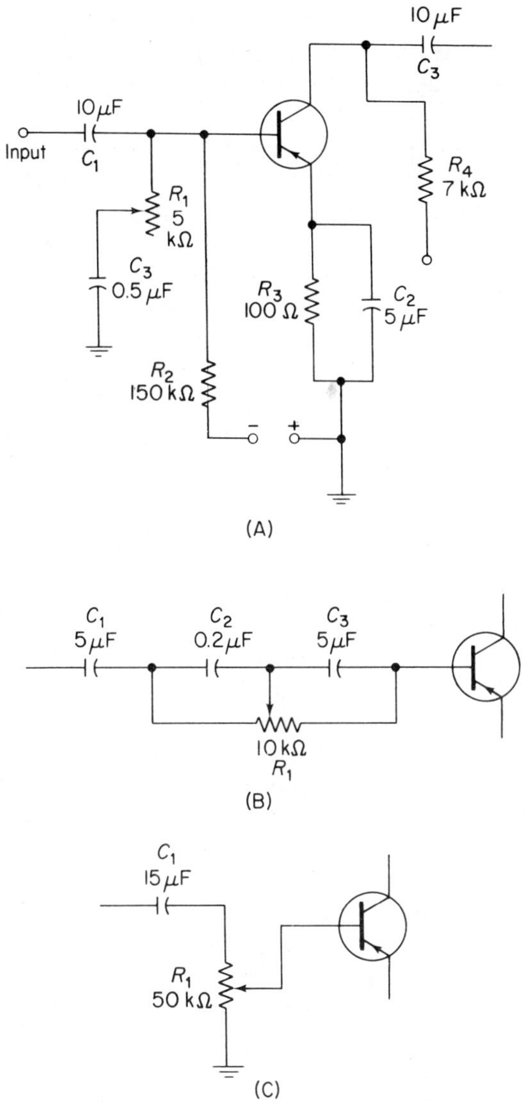

FIGURE 4-8. Tone controls.

frequency response characteristics by permitting the user to diminish either the high- or low-frequency signals as desired. Attenuation is accomplished at a sacrifice in maximum gain, since the diminishing of lower-frequency signals, for instance, will reduce total output and will make it necessary to readjust the gain control to obtain the same (equivalent) sound output level as before.

The control in Fig. 4-8A is a bass tone control consisting of R_1 and C_3. As the resistance of R_1 is reduced, the capacitive reactance of C_3 increasingly shunts higher-frequency signals. This, in effect, accents the bass tones.

A treble control is shown in Fig. 4-8B. When the variable arm of R_1 is positioned at the extreme left, C_2 is effectively shorted, permitting the relatively lower reactance of C_3 to pass most signals at normal attenuation. When the arm is at the extreme right, however, C_3 is shorted, leaving C_2 in series with the signal input. Its higher reactance (because of its lower capacitance) causes an increasingly greater attenuation for signals of lower frequencies. Attenuation of lower-frequency signals causes the higher-frequency signals (by comparison) to predominate. Intermediate settings of R_1 provide various degrees of control.

The simplest and most basic gain control is shown in Fig. 4-8C, where a variable resistor shunts the input to an amplifier. The variable arm selects the degree of signal amplitude required for application to the input of the amplifier. This type of control is often used as the volume control in audio systems or as the gain control, as well as brilliancy control, in television receivers. No impedance matching is accomplished. As the control is varied, impedance changes.

By using an additional resistor in gain control sections, an *L pad* is formed to provide for impedance matching. Pads can be fixed or variable; asymmetrical or symmetrical. Asymmetrical pads are those having dissimilar impedances between input and output. Such pads are used for impedance matching between circuits. Symmetrical pads have identical input and output impedances, and their purpose is to introduce a desired amount of attenuation to decrease signal levels as needed. Both asymmetrical and symmetrical pads may be *unbalanced* (one line grounded and the other above ground) or *balanced* (both lines above ground).

A basic L-type fixed pad is shown in Fig. 4-9A. This pad is designed to match Z_1 and Z_2 and is asymmetrical. It is also known as a *minimum-loss* type since it introduces only a minimum amount of attenuation while matching the impedance of the circuit at the input to the impedance of the circuit connected to the output of the pad.

The L pad can decrease or increase impedance, stepping it down or up as needed. If, for instance, a 300-Ω input is to be matched to a subsequent circuit of 50 Ω, as in Fig. 4-9B, the resistor values shown would be used. The Z_1 section of 300 Ω thus "sees" a resistor of 280 Ω in series with a parallel branch of R_1 (56 Ω) and Z_2 of 50 Ω. By Ohm's law, the total resistance that Z_1 then "sees" is sufficiently close to its own 300-Ω value to form a satisfactory impedance match. The output device, represented by Z_2, "sees" a shunting resistance of 56 Ω, paralleled by a series branch of 280 Ω and 300 Ω. This provides an ohmic value of about 50 Ω (or a value sufficiently close to this even if standard resistor values are used).

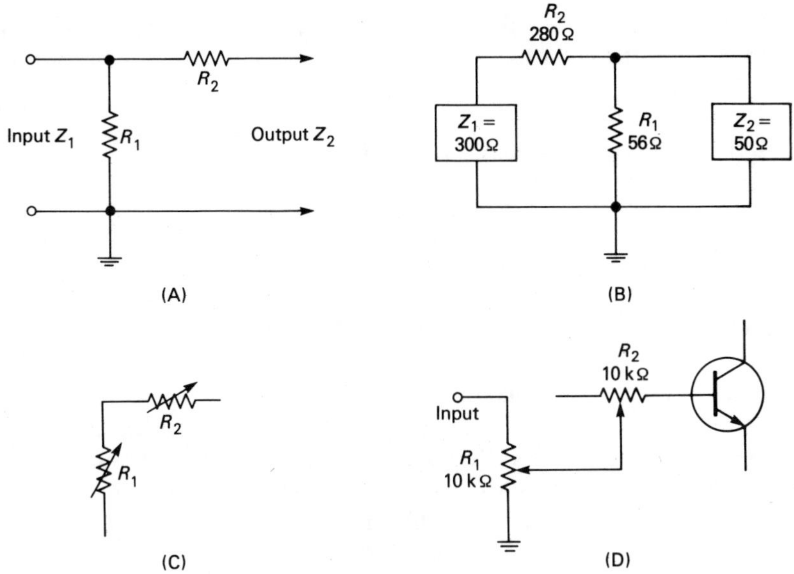

FIGURE 4-9. L pads (fixed and variable).

For the L pad of Fig. 4-9, resistors and impedances have the following relationship:

$$R_1R_2 = Z_1Z_2 \tag{4-38}$$

When Z_1 has an impedance lower than Z_2, the relationship can be expressed as follows (using whole-numbers for convenience in the ratio of the impedances):

$$\frac{R_2}{R_1} = \frac{Z_2}{Z_1} - 1 \tag{4-39}$$

If R_1 is known, the value of R_2 can be found by:

$$R_2 = \left(\frac{Z_2}{Z_1} - 1\right)R_1 \tag{4-40}$$

Thus, in Fig. 4-9B, the value of R_2 is (using Eq. 4-40):

$$R_2 = \left(\frac{300}{50} - 1\right)56 = 5 \times 56 = 280\ \Omega$$

If neither resistor value is known, individual values can be obtained from the following equations:

$$R_1 = \frac{Z_1}{\sqrt{1-(Z_1/Z_2)}} \tag{4-41}$$

$$R_2 = Z_2\sqrt{1-(Z_1/Z_2)} \tag{4-42}$$

The conventional representation for a variable L pad is shown in Fig. 4-9C, though in practical applications two variable resistors are connected to form the network shown in Fig. 4-9D. The value of the 10-kΩ shunt resistance is maintained for the transistor input, regardless of the gain control setting. For maximum gain, the variable arm for R_1 is at the top and the arm for R_2 at the extreme right position. A balanced-circuit L pad is shown in Fig. 4-10A. Because it resembles the letter U turned on its side, it has been known as a *U pad*. Each series resistor is now one-half of the value of R_2 shown in Fig. 4-9A. In Fig. 4-10B values are shown for matching a 50-Ω input to a circuit of 300 Ω connected across the output. Compare these values with those shown in Fig. 4-9B.

Attenuators and pads can also be wired in cascade as shown in Fig. 4-10C. As such they form a *ladder pad*. As more resistors are included in the ladder sequence, attenuation increases.

Resistive networks can also be arranged in a T or H pattern as shown in Fig. 4-11. Figure 4-11A shows the standard symbol for the variable T pad, with actual wiring shown in Fig. 4-11B. The three arms

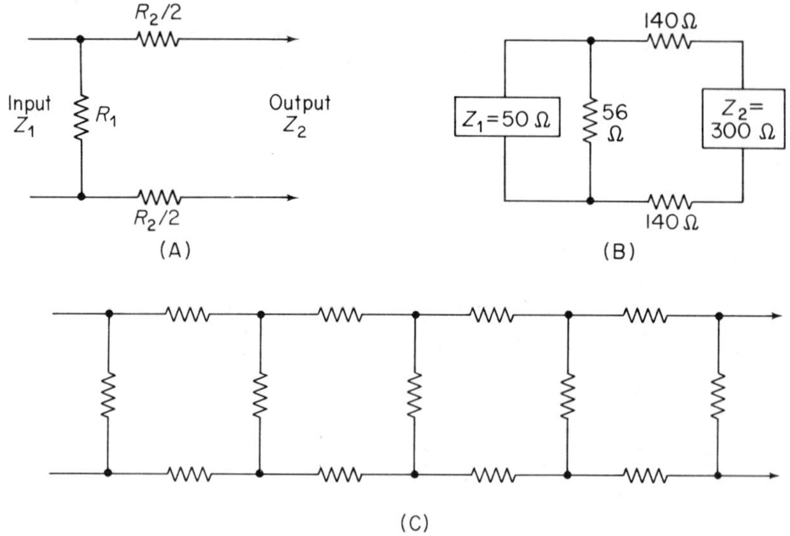

FIGURE 4-10. Balanced L and ladder pads.

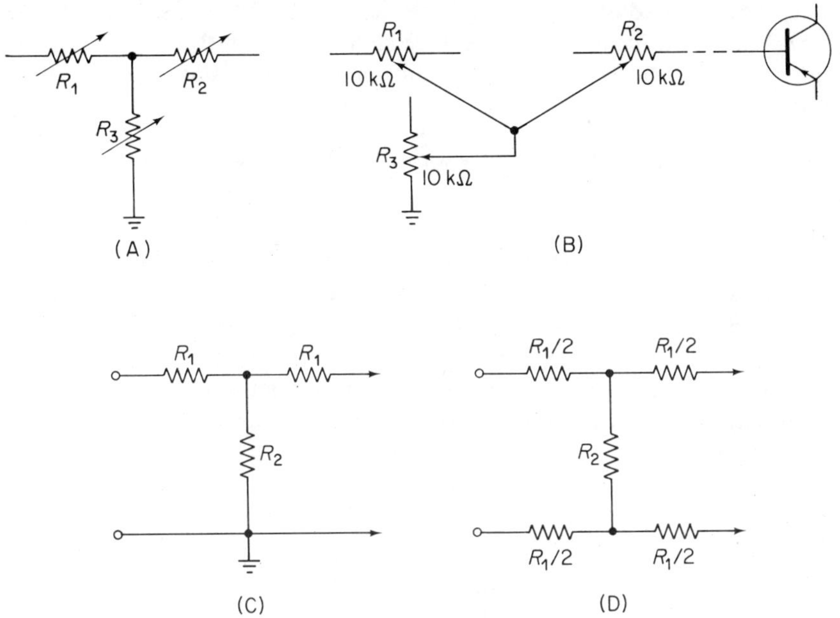

FIGURE 4-11. T and H pads.

move in tandem. For maximum signal transfer, R_1 is at the left, arm R_2 is at the right, and arm R_3 is at the top.

A fixed symmetrical *T pad* is shown in Fig. 4-11C, where the impedance of the input circuitry matches that of the circuit connected to the output. Attenuation of signal is the sole intended end result, with no changes made in impedance relationships. Since no Z matching is needed, all R_1 values are identical, with the three resistors selected to obtain the required degree of signal attenuation. The T pad in Fig. 4-11C is an unbalanced type, with the balanced equivalent shown in Fig. 4-11D. Here the R_1 values must be halved in comparison to the values for the network shown in Fig. 4-11C.

To solve for the R_1 and R_2 values, we must relate them to the ratio of signal-voltage or signal-current attenuation needed. Hence, the equations for finding the resistor values must utilize the ratio of attenuation desired between the input and output of the pad. Either voltage or current can be used. For purposes of illustration, the voltage ratio is shown in the following equations:

$$R_1 = Z\left(\frac{E-1}{E+1}\right) \tag{4-43}$$

$$R_2 = Z\left[\frac{2E}{(E+1)(E-1)}\right] \tag{4-44}$$

Thus, for the T pad at C of Fig. 4-11, if the signal voltage has an amplitude of 0.8 V and is to be attenuated to furnish an output of 0.08 V, the voltage ratio (E) would be 10. If the impedance is 50 Ω, the value of R_1 is found by Eq. 4-43:

$$R_1 = 50\left(\frac{10-1}{10+1}\right) = 50\left(\tfrac{9}{11}\right) = 50 \times 0.8 = 40\ \Omega$$

A symmetrical *pi pad*, unbalanced with respect to ground, is shown in Fig. 4-12A. The balanced version is shown in Fig. 4-12B and is sometimes known as an *O pad* because of its similarity in shape to the letter O. Because impedances are similar at input and output, no matching design is involved and resistance values are chosen for the amount of attenuation needed. As with T pads, equations must utilize attenuation ratios. The voltage-attenuation ratio version is as follows:

$$R_1 = Z\left(\frac{E+1}{E-1}\right) \tag{4-45}$$

$$R_2 = Z\left(\frac{E^2-1}{2E}\right) \tag{4-46}$$

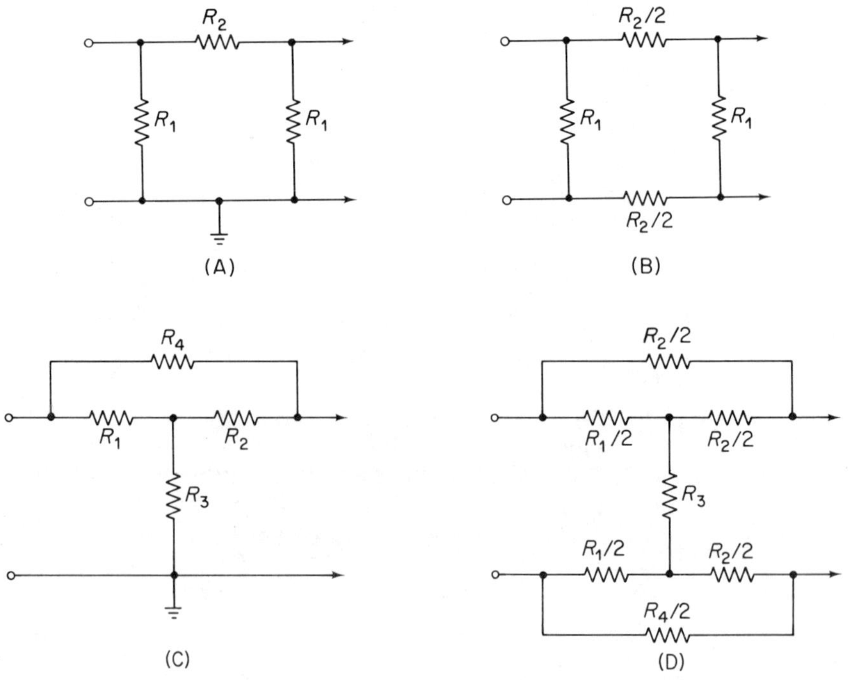

FIGURE 4-12. Pi, O, and bridged T and H pads.

An additional resistor may be bridged across the series resistors of the T and H pads to form what is known as a *bridged pad*, shown in Fig. 4-12C and D. The ohmic values of R_1 and R_2 individually must match Z; hence, only resistors R_3 and R_4 must be calculated. Their equations are:

$$R_3 = \frac{Z}{E-1} \tag{4-47}$$

$$R_4 = Z(E-1) \tag{4-48}$$

4-11. LOW-PASS FILTERS

Low-pass filters transfer low-frequency signals, but attenuate or eliminate high-frequency signals. Thus, as shown in Fig. 4-13, shunt capacitances provide a low reactance for higher-frequency signals, and series inductors offer high reactances against transfer of high-frequency signals. Consequently, low-frequency signals are transferred.

For Fig. 4-13A, the circuit arrangement resembles an inverted capital letter L; hence, it is known as an *L-type filter* as well as a *half section*. Successive half sections can be combined as required to obtain specific characteristics. An added inductor is shown in Fig. 4-13B and is known as a *T filter*.

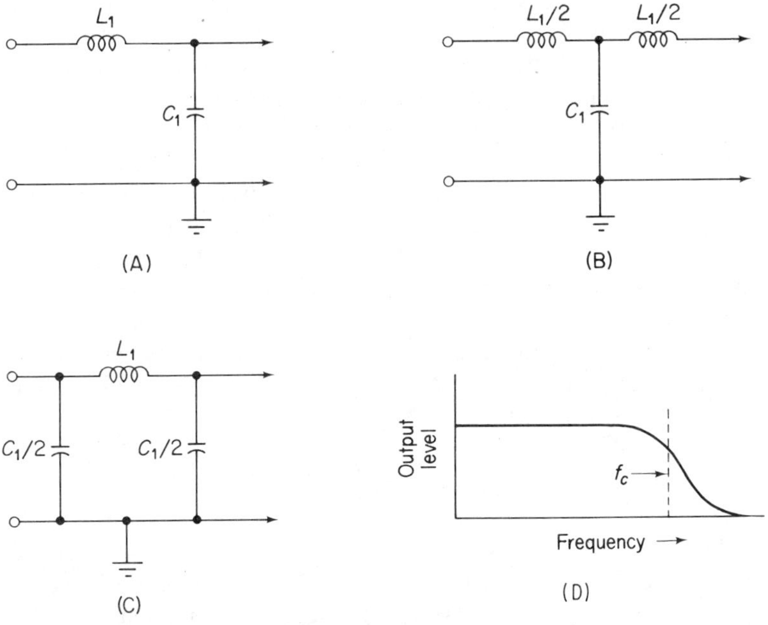

FIGURE 4-13. Low-pass constant-*k* filters.

Figure 4-13C shows an additional shunt capacitance being used for added attenuation of high-frequency signals. The inductor, with shunt capacitances on each side, makes the network appear like the Greek letter pi (π); hence, this type of filter is known as a *π-type filter*. A typical response curve is shown in Fig. 4-13D, where the cutoff frequency (f_c) indicates the signal frequency above which attenuation occurs. Often the f_c refers to the point where 70.7 percent of peak value still exists.

4-12. BASIC FILTER FACTORS

Filter circuitry containing reactive components has a constant Z even though additional half sections are present (or signal voltage amplitudes change). Thus, if the low-pass filter network of Fig. 4-13A had an infinite number of similar sections connected to it in progression, the original impedance of the circuit would still prevail. This results because no resistance was present originally, nor was any added by inclusion of more C and L sections (assuming pure inductances and capacitances). Since neither L or C consume electrical energy, Z remains unchanged.

With an infinite number of sections, the LC filter acquires the electrical characteristics of a transmission line, because electrical energy applied at the input causes current to travel through the successive half sections, as the components of C and L progressively charge and discharge. The values of voltage and current ratios (E/I) determine Z, and for the theoretical infinite line, an ohmic value is obtained indicating the inherent circuit impedance (Z_0), termed the *characteristic impedance*. This term is also applied in relation to the transmission lines used for transferring electric energy between two points. (Characteristic impedance is also known as *iterative*, or *repetitive*, *impedance*, as well as *surge impedance*.) (See Chapter 12, RF Transmission Lines and Antennas.)

When one or more half sections (connected to form a filter) are terminated in a resistance equal to the Z_0, signal current flow equals that which would prevail if the line were infinitely long. A maximum signal-energy transfer from input to output only occurs when the load resistance applied to the output matches the characteristic impedance. The value of Z_0 is found by:

$$Z_0 = \sqrt{\frac{L}{C}} \tag{4-49}$$

The term *constant k* is applied to the filters of Fig. 4-13 to indicate a symmetrical system in which the product of the series and shunt reactances remains fixed in value, regardless of the frequency of applied signal. Thus, for the filter in Fig. 4-13A, the series reactances can be designated as Z_1

(to include any possible resistive components), and the shunt reactances as Z_2. The following relationship prevails:

$$Z_1 Z_2 = k^2 \tag{4-50}$$

This k factor is constant for all signal frequencies, and Eq. 4-50 also applies to the other filters shown in Fig. 4-13. Total inductance values are found by:

$$L = \frac{R}{\pi f_c} \tag{4-51}$$

where R is the terminating resistance
f_c is the cutoff frequency in hertz
L is the inductance in henrys.

As shown in Fig. 4-13B, the series inductors are designated as $L_1/2$ since each (in series) has one-half of the value of total inductance. Similarly, each capacitor is indicated as $C_1/2$ in Fig. 4-13C, since each in shunt contributes to one-half the total capacitance value. Total C is found by:

$$C = \frac{1}{\pi f_c R} \tag{4-52}$$

where R is the terminating resistance
f_c is the cutoff frequency in hertz
C is the capacitance in farads.

The cutoff frequency for the constant-k low-pass filter is found by:

$$f_c = \frac{1}{\pi \sqrt{LC}} \tag{4-53}$$

4-13. *m*-DERIVED LOW-PASS FILTERS

An m-derived filter is formed when another component is added (in series or shunt) to the basic constant-k filter to obtain a sharper and more defined signal-frequency cutoff. Figure 4-14A shows that the added component is L_2, which now forms a series resonant circuit for a specific frequency. At resonance, the impedance of the series-resonant circuit is low, and this fact aids in producing a sharp cutoff in the curve shown in Fig. 4-14B. Hence, this filter uses the resonance to obtain an infinite attenuation at a specific frequency beyond the cutoff (f_c) frequency.

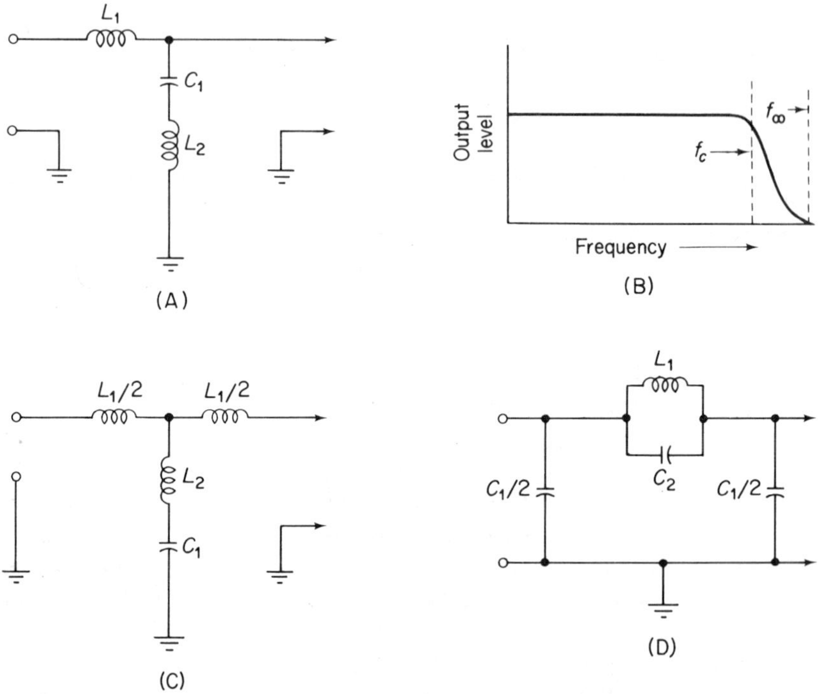

FIGURE 4-14. Low-pass *m*-derived filters.

The component impedances are interrelated by a constant *m*, which (in equation form) is related to the ratio of the cutoff (f_c) to the frequency of infinite attenuation (designated as f_∞). The value of *m* is fractional and generally around 0.6. For a better defined cutoff, *m* is nearer zero. The *m* value for a low-pass filter is:

$$m = \sqrt{1 - \left(\frac{f_c}{f_\infty}\right)} \tag{4-54}$$

The T-type *m*-derived filter, shown in Fig. 4-14C, again uses a series-resonant circuit. In Fig. 4-14D is the π-type *m*-derived filter, with the additional component C_2 forming a parallel-resonant circuit (with high *Z* at resonance) and with sharp attenuation for high-frequency signals.

For the filters of Fig. 4-14, *L* and *C* values are found by the following equations:

$$L_1 = \frac{mR}{\pi f_c} \text{ and } L_2 = \frac{(1-m^2)R}{4m\pi f_c} \tag{4-55}$$

$$C_1 = \frac{m}{\pi f_c R} \text{ and } C_2 = \frac{1-m^2}{4m\pi f_c R} \tag{4-56}$$

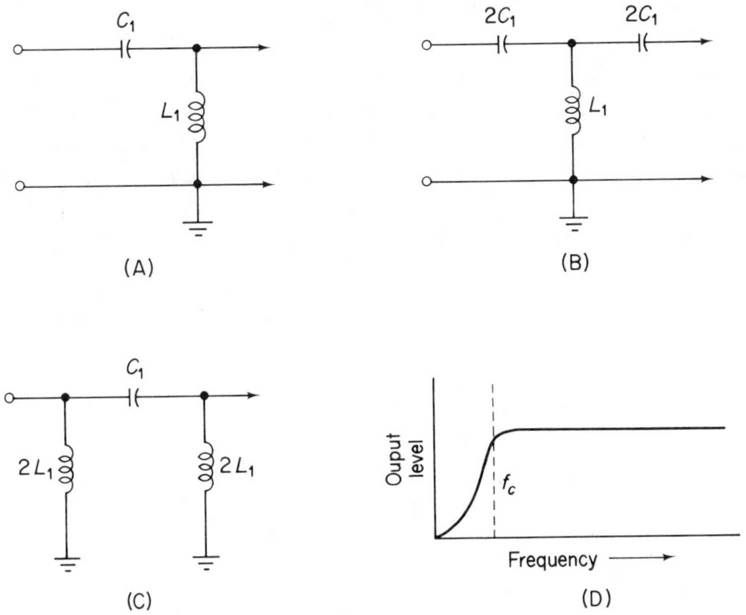

FIGURE 4-15. High-pass constant-k filters.

4-14. (CONSTANT k) HIGH-PASS FILTERS

A filter that easily passes higher-frequency signals, but attenuates signals of lower frequency is referred to as a *high-pass filter*. Several constant-k types are shown in Fig. 4-15. Since the function of the high-pass filter is the inverse of that of the low-pass type, the L and C components are interchanged as shown.

As with the low-pass filters, the impedance Z_o of the section must match that of the terminating (load) resistance for a maximum transfer of signal energy. The factors relating to constant-k filters discussed for the low-pass filters also apply to the high-pass types. The characteristics are shown in Fig. 4-14D, and the cutoff frequency (f_c) now indicates the frequency *below* which attenuation occurs. Related equations, with units identical to the low-pass equations given earlier in Secs. 4-11, 4-12, and 4-13, are:

$$L = \frac{R}{4\pi f_c} \tag{4-57}$$

$$C = \frac{1}{4\pi f_c R} \tag{4-58}$$

$$f_c = \frac{1}{4\pi\sqrt{LC}} \tag{4-59}$$

4-15. *m*-DERIVED HIGH-PASS FILTERS

Like the low-pass types, *m*-derived sections can be designed with the high-pass, constant-*k* types for sharper attenuation around the cutoff point. The basic types are shown in Fig. 4-16, with the series capacitor C_2 added in the circuits of Fig. 4-16A and C. For the circuit in Fig. 4-16D, the addition of L_2 forms a parallel-resonant circuit. The response curve is shown in Fig. 4-16B, with f_c the cutoff point and f_∞ the point of infinite attenuation at the low-frequency end. The following equations apply:

$$m=\sqrt{1-\left(\frac{f_\infty}{f_c}\right)^2} \tag{4-60}$$

$$L_1=\frac{R}{4\pi f_c m} \tag{4-61}$$

$$C_1=\frac{1}{4\pi f_c mR} \tag{4-62}$$

$$C_2=\frac{m}{(1-m^2)\pi f_c R} \tag{4-63}$$

$$L_2=\frac{mR}{(1-m^2)\pi f_c} \tag{4-64}$$

4-16. BALANCED-CIRCUIT FILTERS

The filters shown in Figs. 4-13 through 4-16 are *unbalanced types* in which one line is operated at ground potential and the other above ground (in other words, the filters are unbalanced with respect to ground). All of these filters can be converted to *balanced filters* by using the circuit arrangement shown in Fig. 4-17. In Fig. 4-17A two T-type low-pass filters are connected back-to-back, permitting the placement of the center portion of the composite filter at ground potential. Now, the upper and lower lines are balanced with respect to ground. Similarly, the constant-*k*, high-pass filter can be balanced by using tapped inductors as shown in Fig. 4-17B, or two equal-value inductors can be used at the input and output, with their center common connection at ground.

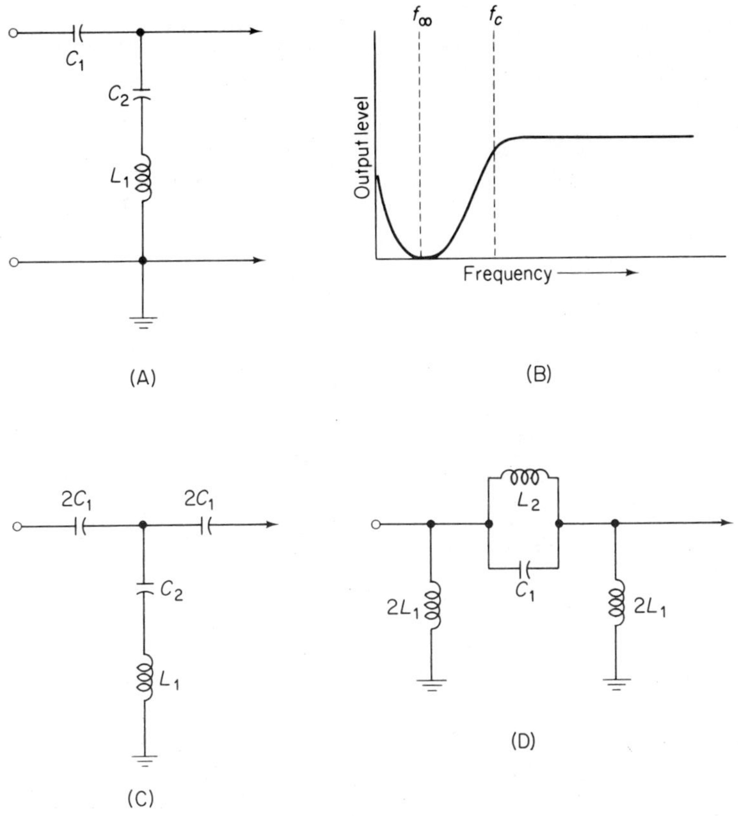

FIGURE 4-16. High-pass *m*-derived filters.

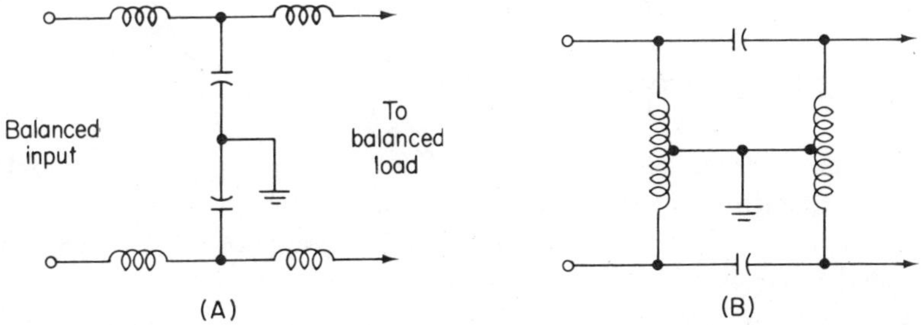

FIGURE 4-17. Balanced filters.

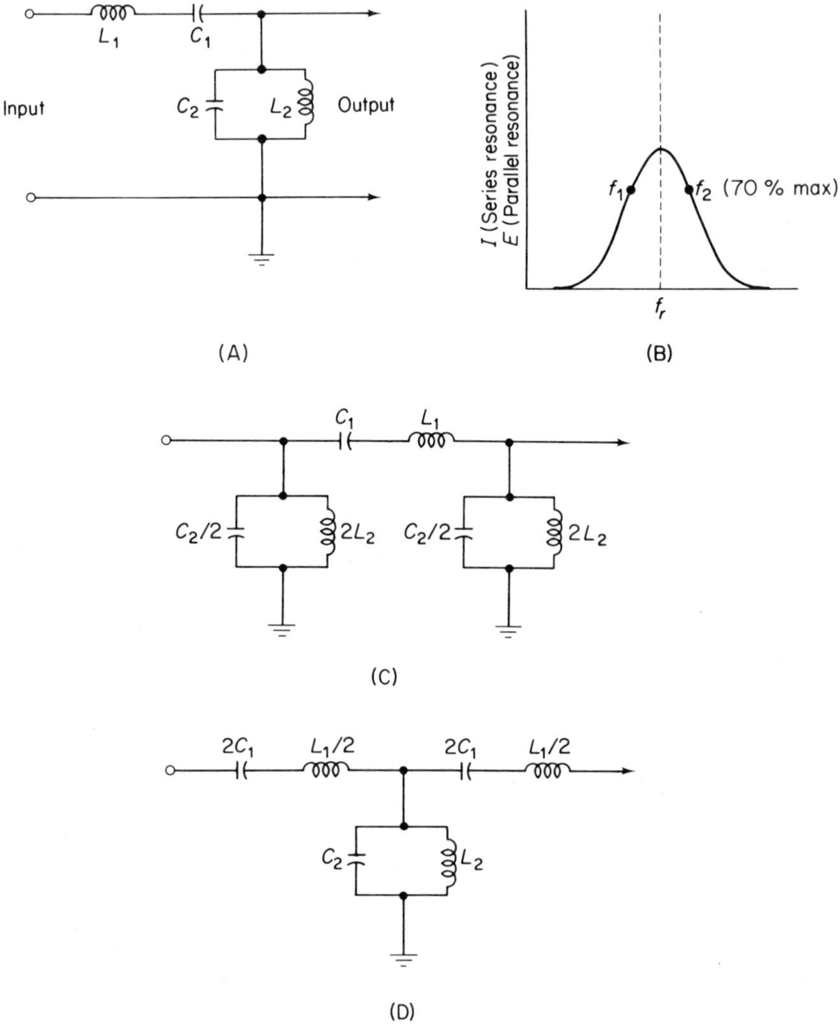

FIGURE 4-18. Bandpass filters.

4-17. BANDPASS FILTERS

When a *group* of signals around a resonant frequency is to be transferred, *bandpass filters* are employed. Several types are shown in Fig. 4-18, with the bandpass characteristics in the graph of Fig. 4-18B. The width of the pass-band is determined by the selectivity (Q) of the component combinations. (See Sec. 4-7.) Unwanted signals, higher and lower in frequency than the cluster around the resonance point, are attenuated or filtered to a negligible amplitude.

The L-type filter is shown in Fig. 4-18A, the *pi*-type in Fig. 4-18C, and the T-type in Fig. 4-18D. Both the series-resonant and the parallel-resonant circuits are tuned to the resonant frequency around which the bandpass is to prevail. Thus, signals having frequencies at or near the resonant frequency meet a low impedance in the series-resonant circuit and are passed through the filter. For the desired signals, the parallel-resonant circuit shunting the output (and also the input in Fig. 4-18C) offers a high impedance, and hence, negligible attenuation. For the unwanted signals, however, series impedance is *high* either below or above resonance, while shunting Z is correspondingly *low*.

The following equations apply:

$$L_1 = \frac{R}{\pi(f_2 - f_1)} \tag{4-65}$$

$$L_2 = \frac{(f_2 - f_1)R}{4\pi f_1 f_2} \tag{4-66}$$

$$C_1 = \frac{(f_2 - f_1)}{4\pi f_1 f_2 R} \tag{4-67}$$

$$C_2 = \frac{1}{\pi(f_2 - f_1)R} \tag{4-68}$$

4-18. BANDSTOP FILTERS

When it is necessary to filter out a group of signals having frequencies around the resonant one but pass signals of frequencies above and below, a *bandstop filter* (or *band elimination filter*) is used. Typical types are shown in Fig. 4-19, with a representative graph of response shown in Fig. 4-19B. (See also Sec. 4-7.)

For the constant-k type shown in Fig. 4-19A, the parallel-resonant circuit (C_1L_1) offers a high Z at resonance, hence attenuating signals at or near the resonant frequency. The series-resonant circuit shunting the output (C_2L_2) has a low Z for signals to be eliminated, offering additional attenuation.

For signals with frequencies above or below the resonance point, the parallel circuit offers low impedance and, thus, passes such signals. Also, the required signals (being off resonance) find a high impedance in the series circuit shunting the output; hence, negligible attenuation occurs.

For the curve in Fig. 4-19B, f_1 represents the low-frequency end of the bandstop span, and f_2 the high-frequency end. This is an inverted selectivity curve, and the width of the bandstop is determined by the Q factors related to selection of the L to C ratios.

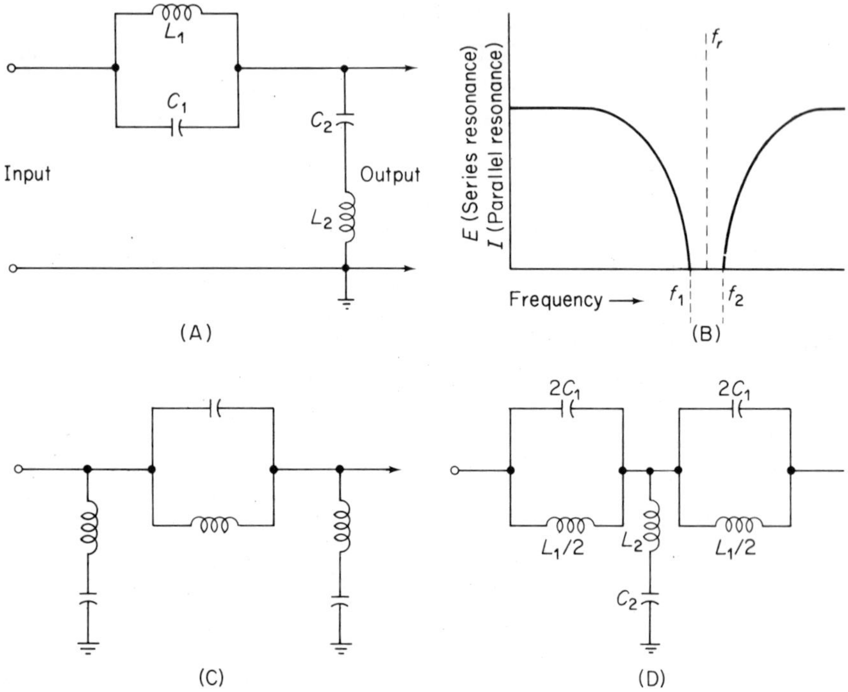

FIGURE 4-19. Bandstop filters.

Appropriate equations for the various components of the bandstop filters are:

$$L_1 = \frac{(f_2 - f_1)R}{\pi f_1 f_2} \tag{4-69}$$

$$L_2 = \frac{R}{4\pi(f_2 - f_1)} \tag{4-70}$$

$$C_1 = \frac{1}{4\pi(f_2 - f_1)R} \tag{4-71}$$

$$C_2 = \frac{f_2 - f_1}{\pi R f_1 f_2} \tag{4-72}$$

4-19. BRIDGE CIRCUITS (*RCL*)

A symmetrical arrangement of components for measuring *R*, *C*, or *L* values by achieving circuit balance is known as a *Wheatstone bridge*, named after Sir Charles Wheatstone (1802–1875), the English physicist who first stressed the importance of this balanced circuit. The basic dc version is shown in Fig. 4-20. As shown in Fig. 4-20A, four resistors form the arms of the bridge network, with the indicating meter connected to opposite junctions of the applied dc source. A galvanometer (*G*) can be used, with a zero-center dial to show unbalance in either direction. Other meters could have been used as shown with the indication *M*, as could an ac source with an ac meter.

For the circuit shown in Fig. 4-20A, a known or standard resistor is designated as R_s, while the unknown resistor under test is designated as R_x. When the bridge is balanced (i.e., when there is a zero reading on meter), the value of R_x can be found by direct or arithmetical comparison with the standard resistor value (R_s).

Figure 4-20B shows one of several conditions of balance. Here all resistors have an equal value; hence, no potential difference exists between the upper and lower meter terminals. The zero reading shows a balanced bridge, and $R_s = R_x$.

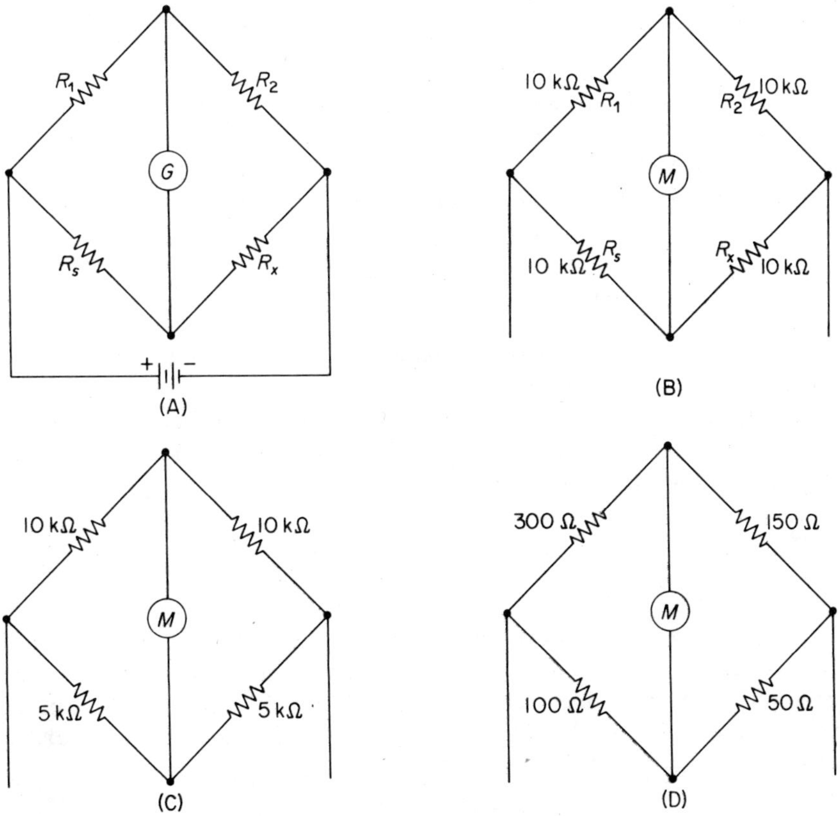

FIGURE 4-20. Wheatstone bridge (dc).

Another balanced condition is shown in Fig. 4-20C. Here, R_1 and R_2 each have a value of 10 kΩ, while R_s and R_x each have a value of 5 kΩ. Since R_1 has the same value as R_2, the applied voltage divides evenly across these two resistors. Similarly, the voltage divides evenly across R_x and R_s, even though they have a value lower than the upper resistors. Thus, the voltage drop across R_2 is the same as that across R_x, and the unknown value of R_x is 5 kΩ, the same as the standard resistor.

Figure 4-20D shows another condition for bridge balance. Here, R_1 has twice the value of R_2, and R_s also has twice the value of R_x. Hence, because R_2 and R_x are proportionately lower than R_1 and R_s, the same voltage drop occurs across R_2 as across R_x, and a balance again prevails. The same balanced condition would have occurred if R_2 had had a value twice that of R_1 while R_x had had a value twice that of R_s. For the various conditions of balance in Fig. 4-20, the following equation yields the value of R_x when the bridge is balanced:

$$R_x = R_s \frac{R_2}{R_1} \tag{4-73}$$

Inductance or capacitance values can also be found with the Wheatstone-bridge principle through use of an ac source, as shown in Fig. 4-21. In Fig. 4-21A, an inductive bridge is shown where the voltage drop across the inductive reactances is compared to the voltages across the resistors. The following equation solves for L_x:

$$L_x = L_s \frac{R_2}{R_1} \tag{4-74}$$

For the capacitance bridge shown in Fig. 4-21B, an inverse reactive function is present because the reactance of a capacitor decreases for higher values of capacitance, while the reactance of an inductor increases for higher values of inductance. Hence, the equation for finding C_x has the R_1 and R_2 designations reversed:

$$C_x = C_s \frac{R_1}{R_2} \tag{4-75}$$

Figure 4-21C shows the *Owen bridge*, which compares inductive and capacitive reactances. The unknown inductance is L_x, and any resistive component of the inductance is designated by R_x. Capacitor C_1 can be varied until a balanced bridge is obtained, or a variable resistor can be placed in series with L_x. For a balanced bridge, L_x is found by:

$$L_x = R_1 R_s C_2 \tag{4-76}$$

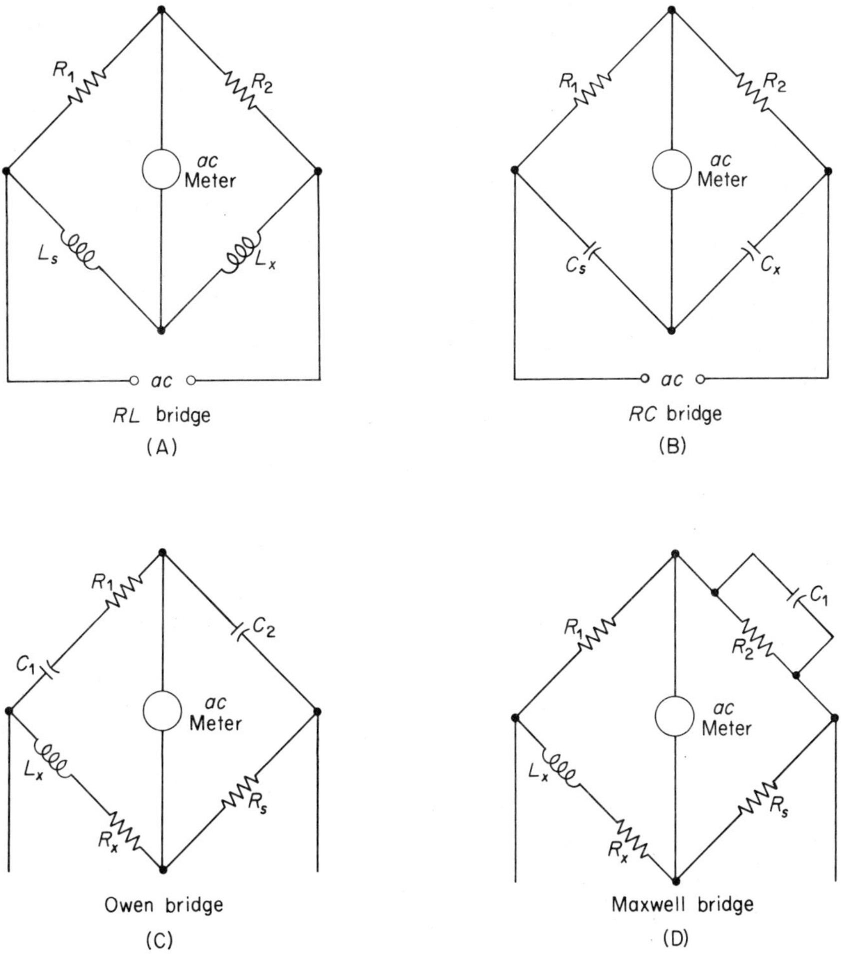

FIGURE 4-21. Various ac bridges.

For finding the value of the resistive component of L_x, the following equation applies:

$$R_x = \frac{C_2}{C_1} R_s \tag{4-77}$$

In the *Maxwell bridge* shown in Fig. 4-21D, the L_x and the resistance (R_x) values of the series arm are found by the following equations:

$$L_x = R_1 R_s C_1 \tag{4-78}$$

$$R_x = \frac{R_1}{R_2} R_s \tag{4-79}$$

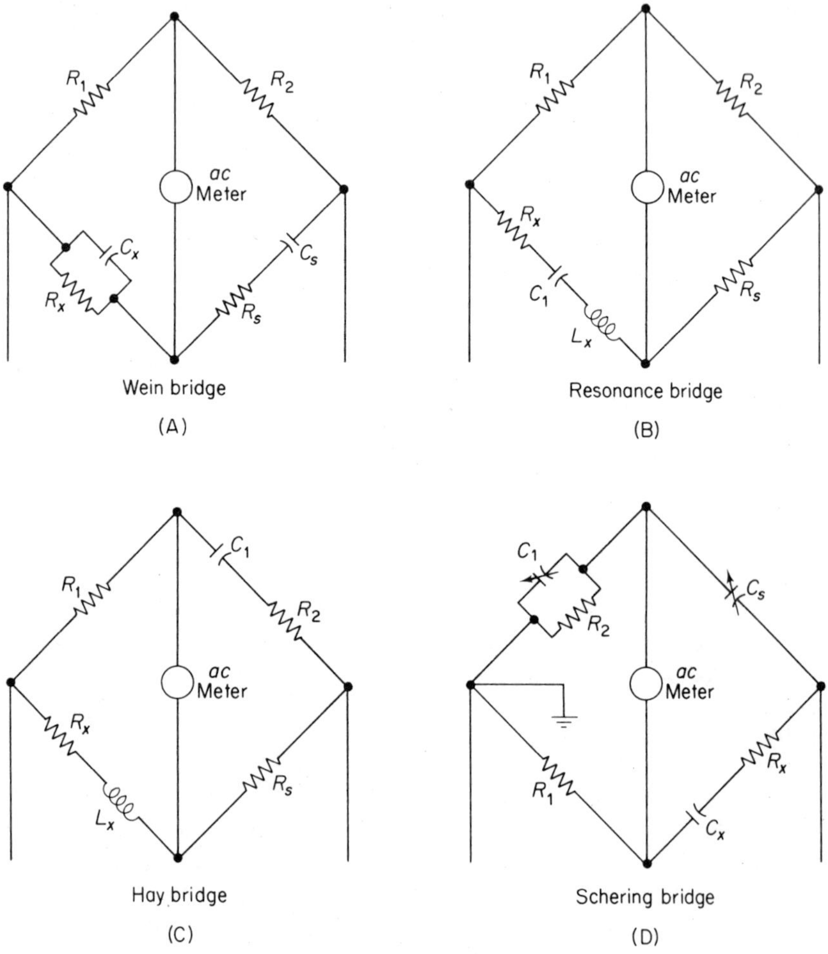

FIGURE 4-22. Various ac bridges (continued).

Additional bridges requiring an ac source are shown in Fig. 4-22. Figure 4-22A shows a bridge circuit useful for measurement of the frequency of ac signals. For measurement of frequency, the following equation applies, provided that $C_x = C_s$, $R_s = R_x$, and R_2 is twice the value of R_1:

$$f\,(\text{in Hz}) = \frac{1}{6.28 R_x C_x} \tag{4-80}$$

A resonance-type bridge is shown in Fig. 4-22B. It is a basic *LCR* type. When the bridge is balanced, the arm consisting of R_x, C_1, and L_x is resonant at the frequency of the applied signal. Hence, the circuit becomes purely resistive since X_L and X_C cancel each other out. This bridge is useful for inductance or impedance measurements. The following equations apply:

$$L_x = \frac{1}{\omega^2 C_1} \tag{4-81}$$

$$R_x = \frac{R_s}{R_2} R_1 \tag{4-82}$$

The so-called *Hay bridge* is shown in Fig. 4-22C and is similar to the Maxwell type shown in Fig. 4-21D. With the Hay bridge, however, C_1 and R_2 are in series instead of in parallel. The Hay bridge is useful for measurement of inductors having fairly high values. The unknown inductance is calculated by the following equation:

$$L_x = \frac{R_1 R_s C_1}{1 + R_2^2 \omega^2 C_1^2} \tag{4-83}$$

In the balanced bridge, the omega values are omitted in the equation for finding R_x:

$$R_x = \frac{R_1 R_2 R_s}{1 + R_2^2} \tag{4-84}$$

Another ac measurement bridge is the *Schering bridge* shown in Fig. 4-22D. For this circuit, a constant voltage is developed across C_x during balancing, and the value of this capacitor is ascertained by the following equation:

$$C_x = \frac{C_1}{R_1} R_2 \tag{4-85}$$

5

Transistors, Bias, and Circuit Formations

5-1. BASIC TRANSISTOR CHARACTERISTICS

Junction transistors are formed by combining two types of semiconductor materials known as *p-type material* (for positive) and *n-type material* (for negative). A combination of a *p* and *n* zone forms a *junction diode*, which conducts current in only one direction (a *rectifier*). When another junction is added, a *transistor* is formed. As shown in Fig. 5-1, two junction-type transistors are commonly used, the *pnp* and the *npn*, each having the symbol shown.

For the *pnp* junction transistor in Fig. 5-1A, the designations of *emitter*, *base*, and *collector* for each lead are used. As shown in Fig. 5-1B, the emitter (E) has an arrow pointing toward the base line when the transistor is a *pnp* type. For the *npn* type shown in Fig. 5-1C, the arrow points away from the base line in the symbol (Fig. 5-1D). Forward bias polarity is indicated by the symbol as shown. Thus, for the *pnp* transistor shown in Fig. 5-1B, forward bias applies a negative potential to the base and a positive potential to the emitter. The collector (C) versus emitter (E) polarity is the reverse of the polarities of the respective *pn* designations shown in Fig. 5-1A. Hence a negative potential is applied to the *p* zone collector, and a positive potential is applied to the *n* zone emitter. For the *npn* circuit shown in Fig. 5-1D, the battery or source potentials must be reversed, so that forward bias will again conform to the junction designation *np* in this instance.

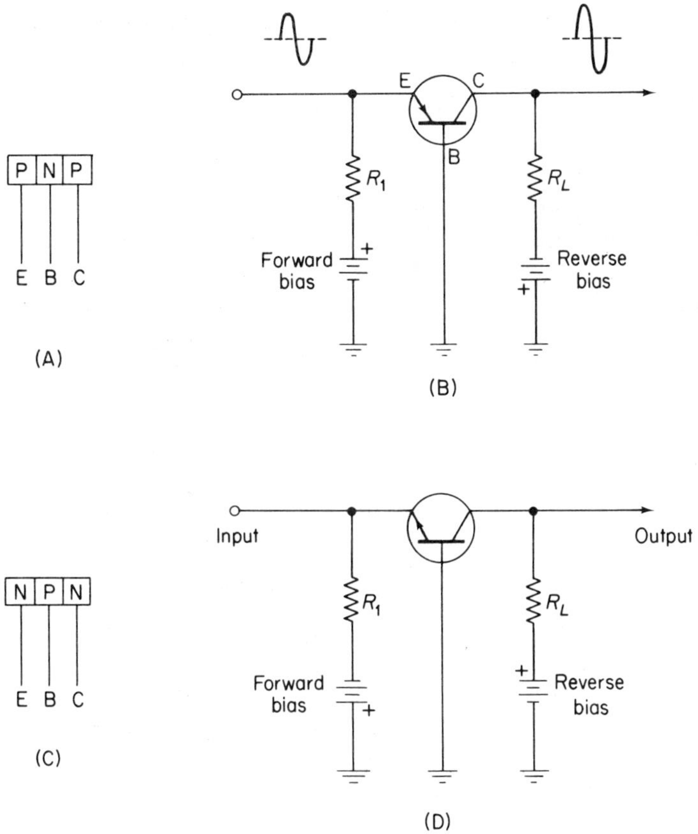

FIGURE 5-1. Grounded-base *pnp* and *npn* circuits.

The circuits shown in Fig. 5-1 are termed *grounded-base circuits*, or *common-base circuits*. Since the base is at ground potential, effective isolation is introduced between the input and output, increasing circuit stability and minimizing internal feedback. Input impedance is low, ranging from 25 to 50 Ω. Output impedance may range up to 1.5 kΩ.

The forward current-transfer ratio is the ratio of the current available at the output to the current circulating in the input circuit. The particular ratio depends on the manner in which the transistor is connected in the circuit. For the common-base circuits shown in Fig. 5-1, the ratio of the dc collector current to the dc emitter current is referred to as *alpha* (α):

$$\alpha = \frac{I_C}{I_E} \tag{5-1}$$

We indicate the change of signal currents by using the differential operator d:

$$d = \frac{dI_C}{dI_E} \tag{5-2}$$

Common-emitter circuitry (grounded emitter) is shown in Fig. 5-2. Again, circuitry and bias depend on whether *npn* or *pnp* transistors are used. For conventional amplifier circuitry, forward bias is applied to the input and reverse bias to the output. For amplification other than Class A, bias changes are necessary. With reverse bias at both input and output, for instance, current cutoff as in Class B or C can be achieved.

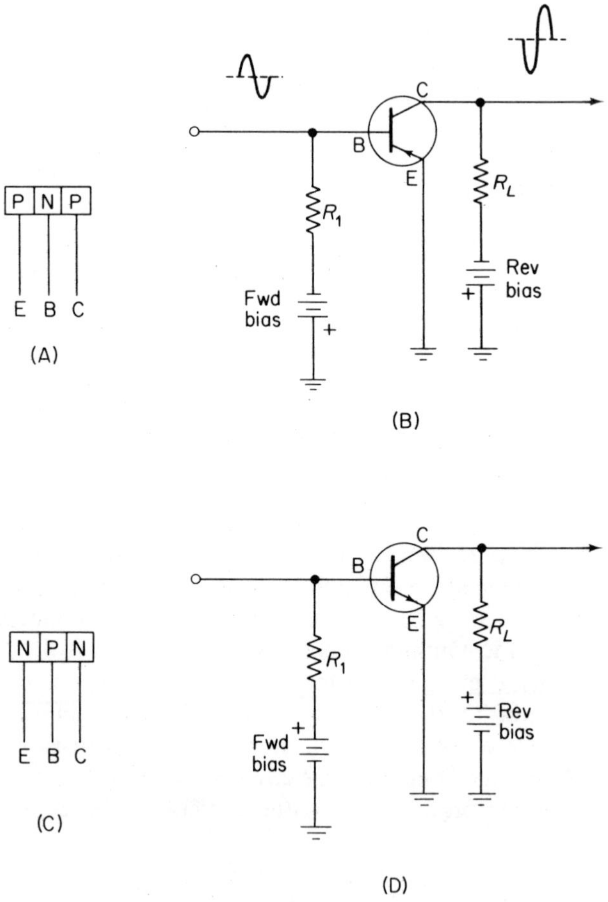

FIGURE 5-2. Common-emitter circuits.

For the common-emitter circuits, the input impedance may range from 25 Ω to 5 kΩ, while the output impedance may be from 50 Ω up to as high as 40 kΩ. Excellent signal-voltage amplification is possible with common-emitter circuitry. For common-emitter circuitry, the forward current-transfer ratio is termed *beta* (β):

$$\beta = \frac{dI_C}{dI_B} \tag{5-3}$$

Characteristic curves of the type illustrated in Fig. 5-3 are used for obtaining information pertinent to the performance of a particular transistor. Such a curve is obtained by plotting the changes in the base current that occur when the input voltage changes. Voltage is applied to the collector side of the transistor, and the collector currents are graphed for various changes of base current. Collector voltages are then changed, and again, collector currents are plotted against base currents.

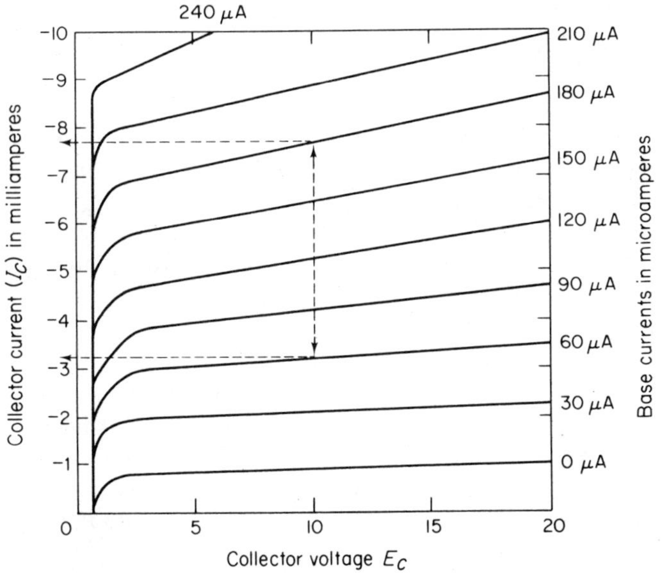

FIGURE 5-3. Typical characteristic curves of a transistor in a grounded-emitter circuit.

A set of transfer-characteristic curves is shown in Fig. 5-4. Such curves are obtained for several base-current values plotted against collector-current and base-to-emitter voltage.

The cutoff frequency of a transistor is that frequency where the value of alpha or beta drops to 0.707 times its 1-kHz value.

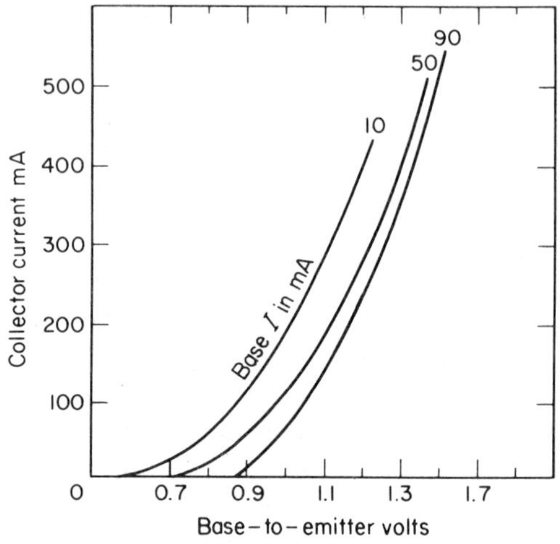

FIGURE 5-4. Transistor transfer characteristics.

5-2. FIELD-EFFECT TRANSISTORS (FET)

The *field-effect transistor* (FET) has high input and output impedances (comparable to vacuum tubes), is suitable for low- or high-frequency signal circuitry, lends itself to a variety of amplifying and switching circuitry (both audio and RF), has excellent thermal stability, and its fabrication is not limited to the few components from which the junction transistor is manufactured. Thus, the FET has found wide application in solid-state circuitry of all types.

Junction-type field-effect transistors are formed in a manner similar to the formation of the junction transistor, where *p*-type material is joined to *n*-type material. The MOSFET (*metallic-oxide semiconductor field-effect transistor*) employs a foundation slab (termed a *substrate*) that is typically an *n*-type silicon slice. The *p*-type regions are *diffused* into the slab and form terminals called *source* and *drain* (*S* and *D*). Another terminal, the *gate* (*G*), is formed by diffusing a *pn* junction into the material. As with transistor types *npn* and *pnp*, the FET units also differ depending on selection of *n* type instead of *p* for specific manufacturing processes. Thus, the FET units are available in *n*-channel or *p*-channel types. [*Channel*, here, refers to the particular *n*- or *p*-type slice (substrate) forming the foundation slab.]

The FET symbols differ from the symbols for transistors to distinguish between gate, source, and drain terminals for the FET as opposed to the base, emitter, and collector of the transistor. Typical FET symbols

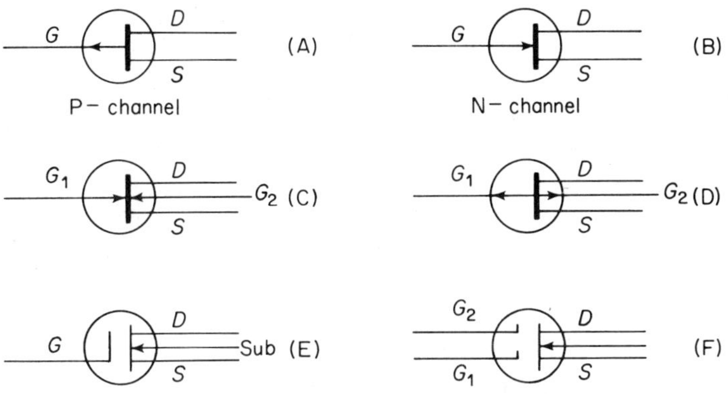

FIGURE 5-5. Typical FET symbols.

are shown in Fig. 5-5. In Fig. 5-5A the *p*-channel type is shown, with the gate arrow pointing away from the vertical connecting line within the symbol. In Fig. 5-5B, the *n*-channel FET is illustrated with the arrow for the gate element pointing to the center vertical bar. As shown in Fig. 5-5C and D, an additional gate element is often added to the slab (but insulated from the first gate). The additional gate forms a *double-gate* FET, useful in circuitry requiring additional signal inputs. The two additional symbols shown in Fig. 5-5E and F indicate the *depletion*-type FET units, where the *sub* designation represents the substrate element terminal. The types in Fig. 5-5E and F are *n*-channel units. For *p*-channel types, the arrow in the symbol would have had to be reversed.

The term *depletion* stems from the basic processes that occur within the transistor during the application of forward and reverse bias, plus signal energy. When major signal energy carriers (such as electrons) are drawn from an area close to a *pn* junction, for instance, the region is called a *depletion area*. Such a depletion area functions as a variable-opening gate which regulates the flow of charges, similar to the base of a junction transistor.

The *n*-channel JFET has a lower channel conduction when the bias input is negative at the gate terminal. This occurs because a negative potential depletes the channel current carriers in the FET. For the *p* channel, however, a positive gate potential decreases conduction, and a negative voltage increases it. The JFET is normally in a conductive state because a conductive channel exists between drain and source elements. Thus, even without a gate-to-source voltage, an internal current path is present. The JFET, for either the *p*-channel or *n*-channel, utilizes reverse bias between the gate-source elements, instead of the forward bias applied to the junction transistors, for the basic amplification circuitry.

For the MOSFET, the gate element within the structure is insulated from the channel by a dielectric material such as silicon dioxide. Because of this insulation characteristic, the MOSFET is also termed an insulated-gate metallic-oxide semiconductor field-effect transistor, or IGFET. Compared to the JFET, the IGFET gate can be biased either forward or reverse. Forward bias provides channel *enhancement*, while reverse bias produces channnel *depletion*. Thus, there are two basic MOSFET units, the enhancement and the depletion types. For the depletion type there is drain current flow without any applied bias to the input elements. When bias is applied, the drain current decreases (depletes) to the particular value required for processing the signal through the circuit.

For the enhancement-type MOSFET there is little current flow without input-element bias. When bias is furnished, there is an increase in drain current (conduction enhanced), and the bias amplitude is set for establishing the operating point upon which the signal develops. MOSFETs have very thin insulation at the gate element, and some units are subject to damage rather easily (even by a static discharge). Hence, such sensitive units are shipped with precautionary devices to minimize damage by electrostatic fields. These devices can consist of shorting wires across terminals. Many MOSFETs are designed with built-in gate-protective devices (such as diodes) that permit current passage in only one direction.

A *common source* (*grounded source*) FET amplifier circuit in basic form is shown in Fig. 5-6. This circuit is comparable to the grounded-

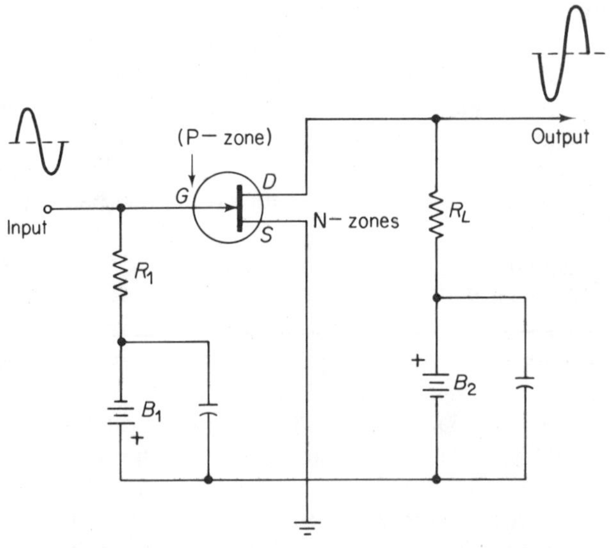

FIGURE 5-6. Common-source FET amplifier.

emitter transistor amplifier discussed earlier in this chapter. The *p* and *n* zones are identified for discussion purposes, though normally only the *G*, *D*, and *S* designations are included. Source and drain output current flow is established by battery B_2, and the current path includes the load resistor (R_L) and the *n* zones. Battery B_1 applies the necessary reverse bias between the gate element and the source element (which is at ground potential). The input signal (if a sinewave) increases or decreases the amplitude of the reverse-bias potential supplied by B_1. Such reverse-bias changes with signal input cause corresponding changes in output current flow and amplification occurs as with the transistor.

As with the grounded-emitter amplifier, there is a phase reversal between the input signal and output signal as shown in Fig. 5-6. If the *n*-channel FET is replaced by a *p*-channel FET, the polarity of both batteries (B_1 and B_2) would have to be reversed. General operation would be the same, however, except that current directions are altered.

5-3. CIRCUIT COMPARISONS

In Fig. 5-7A, the *common-gate* FET circuit is shown. This circuit is comparable to the transistor common-base circuit shown in Fig. 5-7B. For both of these circuits there is no phase reversal between the input and output signals. Since the gate in Fig. 5-7A and the base in Fig. 5-7B are at signal ground, effective isolation exists between input and output circuits, and better performance and stability are realized in some applications. For both circuits the input signal is impressed between ground and the input line. Batteries (or other voltage sources), are bypassed to prevent signal energy from developing across them.

When the positive alternation of the input sinewave signal appears between the source and ground (gate) of the circuit in Fig. 5-7A, the bias from B_1 is reduced. The reduction in bias potential at the source element increases current in the output circuit. Since the voltage-drop polarity across R_L from B_2 is positive toward the drain element, the increase in current flow increases the amplitude of the positive-potential drop across R_L (the same as producing a *positive-polarity* change). Thus, the output signal is in phase with the input signal.

For the circuit in Fig. 5-7B, a positive signal alternation between the emitter and ground (base) of the transistor also decreases bias (in this case the *forward* bias between emitter and base). Forward bias reduction also decreases current flow in the collector circuit, hence the voltage drop across R_L declines. Since, however, the polarity of B_2 places a negative potential at the collector end of R_L, a reduction in the negative voltage drop across R_L raises signal level above ground (more positive), thus

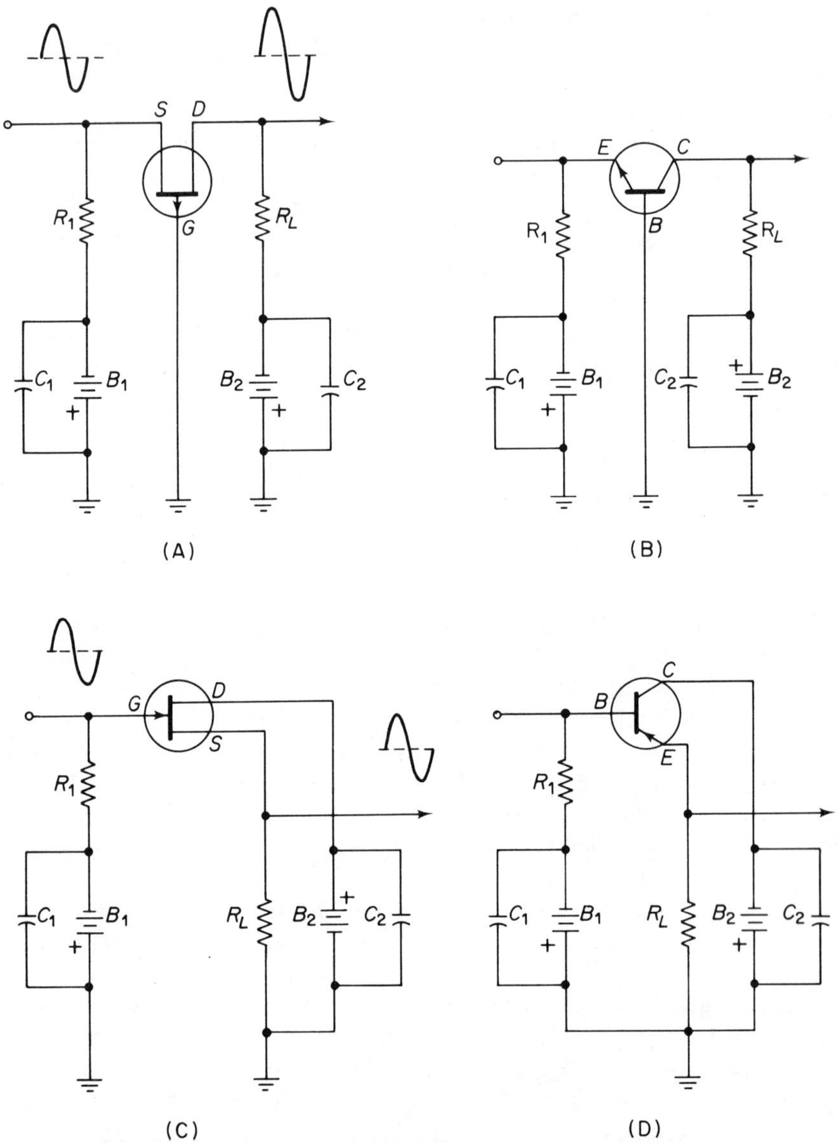

FIGURE 5-7. Common gate, base, drain, and collector circuits.

developing the same phase at output as at the input. Thus, as with the circuit in Fig. 5-7A, the one at Fig. 5-7B also has no signal phase reversal between input and output circuitry.

For both circuits Figs. 5-7A and 5-7B, negative alternations of the input signal also produce the same phase output alternations. Similar results would be obtained if the *p*-channel FET in Fig. 5-7A were replaced with an *n*-channel unit, or the *npn* transistor in Fig. 5-7B were changed to a *pnp* type. In either case the polarities of B_1 and B_2 would have to be reversed.

The circuit in Fig. 5-7C is a *common drain* because the drain element is at signal ground due to C_2. (Without the low reactance of C_2, the drain element would be above ground by the ohmic value of the battery resistance.) Capacitor C_1 also places the bottom of R_1 at signal ground; thus, in effect, bypassing the battery resistance. The output signal is now obtained from a resistor in the *source circuit*, as shown. Such a circuit has no phase reversal between the input signal and the output. Signal voltage gain is less than unity though some signal current gain is possible. The circuit is useful for impedance-matching purposes and for obtaining a low-output impedance (with a high-input impedance). Since the phase of the output signal "follows" that of the input, the circuit has been termed a *source follower*. As such, it resembles the tube-type circuit, where the output is obtained from across a cathode resistor (with the anode placed at signal ground). The tube-type circuit is called a *cathode follower*.

The circuit in Fig. 5-7D is a *common-collector* type because the collector of the transistor is at signal ground due to C_2. The signal output is obtained from across the resistor in series with the emitter, as shown, thus forming an *emitter-follower circuit*. The signal phase at the output again becomes the same as the input. As with the circuits in Fig. 5-7A and B, different type FET and transistor units could have been used (*p* channel for Fig. 5-7C and *npn* for Fig. 5-7D), provided appropriate changes in polarities were made for B_1 and B_2. Operational characteristics other than battery polarities are virtually the same. For the circuit in Fig. 5-7D, as with the FET source-follower and the tube cathode-follower circuit, signal voltage gain is less than unity, though signal current gain can be realized.

5-4. FET AND TRANSFER CHARACTERISTICS

A typical gate-to-drain set of characteristic curves for a field-effect transistor are shown in Fig. 5-8. As was the case with tubes and transistors, such curves provide information on the operational features of particular FETs. Note that the drain-to-source (V_{DS}) voltage is plotted along the *X*

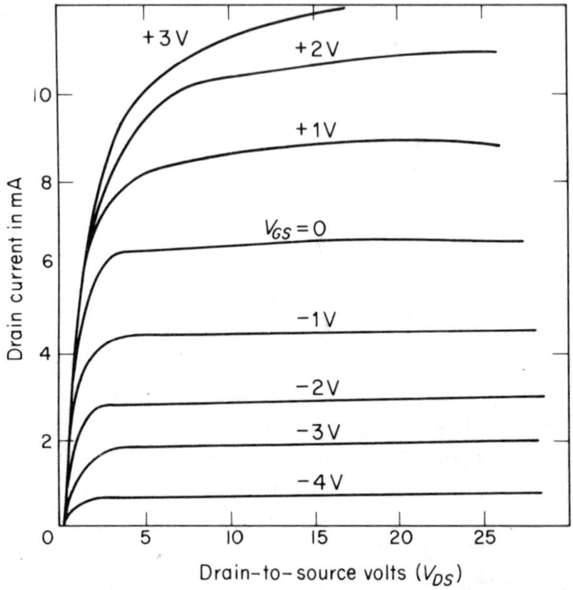

FIGURE 5-8. FET gate-to-drain characteristics.

axis, and the drain current (I_D) is plotted along the Y axis. The various curves represent those obtained for a specific *dc gate* (V_{GS}) *voltage* (voltage between *gate* and *source* terminals).

An important designation in FET characteristics is the *pinch-off voltage* (V_p or V_{po}). This is the point at which the gate-bias voltage, V_{GS}, is such that it causes the drain current to drop to zero for a specific value of V_{DS}. Such a pinch-off voltage is comparable to the plate-current cutoff condition obtained with vacuum-tube characteristics.

Another important FET parameter is *transconductance*, which is expressed as:

$$g_m = \frac{\Delta I_d}{\Delta V_g} \tag{5-4}$$

For the FET, the transconductance is the value in *mhos* obtained by taking the ratio of a small change in drain current to a small change in gate voltage on a chart of gate-to-drain characteristics, like the one shown in Fig. 5-8. Thus, it is a *figure of merit* regarding the ability of the gate voltage to control the drain current.

FET transconductance is usually given with the gate bias at zero, and a minimum g_m is obtained at the pinch-off voltage. If g_m and the load-resistance (R_L) value are known, signal gain is given by:

$$\text{gain} = g_m \times R_L \tag{5-5}$$

The g_m of an FET can be considered to be the signal transfer ratio, indicating the device's sensitivity and behavior to signal changes.

5-5. NETWORK PARAMETERS

Resistive circuits can be analyzed using Kirchhoff's, Thévenin's, and Norton's theorems to set up equivalent circuits. (See Secs. 4-2 to 4-4.) Similarly, the operational characteristics (parameters) of transistors can also be obtained by utilizing equivalent networks. The transistor can be considered as a resistive device as shown in Fig. 5-9A. Here the emitter is indicated by a resistor R_E, the base by R_B, and the collector by R_C. Together they form a T-network of resistors with ohmic values such as would be obtained by making dc measurements. Since this T-network is a *passive network*, it is not a true representation of a transistor because such

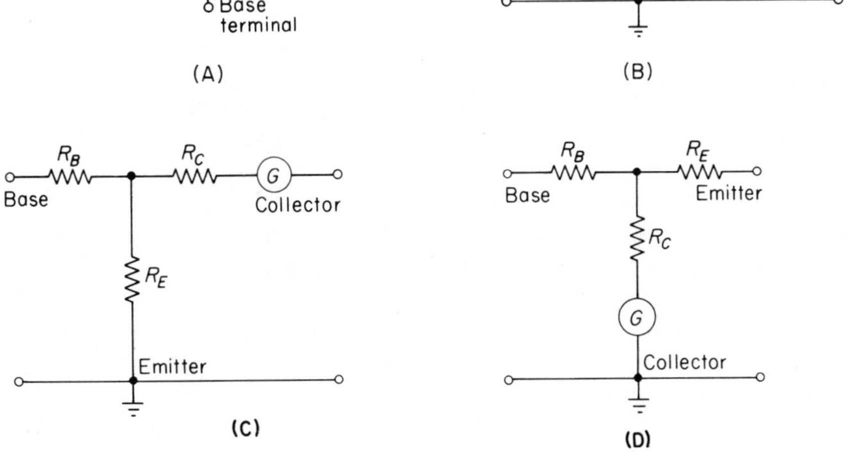

FIGURE 5-9. Equivalent transistor networks.

a three-resistor combination does not have amplifying characteristics. Also, the network in Fig. 5-9A is shown as a three-terminal device. Actually, however, a common input-output lead is present in a transistor circuit, and hence the practical transistor must be represented as a four-terminal network.

The four-terminal equivalent network, shown in Fig. 5-9B, represents the common-base (grounded-base) circuit. Instead of a passive network, a generator (G) is indicated in the collector lead, making this an *active network*. Thus, the amplifying function of the transistor is indicated by the equivalent generator in the output.

The grounded emitter is shown in Fig. 5-9C. For the grounded emitter, the generator in the output line represents the emitter-collector section. Now the left arm of the T-network is shown as R_B for the equivalent base resistance, which now forms the input terminal, and R_E is the representative grounded-emitter resistance. The active network for the grounded collector is shown in Fig. 5-9D.

The active resistance network formations are a close approximation of a transistor's characteristics when low-frequency signals or dc are involved. For high-frequency signals, however, the resistive network converts to an impedance network because the internal capacitances, with their decreasing reactances, are influencing factors. Input and output impedances are also affected by the ohmic value of the load resistance applied to the output, as well as the resistance of the circuit or device applied to the input. Hence, for a true evaluation of circuit parameters, the internal network values must be considered in conjunction with the external networks so that maximum signal-power transfer and maximum circuit efficiency are obtained. In the discussions that follow, we will be concerned primarily with the resistive characteristics of the equivalent networks so as to obtain a clearer understanding of the notation employed and the methods utilized.

As discussed in Sec. 4-3, for convenience in analyzing networks it is expedient to consider the network as a black box wherein we have internal components of unknown values. To analyze the internal circuit, we read voltages and currents or apply test signals to the input and output terminals and evaluate their effects. The voltage and current measurements are also undertaken during the open circuit or short circuit of either the input or output terminals.

The four-terminal equivalent network of a triode transistor can be represented as a black box, as shown in Fig. 5-10. Here, V_1 is the input voltage, V_2 the output voltage, I_1 the input current, and I_2 the output current. The resistance parameters of the transistor so represented have been symbolized by the so-called *R-parameters* as well as by the more

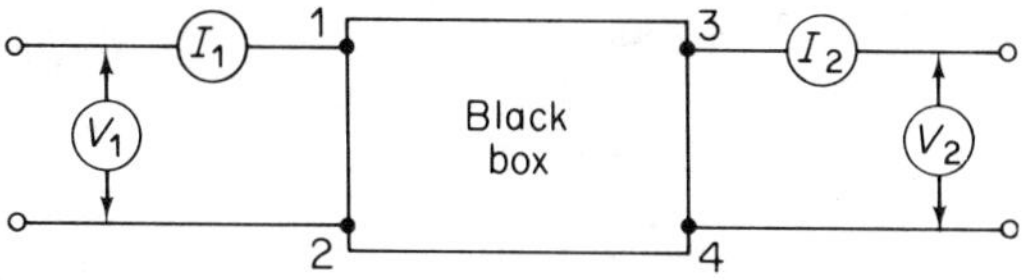

FIGURE 5-10. Black box concept.

widely used h-parameters. Initially, we will consider the R-type parameters, since they serve as a more solid foundation for understanding the h (hybrid) types.

The input resistance is notated as R_{11}, to identify that this R value is obtained by using the V_1 and I_1 values. Thus the first 1 of the subscript indicates the V_1 voltage and the second 1 of the subscript the I_1 current. Thus, R_{11} is a measure of the resistance with the test voltage V_1 applied to the input terminals 1 and 2, with the output terminals 3 and 4 open; that is, $I_2=0$. Similarly, R_{21} indicates the forward transfer resistance, with the test voltage V_1 applied to the input terminals again and the ratio of V_2/I_1 taken for the R_{21} value. When the test voltage is applied to the output terminals 3 and 4 and the input terminals left open ($I_1=0$), we obtain

$$R_{12}=\frac{V_1}{I_2}=\begin{array}{c}\text{reverse transfer resistance}\\ \text{(feedback resistance)}\end{array} \tag{5-6}$$

$$R_{22}=\frac{V_2}{I_2}=\text{output resistance} \tag{5-7}$$

From the foregoing we can derive the loop equations for the transistor network.

$$V_1=R_{11}I_1+R_{12}I_2 \tag{5-8}$$

$$V_2=R_{21}I_1+R_{22}I_2 \tag{5-9}$$

The amplifying ability of the transistor network relates to the mutual resistance (r_m), and current amplification is referred to as *alpha* (α) discussed earlier. Related to the R-parameters, these are:

$$r_m=R_{21}-R_{12} \tag{5-10}$$

$$\alpha=\frac{R_{21}}{R_{22}} \tag{5-11}$$

The R-value relationships in Fig. 5-9A (common base) become:

$$R_E = R_{11} - R_{12} \tag{5-12}$$

$$R_C = R_{22} - R_{21} \tag{5-13}$$

$$R_B = R_{12} \tag{5-14}$$

The equivalent generator voltage is equal to $I_1(R_{21} - R_{12})$. The resistive parameters can also be utilized for the dynamic characteristics of the network under signal conditions. Using the lower case delta to indicate a quantity change, and holding I_C constant, we get

$$R_{11} = \text{slope of curve } dV_E/dI_E$$

$$R_{21} = \text{slope of curve } dV_C/dI_E$$

Holding I_E constant, produces the following:

$$R_{12} = \text{slope of curve } dV_E/dI_C$$

$$R_{22} = \text{slope of curve } dV_C/dI_C$$

For dynamic conditions where ac signals are involved, consideration must be given to reactive components as well as to resistive elements, hence the designations are in Z notation instead of R. The black-box electronic circuit input has an impedance, and with an open circuit at the output ($I_2 = 0$), we obtain

$$Z_{11} = \frac{V_1}{I_1}(I_2 = 0) \tag{5-15}$$

With an open circuit at the output, we obtain the forward transfer impedance comparable to R_{21}:

$$Z_{21} = \frac{V_2}{I_1}(I_2 = 0) \tag{5-16}$$

The reverse transfer impedance is obtained with the input circuit open ($I_1 = 0$) producing:

$$Z_{12} = \frac{V_1}{I_2}(I_1 = 0) \tag{5-17}$$

The output impedance is also obtained with the input held in the open-circuit condition:

$$Z_{22}=\frac{V_2}{I_2}(I_1=0) \tag{5-18}$$

We can now rewrite the loop equations given earlier (Eqs. 5-8 and 5-9) as follows:

$$V_1=Z_{11}I_1+Z_{12}I_2 \tag{5-19}$$

$$V_2=Z_{21}I_1+Z_{22}I_2 \tag{5-20}$$

5-6. HYBRID (*h*) PARAMETERS

The *R*-parameters were obtained under open-circuit conditions and represented *constant-voltage* conditions. As discussed in Chap. 4, it is often convenient to use the *constant-current* analysis, shorting out terminals as required. By combining the constant-voltage and constant-current approaches, a more desirable type of parameter is obtained. This system is in general use by transistor manufacturers. The combining process has led to the term *hybrid* or *h-parameter*. These parameters are primarily used for obtaining the operational characteristics of *bipolar* transistors. The parameters used for the unipolar transistors (FET) are the *Y* types discussed later.

For the *h*-parameters, the following notation applies for the black box concept shown in Fig. 5-10:

$h_{11}=V_1/I_1$	(an input *impedance* parameter, with output terminals 3 and 4 shorted, and $V_2=0$)
$h_{12}=V_1/V_2$	(a reverse-transfer *voltage ratio*, with input terminals 1 and 2 open, and $I_1=0$)
$h_{21}=I_2/I_1$	(a forward-transfer *current ratio* with output terminals 3 and 4 shorted, and $V_2=0$)
$h_{22}=I_2/V_2$	(an output *admittance* term, with input terminals 1 and 2 open, and $I_1=0$)

Basic calculations can be used if it becomes necessary to convert *R* to *h* or *h* to *R*. Parameter R_{11}, for instance, is equal to $(h_{11}h_{22}-h_{12}h_{21})/h_{22}$. Similarly, $R_{12}=h_{12}/h_{22}$ and $R_{21}=h_{21}/h_{22}$.

The equations for the *R* and *Z* parameters (Eqs. 5-8, 5-9, 5-19, and 5-20) involved input voltage and output voltage (V_1 and V_2). For the *h*-parameters, however, the equations relate to input voltage and output current, as follows:

$$V_1 = H_{11}I_1 + H_{12}V_2 \tag{5-21}$$

$$I_2 = H_{21}I_1 + H_{22}V_2 \tag{5-22}$$

Standards have been adopted for letter subscripts to allow easier identification of the *h*-parameters. The first subscript designates the characteristic, *i* for input, *o* for output, *f* for forward transfer, and *r* for reverse transfer. The second subscript designates the circuit configuration, with *b* for common base, *e* for common emitter, and *c* for common collector. Thus, h_{11} can be indicated as h_{ib} for the input *h* of a common-base network. Similarly, h_{12} can be written as h_{rb} for reverse transfer in the common-base network. This avoids the confusion that might result from simply using h_{11}, for instance, without designating whether it is in reference to common base, common emitter, or common collector.

Figure 5-11A shows a basic grounded-emitter circuit. Applied to the input is the signal voltage to be amplified. This could be symbolized as E_S for *signal voltage*, or as E_G for *generator voltage* as shown. The resistance associated with the input signal is marked R_G. The load resistance applied to the output is indicated by the standard R_L symbol. The dc power sources E_1 and E_2 are effectively bypassed by capacitors C_1 and C_2, hence they are not part of the active parameter analysis.

The equivalent circuit for the grounded emitter is shown in Fig. 5-11B with appropriate hybrid symbols with letter subscripts. The base current is indicated as i_B, and collector current as i_C. The input voltage e_G also develops across R_G, hence the actual voltage applied to the base and emitter is indicated as e_I. The output voltage across the load resistor is shown as e_o. The emitter input resistance is given as h_{ie}, and the output admittance or conductance is given as h_{oe}, measured in mhos. Note the use of the reverse-voltage transfer ratio symbol h_{re} for the emitter circuit. (In a common base this would be h_{rb}.) The forward-current ratio is designated as h_{fe}, indicating the emitter designation.

The forward current-transfer ratio h_{fe} is now dI_C/dI_B (with $E_o = 0$), which is the same as the Eq. (5-3) given earlier for signal current gain β (beta). Manufacturers have used A_I for signal-current gain, symbolizing current amplification. The full equation is

$$A_I = \frac{i_C}{i_B} = \frac{h_{fe}}{1 + h_{oe}R_L} \tag{5-23}$$

While this equation refers to the common-emitter circuit of Fig. 5-11, it also applies to grounded-base and grounded-collector circuits. In

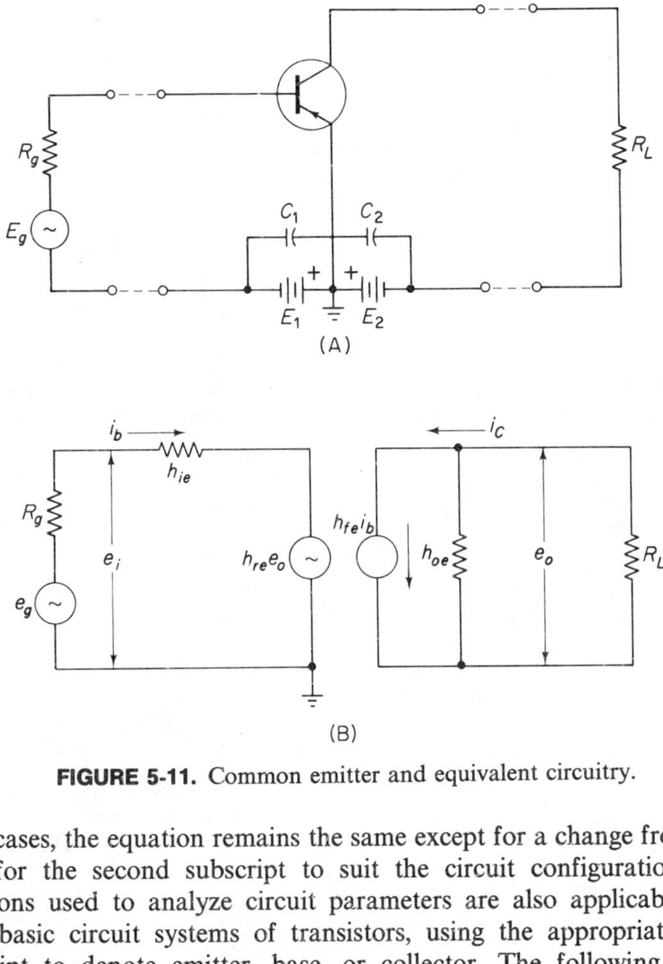

FIGURE 5-11. Common emitter and equivalent circuitry.

those cases, the equation remains the same except for a change from *e* to *b* or *c* for the second subscript to suit the circuit configuration. Other equations used to analyze circuit parameters are also applicable to the three basic circuit systems of transistors, using the appropriate second subscript to denote emitter, base, or collector. The following example shows the application of Eq. 5-23:

Example

A transistor has a low-signal designation of $V_1 = 5$ V, and $I_b = 0.1$ mA. The manufacturer's *h* ratings are

$h_{ie} = 2{,}800\ \Omega$
$h_{oe} = 43\ \mu$mhos
$h_{fe} = 110$
$h_{re} = 7.5 \times 10^{-4}$

Assume a load resistance of 10,000 Ω is to be used. What is the current gain?

Solution

$$A_I = h_{fe}/1 + h_{oe}R_L$$

$$= \frac{110}{1+(43\times 10^{-6}\times 10{,}000)} = 77$$

The input resistance R_I can be found by the following equation:

$$R_I = h_{ie} - \frac{h_{fe}h_{re}R_L}{1+h_{oe}R_L} \tag{5-24}$$

Using the h values given above for the transistor, with a load resistance of 10,000 Ω, the following equation shows the application of Eq. (5-24):

$$R_I = 2{,}800 - \frac{110\times 7.5\times 10^{-4}\times 10{,}000}{1+(43\times 10^{-6}\times 10{,}000)} = 2{,}223\ \Omega$$

The signal-voltage gain of the transistor circuit is found by:

$$A_E = \frac{E_o}{E_i} = \frac{1}{h_{re} - \dfrac{h_{ie}}{R_L}\left(\dfrac{1+h_{oe}R_L}{h_{fe}}\right)} \tag{5-25}$$

Again, using the values for the transistor given as an example, the voltage amplification is found:

$$A_E = \frac{1}{0.00075 - \dfrac{2{,}800}{10{,}000}\left(\dfrac{1+(43\times 10^{-6}\times 10{,}000)}{110}\right)} = 274.$$

The power gain of the transistor circuit is found by multiplying the signal-current gain A_I by the signal-voltage gain A_E:

$$A_P = A_E A_I \tag{5-26}$$

Applying the two values previously obtained for the transistor as an example, we find the power gain to be:

$$A_P = 274\times 77 = 21{,}098$$

5-7. Y-PARAMETERS

As mentioned earlier, the admittance Y-parameters are most useful for investigating the operational characteristics of the field-effect transistor. Since $Y=1/Z$, the following replace the h notations given earlier for the black box of Fig. 5-10:

$Y_{11}=I_1/V_1$	(an input admittance parameter, with output terminals 3 and 4 shorted, and $V_2=0$)
$Y_{12}=I_1/V_2$	(reverse transfer admittance, with input terminals 1 and 2 shorted, and $V_1=0$)
$Y_{21}=I_2/V_1$	(forward transfer admittance with output shorted, and $V_2=0$)
$Y_{22}=I_2/V_2$	(output admittance with input shorted, and $V_1=0$)

Instead of the input-voltage and output-current h equations (5-21 and 5-22), the FET equations for Y-parameters involve input current I_1 and output current I_2:

$$I_1=Y_{11}V_1+Y_{12}V_2 \tag{5-27}$$

$$I_2=Y_{21}V_1+Y_{22}V_2 \tag{5-28}$$

As letter subscripts were used for the easier identification of the h-parameters, i, o, f, and r can be used for FET units to describe parameters of input, output, forward transfer, and reverse transfer, respectively. A second subscript is used to identify gate, source, or drain. Thus, the I_1 and I_2 equations (5-27 and 5-28) for *common-source* circuitry become:

$$I_g=Y_{is}V_g+Y_{rs}V_d \tag{5-29}$$

$$I_d=Y_{fs}V_g+Y_{os}V_d \tag{5-30}$$

For common-gate or source-follower design, the second subscripts of Eqs. 5-29 and 5-30 are changed accordingly. Thus, for common-gate circuitry,

$$I_s=Y_{ig}V_s+Y_{rg}V_d \tag{5-31}$$

$$I_d=Y_{fg}V_s+Y_{og}V_d \tag{5-32}$$

5-8. LOAD-LINE FACTORS

The characteristic curves shown earlier in this chapter for transistors indicate static conditions. Thus, while such characteristic curves show the amount of output current that flows through the transistor for given bias and collector voltages, they are not indicative of the *dynamic characteristics* of the transistor; that is, the curves do not show characteristics that are established when a *signal* voltage is applied to the base input of a transistor. During signal-voltage input, the output current varies by an amount established by the amplitude of the input signal and the signal gain of the transistor. In order to illustrate the conditions that occur when the transistor is operating with a signal input and is amplifying, a *load line* must be drawn. A typical example is shown in Fig. 5-12.

Note the dashed line curve in Fig. 5-12. This represents the constant power dissipation line (in watts) for the collector side as specified for a particular transistor. Thus, for the transistor graphed in Fig. 5-12 the 48 mW is the maximum energy dissipation before overload occurs. This dissipation curve is plotted along points established by the product $I_C V_C$. Thus, at any point along the dashed curve the current-voltage product equals 48 mW for this transistor. Thus, to stay within the dissipation rating of this transistor, the load line must be drawn in the graph area below and to the left of the dissipation line. Maximum power gain of the transistor is obtained when the load line is drawn tangent to the dissipation line. The

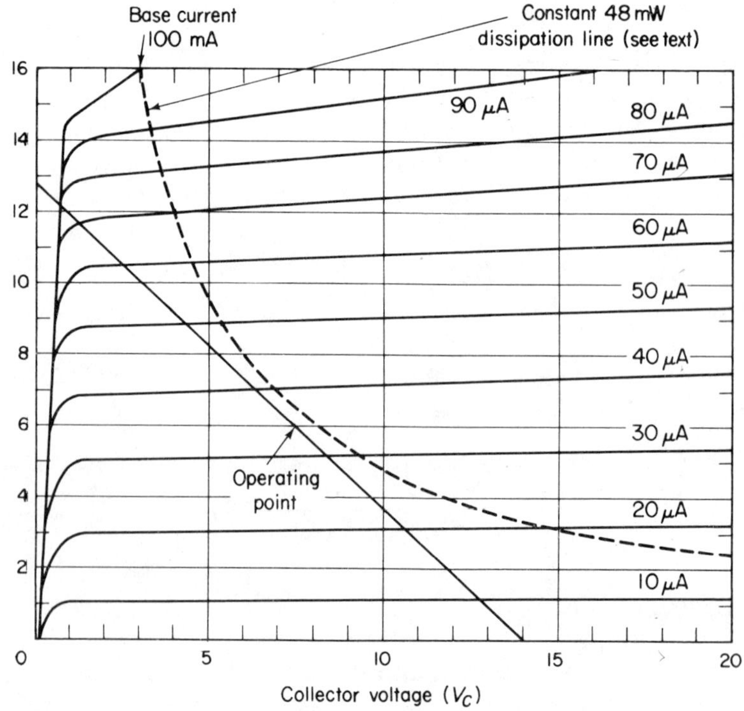

FIGURE 5-12. Load line and power dissipation line.

load impedance (or resistance) may be calculated by Eq. 5-33, which is actually a computation of the *slope* of the load line:

$$R_L = \frac{dV_C}{dI_C} \tag{5-33}$$

The operating point has been selected so a linear signal swing for Class A operation is available above and below the operating point. The point is at 7.5 V for V_C, 6 mA for I_C, and 35 μA for I_B as shown in Fig. 5-12. At the operating point, $I_C V_C = 0.006 \times 7.5 = 45$ mW, which is below the maximum permitted according to the power dissipation line. Similarly, no other portion of the load line touches or extends to the right or above the dissipation line.

To determine the load resistance, we use Eq. 5-33, $dV = 0$ to 14, and $dI = 0$ to 12.8 mA. Thus, we obtain

$$14/12.8 \times 10^{-3} = 1093.7\ \Omega$$

For Class A operation, the signal swing along the load line must not encroach on the base-current curvatures at the left. The operating point, as well as the load-line slope, can be altered to provide for a different value of load resistance, greater signal swing, etc. In Fig. 5-13 for instance, two load

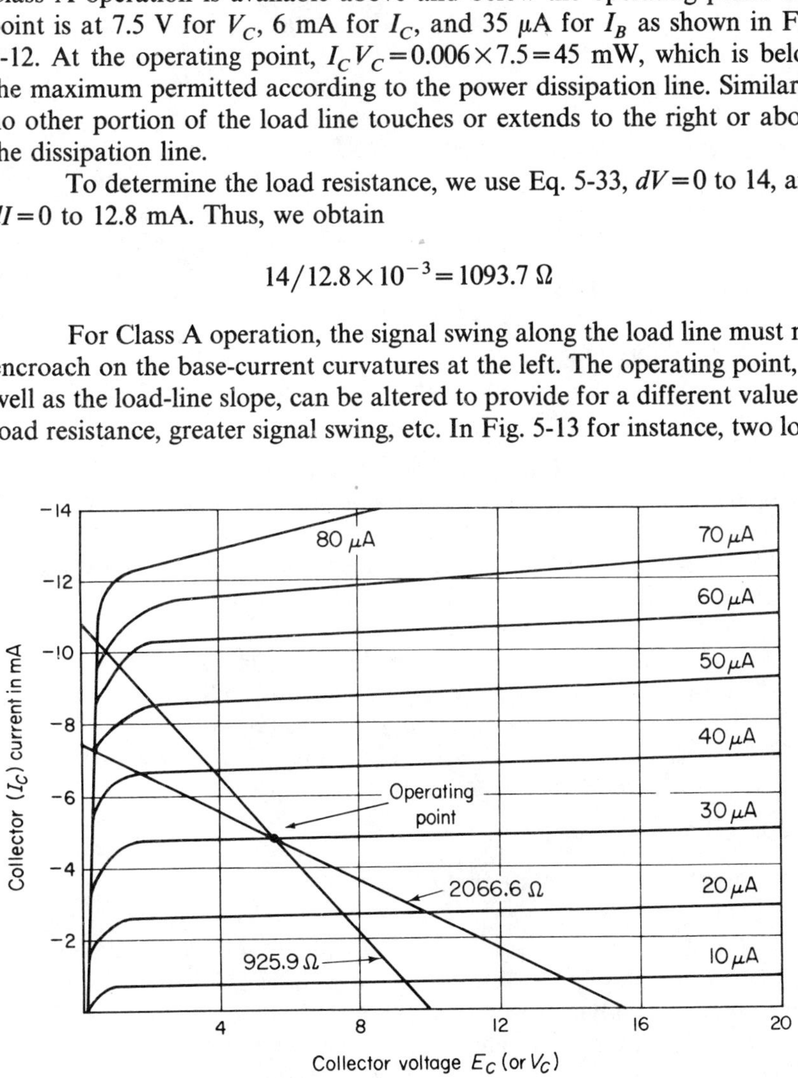

FIGURE 5-13. Load line comparisons.

lines are shown for comparison purposes. Though both use the same operating point, each could have had a different operating point if desired.

The steeper load line has a $dV=0$ to 10 and a $dI=0$ to 10.8 mA:

$$R_L = 10/10.8 \times 10^{-3} = 925.9\ \Omega$$

For the other load line, however, a greater ohmic value is obtained:

$$R_L = 15.5/7.5 \times 10^{-3} = 2066.6\ \Omega$$

The primary purpose of a signal-voltage amplifier is to increase signal voltage (and not necessarily power), hence the load resistor is made fairly large in audio applications. (In RF circuitry, a parallel-resonant circuit may be present at the output of the amplifier, presenting a high impedance without load and a reduced impedance with load.)

Even in signal-voltage amplifiers, the amount of power output can be determined once the load line has been drawn. The equation that applies is the one also used in power amplifiers.

$$\text{Power output} = \frac{(E_{max} - E_{min})(I_{max} - I_{min})}{8} \qquad (5\text{-}34)$$

The power-output formula is based on the fact that the alternating components of voltage and current have peak amplitudes that are one-half of the total swings of these waveforms. The power delivered to the load resistor is equal to one-half of the product of the peak ac signal voltage and the peak signal current. In dc circuits, the power in watts is equal to the product of voltage times current, and in resistive ac signal circuits, such as amplifiers, the same calculations apply. Therefore, if the extent of the signal swings are multiplied, and the result again multiplied by a factor that takes into consideration the effective values (as required in ac calculations), the result will be the average power delivered to the load resistor, as derived from Eq. 5-34 for power output.

5-9. *RC* VS. POWER AMP LINES

For the resistance-capacitance coupled *RC* amplifier stage shown in Fig. 5-14A, the supply voltage indication on a load-line drawing is represented by the right-hand termination of the load line at the zero collector-current line. Thus, for the characteristic curves shown in Fig. 5-15, the supply voltage is -28 V if this is a resistance-coupled (small-signal) amplifier. The signal-voltage swing across the load resistor for a signal

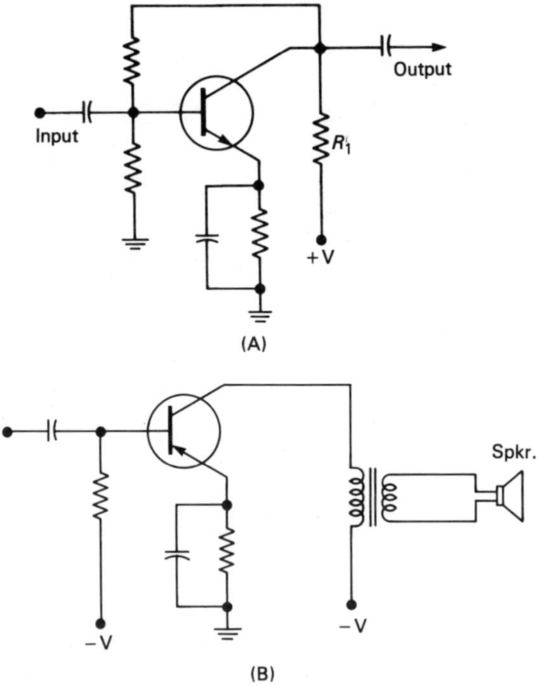

FIGURE 5-14. Signal voltage and power amplifiers.

input can then reach the maximum value of −28 V, because this is the highest potential available from the power supply. The operating voltage is −12 V, since this is the drop across the load resistance in the absence of an input signal.

When the amplifier stage has an output transformer such as in Fig. 5-14B, the actual supply voltage would only be −12 V for this transistor, the same as the operating voltage for the dynamic load line. Its function, in relation to the dynamic characteristic with an input signal is, however, essentially the same as that which would occur with an actual load resistor in series with the supply. In a transformer-coupled system, the actual load is that which is applied to the secondary of the output transformer (such as the voice coil of a loudspeaker or the inductor in a tape-recording head). Thus, if the input signal applied across the base-emitter swings in a positive direction (less forward bias for a *pnp* transistor), there is a sudden change in current through the inductor making up the transformer primary. Hence, a voltage is induced across the inductor, which *adds to the collector-supply potential.* The effect is an *instantaneous* increase in collector potential to a value considerably above that of the operating potential (and thus substantially above the collector-supply potential).

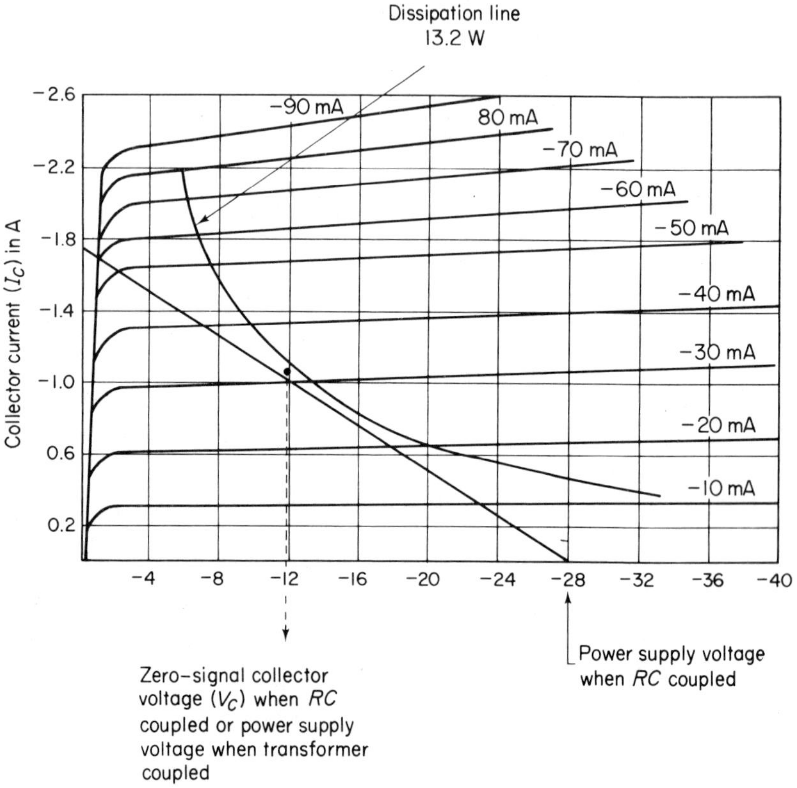

FIGURE 5-15. Dynamic load line factors.

When the input signal swings in the opposite direction (and increases forward bias), a sudden current change again occurs in the transformer primary, thus inducing a voltage across the primary opposite to the previous voltage change. Hence, collector-voltage signal swing reaches values both above and below the normal operating potential.

Note the constant power-dissipation line. At 13.2 W the load line is close to the curve for obtaining maximum power output. The ohmic value of the load line is obtained from Eq. 5-33:

$$R_L = \frac{dV_C}{dI_C} = \frac{(0 \text{ to } 28)}{(0 \text{ to } 1.76)}$$

$$= 15.9\ \Omega$$

With such a low value, direct coupling of the collector output to the voice coil is possible. The 1.76 in the foregoing example is an approximate value, but sufficiently close for practical purposes. Similarly, the load resistance can be considered to have a value of 16 Ω for all practical purposes.

The actual signal-power output depends on the magnitude of the applied input signal and how nearly it causes a full swing of collector current. The percentage of collector efficiency can be found by:

$$p_{\text{eff}} = \frac{\text{signal-power output}}{\text{dc input power}} \times 100 \text{ (percent)} \tag{5-35}$$

Because variations in the amplitude of the input signal alter loading effects on the amplifier, Equation 5-35 applies only to constant-amplitude sinewave-type test signals which present a constant load. For Fig. 5-15 the efficiency percentage is:

$$p_{\text{eff}} = \frac{4.5 \text{ W}}{12 \text{ W}} \times 100 = 37 \text{ percent}$$

6

Basic Linear Circuitry

6-1. CLASSES OF AMPLIFIERS

There are various classes of audio and RF amplifiers and their basic characteristics can best be illustrated by the graphs shown in Fig. 6-1. The classifications apply equally to *pnp* and *npn* bipolar junction transistors or to the *p*-channel and *n*-channel FET units. For convenience, the graphs shown in Fig. 6-1 are referenced to the *n*-channel JFET, where a lower channel conduction occurs when the bias applied to the input terminals is negative. (See Sec. 5-2, Field-Effect Transistors.)

Alphabetical designations are used to identify the amplifier classes. For Class A operation, the bias is such that operation is on the linear portion of the characteristic curve of the transistor. The input signal does not reach the current cutoff or saturation level. There is a minimum of harmonic distortion compared to the characteristics of other amplifier classes. However, efficiency (conversion of dc power to signal power) is relatively low and depends on the exact bias and signal amplitudes used. For Class A amplifiers, efficiency may range between 10 and 15 percent. Class A amplifiers are extensively used as small-signal amplifiers as well as power amplifiers in television and radio receivers.

As shown in Fig. 6-1, Class AB_1 has a larger signal-input characteristic and is useful where more output power is required than obtained from Class A. The bias is usually set so that the no-signal idling current permits the input signal to swing the collector current to the cutoff point as well as

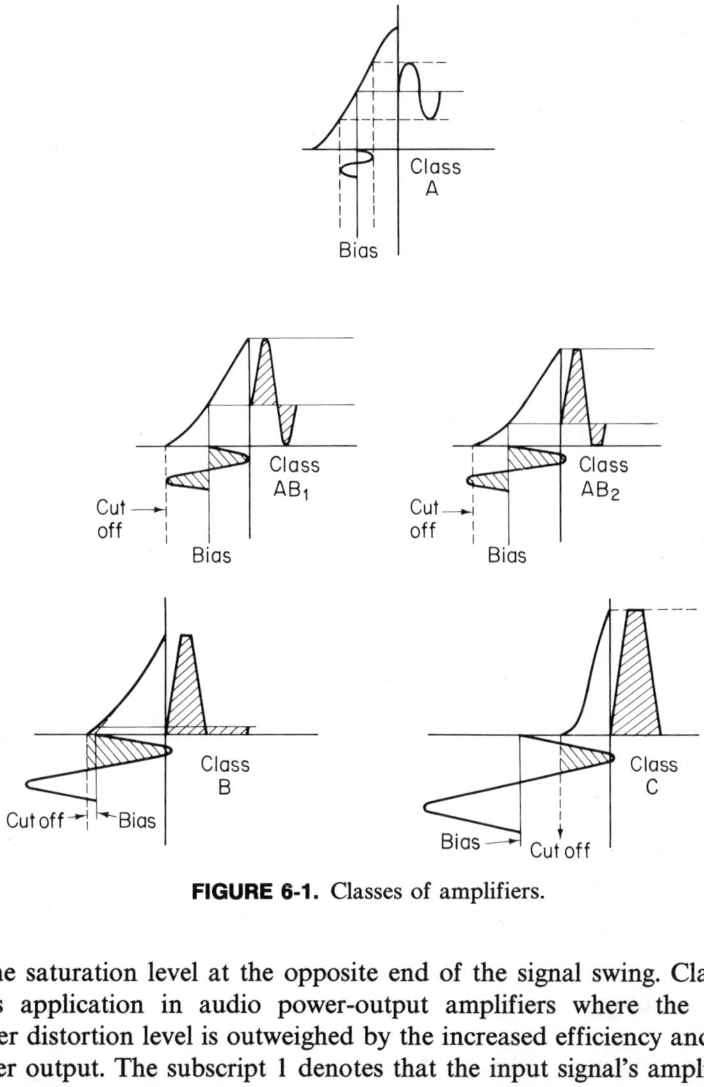

FIGURE 6-1. Classes of amplifiers.

to the saturation level at the opposite end of the signal swing. Class AB_1 finds application in audio power-output amplifiers where the slightly higher distortion level is outweighed by the increased efficiency and signal power output. The subscript 1 denotes that the input signal's amplitude is held just below the point where saturation occurs for collector current. Efficiency for this class of amplifier varies between 20 and 35 percent, depending on the bias level, supply potentials, and other design factors.

Class AB_2 operational characteristics are also shown in Fig. 6-1. Bias voltage level is selected to lie on the lower portion of the curve. The input signal has sufficient amplitude to drive the output current into the cutoff as well as the saturation region. Output power and efficiency are increased over the AB_1 type, though distortion also increases as shown by the output signal waveshape. Distortion is high because of operation on the nonlinear portion of the curve and the high-level drive of the input signal (which causes signal clipping).

The input signal for Class AB_2 must have sufficient amplitude to achieve the swing needed. Push-pull or complementary-symmetry operation is preferable (see Secs. 6-2 and 6-3) since these circuits reduce distortion while at the same time increasing signal power output. Efficiency ranges from 35 to about 50 percent, depending on bias and signal-input drive factors.

Schematically, the circuits for Classes AB_1 and AB_2 resemble those for Class A. The differences are found in the higher-power dc supplies, bias differences, and input-signal amplitudes of the former two. They can be single-ended or push-pull (as described later in this chapter) and can be used for audio or RF.

The Class B type (shown in Fig. 6-1) can also be used for either RF or audio, though for audio the push-pull circuit must be used to minimize the possible distortion. The Class B amplifier is biased approximately at cutoff, though often the term *projected cutoff* is used to designate operation at a bias point that is obtained when the linear portion of the curve is projected downward to meet the horizontal line of the graph. Class B is characterized by high efficiency (from 60 to 70 percent), but also by high distortion as compared to other types (in audio-amplifier applications). However, distortion for RF signals is lower.

The Class C amplifier can be used for RF signals only (RF power amplifiers in transmitters) because bias is beyond the cutoff point; for audio signals some portions of the waveform would be lost. Collector current flows for only a portion of the applied input signal, and a high order of efficiency is obtained. With a well-designed Class C stage, efficiency may be in excess of 90 percent.

NOTE: The special type Class D is discussed in Sec. 6-8.

6-2. PUSH-PULL AMPLIFICATION

Two FET units or bipolar transistors can be used in a symmetrical circuit arrangement known as *push-pull*. This produces a greater signal power output than can be obtained from a single unit. Typical circuits are shown in Figs. 6-2 and 6-3. Push-pull operation requires 180° phase difference between the signals applied to the input element of the push-pull transistors or FETs. One method for obtaining such phase splitting is to use an interstage transformer between the small-signal amplifier output and the two push-pull units as shown in Fig. 6-2.

The transformer secondary winding has a center tap that effectively splits the signal waveform into two parts, each of which is out of phase

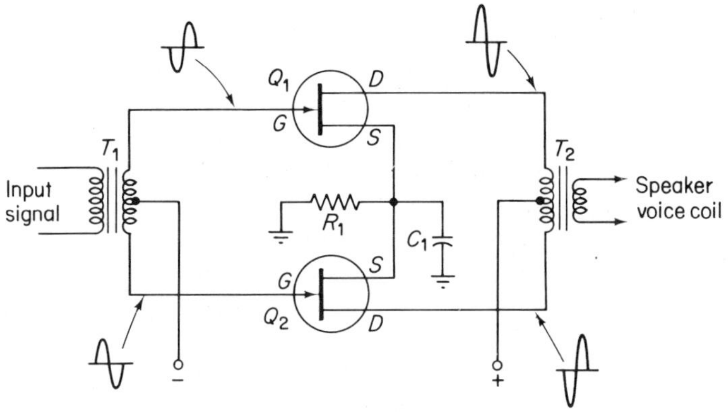

FIGURE 6-2. FET push-pull amplifier.

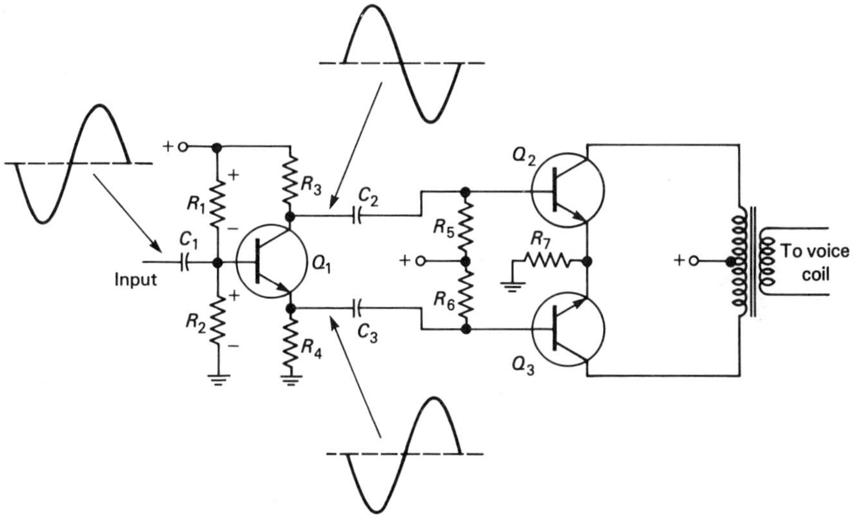

FIGURE 6-3. Split-load phase inversion.

with the other. Since there is a phase reversal in the *common-source* or the *common-emitter* type amplifier, the signal developed at the drain element of Q_1 in Fig. 6-2 is out of phase with the signal at the drain of Q_2. Thus, while current through one-half the primary T_2 increases, current through the other one-half decreases. Hence, as one drain side of the transformer becomes more positive, the other side becomes more negative. The combined current changes produce the output signal.

The opposing current changes in the push-pull transformer tend to reduce transformer core saturation as well as harmonic distortion.

6-3. PHASE INVERSION

Instead of employing the interstage transformer T_1, as in Fig. 6-2, to obtain the necessary out-of-phase signals for the push-pull transistors, these signals may be obtained by the split-load phase inversion system shown in Fig. 6-3. Here the emitter-follower circuit principle is combined with the collector load resistor output, thus effectively splitting the load resistor into the dual arrangement, with 180° phase differences between the two signals. Resistors R_3 and R_4 are of equal value, with equal-value direct current through them, and equal-amplitude signal voltages across them.

A paraphase circuit for obtaining the required phase splitting is shown in Fig. 6-4. Here, Q_2 is used specifically for producing the 180° phase shift of the signal. Resistors R_1, R_2, R_3, and R_4 are the voltage dividers used to obtain the necessary forward bias (as were R_1 and R_2 for Fig. 6-3).

The load resistors across which the amplified signals develop are R_6 and R_7. Two additional resistors, R_8 and R_9, span the two collectors as shown in Fig. 6-4, and it is from their junction that the signal for the base

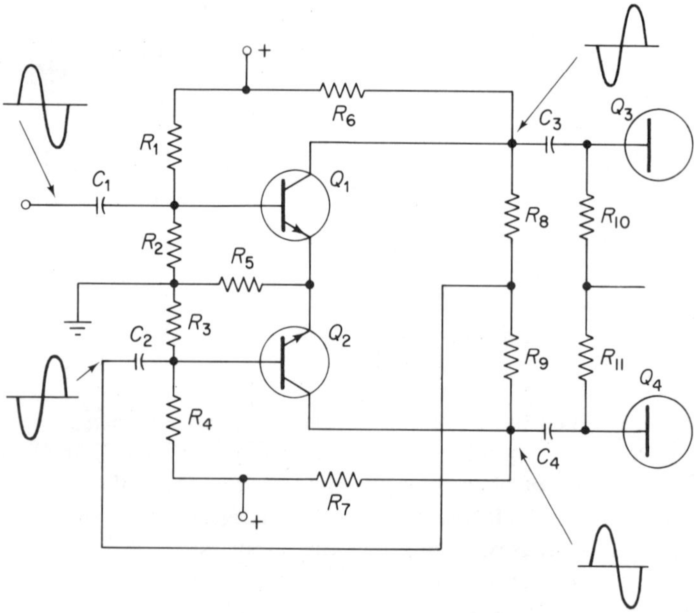

FIGURE 6-4. Paraphase circuitry.

input of the inverter transistor Q_2 is obtained. A balanced circuit is obtained by using matched components for upper and lower sections.

The phase and amplitude of the signal applied to the base of Q_2 are automatically obtained by the self-balancing aspects of the paraphase circuitry. If, for instance, there were no signal at the base of Q_2, the signal derived from R_8 and fed to the input of Q_2 would have a proper phase to start the system in symmetrical operation. Hence, an output develops across R_9, and this output tends to oppose that across R_8. Cancellation, however, cannot occur. Thus, the system is self-balancing.

A complementary-symmetry phase-inversion system can also be employed, as shown in Fig. 6-5. Here phase splitting occurs because the output signals from Q_1 are applied to the base-inputs of the two common-emitter circuits, each of which consists of a *pnp* transistor and an *npn* transistor. Phase splitting results from the signal effect on the base inputs of the dissimilar transistors. If, for instance, a positive alternation of the input signal appears at the base of Q_2, that alternation aids forward bias,

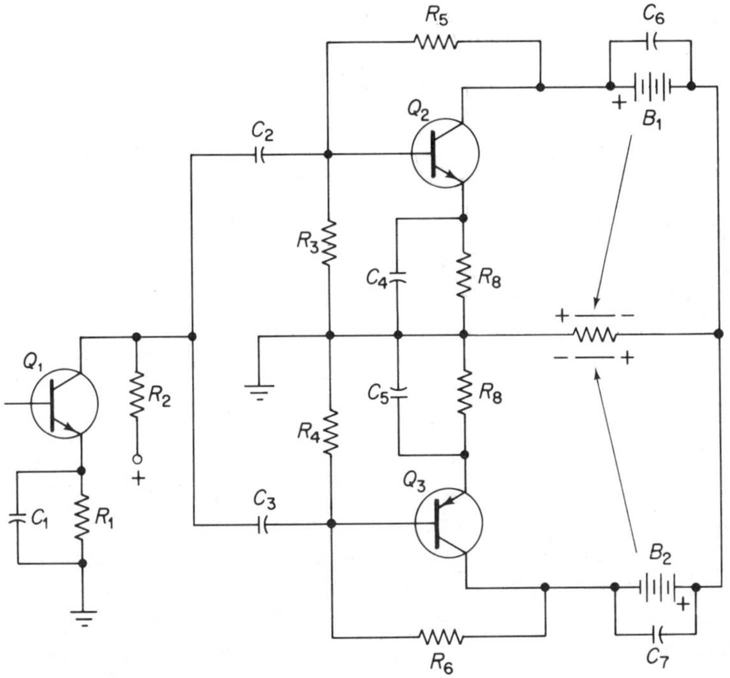

FIGURE 6-5. Complementary-symmetry amplifier.

hence conduction through Q_2 increases. For the positive signal alternation at the input of Q_3, however, the result is a decrease in the forward bias and a lowering of conduction through Q_3. Thus, the equivalent effects of phase inversion are obtained.

6-4. RF AMPLIFIERS

A typical RF amplifier using an FET unit is shown in Fig. 6-6. The input signal from a previous stage is applied to a tap on the inductor of the input resonant circuit. The input resonant circuit is coupled to the gate input of the FET by the 500-pF series capacitor, as shown in the figure, to prevent shorting the negative supply potential at the gate input to ground. An RF choke coil isolates the gate signals from the power source at both the gate section and the drain section. The output signal develops across the high impedance of the parallel-resonant circuit at the output.

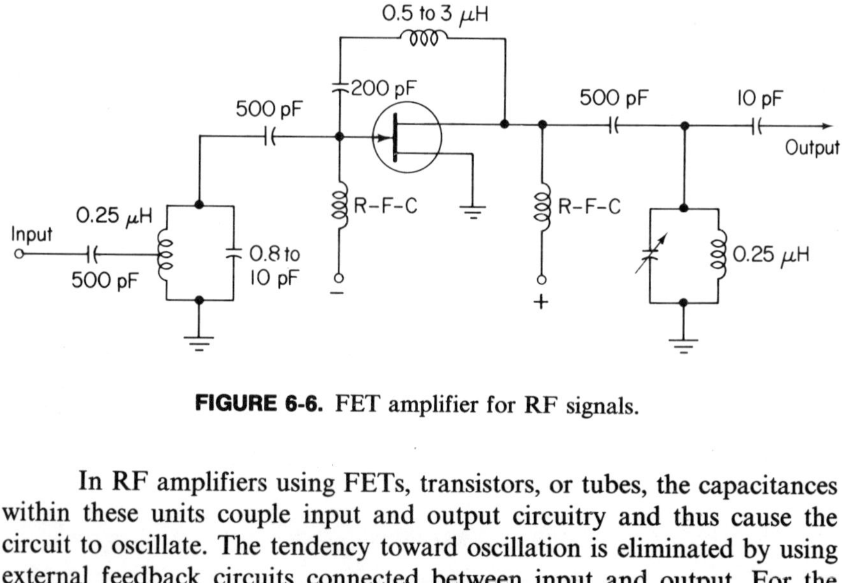

FIGURE 6-6. FET amplifier for RF signals.

In RF amplifiers using FETs, transistors, or tubes, the capacitances within these units couple input and output circuitry and thus cause the circuit to oscillate. The tendency toward oscillation is eliminated by using external feedback circuits connected between input and output. For the circuit shown in Fig. 6-6, both an inductor and a series capacitor are employed between drain and gate elements. This procedure is usually called *neutralization*—indicating cancellation of reactive coupling. If cancellation involves both resistance and reactance, the term *unilateralization* is applied to the procedure.

A grounded-emitter RF amplifier is shown in Fig. 6-7A. (The signal in the emitter is at *ground* potential by virtue of the low reactance of C_4.)

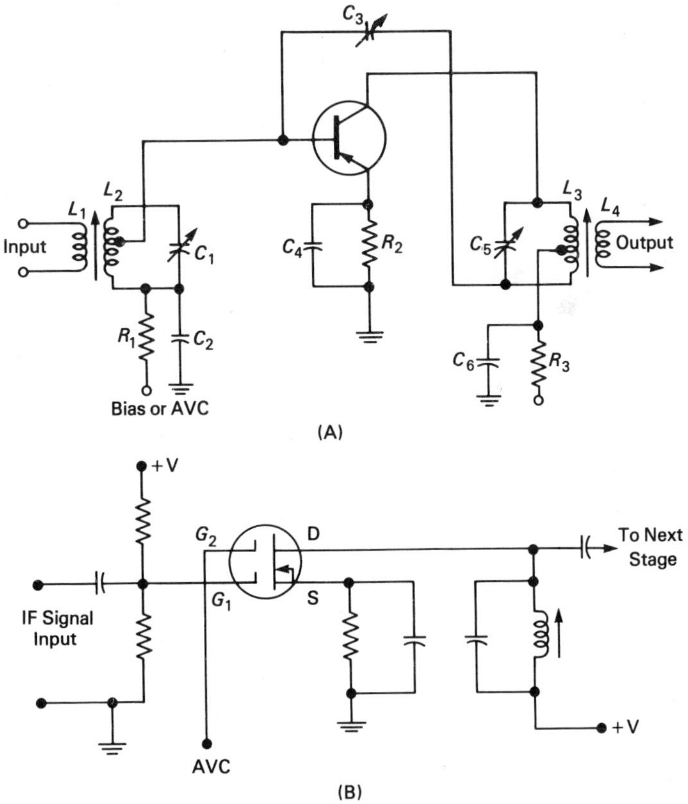

FIGURE 6-7. Common-emitter RF amplifier.

Such a circuit is also used in receivers where R_1 is fed a regulating voltage from the automatic volume-control (AVC) detector.

Inductor L_2 is tapped by the base input for impedance-matching purposes. Inductor L_3 is also tapped, with C_6 placing this tap at ground and splitting the top and bottom of the resonant circuit into individual sections with a 180° phase difference in the signal. The lower portion thus serves as a feed point for the neutralization capacitor C_3, which is adjusted until circuit stability is obtained. Tuning for intermediate-frequency (IF) type RF amplifiers is usually effected by adjustment of the metallic cores since only a single frequency is involved and only slight adjustments are required. Capacitors C_1 and C_5 can be used for more extensive tuning.

In Fig. 6-7B is shown a dual-gate FET used in an intermediate-frequency amplifier stage such as follows the tuner in superheterodyne receivers. The IF input signal is applied to gate G_1 as shown and the AVC (or AGC in television receivers) is applied to the second input (G_2). The remainder of the circuit is conventional with the stabilizing resistor-capacitor network to ground from the FET source element, and the output obtained from the drain element. A resonant-circuit tuned section between the drain element output and the next stage permits tuning by the variable inductor core.

6-5. VIDEO AMPLIFIER

Video amplifiers function in a manner similar to audio types, except that the video amplifiers are designed to handle the extensive frequency range of video signals, which may extend from about 30 Hz to 4 MHz. A typical video amplifier is shown in Fig. 6-8. Resistor R_5 adjusts emitter impedance and, hence, regulates the gain of the video amplifier transistor. Thus, the contrast level of the picture is regulated by adjustment of R_5.

Picture brilliance is regulated by adjustment of R_7, which varies the voltage applied to the cathode and, hence, alters the bias (i.e., potential difference between grid voltage and cathode voltage). Inductors L_1 and L_2 are *peaking coils*, which extend the frequency response of the amplifier for handling the wide range of video signals. Essentially, L_2 forms a parallel-resonant circuit with shunt capacitances. The circuit raises impedance and minimizes the shunting of high-frequency signals. Inductor L_1 with R_4 forms an impedance for isolating the shunting capacitances of the input and output circuitry from the collector of the video amplifier to the cathode (or grid) circuits of the picture tube.

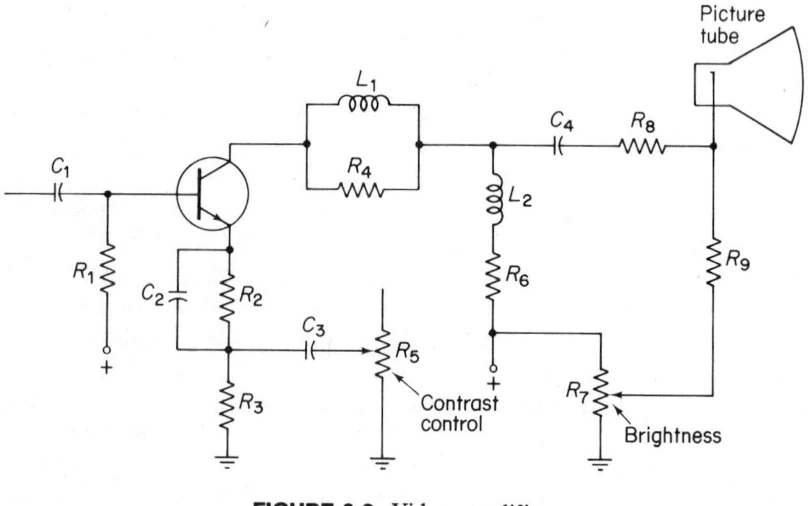

FIGURE 6-8. Video amplifier.

6-6. CLASS C AND AM

A push-pull Class C amplifier modulated by an audio, video, or other low-frequency range signal is shown in Fig. 6-9. The RF input from a previous stage of amplification (or from an oscillator) is applied to the input resonant circuit by the transformer arrangements of L_1 and L_2. Cross-neutralization is used which consists of circuitry where NC_1 provides feedback coupling between the collector of Q_2 and the base input of Q_1, while NC_2 crosses from the collector of Q_1 to the base of Q_2. Split-stator capacitors are used for the output-resonant circuit, wherein the rotor is at ground, minimizing shock hazards in high-power transmitters.

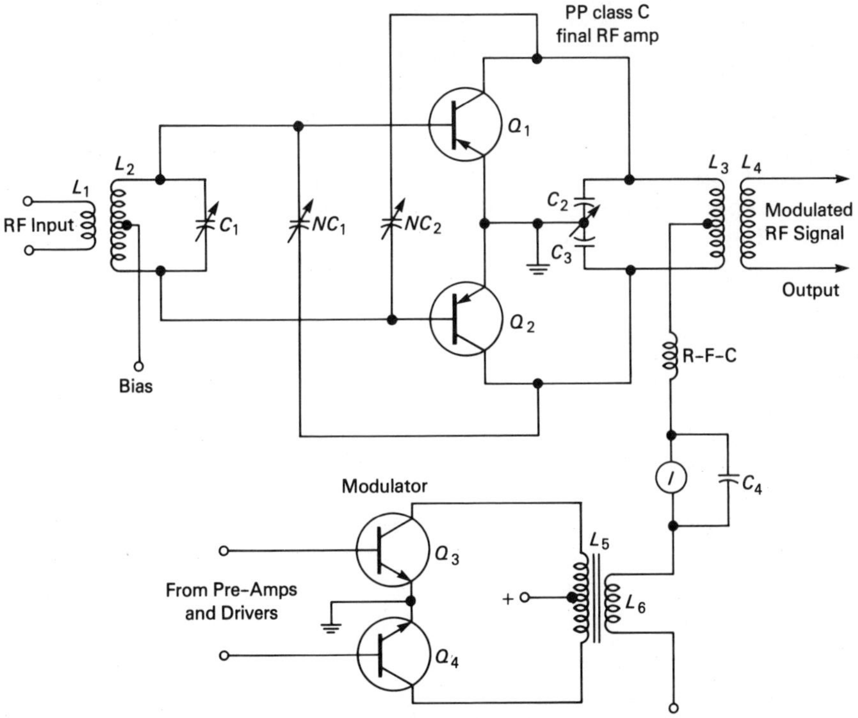

FIGURE 6-9. Push-pull class C and modulator.

The output from the push-pull modulator is applied to a modulation transformer primary L_5. When the signals appear across L_6, which, is in series with the power supply, the signal voltages add to and subtract from the potentials applied to the collectors of Q_1 and Q_2 (or to the anodes of transmitting Class C tubes). Consequently, the applied Class C collector voltages vary in relation to the amplitude changes of the modulating signal. Hence, amplitude-modulation is produced. The result is the formation of sidebands. (See also Chapter 16.)

If the final Class C stage is modulated and no additional RF amplification follows it, the system is referred to as *high-level modulation.* This indicates that modulation occurs at the highest RF power level, regardless of the type of modulation employed. (The modulating signal could also have been applied to the base input circuits for producing AM.) When the modulated Class C amplifier is followed by one or more Class B amplifiers, the system is called *low-level modulation,* since modulation occurs at a level lower than that of the final output power from the last stage.

For 100 percent modulation, the output power of the *modulator* (Q_3 and Q_4) must be one-half the Class C input power—the product of the Class C amplifier supply voltage and direct current. The input signal to the base inputs of the Class C amplifier transistors is called *excitation* and must not be confused with the term *input power,* which relates to dc potentials and currents.

The *modulation percentage* is defined as how much less the modulating power is than the value that is one-half of the carrier amplifier input power. In adjustment or testing procedures, a constant-amplitude modulating signal is used. The following equation applies to such a situation:

$$P_a = \frac{m^2 p_i}{2} \qquad (6\text{-}1)$$

where P_a is the required modulator audio or video power
m is the percentage of modulation in decimal form, as 0.5 for 50 percent modulation
p_i is the Class C input power (dc).

Hence, if the input power to the Class C stage is 2 kW, for 100 percent modulation we obtain the following audio power requirement:

$$P_a = \frac{1 \times 2000}{2} = \begin{array}{l}\text{1000 watts (1 kW)}\\ \text{required modulating power}\end{array}$$

6-7. AM AND FM DETECTORS

Detection is also known as *demodulation* since the process is the inverse of modulation. The simplest form of detection is the use of a solid-state diode, though a vacuum tube can also be used. The rectifying principle of the diode, which permits current flow in only one direction, is the basis for the detection process in both AM and FM, as shown in Fig. 6-10.

An AM diode detector is shown in part A. The resonant circuits at the input are tuned to the signals obtained from the intermediate-frequency (IF) amplifiers. For positive signal alternations across L_2, the diode conducts and produces positive pulses (as shown) with amplitudes that vary as the composite-signal input varies. (The composite signal consists of the carrier plus the sidebands.) During negative alternations the diode does not conduct. Thus, the diode rectifies the RF signal energy, and, when this appears at the output, capacitor C_3 filters the pulsating dc and produces the audio signal (representative of the envelope shown in dotted outline for the rectified signal). By tapping the bottom of R_1 with a resistor and an audio bypass capacitor, a voltage is obtained for AVC purposes. As the average carrier amplitude increases (to produce a louder

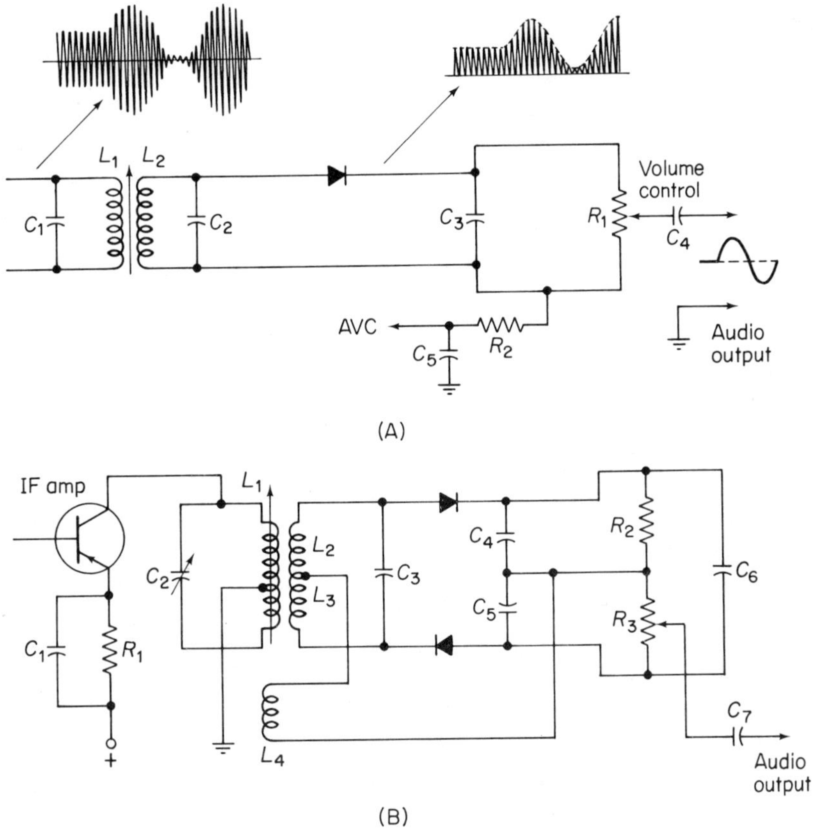

FIGURE 6-10. AM and FM detection systems.

signal), more AVC voltage is fed to earlier RF stages to decrease gain and automatically maintain the volume as set by the listener.

Figure 6-10B shows a typical FM detector. Here, two diodes are used in a special circuit, called a *ratio detector*, wherein L_4 samples some of the signal at L_1 and makes phase comparisons with the signal appearing across L_2 and L_3. As the carrier frequency shifts during frequency modulation, the frequency changes are converted to representative audio voltages and obtained from across R_3 (which also acts as a volume control).

During the detecting process of the ratio detector, one diode conducts more than the other, causing the ratio of voltages across the output resistors to change, while keeping the total voltage across R_2 and R_3 the same. Capacitor C_6 shunts the two resistors and is selected to have a high capacitance value (usually several microfarads). This capacitor charges to the voltage (dc) value appearing across the output resistors. Since C_6 opposes a voltage change, it maintains the voltage across the resistor combination at a constant level. Thus, sudden changes, which occur because of sharp static bursts or noise pulses, are minimized. A similar circuit, called a *discriminator*, has the two diodes wired in the same direction. The discriminator requires an amplitude-clipping stage (sometimes called a *limiter)*, which precedes the detector to eliminate amplitude modulation in the form of noise signals. The ratio detector, however, is insensitive to most noise or AM-type signals.

6-8. CLASS D AMPLIFICATION

The Class D amplifier is a special high-efficiency type that employs pulses in modulated form. In one system the pulses have an amplitude that corresponds to the signal amplitude as shown in Fig. 6-11. This system is also known as *pulse-amplitude modulation* (PAM) and is also discussed in Chapter 16, Sec. 16-3. With Class D amplification it is possible to achieve a high degree of efficiency, and signals can be driven into higher peak-current amplitudes than is possible with conventional A, AB, and B amplifiers.

As shown in Fig. 6-11A, the pulse amplitudes coincide with the modulating sinewave signal and also change polarity as shown. An alternate method is to utilize single-polarity pulses as shown in Chapter 16, Fig. 16-4. For the system shown in Fig. 6-11B, the input signal is applied to a pulse modulator, and the signal is converted into an amplitude-modulated pulse train. Though a sinewave is shown as the modulating signal, complex audio waves could, of course, be used. After amplification, the modulated signal tends to have sawtooth characteristics because of the spaces between

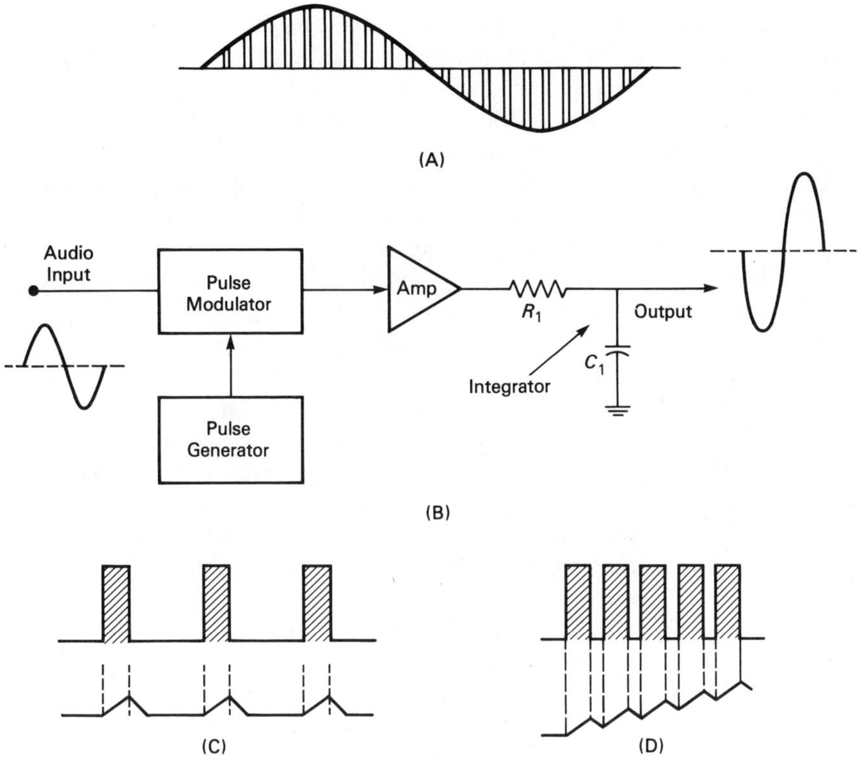

FIGURE 6-11. Class D system.

pulses and the amplitude-changing peak of each pulse. Consequently, an integrator system is utilized to accumulate the change from pulse to pulse so the waveshape conforms to the original modulating signal waveshape in all respects except amplitude.

The integrator circuit system is also used for the alternate pulse modulation systems to assure a smooth change amplitude pattern. Thus, for the system where a constant pulse amplitude is maintained, but the pulse widths are varied, most of the circuitry is similar, though a pulse-width modulator is used instead of the one shown in Fig. 6-11B. (For pulse-width modulation factors, see Chapter 16, Sec. 16-6.)

The principles of integrator applications to pulse trains are shown in Fig. 6-11C and D. (See also Chapter 4, Sec. 4-8, Integration Circuitry.) When widely spaced pulses are used with a long time constant during integration, low-amplitude triangular waveforms are produced as shown in Fig. 6-11C. This comes about because the output capacitor of the integrator (see Fig. 4-6) charges only to a small portion of the total pulse amplitude because the pulse is of such short duration with regard to the time constant. During the intervals between pulses, the capacitor discharges, hence the triangular waveshape. When the interval between pulses is shorter than the pulse width, as shown in Fig. 6-11D, the integration process tends to become a true summation device. This is so because successive pulses of the pulse train cause a gradual rise of the output waveform amplitude as shown. For the first pulse, the capacitor charges to a certain value, dependent on pulse width. Assume that the charge is 2 V. If the interval between pulses is one-fourth of the duration, the capacitor discharges to 1.5 V. During the next pulse duration it gains another 2 V of charge, bringing it to a total of 3.5 V. During the next interval between pulses it loses 0.5 V, for a net charge of 3 V. For the next pulse, it gains another 2 V, and continues in like manner until the charge approaches that of the pulse magnitude. This principle is used in television. The vertical sweep oscillators, which trace the vertical portions of the picture, are triggered by such an accumulation of charges on an integrator capacitor. Successive incoming pulses applied to the integrator gradually build up the voltage until it reaches the proper level to initiate the triggering process.

7

AM, FM, TV, and CB Listings

7-1. U.S. PUBLIC ENTERTAINMENT BROADCAST ALLOCATIONS

Frequency allocations for the various public entertainment broadcasting in the United States are under the jurisdiction of the Federal Communications Commission. Spectrum space information in this chapter is followed by listings showing the frequency span for each television station. In addition the picture and sound carrier frequencies are also shown for reference and comparison purposes.

The standard television signal structure is shown in Fig. 7-1, and since it is made up of a number of individual signals it is called a *composite* signal. In addition to the video information signal there are blanking pulses as well as vertical and horizontal synchronizing pulses needed to lock in the vertical and horizontal sweep oscillators of the receiver. Two fields are shown, and these make up the frame of the telecast signal. Scanning data and other related information are given later in this chapter.

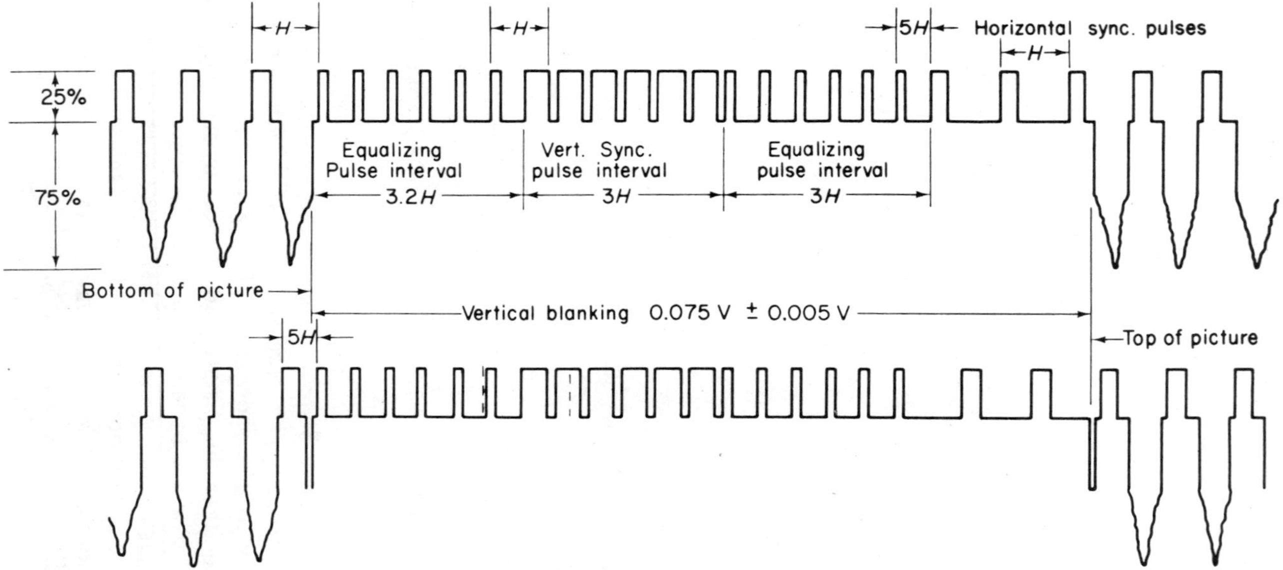

FIGURE 7-1. Composite TV signal.

AM RADIO STATION ALLOCATIONS

550 kHz to 1,600 kHz
(Nominally 10-kHz bandwidth per station)
Preferred intermediate frequency (IF) 455 kHz

FM RADIO STATION ALLOCATIONS

88 MHz to 108 MHz
(200-kHz bandwidth per station)
Preferred intermediate frequency (IF) 10.7 MHz

VHF TELEVISION STATION ALLOCATIONS

(6-MHz total bandwidth, including video and audio)
Preferred intermediate frequency (IF):
Picture carrier 45.75 MHz
Sound carrier 41.25 MHz
Picture and sound IF heterodyned to produce final sound IF of 4.5 MHz

TABLE 7-1. VHF Television Station Allocations (U.S.)

Channel Number	Frequency (MHz)	Video Carrier	Sound Carrier
1	Not used		
2	54–60	55.25	59.75
3	60–66	61.25	65.75
4	66–72	67.25	71.75
5	76–82	77.25	81.75
6	82–88	83.25	87.75
——FM Band (88 MHz to 108 MHz)——			
7	174–180	175.25	179.75
8	180–186	181.25	185.75
9	186–192	187.25	191.75
10	192–198	193.25	197.75
11	198–204	199.25	203.75
12	204–210	205.25	209.75
13	210–216	211.25	215.75

TABLE 7-2. UHF Television Station Allocations (U.S.)

Channel Number	Frequency Range, MHz	Picture Carrier, MHz	Sound Carrier, MHz
14	470–476	471.25	475.75
15	476–482	477.25	481.75
16	482–488	483.25	487.75
17	488–494	489.25	493.75
18	494–500	495.25	499.75
19	500–506	501.25	505.75
20	506–512	507.25	511.75
21	512–518	513.25	517.75
22	518–524	519.25	523.75
23	524–530	525.25	529.75
24	530–536	531.25	535.75
25	536–542	537.25	541.75
26	542–548	543.25	547.75
27	548–554	549.25	553.75
28	554–560	555.25	559.75
29	560–566	561.25	565.75
30	566–572	567.25	571.75
31	572–578	573.25	577.75
32	578–584	579.25	583.75
33	584–590	585.25	589.75
34	590–596	591.25	595.75
35	596–602	597.25	601.75
36	602–608	603.25	607.75
37	608–614	609.25	613.75
38	614–620	615.25	619.75
39	620–626	621.25	625.75
40	626–632	627.25	631.75
41	632–638	633.25	637.75
42	638–644	639.25	643.75
43	644–650	645.25	649.75
44	650–656	651.25	655.75
45	656–662	657.25	661.75
46	662–668	663.25	667.75
47	668–674	669.25	673.75
48	674–680	675.25	679.75

(*Continued*)

TABLE 7-2. (continued)

Channel Number	Frequency Range, MHz	Picture Carrier, MHz	Sound Carrier, MHz
49	680–686	681.25	685.75
50	686–692	687.25	691.75
51	692–698	693.25	697.75
52	698–704	699.25	703.75
53	704–710	705.25	709.75
54	710–716	711.25	715.75
55	716–722	717.25	721.75
56	722–728	723.25	727.75
57	728–734	729.25	733.75
58	734–740	735.25	739.75
59	740–746	741.25	745.75
60	746–752	747.25	751.75
61	752–758	753.25	757.75
62	758–764	759.25	763.75
63	764–770	765.25	769.75
64	770–776	771.25	775.75
65	776–782	777.25	781.75
66	782–788	783.25	787.75
67	788–794	789.25	793.75
68	794–800	795.25	799.75
69	800–806	801.25	805.75
70	806–812	807.25	811.75
71	812–818	813.25	817.75
72	818–824	819.25	823.75
73	824–830	825.25	829.75
74	830–836	831.25	835.75
75	836–842	837.25	841.75
76	842–848	843.25	847.75
77	848–854	849.25	853.75
78	854–860	855.25	859.75
79	860–866	861.25	865.75
80	866–872	867.25	871.75
81	872–878	873.25	877.75
82	878–884	879.25	883.75
83	884–890	885.25	889.75

7-2. TELEVISION SIGNAL DATA

In television transmission, various signals are combined to form a *composite* signal containing picture information and various pulses for synchronizing the beam sweep within the picture tube. The standard television composite signal is shown in Fig. 7-1. Horizontal blanking pulses blank out the screen during the retrace of the electron beam as it sweeps across the picture tube. Synchronizing pulses are mounted on the flat portion of the blanking pulse (termed the *pedestal*) to lock in the sweep circuits of the receiver. Picture (video) information occurs between blanking pulses. The picture tube beam sweeps across the picture tube and progressively downward forming what is called a *field*. Alternate fields interlace with preceding ones, and two fields form a *frame*. Equalizing pulses maintain horizontal synchronization during vertical blanking (when the beam retraces from the bottom of the screen to the top). Vertical sync pulses consist of 6 blocks so as to maintain horizontal synchronization during vertical beam control.

TELEVISION TRANSMISSION FACTORS

One frame = 33,334 μs (microseconds)
One field = 16,667 μs
One horizontal sweep cycle (start of one horizontal line trace to start of next) = 63.5 μs (See Fig. 6-2.)
Horizontal blanking interval = 10.16 μs to 11.4 μs
Horizontal trace (without blanking time) = 53.34 μs
Horizontal sync pulse duration = 5.08 μs to 5.68 μs
Vertical sync pulse interval (total of six vertical blocks) = 190.5 μs
Vertical blanking interval = 833 μs to 1300 μs for each field
Vertical scan frequency (monochrome) = 60 Hz
Vertical scan frequency (color) = 59.94 Hz
Horizontal scan frequency (monochrome) = 15,750 Hz
Horizontal scan frequency (color) = 15,734.264 Hz
Total frequency span for an individual station (monochrome or color) = 6 MHz
Picture carrier is nominally 1.25 MHz above the lower end of the channel (monochrome or color)
Vestigial sideband transmission is used for both monochrome and color
Aspect ratio of monochrome or color picture is 4:3
Scan lines per frame (mono or color) = 525 (interlaced)
Scan lines per field (mono or color) = 262.5
The frequency-modulated sound carrier is 4.5 MHz above the picture-carrier frequency (mono or color), with maximum deviation 25 kHz each side of center frequency
The effective radiated power of the audio may range from 50 to 70 percent of the peak power of the picture-signal carrier

7-3. COLOR TELEVISION FACTORS AND TERMS

The color video signal corresponds to a brightness component transmitted as an amplitude-modulated (AM) video carrier, plus a pair of color signals transmitted as AM sidebands that are produced by a phase-modulated carrier. Hence, two subcarriers 90° apart are involved, and both have a common frequency related to the color-picture carrier frequency of 3.579,545 MHz.

The modulated color carriers are suppressed at the transmitter, and only sideband signals are telecast. An independent carrier oscillator is used at the receiver and synchronized by a color burst signal on the horizontal *pedestal.* A minimum of 8 cycles comprise the burst signal, the frequency of which is identical to the one used at the transmitter: 3.579,545 MHz. The burst signal is omitted following equalizing pulses and is also absent during the vertical pulse interval [or during monochrome (black-and-white) transmission].

The brightness, or luminance, portion of the video signal is also referred to as the *Y signal.*

Hue is the term that identifies a color (such as blue hue, green hue, etc.).

Brightness refers to the intensity of a color.

Saturation refers to the degree to which a color is diluted with white. The less white a color contains, the higher its saturation.

The *Y signal* consists of predetermined levels of each of the primary colors—red, blue, and green—to correspond to the proportions to which the average eye responds. The Y signal thus contains 0.59 green, 0.30 red, and 0.11 blue.

The *I signal* consists of combinations of B−Y and R−Y signals, and its proportions are: −0.27 blue−Y; and 0.74 red−Y.

The *Q signal* (B−Y and R−Y) consists of 0.41 blue−Y, and 0.48 red−Y.

Color television signal phase relationships are shown in Fig. 7-2 and these show how the color signals are derived using R−Y and B−Y demodulators (or I/Q detectors). Note that the B−Y signals are displaced 33° clockwise from the Q signals, and the R−Y signals are likewise displaced 33° clockwise from the I signals. The relative positions of the primary colors are represented by dashed lines. The lower portion of Fig. 7-2 has been enlarged in Fig. 7-3 to show how the same resultant color is obtained for signal voltages of either I/Q or R−Y/B−Y, using saturated green as an example.

If an amplitude of −0.52 is taken along the −Q axis and −0.28 along the −I axis as shown, we would use these points to draw a parallelogram as shown by the dashed lines in Fig. 7-3. This parallelogram

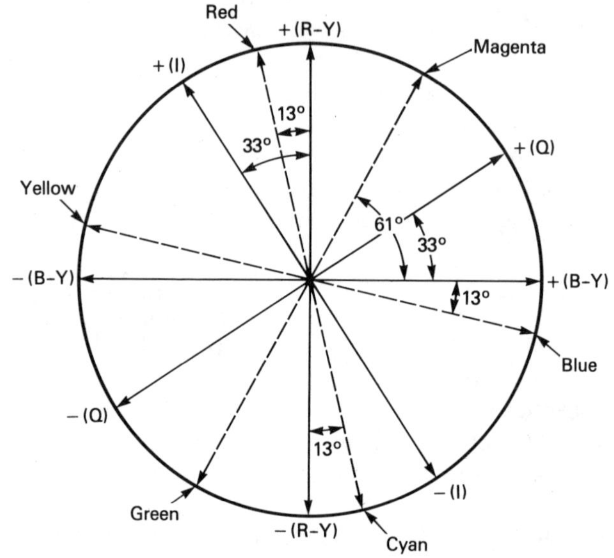

FIGURE 7-2. Phase relationships of color TV signals.

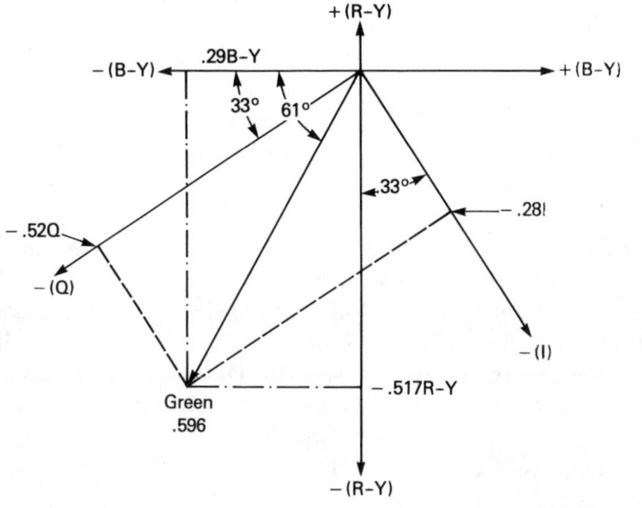

FIGURE 7-3. Green obtained from either I/Q or R-Y/B-Y.

indicates the amplitude of the vector addition of these two $-Q$ and $-I$ amplitudes. The result is 0.596, which represents the amplitude of the saturated green signal. Note that this identical amplitude for the saturated green signal can be obtained by taking an amplitude of 0.29 on the $-B-Y$ axis and -0.517 on the $-R-Y$ axis. Completing a parallelogram from these two points (the dot-dash line representation) produces the same amplitude obtained for the I/Q signal parallelogram. Similarly, all the other colors produce identical vectors for certain values of I and Q or of $R-Y$ and $B-Y$. The particular design of the demodulator system in the color receiver determines whether I/Q signals are produced or $R-Y$ and $B-Y$.

7-4. CB RADIO AND AMATEUR (HAM) ALLOCATIONS DATA

A Citizens' Band (CB) radio station is defined as a Class D radio-telephony radio station. Forty channels have been allocated having a frequency span from 26.965 MHz to 27.405 MHz, as shown in Table 7-3. Note that in the numbering sequence Channel 22 is followed by 24, and 25 is before 23. This has been done to keep the *frequency change* at a

TABLE 7-3. CB Listings

Channel	Frequency	Channel	Frequency
1	26.965 MHz	11	27.085 MHz
2	26.975	12	27.105
3	26.985	13	27.115
4	27.005	14	27.125
5	27.015	15	27.135
6	27.025	16	27.155
7	27.035	17	27.165
8	27.055	18	27.175
9	27.065	19	27.185
10	27.075	20	27.205
21	27.215	31	27.315
22	27.225	32	27.325
24	27.235	33	27.335
25	27.245	34	27.345
23	27.255	35	27.355
26	27.265	36	27.365
27	27.275	37	27.375
28	27.285	38	27.385
29	27.295	39	27.395
30	27.305	40	27.405

progressively higher sequence. Manufactured units, however, have a proper sequence on tuning dials that show the entire 40 channels. Actually the channel *number* designation has been left out of the rules by the FCC. Instead, channel identification is solely by its designated center frequency. The altered sequence in Table 7-3 comes about because the older allocations were changed and two channels were added between the previous Channels 22 and 23. The EIA proposed that the new channels be designated as No. 24 and No. 25, with the sequence shown in the table.

Except for the channel-selector unit, all equipment, components, and carrier-frequency generating circuitry must be housed within a cabinet and unavailable from the outside. Harmonic and other spurious signals appearing at the output of a CB transmitter must be diminished (attenuated) by at least 60 dB below the fundamental frequency power output in watts. The latter is designated as 12-W peak envelope power (P.E.P.) SSB max., and 4 W AM max. All 40 channels can employ single sideband (SSB) transmission using either the upper sideband (USB) or the lower sideband (LSB).

Ham radio stations have a wider latitude of operation because of the special license issued. They operate in a number of so-called *bands* often referred to in relation to wavelength in meters. Operation is in both the VHF and UHF regions, with widely used bands covering those shown in Table 7-4.

TABLE 7-4. Amateur Listings

160-meter band	1.8	to	2.0 MHz
80-meter band	3.5	to	4.0 MHz
40-meter band	7.0	to	7.3 MHz
20-meter band	14.0	to	14.35 MHz
15-meter band	21.0	to	21.45 MHz
10-meter band	28.0	to	29.7 MHz
6-meter band	50.0	to	54.0 MHz
2-meter band	144.0	to	148.0 MHz

7-5. GENERAL FREQUENCY DESIGNATIONS

VLF	(very low frequencies)	3 Hz to	30	kHz
LF	(low frequencies)	30 kHz to	300	kHz
MF	(medium frequencies)	300 kHz to	3	MHz
HF	(high frequencies)	3 MHz to	30	MHz
VHF	(very high frequencies)	30 MHz to	300	MHz
UHF	(ultrahigh frequencies)	300 MHz to	3,000	MHz
SHF	(superhigh frequencies)	3 GHz to	30	GHz
EHF	(extra-high frequencies)	30 GHz to	300	GHz

7-6. MILITARY FREQUENCY DESIGNATIONS

P band	225 MHz to	390	MHz
L band	390 MHz to	1,550	MHz
S band	1,550 MHz to	5,200	MHz
X band	5,200 MHz to	10,900	MHz
K band	10,900 MHz to	36,000	MHz
Q band	36 GHz to	46	GHz
V band	46 GHz to	56	GHz

7-7. THE INTERNATIONAL MORSE CODE

A	·—	N	—·	1	·————
B	—···	O	———	2	··———
C	—·—·	P	·——·	3	···——
D	—··	Q	——·—	4	····—
E	·	R	·—·	5	·····
F	··—·	S	···	6	—····
G	——·	T	—	7	——···
H	····	U	··—	8	———··
I	··	V	···—	9	————·
J	·———	W	·——	Ø	—————
K	—·—	X	—··—		
L	·—··	Y	—·——		
M	——	Z	——··		

Period (.)	·—·—·—
Comma (,)	——··——
Interrogation (?)	··——··
Quotation mark (")	·—··—·
Colon (:)	———···
Semicolon (;)	—·—·—·
Parenthesis ( )	—·——·—

Zero (Ø) is often transmitted as a long dash. The following letter combinations are transmitted without any space between:

Wait sign (AS)	·—···
Double dash (Break)	—···—
Error (erase sign)	········
Fraction bar (/)	—··—·
End of message (AR)	·—·—·
End of transmission (SK)	···—·—
International distress signal (SOS)	···———···

8 Digital Data

8-1. DIGITAL LOGIC BASICS

Audio or RF amplifiers and similar circuits are *linear*. Digital circuits, as shown in Chapter 9, handle pulse-type signals instead of the sinewave or composite (fundamental plus harmonics) signals. The digital circuits are used extensively in computers, calculators, microprocessors, video games, quartz-crystal pulse generators for timing, and in many other similar applications.

For circuits to be capable of handling number representations, extremely *precise and accurate* circuit parameters are necessary. Such strict requirements cannot be obtained with circuits operating on the linear portion of the characteristic curves because of the variance in transistor, circuit, and component characteristics. The only practical procedure is to use *on* and *off* states, since these exist for any type transistor or solid-state component. Thus the error possibilities are minimized because the performance does not depend on intermediate levels of current or voltage but rather on just the two states of *conduction* and *nonconduction*.

Adapting the nonconducting and conducting states of transistors or diodes to arithmetic processes means that we are limited to two numerals, 1 and 0. Thus utilization is made of base-two arithmetic systems rather than the more familiar base-ten system. The base-two system is termed *binary*, and a comparison of binary and base-ten is given in Table 14-12. (See also Tables 14-14, 14-15, and 14-16.)

In the design of logic circuitry, consideration is given to the two states of conducting and nonconducting by extensive use of switching or gating circuits. The signals used in digital circuitry are pulses, and the presence or absence of a pulse signal is related to numerals 1 and 0. During design of digital systems the polarity of a pulse is selected to represent either the 1 or 0 value. Thus, if a positive pulse is to represent logic 1, then the absence of a pulse (or the presence of a negative pulse) would represent 0. Similarly, if the system is to use negative pulses to represent logic 1, any positive pulse (or the absence of any pulse) would then denote 0. (See Fig. 8-1.)

In the binary system there is a progressive power value increase for digits to the left of the decimal point, and each successive digit doubles in value. Thus, 001 represents base-ten 1, and 010 represents 2. The 100 equals 4, and 1000 equals 8, etc. The power relationships of binary and place values are:

etc.	10	9	8	7	6	5	4	3	2	1	Place
←	2^9	2^8	2^7	2^6	2^5	2^4	2^3	2^2	2^1	2^0	Power
	512	256	128	64	32	16	8	4	2	1	Value

These power relationships permit us to find the value of any combination of 1's and 0's in the binary system. Hence, the binary (base-two) number 101 equals 5 because the right digit has a value of 1 and the left digit, being in third place, has a value of 4 and $4+1=5$. Similarly, the number 1101 has a value of 13, since the right numeral has a value of 1, the third from the right has a value of 4, and the fourth from right has a value of 8; thus we have $8+4+1=13$.

All arithmetic operations performed in the base-ten system can be duplicated in the base-two. In fact all calculators, computers, and microprocessors utilize the binary system to perform all arithmetic functions, and the final results are converted to the base-ten system before being displayed on read-out devices. With base-two the logic that applies differs from base-ten, but the end results are the same. Thus, in binary addition, $1+1=0$, with 1 to carry, and the sum is thus binary 10 having a base-ten equivalent of 2. Similarly, subtracting binary 10 (base-ten value of 2) from binary 101 (base-ten value of 5) gives us binary 11 with a base-ten value of 3. Such a subtraction process in binary also utilizes the borrow principle as in base-ten. Thus, in the operation $101-10$, the right-hand digits (first-place digits) are subtracted, $1-0=1$. With the second-place digits, we are unable to subtract 1 from 0, hence a 1 is borrowed from the next place as with base-ten subtraction processes. Actually it involves subtracting binary 1 from 10 (value$=2$); thus, the remainder would be 1.

The examples that follow give additional illustrations of the binary mathematical processes.

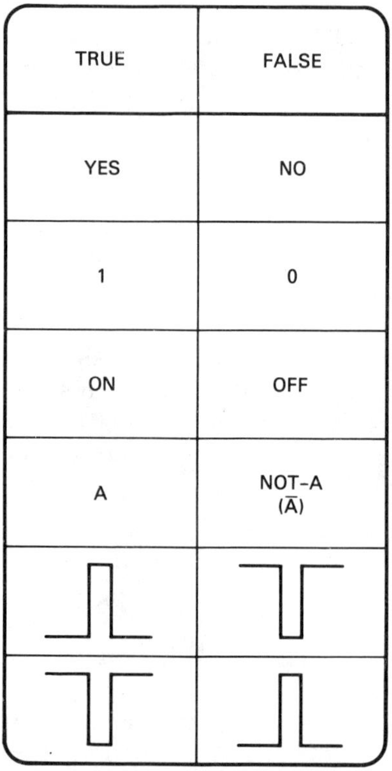

FIGURE 8-1. Logic equivalencies.

8-2. BINARY MATH

In binary addition, $1+1=0$, with 1 to carry. Thus, $1+1=10$, where the first-place bit is the 0, and the second-place bit represents the carry number. The following are additional examples:

11 (3)	addend	01 (1)	11 (3)
+100 (4)	augend	+101 (5)	11 (3)
111 (7)	sum	110 (6)	101 (5)
			1011 (11)

In subtraction, the *borrow* principle must be used as it is in base-ten subtraction.

111 (7)	minuend
−11 (3)	subtrahend
100 (4)	remainder

110 (6)	10101 (21)
−1 (1)	−1001 (09)
101 (5)	1100 (12)

For multiplication the multiplicand is set down once to represent the first-order multiplier and then set down again, but moved to the left by one place, to indicate the second-place multiplier function if one exists. Addition of the partial products thus formed provides the product as shown in the following examples:

101	(5) multiplicand	110	(6)
×11	(3) multiplier	×101	(5)
101	partial products	110	
101		000	
1111	(15) product	110	
		11110	(30)

The procedure for division of binary numbers is similar to that used for base-ten numbers:

$$\begin{array}{l} \text{Dividend} \\ \text{Divisor} \end{array} \frac{1100\ (=12)}{100\ (=04)} = \text{binary } 11\ (=3) \text{ quotient}$$

The following are additional examples:

10
111)1110
111
0

11
110)10010
110
110
110

In the second example shown above, the binary number 110 (6) is larger than the first three digits in the dividend, 100 (4); hence the 110 must be placed to the right (by one digit) so that it goes under the 1001 grouping, thus following the general rule in base-ten divisions.

The divisor 110 "goes into" the 1001 portion of the dividend and when subtracted from it gives a result of 11. When the last 0 in the dividend is then brought down, the result is 110, thus concluding the division.

8-3. COMPLEMENT NUMBERS

By using the principle of *complementing* in arithmetic operations, it is possible to perform subtraction by *addition*. This method simplifies subtraction procedures in computers because it makes possible both addition and subtraction by common circuitry. The process involves changing the subtrahend to its complement for either the base-ten number or the binary number as shown by the examples that follow.

$$\begin{array}{rl} 8264 & \\ -1623 & \text{(standard subtraction)} \\ \hline 6641 & \end{array}$$

$$\begin{array}{rl} 8264 & \\ +8376 & \text{(complement of 1623)} \\ \hline 16640 & \\ +1 & \text{(end-around carry of left-most bit)} \\ \hline 6641 & \end{array}$$

In the foregoing, note that the subtrahend is changed by the setting down of the difference between each digit and 9, and then adding this complement to the minuend. The leading digit of the remainder (the digit 1) is now shifted to the units position and added, yielding the correct answer. The shift process is termed the *end-around carry*.

In the binary system the complement is easily formed by changing all 1's to 0's and all 0's to 1's:

$$\begin{array}{lr} \text{standard} & 1101 \\ \text{subtraction:} & -0101 \\ \hline & 1000 \end{array} \qquad \begin{array}{lr} \text{complement} & 1101 \\ \text{method:} & +1010 \\ \hline & 10111 \\ & +1 \\ \hline & 1000 \end{array}$$

The subtrahend must have as many binary digits (0 and 1) as the minuend in order that error be prevented. Thus, in the foregoing, 101 was changed to 0101 to form the proper complement.

8-4. FRACTIONAL AND NEGATIVE BINARY NOTATION

In the base-ten system, the place representation to the *left* of the decimal point is in the order of units, tens, hundreds, thousands, tens of thousands, etc. In the binary system, the order is units, twos, fours, eights, sixteens, etc. (See Tables 14-12 and 14-13.) In base-ten notation, the place representation to the *right* of the decimal point is in the order of tenths, hundredths, thousandths, etc. In the binary system, however, the order to the right is *halves*, *fourths*, *eighths*, *sixteenths*, etc. Thus, while in the base-ten system 3.1 represents "three and one-tenth," in the binary system 11.1 equals "three and *one-half*." Similarly, 0.01 equals "one-fourth," 0.001 equals "one-eighth," etc. In base-ten the number 0.11 equals $\frac{11}{100}$, but in binary 0.11 represents $\frac{3}{4}$ because two places to the right of the binary point (decimal point) indicates fourths, and the number 11 in binary is *three* in the base-ten system. Similarly, 0.011 in binary equals $\frac{3}{8}$ and 0.0011 equals $\frac{3}{16}$ in base-ten. Some random numbers are shown below for added illustration:

101.1	$=6\frac{1}{2}$
111.11	$=7\frac{3}{4}$
1010.101	$=10\frac{5}{8}$
11.1001	$=3\frac{9}{16}$
101.00101	$=5\frac{5}{32}$
100.10001	$=4\frac{17}{32}$
1001.110	$=9\frac{6}{8}=9\frac{3}{4}$
1.1010	$=1\frac{10}{16}=1\frac{5}{8}$

A number (binary) in a computer is designated as a negative number when it is preceded by a sign bit consisting of an extra 1 bit. Thus, if the magnitude of a number is four significant digits, e.g., 1010, the number is positive if preceded by a zero, i.e., 01010. If it were 11010, the computer circuitry would recognize the left-most 1 as the sign bit identifying the 1010 as a negative number. (In the foregoing, a 4-bit number was used for explanatory purposes. In the computer, a register has a digit capacity dependent on design and may have 32 bits, 64 bits, etc.)

The complement principle described in Sec. 8-3 lends itself to negative binary number representations, permitting execution of arithmetical processes in binary form. Thus, the binary positive number 101 (5) becomes 010 when it takes a negative value. The arithmetical operations follow the end-around carry principles used with complement numbers as the following procedure shows. (For simplicity, the sign bit is not shown.)

Procedure:

$$7+(-3)=4$$

111	(7)
+ 100	(complement of 3)
1011	
+1	(end-around carry)
100	= +4

8-5. NUMBER SYSTEMS

Data relating to base-ten notation is given in Tables 14-12 and 14-13 in reference to the binary system, and the octal system is described and illustrated in Table 14-14. The following table lists other number systems and their respective radices:

Number System	Base of Radix	Number System	Base of Radix
Binary	Two	Sextodecimal	Sixteen
Ternary	Three	Septendecimal	Seventeen
Quaternary	Four	Octodenary	Eighteen
Quinary	Five	Novendenary	Nineteen
Senary	Six	Vicenary	Twenty
Septenary	Seven	Tricenary	Thirty
Octonary (or Octal)	Eight	Quadragenary	Forty
Novenary	Nine	Quinquagenary	Fifty
Decimal	Ten	Sexagenary	Sixty
Undecimal	Eleven	Septuagenary	Seventy
Duodecimal	Twelve	Octogenary	Eighty
Terdenary	Thirteen	Nonagenary	Ninety
Quaterdenary	Fourteen	Centenary	Hundred
Quindenary	Fifteen		

9

Digital Circuits

9-1. THE FLIP-FLOP CIRCUIT

Compared to television and other electronic systems, there are not many different types of circuits used in digital logic processes. Primary circuits consist of those that generate the pulse signals for the system, those used for counting purposes, and those that perform switching or gating functions. These circuits are interconnected in sequence, and the same circuits are used many times over in calculators, computers, industrial control counting systems, and similar applications. Other than the foregoing, circuitry such as the conventional power-supply systems, amplifiers, and similar signal processors are, of course, also used in digital applications. In digital systems the *flip-flop* is widely used in computers for counting and calculating purposes. Also called the *Eccles-Jordan* flip-flop after its originators, the circuit is extensively applied in industry for counting, forming switching networks, and for control purposes. The circuit is *bistable*; that is, it produces no output signal unless a signal is applied to its input. It has two possible states, sometimes represented as 1 and 0 on schematics, or as Q and $\overline{Q}$. The overbar denotes the negated output.

A typical flip-flop circuit is shown in Fig. 9-1. In such a circuit, one transistor conducts and the other is at cutoff, with the collector circuitry holding these stable states only as long as power is applied. The circuit is symmetrical, as shown in the figure, so that an output is obtainable from either collector circuit. The flip-flop is assumed to be representative of "0"

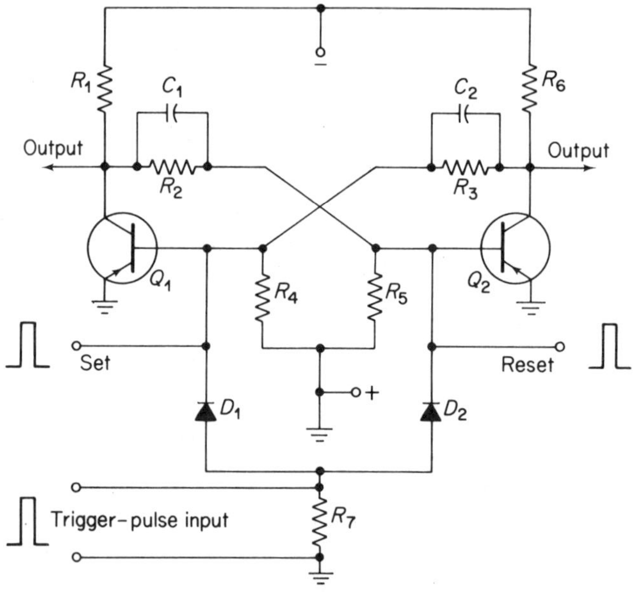

FIGURE 9-1. Basic flip-flop circuit.

for a certain status. We will designate the "0" state for the flip-flop when Q_1 is conducting and Q_2 nonconducting.

When Q_1 conducts, the voltage drop across R_1 brings the collector of Q_1 near the ground (+) potential, which is coupled to the base of Q_2. Here, it places a reverse bias at the base of Q_2 and prevents conduction. Under these conditions there is no voltage drop across R_6, and a negative potential is applied to the base of Q_1; the potential holds Q_1 in the conducting state.

If a positive pulse is applied to the SET input, that pulse overcomes the negative forward bias at the base of Q_1 and causes this transistor to become nonconducting. Now the voltage drop across R_1 will decline and the base of Q_2 will obtain the forward bias necessary for it to go into conduction. Thus, the second stable state has been reached—the state represented by "1" or the *on* state. At this point the entry of another pulse at the SET input will be ineffective since the flip-flop is in the *set* state. To reset it to zero, a positive pulse must be applied to the base of Q_2, as shown in Fig. 9-1, thus causing this transistor to become nonconductive. The transistor, in its turn, causes Q_1 to become conductive and again the "0" state results.

As shown, two diodes, D_1 and D_2, (*steering diodes*), can be used to apply a positive pulse to both base circuits at once. Thus, this input across R_7 is called a *trigger* input because it can perform the functions of both set and reset. Each positive input pulse will trigger the flip-flop to return to the other state (from "1" to "0", or from "0" to "1").

Since only the "0" and "1" states are possible, the flip-flop systems employ *binary* representations having base 2. Tables are given in Chap. 14, and binary arithmetic data are found in Chap. 8.

A square or rectangle is generally used as the symbol for the flip-flop circuit as shown in Fig. 9-2A. Here the inputs are identified by T for trigger, R for reset, and S for set. Outputs are designated as Q for logic 1 and $\overline{Q}$ for 0. Variations are found in the basic flip-flop circuitry; for example, note the JK flip-flop shown at B. This flip-flop combines the basic functions found in the reset and trigger flip-flop circuit, plus providing for clocked operation. The clock input line is identified as CP (clock pulse). The JK flip-flop shown is also called the *synchronous* type. (See also Sec. 9-4.)

For the JK circuit represented in Fig. 9-2B, the set, reset, and trigger modes illustrated in Fig. 9-1 are achieved as follows: When J=1 and CP=1, the set mode is initiated. When K=1 and CP=1, the reset function is initiated. When inputs J, K, and CP have simultaneous applications of logic 1, the trigger mode is obtained. The clock is essentially a precisely timed signal generator that originates the pulses used throughout a particular digital system. When the clock is applied to a chain of flip-flop

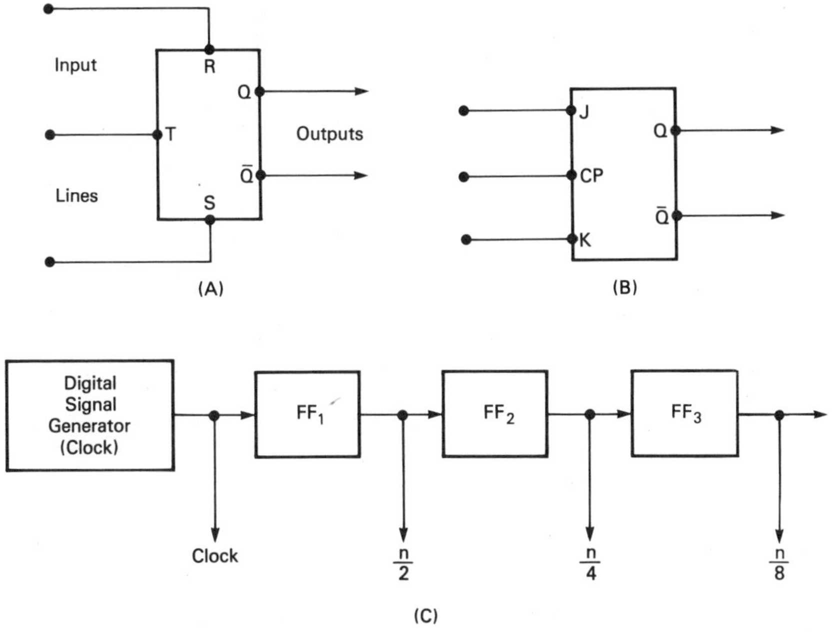

FIGURE 9-2. Flip-flop symbols and counter.

stages as shown in Fig. 9-2C, a count division is available because the number of logic 1 pulses entering the first flip-flop will produce only half as many logic 1's at the output. Since this same division-by-two prevails for the second flip-flop, the output here would be one-fourth the number of logic 1 pulses produced by the clock. Thus, successive flip-flop stages can divide by two for as long a train as needed.

9-2. *OR* AND *AND* LOGIC GATES

Logic gates (or *switches*) are used extensively in digital computers and counting devices for performing certain functions of combining counts or providing an output when pulse coincidence prevails at the input. Typical diode-type logic circuits are shown in Fig. 9-3, as are the symbols that apply. Only two inputs are shown, though more are used when necessary.

For the positive signal OR gate, when a positive pulse is applied to A, *or* B, *or* to both inputs, the positive voltage of the pulse adds to the applied positive voltage, thus increasing conduction and producing an

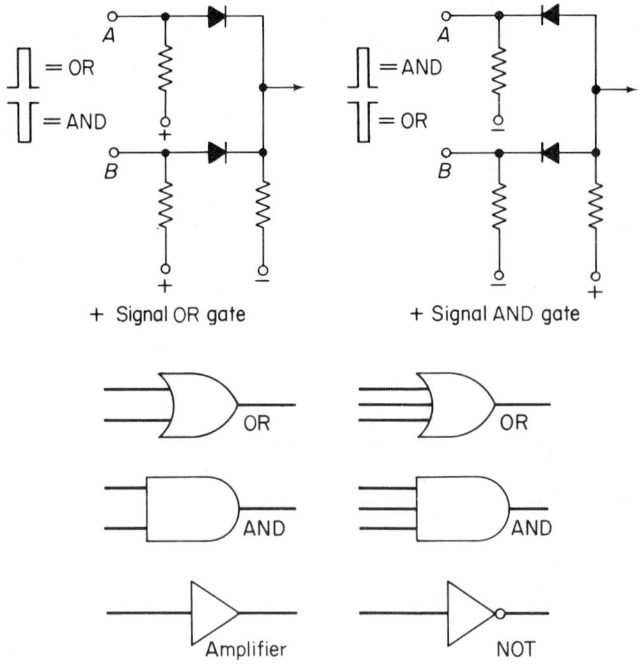

FIGURE 9-3. OR-AND gates and symbols.

output. We can say that either an A input *or* a B input, *or* both, produce an output. If a negative pulse is applied to A, however, the pulse overcomes the applied positive potential to the upper diode. But since the lower diode still conducts, some current will flow through the output resistor. When, however, both negative pulses are applied, neither diode conducts, and there will be sudden voltage change at the output as conduction through the resistor stops. Thus, it is necessary to apply a pulse at both A *and* B to produce an output.

For the positive-signal AND gate, the opposite polarity pulses form the OR and AND switches as Fig. 9-3 shows. Here, a designer can form logic circuits by using either positive or negative pulses as desired. The output from one such gate can be applied to the input of another.

The OR and AND gate symbols are shown in Fig. 9-3 for two- or three-input types. For reference, an amplifier symbol is also shown, as well as a *NOT* circuit. This is the logical term applied to a circuit that inverts the polarity of a pulse (the output is *not* the same as the input).

9-3. *NOR* AND *NAND* LOGIC GATES

When transistors are used to form logic OR and AND gates of the type discussed in Sec. 9-2, the output can be obtained from the emitter—as in an emitter-follower device to prevent reversal of pulse polarity. If the output is obtained from the collector, phase inversion occurs, and the NOT function described in Sec. 9-2 prevails. Thus, for the OR function in Fig. 9-4, a NOT function also occurs, this NOT-OR function being designated as a *NOR circuit*. The symbol has the small circle denoting the NOT function, as shown.

For the AND logic function, the transistors are wired in series. Thus, a negative pulse must be applied to both inputs to furnish the necessary bias potentials to permit each to conduct. A *coincidence gate* or *AND circuit* is formed, but the NOT function of phase reversal produces a NOT-AND circuit, or NAND gate, as shown. Again, the small circle is added to the AND symbol to denote the NOT function.

Truth tables are often used to depict the logic that applies to the various circuits. Symbols A, B, C, etc. can be used to designate various inputs, or 1 and 0 numerals used for the inputs. Thus, for an OR circuit with three inputs, we would obtain an output for any single input or combination as shown in Tables 9-1 and 9-2.

The plus sign (+) in the foregoing tables represents the *logical connective* for the OR function. For the AND function the multiplication sign is used, either by a lower-case ×, a raised dot, or by the algebraic

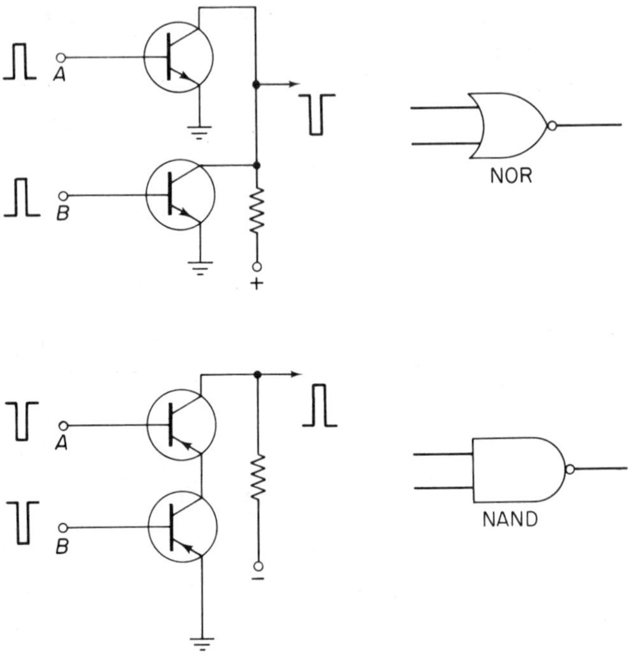

FIGURE 9-4. NOR and NAND circuits.

TABLE 9-1. OR Logic (A+B+C)

0+0+0=0
A+0+0=1
0+B+0=1
0+0+C=1
A+B+0=1
0+B+C=1
A+0+C=1
A+B+C=1

TABLE 9-2. OR Logic (0+1)

0+0+0=0
1+0+0=1
0+1+0=1
0+0+1=1
1+1+0=1
0+1+1=1
1+0+1=1
1+1+1=1

TABLE 9-3. AND Logic (ABC)

0×0×0=0
A×0×0=0
0×B×0=0
0×0×C=0
A×B×0=0
0×B×C=0
A×0×C=0
A×B×C=1

method of placing letter symbols close together. Thus, for three inputs we can express it as A×B×C, A·B·C, or as ABC. For a three-input AND circuit, no output is obtained until coincidence in inputs appears as shown in Table 9-3.

9-4. LOGIC-CIRCUIT COMBINATIONS

Several interconnections of OR, AND, and NOR gates are shown in Fig. 9-5. For the first one shown, a two-input OR circuit has its output applied to one of the inputs of an AND circuit. The OR circuit has the inputs designated as A and B, while input C is applied to the second terminal of the AND gate as shown. Since the AND circuit is a coincidence gate, it must have both inputs present to obtain an output. Thus, an output from the OR circuit must be combined with a signal at the C input to the AND circuit. Since the OR circuit produces an output for either A *or* B, the logic expression is $(A+B)\cdot C$, meaning that either A *or* B *or* both must be present in conjunction with C to produce an output from the AND circuit.

The second circuit shown in Fig. 9-5 has a three-input AND gate feeding a two-input NOR circuit. Since the NOR circuit produces an output for any one or more inputs, the logic expression for this logic-circuit combination is $\overline{ABC+D}$. The overbar indicates the negation of the expression because of the NOR function. Thus, the output is a NOT function of A *and* B *and* C *or* D.

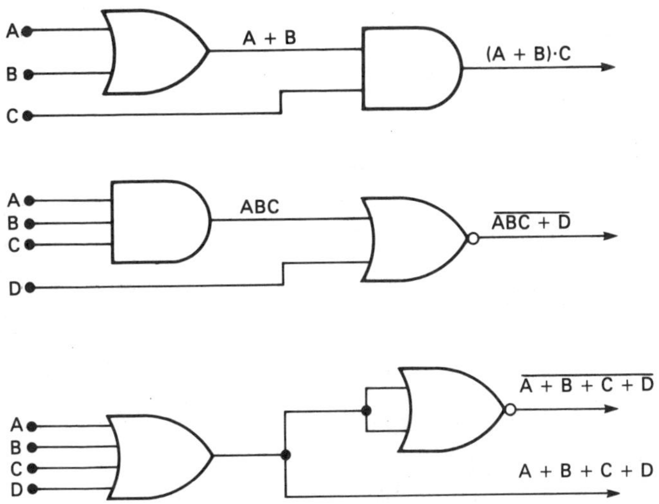

FIGURE 9-5. Logic interconnections.

For the third interconnected circuitry of Fig. 9-5 we have a four-input OR gate with a dual output line; one of which feeds a NOR circuit with the two input lines shorted. This circuit functions purely as a NOT or *negating* unit without amplification. Dual outputs are obtained, with the NOT circuit output having the overbar to indicate negation. Since only the OR function is utilized, the expressions are $\overline{A+B+C+D}$ and $A+B+C+D$.

The symbols shown in Fig. 9-6 represent the *exclusive* OR and NOR gates. These are special digital sections used in logic arithmetic processes, wherein the circuit adds without carry. Thus, an input at either input gate alone produces an output. If signals are applied to the two inputs simultaneously, the output is 0. If the output from such a circuit is negated as shown in Fig. 9-6B, the inversion of the output logic forms an exclusive NOR circuit.

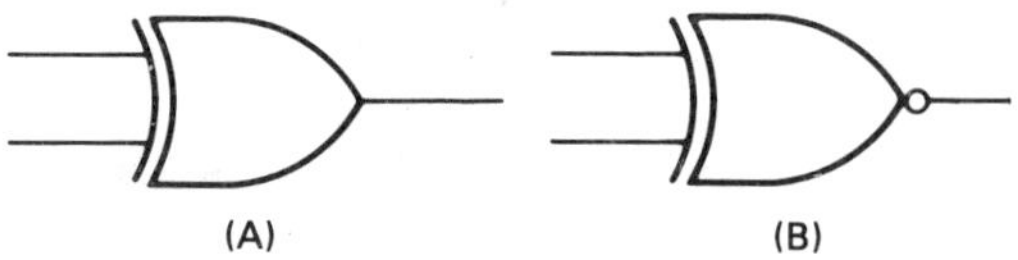

FIGURE 9-6. Exclusive OR and NOR symbols.

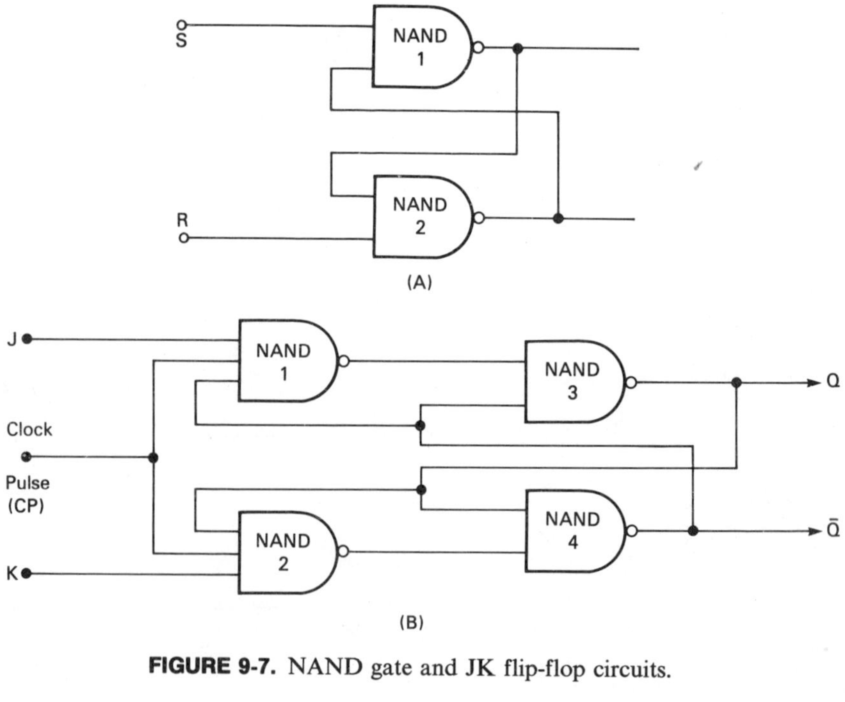

FIGURE 9-7. NAND gate and JK flip-flop circuits.

The flip-flop circuits discussed in Sec. 9-1 and illustrated in Fig. 9-2 can also be used to form logic circuits as shown in Fig. 9-7. In Fig. 9-7A the set-reset flip-flop is shown, using two NAND gates. (NOR gates could also be used, with a reversal of the S and R inputs for the same Q and $\overline{Q}$ outputs.) For the circuit shown the output of NAND gate No. 1 provides for the logic 1 or Q output, while for NAND gate No. 2 the output line supplies the 0 or negated $\overline{Q}$. Note that the output from the first NAND also feeds the other input line for NAND gate No. 2, while the output from the latter is also applied to the second input line of NAND No. 1.

As shown in Fig. 9-7B, the JK flip-flop circuit is constructed by adding two additional NAND circuits to the inputs of the reset-set flip-flop shown at A. The Q and $\overline{Q}$ outputs from the set-reset section (NAND gate No. 3 and gate No. 4) are fed back to one of the inputs of the JK NAND gate sections as shown. The third input line to the NAND gates 1 and 2 is for clock pulse input. The input pulses that produce an output for the JK flip-flop circuit given in Sec. 9-1 apply here also.

10

Integrated Circuits

10-1. FUNDAMENTAL ASPECTS

The integrated circuit is one of the most significant advances in electronic technology. The IC permits the assembly of thousands of solid-state components into a microminiature structure called a *chip*. A single IC can contain a complete stereo hi-fidelity audio amplifier section of a receiver, or a complete microprocessor, as well as a number of other electronic devices such as video games and hand-held calculators. Hence such ICs eliminate much of the component mounting and printed circuit wiring that had to be done heretofore.

There are three basic categories of ICs. The SSI represents the small-scale integrated circuitry that contains amplifier circuits, signal processors, and signal generators. The MSI represents the medium-scale integrated circuit widely used for calculator and computer circuitry. The third type is the LSI indicating large-scale integration of complex circuit combinations forming microprocessors and other complete electronic systems. Thus, the ICs range from small signal types with comparatively few circuits to the multiple signal units containing numerous interconnected circuit combinations.

Many electronic systems utilize several ICs. The television receiver is a typical example. Here, several integrated circuits are interconnected to perform sweep signal generation and processing, detection and amplification of video and sound signals, generation and synchronization of the subcarrier oscillator, as well as forming the circuitry for AGC and AFC purposes. Thus the only external wiring needed is that interconnecting the IC units to each other and to the necessary variable resistors for regulating tone, volume, and other functions under the control of the listener or viewer.

The basic advantage of the microminiature chip, in addition to its size, is its ability to apply various processing procedures to a given signal. In almost all electronic systems the signal detection, generation, and processing is involved in the early stages, and signal amplitude is not of particular importance in these stages. It is only when the final results or processes have been performed that the signal needs to be raised in power for application to loudspeakers, picture tubes, and similar load devices. An IC of small dimensions can perform all the necessary processes utilizing microvolts of signal amplitudes; thus power, space, and bulky components and wiring are eliminated.

Initial aspects of an IC formation involve planning by the engineers regarding the sequential paths the signal must undertake and the particular processes applied to it. Thus, the design engineers must set down the various conduction paths between individual components and circuits within the IC. Large-scale schematics are used to indicate component locations and interconnections of all the components within the IC such as resistors, diodes, capacitors, and transistors. When the routing and processing circuitry has been finalized it is reduced photographically to microminiature dimensions on a plastic film usually deposited on a semiconductor foundation slab such as a silicon wafer. Such a wafer is usually called a *substrate*. (One of the terminals of the field-effect transistor is sometimes called a sub, substrate, or bulk element indicating direct connection to the foundation slab.)

In modern IC manufacturing, many methods are available using various techniques to build up the IC. Included are such processes as the etching away of certain portions of the structure by acid; thermal processing of the structure; chemical etching; and mask fabrication techniques. Some photo-etching procedures are sometimes utilized as well as diffusion and vacuum deposition processes. Certain atomic elements and chemical impurities are thermally processed onto the substrate to form the basic structure of the semiconductor elements. The impurities are dissimilar elements that are injected to form *n*-zones or *p*-zones as needed.

Step-by-step explanations of all the processes available to the design engineer for manufacturing ICs would involve several volumes. A general comprehension of the techniques involved can be acquired, however, by becoming acquainted with one of the basic processes, as described in Sec. 10-2.

10-2. BASIC IC FABRICATION

Though the IC chip is of microminiature proportions and in many cases smaller than the eye of a needle, almost all of the basic electronic components can be formed and interconnected in the structure. Not all components are equal in the amount of processing required to form them. The more easily formed units consist of junction transistors, FETs, junction diodes, and resistors. Capacitors are somewhat more difficult than the aforementioned but can be included wherever needed and hence do not present major obstructions in manufacturing processes. Inductors are virtually impossible to produce in integrated circuit form, though the characteristics of inductance can be simulated.

During IC manufacture, the components are interconnected on the same surface or plane of the foundation material, and the procedure is often called a *planer* process. One process consists of diffusion, oxidation, and additional processing for elimination of unwanted elements or sections. The diffusion process involves the intermixing of atomic structures to the precise degree essential in the production of the characteristics needed in a particular IC. Oxidation is used to combine oxygen with an element to alter the structure as needed. A basic process involving these principles is shown in Fig. 10-1. The fusing together of an *n*-layer and a *p*-substrate are shown in Fig. 10-1A. This process forms a *p*-zone impurity through the *n*-layer structure shown in Fig. 10-1B. Hence, so-called *n* zones are formed, and this diffusion process is known as *isolation diffusion*. The isolation of the *n*-zone regions form *p-n* junctions, and the basic sections of a diode are thus formed, with the cathode and anode terminals permitting

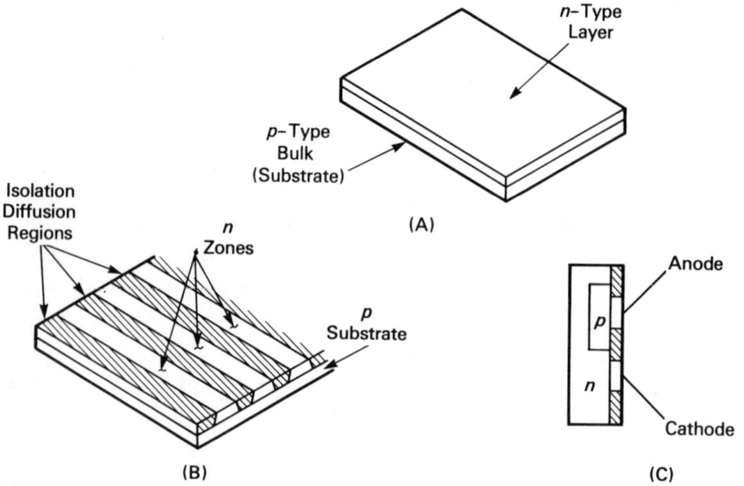

FIGURE 10-1. Basic formation of an IC.

the terminal contacts as illustrated in Fig. 10-1C. Since the production of the diode consists of forming *p-n* junctions, a continuation of the process forms the triode for junction transistors by reemploying the diffusion process. Thus, the *npn* transistor is formed, which is the most widely utilized in IC structures because its production process is less complex than that of the *pnp* transistor. If certain requirements call for a *pnp* type, however, it can be processed as is the case with complementary circuitry utilizing an *npn* as a complement of a *pnp* in a specific circuit. The *npn* formation is shown in Fig. 10-2A. The respective elements of base, emitter, and collector are formed by the diffusion process and these are represented in the standard symbol shown in Fig. 10-2B.

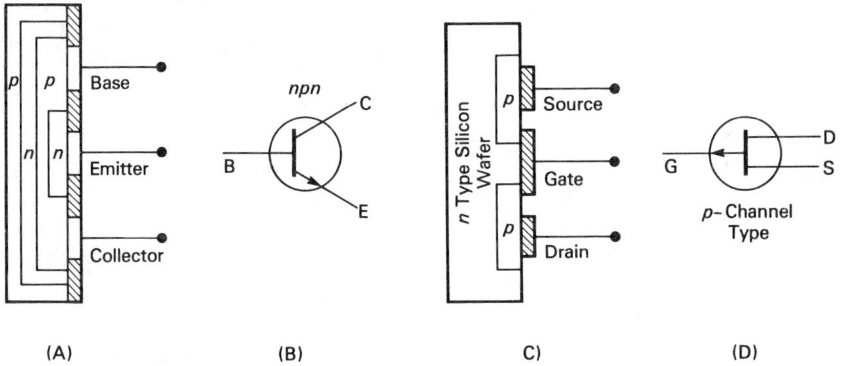

FIGURE 10-2. Junction (*npn*) transistor and *p*-channel FET.

The FET unit is formed in an IC using similar processes. For the FETs a substrate foundation slab formed of *n*-type silicon can be used, with *p*-type diffusions utilized for production of the source and drain regions by masking processes. Oxide is thinly formed over the surface, and an etching process produces openings for *windows* situated over the *p*-regions as shown in Fig. 10-2C. Next a metallic evaporation process involving the entire surface area is performed. Thus, metallic contacts with a drain and source element windows remain, as well as a metallic span over the peak regions separated by an oxide film. For the JFET the gate element is formed by a *p-n* junction diffused into the channel material. The polarities of the slab and regions are established as shown in Fig. 10-2C (whether a *p*-channel or an *n*-channel FET is formed). The *p*-channel type is shown in Fig. 10-2C and the standard symbol at Fig. 10-2D. For the *n*-channel type the processed structure formed is illustrated in Fig. 10-3A and the standard symbol in Fig. 10-3B. The dual-gate FET is structured by adding a gate element to the slab as shown in Fig. 10-3C. This gate element is insulated from the first gate element. The standard

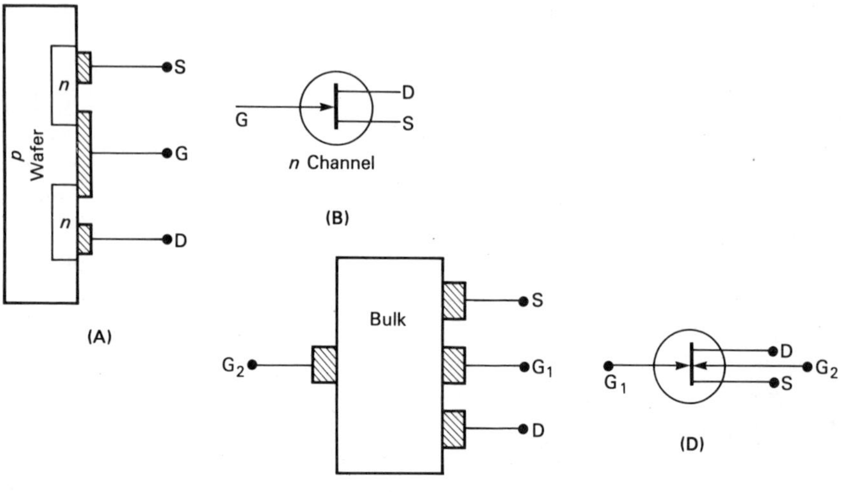

(C)

FIGURE 10-3. FET n-channel and dual gate.

symbol is shown in Fig. 10-3D for identification purposes. The p-channel unit is formed by a reversal of the diffusion zone polarities during the processing.

In any semiconductor there are specific conduction sections, and hence specific resistances are present in these areas. The ohmic value of such resistances can be changed by altering the thickness of the conduction region. The resistance can also be changed by varying the amount of impurities that are incorporated into the basic IC structure. Thus, the equivalent of resistors can be formed within the IC, and the ohmic value needed can be established during the manufacturing process. Generally resistance values below 50 kΩ present no major fabrication difficulties. Substantially higher values require more critical procedures and hence higher manufacturing costs.

The formation of a diode and a resistor is shown in Fig. 10-4. In this structure an n-zone is diffused into a p-type wafer for the diode formation, with the cathode and anode regions as indicated. Next a p-zone diffusion is formed into the n-zone to structure the resistor. The pn junction with reverse bias also has capacitance and hence is utilized to form capacitors within the integrated circuit structure. When reverse bias is applied there is no conduction, and hence the normal characteristics of all capacitors have been achieved. Thus, the interelement capacitances of the solid-state semiconductor serves as the capacitor for ICs. Usually, however, the capacitance value is related to the amplitude of the applied voltage because the latter alters the width of the depletion region, and

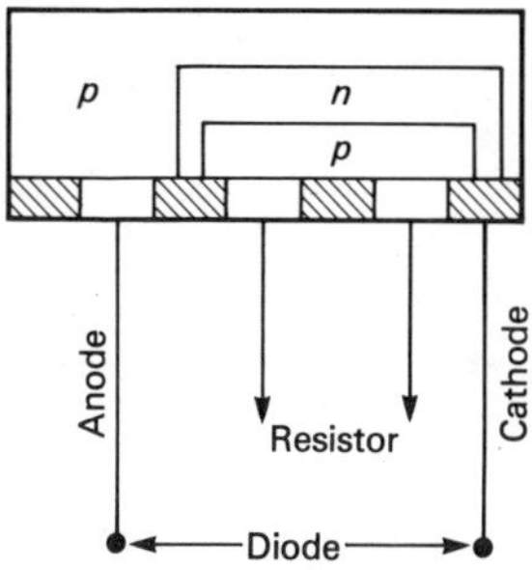

FIGURE 10-4. Formation of resistor and diode in an IC.

hence the dielectric of the capacitance is formed. Thus, this characteristic is considered during design so the proper value of capacitance will be obtained in the final IC that results. A variety of values can be produced, ranging from a low of 15 pF to a high of 100 pF. The variation of capacitance with applied voltage is the basic principle of the varactor diode wherein the capacitance can be altered by changing the applied voltage and thus simulating a variable capacitor. (See Sec. 11-7.)

For comparison purposes, a highly magnified section of an integrated circuit segment in comparison to the actual circuitry formed is shown in Fig. 10-5. Here a portion of an amplifier system is illustrated

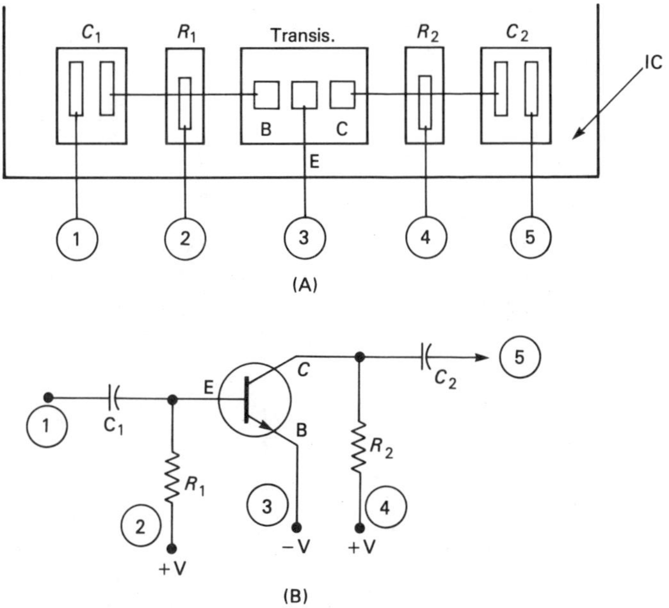

FIGURE 10-5. IC section and equivalent circuit.

having an input capacitor C_1 and an input resistor R_1. The output from the collector circuit is connected to the load resistor R_L, and the signal developed across this resistor is coupled to a subsequent stage by capacitor C_2. All the interconnecting wires for the actual circuit are also interconnected within the IC as shown. Equivalent circuit sections for A and B are identified by encircled numerals.

10-3. IC HOUSINGS AND SYMBOLS

Though some ICs have been manufactured with circular or square housings, the form shown in Fig. 10-6A is widely used. The number of terminal prongs varies depending on the number of circuits contained within the IC and the required terminals linking the internal structure to the external prongs of the IC. The latter point downward from the IC housing to permit the insertion of the IC into a matching socket. Instead of a socket, however, some ICs are inserted into a matching set of pre-punched holes in a printed-circuit board. In the latter instance the prongs are soldered to the printed-circuit board wiring network, and hence the IC is not readily removed or replaced. Some ICs measure 1 cm by 2 cm while

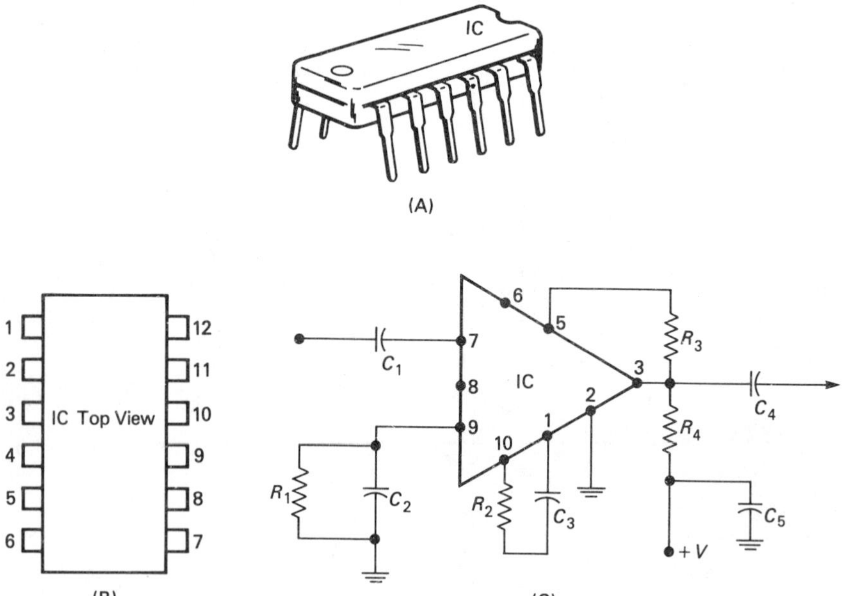

FIGURE 10-6. ICs and typical schematic.

others are substantially larger. When more terminals are needed because of a greater amount of internal circuitry, size increases proportionately. This is shown in Fig. 10-6B, where the numbering sequence is also illustrated. The start is at the top where an indentation is present in the IC to identify the beginning of the numbering sequence as well as the termination.

When the IC is represented in a schematic drawing, it may be as shown in Fig. 10-6B, though the triangular form shown in Fig. 10-6C is used frequently. When a triangular form is used, only the terminals connected to internal components are generally illustrated, thus some numbers in the sequence will be missing. External components are generally necessary not only to link the IC to other circuitry in the television receiver, computer, or other system utilized, but also to add components having a physical size that inhibits their usage within an IC. Thus, for the amplifier illustrated in Fig. 10-6C, capacitor C_1 is needed for the input-coupling capacitor to terminal 7. The shunting resistor and capacitor, R_1 and C_2, from terminal 9 are in series with the internal emitter of the IC's input transistor to ground. This *RC* network contributes to thermal stability. For the IC shown, pin 2 connects internal circuitry to external chassis ground. A feedback loop is formed by resistor R_2 and capacitor C_3 connected between terminals 1 and 10. The output, obtained from terminal 3, is coupled to the next stage by capacitor C_4. Resistor R_4 is the load resistor and the bottom is bypassed by capacitor C_5 as a direct return path for the signal energy from the internal IC network.

10-4. EXAMPLES OF TYPICAL ICs

A typical multicircuit IC is shown in Fig. 10-7. Here 18 terminals are available, and the IC contains two independent amplifier systems for stereo reproduction. Many such ICs contain all the stages from the preamplifier to the output power amplifiers. If the audio power amplifier requirements are approximately 5 W or more, the IC may only contain the final drivers that precede the power amplifier stages and the latter would be a separate circuitry. For the IC in Fig. 10-7 the stereo sections contained therein are designed for a low power output phonograph or tape amplifier system. As mentioned earlier, additional components must, of course, be added such as volume and tone controls, on/off switches, and power supply potentials.

The individual stereo systems for the left and right channels are represented in triangular form for the IC of Fig. 10-7. Thus, the left channel triangle is representative of the combined preamplifiers, driver stages, and output amplifiers. An identical array of circuitry prevails for

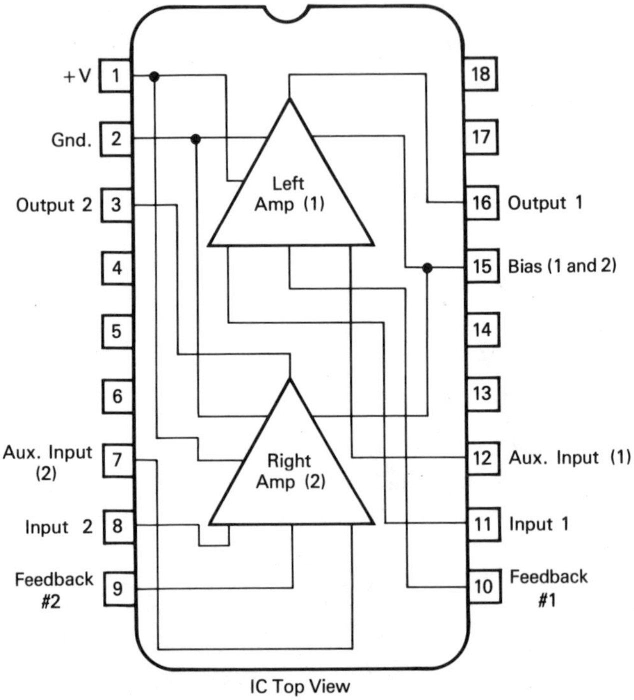

FIGURE 10-7. Stereo amplifiers.

the right-channel triangle. As is often the case with ICs, all output terminal prongs are not necessarily utilized or interconnected internally. For convenience, the general practice is to have the housing contain a full complement of output terminals even though a few may not be used. For the ICs shown, the right channel input and output lines are at the left and the left channel lines appear at the right.

Terminal No. 1 applies a positive voltage to both channel circuits as shown by the line entering the center left portion of the triangles. The particular placement of the lines to the triangles is arbitrary, though the general practice is to indicate input lines at the opposite ends of a triangle point while the point itself applies to the output terminal. Ground connections are made to terminal 2, which connects to both channels' circuitry. Dual inputs are provided for each channel; the auxiliary input having an impedance suitable for tape decks and the other input having a low impedance for magnetic cartridges. Feedback terminals 9 and 10 provide for setting the degree of feedback for the most desired balance between harmonic distortion reduction and output power. With the greater amount of feedback the distortion is decreased to a greater extent, but less power output is obtainable at peak levels. Bias input terminals are also provided so that the bias applied by the series resistors within the IC can be altered for a change of performance characteristics for an individual channel.

Fig. 10-8 shows a typical IC arrangement for a single-channel system. An amplifier system is fed by a detector circuit so that this IC not only demodulates the signal but also amplifies the audio signal obtained during detection. The audio amplifier section usually contains a preamplifier, a driver amplifier stage, and a final audio output amplifier. When more extensive signal processing is required, of course, a greater number of interconnected circuits would be wired in sequence; and a greater number of output terminals than are shown in Fig. 10-8 would be necessary. For the arrangement shown, terminals are needed for connections to ground (negative), positive voltage, volume control, signal input, signal output, and AVC—requiring use of only 6 of the 10 terminals available. An AVC signal output is provided from the detector circuit for volume control purposes. This signal is fed to the RF and IF stages of the receiver and alters the bias of these stages to maintain a volume level that is fairly constant for reasonable changes to the signal level of the station tuned in. For Fig. 10-8 pin 8 is for connection to the external volume control. A similar circuit arrangement for an IC by another manufacturer may have different terminal locations than those shown in Fig. 10-8. Hence, for

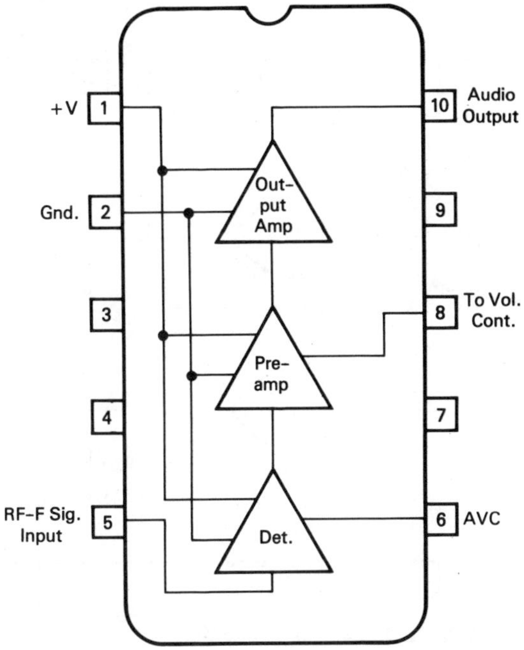

FIGURE 10-8. AM detector and amplification IC.

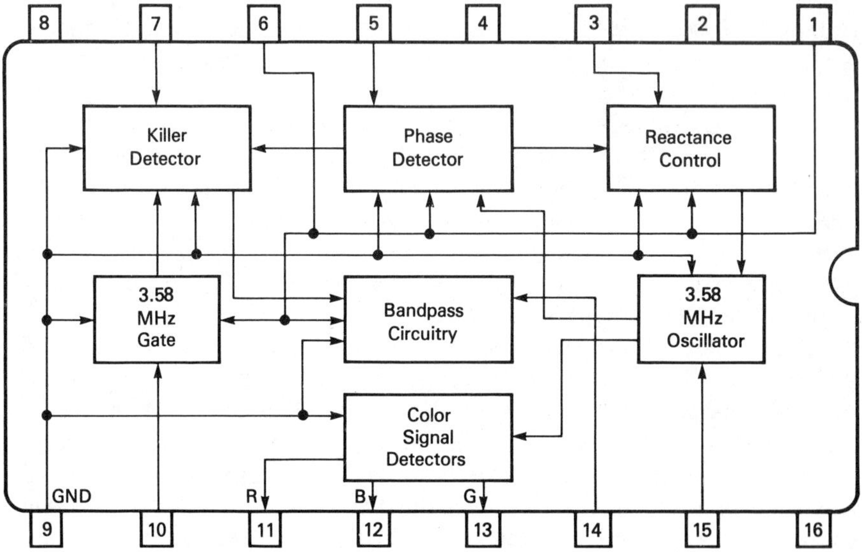

FIGURE 10-9. Color TV circuitry in a single IC.

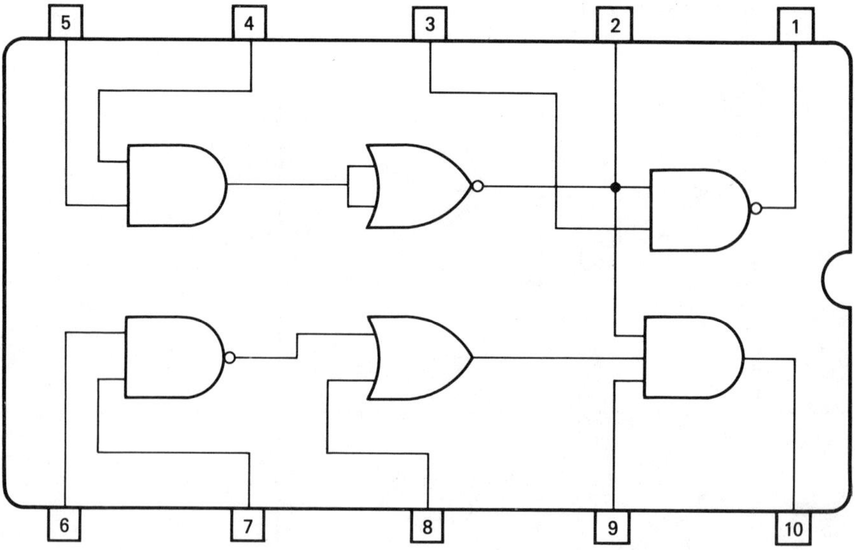

FIGURE 10-10. Logic circuitry in an IC.

positive identification of the terminals of any specific IC, the data sheet furnished by the manufacturer must be consulted.

A multicircuit IC used in color television receivers is shown in Fig. 10-9. This 16-pin IC contains most of the color signal-processing sections. The color killer detector prevents color circuits from functioning during reception of a black and white signal, thus minimizing the distortion effects that would otherwise occur. The 3.58-MHz gate supplies the sync signals for locking in the color subcarrier oscillator. The latter is a crystal-controlled signal generator that is locked in by reactance control circuitry under the control of the phase detector. When the oscillator tends to shift in phase, the phase detector produces a correction signal for frequency lock-in purposes. The color signals are mixed with the subcarrier signal and detected to produce the video signals of blue, green, and red.

Numerous logic circuits are also contained in ICs, and a typical example is shown in Fig. 10-10. (See also Chapters 8 and 9.) For the 10-terminal IC of Fig. 10-10, terminals 4 and 5 are applied to an AND circuit that feeds a NOT circuit (phase inverter). The output from the latter, plus inputs from terminals 2 and 3, feed a NAND circuit. The output from the latter is available from terminal 1 of the IC. Another group of logic circuits consists of a NAND gate, an OR circuit and a 3-input AND circuit having its output available from terminal 10. Note the linkage of the two output circuits by a common input terminal. Other such ICs may contain as many as 40 terminals (for some microprocessors), or others may contain less, depending on need.

11

Power Supplies and Oscillators

11-1. GENERATION OF DC AND AC SIGNALS

Power supplies are used extensively to convert the alternating current characteristics of the electric energy supplied to homes and industry to direct current. The dc is needed to operate solid-state devices such as home radio, television, and high-fidelity equipment. Because ac is essentially an audio signal (60 Hz) its direct use for power sources is not feasible because of the introduction of hum. In addition, a unidirectional electric power is needed to provide the energy for amplifiers and other circuits. Thus, in essence, the power supply generates a dc signal energy suitable for battery replacement in powering electronic devices.

Generators of ac signals are also widely used in all branches of electronics. Such generators are called *oscillators*, and they produce a signal having a specific frequency for use in tuners and in test equipment. Such circuits also form the generators of the sweep signals in television receivers and oscilloscopes. Oscillators can be designed around resonant circuits or by use of RC or RL circuits as discussed in this chapter.

11-2. POWER SUPPLIES

Half-wave and full-wave power supply systems are illustrated in Fig. 11-1. In part A the half-wave supply uses a transformer for stepping up or reducing the line voltage as required. (The line voltage could have

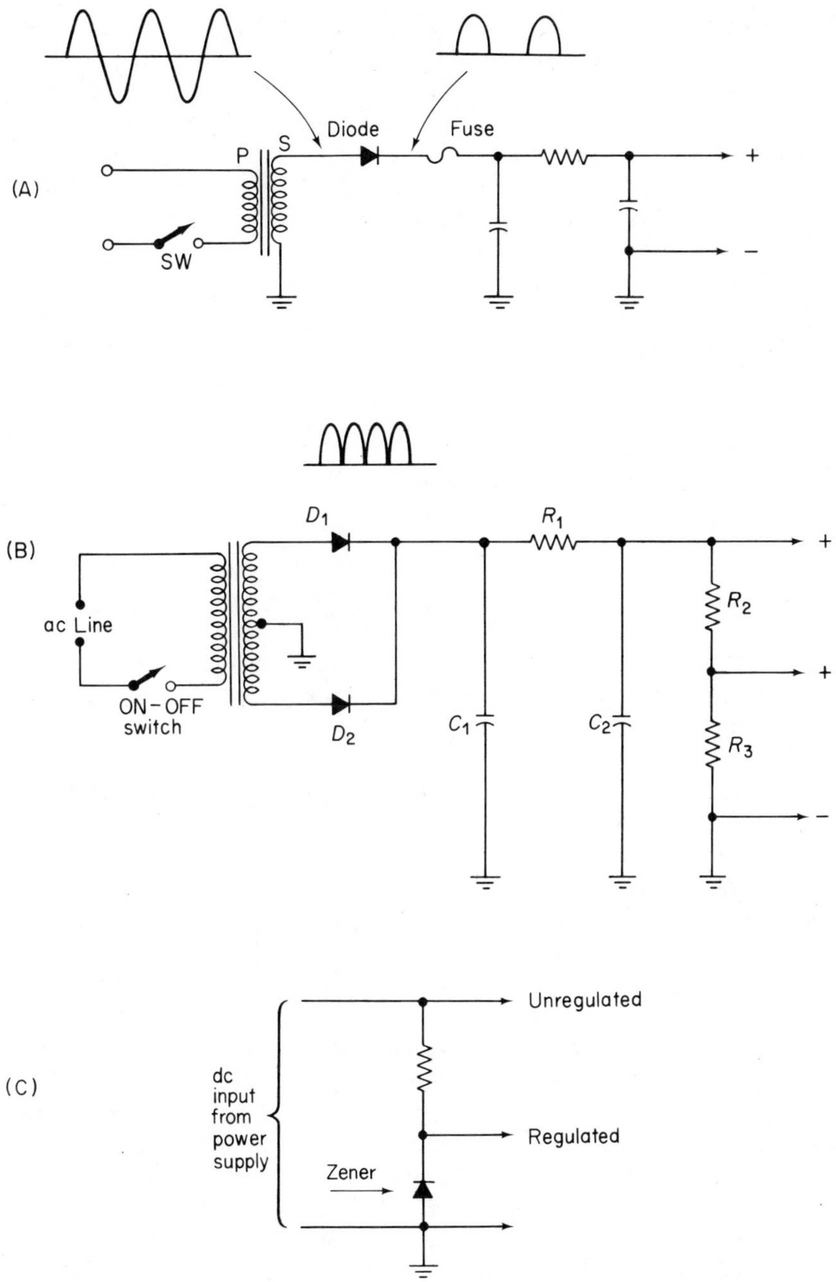

FIGURE 11-1. Half- and full-wave power supplies.

been rectified directly without the transformer, though one side of the ac line would then have to be at ground potential for the supply.)

The diode, having unidirectional current characteristics, passes only the positive pulses for the supply shown in part A. Thus, there are $\frac{1}{120}$-s gaps between pulses, and there is great demand on the filter network of resistors and capacitors for filtering the ripple component from the dc output. (On occasion, a series inductor, a *filter choke*, is used to present a high reactance for the ripple component.)

For the full-wave supply shown in Fig. 11-1B, a tapped transformer is used. Thus, for the same output voltage as produced by part A, the unit in part B requires twice the voltage across the secondary of the transformer. This results because diodes D_1 and D_2 pass current alternately: one for the positive portions of the sinewave signal; the other for the negative portions. Filtering requirements are less critical than they are for the circuit of part A because the pulsating dc produced has no intervals between pulses.

As the load that is connected across a power supply draws more current from the supply, the voltage drops increase across the power supply units (series resistors, transformer-winding resistances, etc.), and consequently, output voltage decreases. This variation of voltage output with respect to the amount of current drawn from the power supply is termed *voltage regulation*. The percentage of voltage regulation of a power supply is given by the following equation:

$$\text{percent voltage regulation} = \frac{\text{no-load } E - \text{full-load } E}{\text{full-load } E} \times 100 \qquad (11\text{-}1)$$

Equation 11-1 takes into consideration the proportion of voltage increase and decrease that accompanies a change of load on a power supply. Such a load consists of the radio, amplifier, or other device attached to the power supply, which draws current and power from the supply.

Regulation can be improved by increasing the size of filter capacitances and by using a choke-input filter or special regulating devices such as *Zener diodes*. These are wired into the circuit, as shown in Fig. 11-1C, in reverse to the normal conduction path of the diode. As the reverse voltage on a Zener is gradually increased, the so-called *Zener region* of the diode's characteristics is reached, at which time the Zener maintains a constant voltage output despite changes (within certain limits) of the load current. The resistor in series with the Zener sets the range of operation, and under average load conditions, the voltage applied to the Zener is somewhat higher than that from the output of the Zener so that it can vary upward and downward as required. Zeners are rated in the wattage and voltage (regulated output) obtained from them.

11-3. CRYSTAL OSCILLATOR

The frequency-stabilizing characteristics of the piezoelectric quartz crystal are utilized in transistor, vacuum-tube, or FET oscillators to produce a stable output signal. The crystal slab is a transducer and, if voltage is applied across it, a distortion occurs in its shape, which now converts electric energy to mechanical. Under pressure or strain, the crystal will also generate voltage. The resonant frequency of the crystal is related to its thickness and the axis along which the crystal slab was cut. The following equation applies:

$$f_r = \frac{k}{t} \tag{11-2}$$

where k is a constant dependent on type of cut
f_r is the resonant frequency in kHz
t is the thickness in inches.

If the frequency is taken in MHz, the thickness will be given in thousandths of an inch. For the *X cut*, k reaches a maximum value of 112.6, while the *AT cut* yields k values of no more than 66.2. The *Y cut* gives a maximum k of 77.0, and the *BT cut's* maximum is 100.78.

During the grinding of a crystal for a specific frequency, the following variation of Eq. 11-2 is useful:

$$t = \frac{k}{f_r} \tag{11-3}$$

A typical crystal oscillator circuit is shown in Fig. 11-2. Instead of the FET unit shown, a junction transistor could have been used. For the

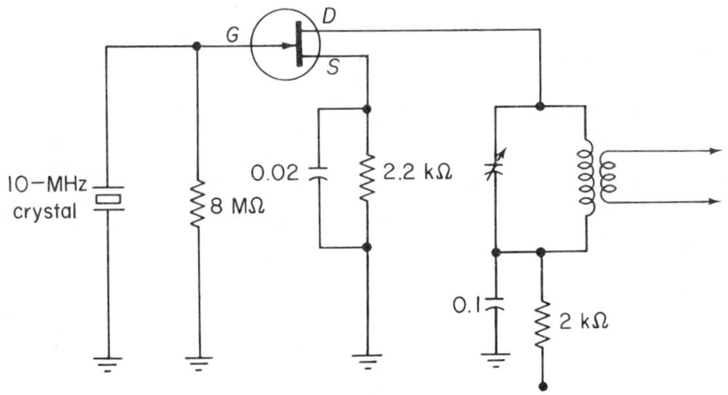

FIGURE 11-2. FET crystal oscillator.

circuit shown, the crystal behaves like a resonant circuit at the gate side, with inter-element capacitances of the FET providing the necessary coupling between input and output to sustain oscillations. The variable capacitor in the output resonant circuit permits tuning this section to the proper frequency so that the crystal will oscillate at its resonant frequency.

11-4. VARIABLE-FREQUENCY RF OSCILLATORS

A variable-frequency RF oscillator is shown in Fig. 11-3. A *pnp* transistor is used, and the type of oscillator so formed is the *Hartley oscillator*, wherein a tap on the resonant-circuit inductor (L_1) effectively divides it into two sections: one coupled to the base via C_1; the other coupled to the collector via C_3. The tap is at ground potential, as the figure shows. A radio-frequency choke (R-F-C) is in series with the negative supply potential to the collector for signal isolation purposes.

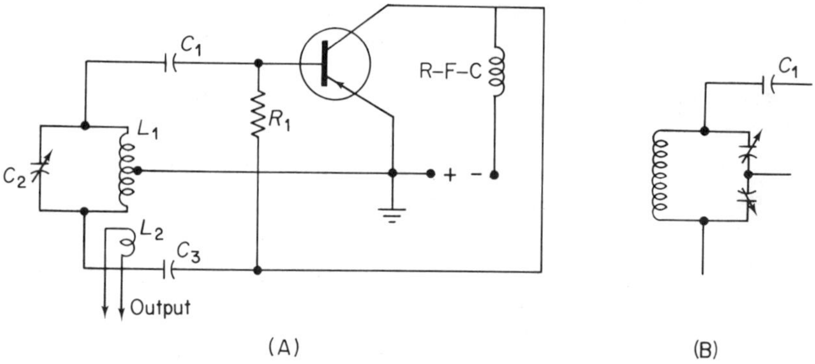

FIGURE 11-3. Variable-frequency RF oscillator.

If the ground tap is placed at the junction of two capacitors as shown in Fig. 11-3B, an oscillator is again formed. Such an apparatus is called a *Colpitts oscillator*. As with the Hartley, the division of the resonant circuit provides coupling of the amplified output signal energy to the input circuit to sustain oscillation.

11-5. RELAXATION OSCILLATORS

Relaxation oscillators are nonresonant types that utilize resistance-reactance combinations for generating signals by periodic blocking of conduction through one or more transistors (or tubes). Such oscillators are useful for generation of pulse or squarewave type signals, and are employed extensively in television receivers for production of the vertical and horizontal sweep signals.

Typical relaxation oscillators are shown in Fig. 11-4. The one in part A is a *blocking oscillator*, and a transformer is utilized as the figure shows. The amplified output appears across the transformer primary L_1 and is transferred to L_2 and also coupled back to the base input of the transistor via the 10-μF capacitor. The feedback signal is sufficiently high to drive the base input bias between the saturation point and the nonconduction region. This periodic blocking of conduction generates the output signal, the frequency of which is dependent on the values of the transformer inductors, the base resistor, and the coupling capacitor.

The oscillator shown in Fig. 11-4B utilizes another transistor instead of the transformer, and this oscillator is a *multivibrator*. Conduction of one

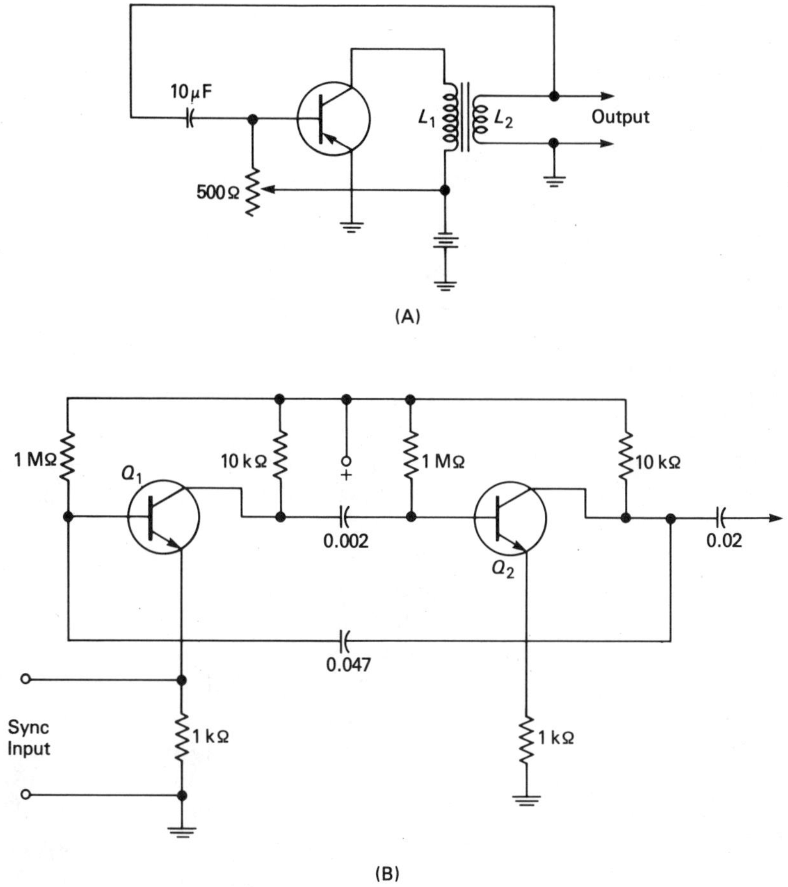

FIGURE 11-4. Relaxation oscillators.

transistor occurs during the period in which the other exists in a nonconducting state. When the holding potentials drain through the capacitances (inter-element and coupling), the nonconducting transistor goes into conduction, and its collector output signal causes the other transistor to go into a nonconducting state. The process continues and produces the output signals.

Relaxation oscillators can be synchronized by an incoming signal that triggers one transistor into conduction at or near the frequency of the oscillator. Thus, the frequency of the relaxation oscillator can be under the direct control of another signal-generating system. In television, for instance, synchronizing pulses are transmitted by the TV station along with the video and sound information. At the receiver, these sync pulses are used to lock in the vertical and horizontal sweep oscillators to keep them in perfect synchronization with the one at the station. This assures proper picture lock-in, for both the vertical scan and the horizontal trace.

11-6. MIXER (CONVERTER) CIRCUIT

A *mixer* (*converter*) *circuit* is used in the superheterodyne receivers where the incoming signal, to which the receiver is tuned, is mixed with a signal obtained from a signal generator in the receiver, the *local oscillator*. The purpose of the mixer is to mix the two signals to produce an intermediate-frequency (IF) signal of constant frequency. This process is called heterodyning. It permits proper design of RF stages for maximum gain and optimum selectivity, while eliminating the Q changes with variations in the inductor-capacitor ratios. These latter changes would occur if all RF stages were constantly retuned to resonance for various stations.

A typical mixer stage is shown in Fig. 11-5 (this is the type used in radio receivers). Circuits similar to this are also used in television and related receivers because virtually all standard receiving systems employ the superheterodyne principle. For the circuit of Fig. 11-5, an additional RF stage could have preceded the mixer when greater signal gain and sensitivity were required in the tuner section.

As the figure shows, the input transformer often consists of a ferrite-rod antenna section, which acts as the resonant circuit tuned to the station being received. The signals are applied to the base circuit of the mixer Q_1, where they are heterodyned with the signal developed in the oscillation section. This section consists of inductor L_4 and the feedback coil L_3. The primary tuning capacitors are C_3, for the input to the mixer, and C_6, for the oscillator section. Each of these is shunted by a so-called *trimmer capacitor* for precise adjustment to permit proper *tracking* (i.e., the

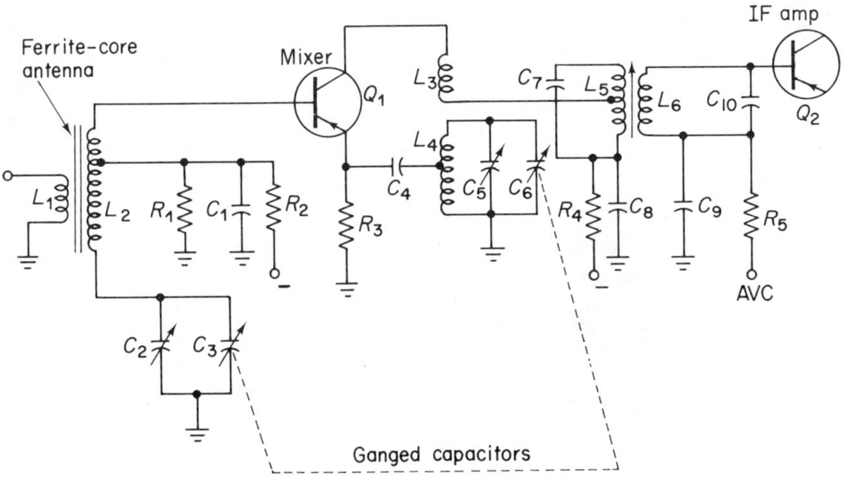

FIGURE 11-5. Radio tuner system.

proper tuning coincidence of the two circuits for the tuning range available).

Usually the local oscillator circuit maintains a frequency higher than that of the incoming signal by the frequency of the IF circuitry. Thus, if a 1000-kHz station were tuned in, the oscillator would have to maintain a 1455-kHz frequency in order to produce 455-kHz IF. Capacitors C_3 and C_6 have their rotors mounted on a common shaft. This ganging permits the two to be tuned in frequency-difference coincidence. Hence, if C_3 were tuned to 600 kHz, the oscillators would be tuned to 1055 kHz, again producing 455-kHz IF.

For public FM reception in the 88- to 108-MHz range, a commonly used IF is 10.7 MHz. Thus, if a 100-MHz station is tuned in, the oscillator generates a 110.7-MHz frequency, producing the 10.7-MHz IF. The mixing produces sum and difference frequencies, but the unwanted signals are rejected by the IF amplifier stages that are tuned to the IF frequency. These stages reject signals above the required bandpass.

11-7. VARACTOR AND REACTANCE CIRCUITRY

Circuits that exhibit reactive characteristics are useful for the production of frequency modulation. Audio signals are applied to the reactance circuit which in turn shifts the frequency of the variable-frequency oscillator that is producing the carrier. Such circuits are also useful for control purposes, such as in color television receivers where the color carrier generator (3.58 MHz) oscillator must be kept in phase with the transmitted color signal. A typical reactance circuit is shown in Fig. 11-6, where an FET is used. A junction transistor could also be used in such an application. The drain and source elements of the FET are connected across the resonant-circuit inductor of the oscillator (using capacitor coupling where dc isolation is required). Thus, the signal from the oscillator appears across the series network composed of C_1 and R_1. The capacitance value of C_1 is chosen so that its reactance is approximately 10 times as great as the ohmic value of R_1. Hence, current for the *RC* network leads the signal voltage obtained from the oscillator, as shown in part C. However, since the signal applied to the gate input of the FET is obtained across R_1 only, the voltage at the gate will be in phase with the *RC* network current as there can be no phase shift across a pure resistance. Because the signal *current* through the FET source-drain section is in phase with the *voltage* at the gate, the drain current leads the oscillator signal voltage by 90° as shown in part C.

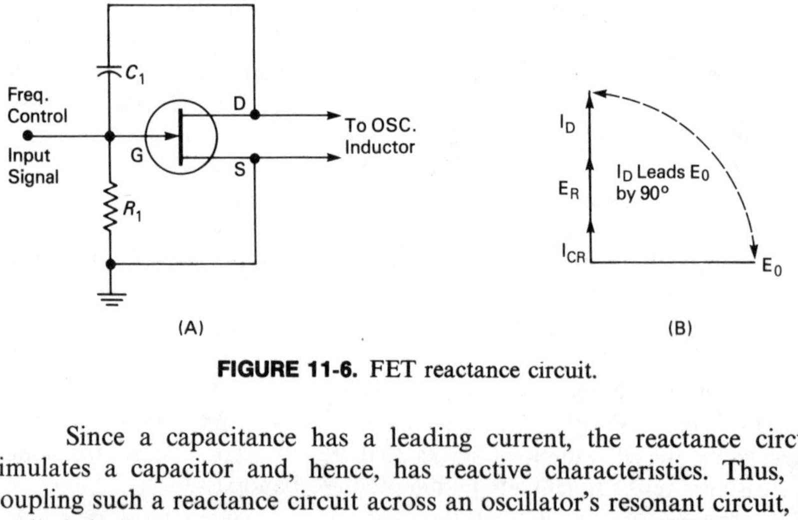

FIGURE 11-6. FET reactance circuit.

Since a capacitance has a leading current, the reactance circuit simulates a capacitor and, hence, has reactive characteristics. Thus, by coupling such a reactance circuit across an oscillator's resonant circuit, an applied shunt capacitance results that affects oscillator tuning. If an audio signal is applied to the gate input, the signal alters the reactance at the audio-frequency rate and shifts the frequency of the oscillator accordingly.

Special diodes called *varactors* (*variable reactors*) are also used extensively for tuning purposes in receivers. These diodes permit push-button tuning or continuously variable tuning, as determined during design. The varactor diodes simulate capacitance that is variable depending on the applied potential. In these units the inter-element capacitances of the solid-state depletion region exhibit nonlinear characteristics when the applied voltage is gradually changed in value. When reverse bias is applied, the varactor is nonconducting for dc, and a specific value of capacitance is present. Thus, as shown in Fig. 11-7A, two such units can be used back-to-back to form the variable tuning element across an oscillator inductor. For any voltage variation at the junction of the two diodes, the capacitance is changed and the oscillator's signal frequency changes. The oscillator output is obtained from coupling capacitor C_3. The latter, with C_2, isolate the power-supply potential applied to the resonant circuit and prevent the voltage from entering the line to the emitter resistor R_3. Capacitor C_1 bypasses undesired signal variations that may cause incorrect tuning. If dc is the control potential, C_1 bypasses all ac components. If low audio is the control signal (as in FM generation) then C_1 bypasses RF signals.

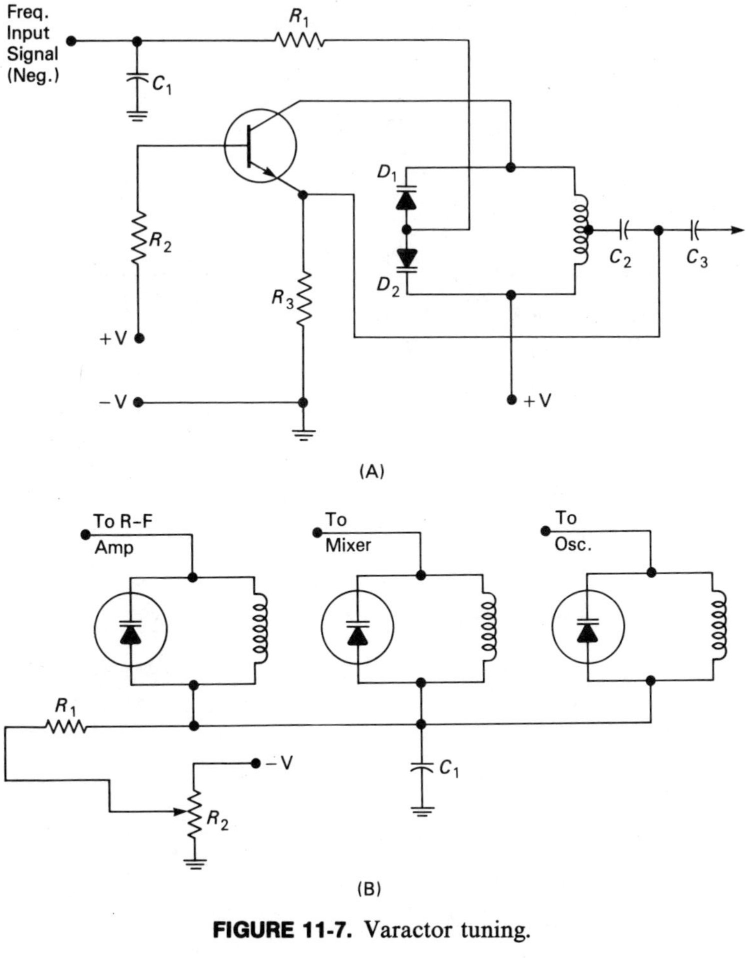

FIGURE 11-7. Varactor tuning.

Varactor tuning for the front end (tuner) of a receiver is shown in Fig. 11-7B, using a single diode for each resonant circuit. Here resistor R_2 permits regulation of the amount of potential applied to the varactor diodes and thus permits tuning as would be the case with a variable capacitor function. If resistor R_2 is replaced by a series of push-buttons applying various voltages to the varactors, each push-button's voltage control can be adjusted so each button tunes to a different station. Resistor R_1 is a limiting unit that prevents complete grounding of the bottom of the resonant circuits when the variable arm of R_2 is turned all the way down. Capacitor C_1 bypasses unwanted signal variations that might affect proper tuning. The oscillator inductor would have less turns of wire, so the resonant circuit formed with the varactor tunes higher to produce the intermediate frequency signal output needed for the IF stages that follow the tuner.

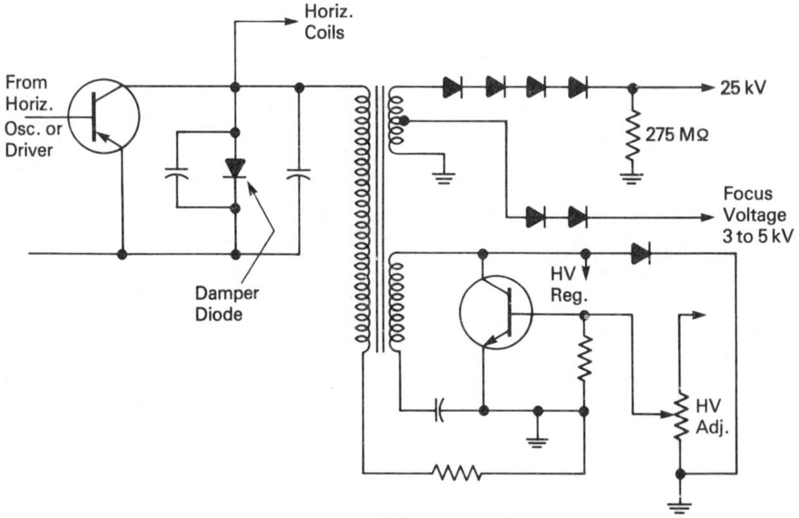

(A)

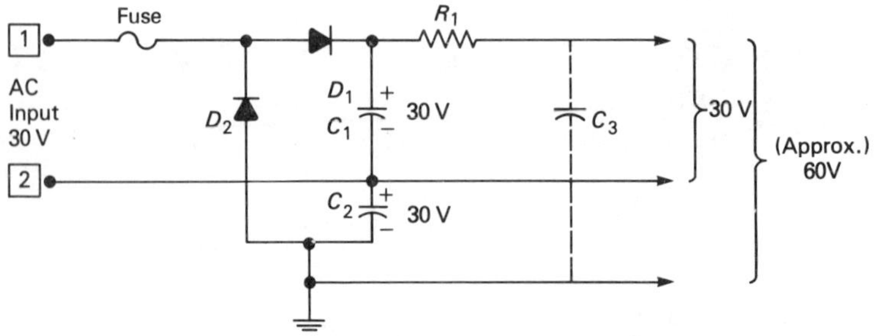

(B)

FIGURE 11-8. HV and doubler systems.

11-8. SPECIAL POWER SUPPLIES

Two special type power supplies are shown in Fig. 11-8. Part A shows the high-voltage system used in color television receivers for obtaining approximately 25 kV for the color picture tube. This high-voltage system is also part of the horizontal output amplifier of the television receiver. The output from the amplifier transistor (at the collector) is applied to the horizontal deflection coils for sweeping the electron beam within the picture tube. (The combination of vertical sweep and horizontal sweep coils is termed a *yoke*.) The pulses developed in the horizontal output amplifier section are stepped up by the transformer shown, and silicon rectifiers are used to obtain the required high voltage (dc type).

The secondary winding is tapped as shown for obtaining the 3 to 5 kV needed for the focus electrode of the picture tube. A special voltage-regulating transistor is used in the secondary circuitry for stabilization of the high voltage. The base of the regulator transistor connects to a variable resistor for precise setting of the high-voltage amplitude. The damper diode in the collector-emitter side of the output transistor eliminates positive-peak transients.

Another special type power supply is shown in Fig. 11-8B, where a voltage doubling principle is utilized. Here, two capacitors charge alternately to the peak voltage rectified, and the doubled output amplitude is obtained from across the two in series as shown. In order to describe circuit operation, the input terminals have been identified as (1) and (2). When terminal (1) is positive and terminal (2) negative, electron flow starts at terminal (2), and in flowing back to terminal (1), capacitor C_1 is charged to the peak amplitude of the rectified voltage passed by diode D_1. For the next alternation arriving at terminals (1) and (2), terminal (1) is negative and electron flow is now through D_2, charging capacitor C_2 for a return path to terminal (2). The two capacitors, in series, thus furnish double the input voltage. (This is an approximation, since there is a voltage drop across the series filter resistor R_1, and the output voltage is also dependent on the load current drawn. If the current drain on the series capacitors is more rapid than the successive alternations of rectified ac that feed them, the output voltage declines proportionately.)

12

RF Transmission Lines and Antennas

12-1. BASIC TRANSMISSION LINES

Modern electronic practices use transmission lines for a variety of purposes, including the following:

1. Conveying electronic data between specific points.
2. Acting as reactive or resonant sections for forming filters, traps, etc.
3. Behaving as a transformer for matching impedances.
4. Forming delay lines to introduce a required degree of delay for signals when necessary.

Transmission lines are used in various lengths, extremely short sections being employed as reactive or resonant components. In such applications, length determines the primary characteristic (covered later in this chapter). For communication purposes, long lengths are used for linking signal information.

Four basic transmission-line types are shown in Fig. 12-1. Figure 12-1A shows the so-called *open-wire* line, which consists of two conductors spaced by plastic or ceramic insulators. When any metal objects or wires are brought into close proximity, capacitance exists between them. Thus, the term *dielectric* is applied to the space for the air or insulation material, just as it is with standard capacitors. In the open-wire line, the dielectric is air. Such a line is characterized by low loss, since other dielectric materials

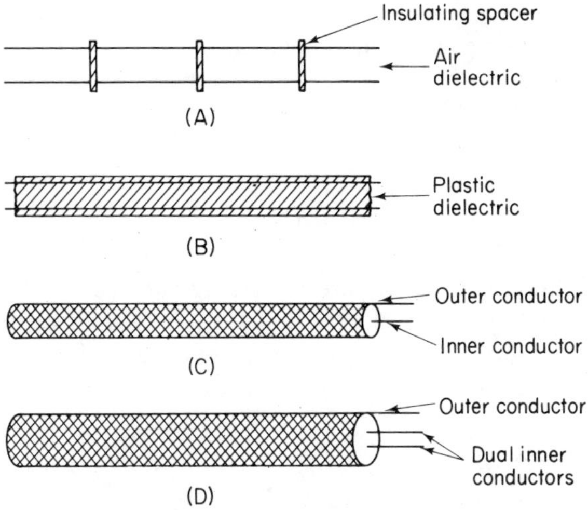

FIGURE 12-1. Basic types of lines.

(such as plastics) usually introduce some shunt resistance, which consumes some signal energy. Its disadvantages lie in the wider spacing necessary to achieve the same impedances as is the case with plastic dielectric lines, plus greater radiation losses.

The plastic dielectric, two-wire line shown in Fig. 12-1B is the common *twin lead* used in television receiver installations. Such a line is standardized at 300-Ω characteristic impedance, and the flexible insulation with less than $\frac{1}{2}$-inch spacing between wires provides for convenient installation in feeding through walls, etc. Losses are somewhat greater than for the open-wire line, and some signal (interference) pickup may occur along such a line.

The transmission line in Fig. 12-1C is referred to as a *coaxial cable* or *concentric line*. The inner conductor (of solid or stranded wire) is held at the center of the cable by a flexible plastic insulation or washerlike dielectric insulators at fixed points within the line. The outer conductor may be a metal tube or metallic braid (to provide for flexibility). This outer conductor is usually placed at ground potential, thus forming an unbalanced line, just as the unbalanced filter sections discussed earlier. Coaxial cable, because of the outer conductor shielding the inner, is superior to other types in terms of minimum radiation loss or interference pickup. Signal attenuation, however, is generally higher.

Coaxial cable finds some application in receiver installations where connections must be made to remote antennas with a minimum of noise pickup. This cable finds extensive usage in the interconnection of microphones, studio equipment, transmitter outputs to antennas, ultrahigh frequency filter networks, and in similar applications. For balanced systems, the two-wire coaxial line shown in Fig. 12-1D is used, with the shielded outer conductor at central ground potential with respect to the dual inner lines.

12-2. CHARACTERISTIC IMPEDANCE

When the electric pressure of voltage forces current through a conductor, magnetic and electrostatic fields are created in the vicinity of the conductor. Figure 12-2A shows these fields (sometimes called lines of force) as they exist between the two current-carrying wires of a typical two-wire line.

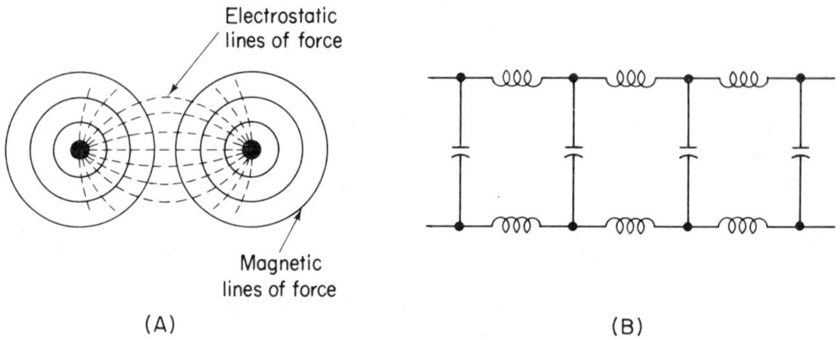

FIGURE 12-2. Transmission line characteristics.

The amplitude of the fields between the wires depends on the amount of current flow plus the applied potential causing the current. Such fields exist for either ac or dc, though for ac the lines of force collapse as each ac alternation drops to zero and build up again (in opposite polarity) as the next ac alternation drives to peak amplitude.

As shown in Fig. 12-2B, each transmission line has a specific amount of inductance per unit length of line (as does any length of wire). Since the close proximity of two wires forms a capacitance, a certain amount of capacitance is also present per unit length. However, the capacitance is represented as being in shunt instead of in series as is the case with inductance. Some resistance is also present in the wire, though it is generally kept at a negligible value through the use of larger size conductors. For dielectric materials other than air, some shunt resistance may also occur, particularly if the leakage resistance of the dielectric material is increased by moisture or inherent impurities.

As with the filter sections discussed in Chapter 4, the repeated units of inductance and capacitance along the line set up a characteristic impedance, and the same Z_o equation applies: $Z_o = \sqrt{L/C}$. For a given transmission line, the impedance remains the same, regardless of the line length. Thus, whether a 300-Ω twin lead is 10 feet or 100 feet long, Z_o remains at 300 Ω.

When air insulation is used in a *parallel-wire line* such as in Fig. 12-1A, the following equation can be used for Z_o:

$$Z_o = 276 \log \frac{2b}{a} \qquad (12\text{-}1)$$

where b is the spacing (center-to-center) between wires
a is the radius of each conductor.

Because b/a is a ratio, values can be in inches, feet, millimeters, etc., and the characteristic impedance (Z_o) value will be the same. If the inductance and capacitance values were taken over a long section of line, the surge impedance value would remain the same, since for each increase in series inductance, there would be a corresponding increase in shunt capacitance, thus maintaining the same L/C ratio. This is born out in the following example where the earlier Z equation is used:

Example

An air-dielectric transmission line has an inductance value of 0.36 mH and a capacitance of 0.001 μF per unit length. What is the impedance?

Solution

$$Z_o = \sqrt{\frac{L}{C}} = \sqrt{\frac{0.36 \times 10^{-3}}{10^{-9}}}$$

$$= \sqrt{0.36 \times 10^{6}}$$

$$= 0.6 \times 10^{3}$$

$$= 600\ \Omega$$

For the coaxial cable in Fig. 12-2C, the characteristic impedance may be found by the following equation:

$$Z_o = 138 \log \frac{b}{a} \qquad (12\text{-}2)$$

where b is the inside diameter of the outer conductor
a is the outside diameter of the inner conductor.

When the coaxial cable's dielectric material is something other than air, Eq. 12-2 should be multiplied by the results of the following formula:

$$\frac{1}{\sqrt{k}} \qquad (12\text{-}3)$$

where k is the *dielectric constant* of the material.

When discussing transmission-line characteristics, the general practice is to call the signal source the *generator* and the signal recipient unit the *load*, in cases where power is consumed or radiated (as in transmitting antennas). Such designations are convenient because they allow us to dispense with repeated references to the transmitter, the receiver, the antenna, etc. Thus, a generator could be a transmitter with an antenna as the load, while in the receiver the antenna is the generator and the receiver the load.

As for the filter sections discussed earlier and also for other generator-load combinations, the maximum available signal power is transferred between generator and load only when the impedance of one matches that of the other.

12-3. FLAT (UNTUNED) LINES

As will be shown later, transmission lines can be utilized in such a manner that advantage is taken of their inherent resonant characteristics. If, however, the resonant factors are ignored, the line impedance must match that of the generator and load for a maximum signal energy transfer. In such an instance, the transmission line is termed a *flat* or *untuned line*. Such a nonresonant line is "flat" regarding power values along the line, since voltage and current values remain unchanged, as does impedance. Such is not always the case, as will be discussed more fully later for the resonant-type line.

For an ac signal applied to a transmission line, the lines of force shown in Fig. 12-2A are equal but opposite for the two wires, since current flow at any instant is in one direction for a particular wire and in the opposite direction for the other wire. Thus, the fields tend to oppose, or even cancel, each other, depending on the proximity of the wires. Radiation losses are reduced to a greater degree as the wires are brought closer together. However, since spacing alters Z_o (Eq. 12-1), the wires may have to be farther apart than desirable in order to obtain minimum losses.

12-4. STANDING WAVES

Discussions of transmission-line factors necessitates repeated reference to the specific wavelength of the line, since line length relates to inductive, capacitive, or resonant characteristics.

When a transmission line's output impedance matches the generator's impedance, the maximum amount of available signal energy enters the line and travels toward the load terminating the line. If, however, the load is not matched to the line, all the signal energy is not accepted and some reflects back to the generator—the greater the mismatch, the greater the amount of energy returned along the line. Hence, some signal energy travels along the line toward the load, while some is returning along the line back to the generator.

The signal travel in both directions causes the primary signals and the reflected signals to be intermixed along the line, resulting in out-of-phase conditions in some sections, and in-phase conditions at others. Consequently, at places where voltages are in phase, their amplitudes are high; while at sections where out-of-phase conditions prevail, low or zero voltage occurs. Similarly high and low amplitudes prevail for current values along the line where reflections are present.

When the high- and low-amplitude points of voltage and current along the line remain at fixed positions, the waves produced are called *standing waves*. High points of voltage or current are termed *loops*, while low or zero amplitude points are called *nodes*. Since voltage and current amplitudes vary along a line with standing waves, the line impedance no longer would be constant, but would depend on the voltage-current ratio prevailing at a particular point.

An extreme condition of mismatch prevails if the transmission line is either open or shorted at the terminating end away from the generator. In such instances, all signal energy is returned to the generator, since no load resistance is present to consume the energy. With an open line, the impedance is infinitely high, whereas the shorted (closed) line drops the impedance to zero. The voltage and current relationships form out-of-phase conditions as shown in Fig. 12-3 for the various lengths of lines (both open and shorted).

Figure 12-3A shows a line that is a half wavelength long and open ended. Current and voltage distribution along such a half-wavelength line results in a voltage loop at the end, plus a current node. When the wave of signal energy reaches the end of such a line, the current drops to zero, and the resultant collapsing fields cut the conductor ends and induce a voltage having a peak value as shown, with a high impedance. For a half-wavelength line, a high-impedance condition also prevails at the generator

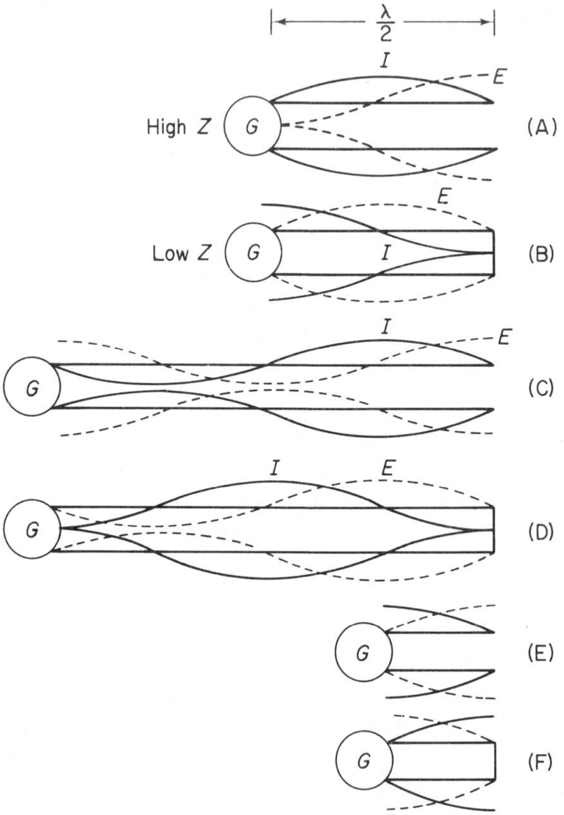

FIGURE 12-3. Characteristics of open and closed lines.

(though the voltage loop here is 180° out of phase with that at the end of the line). While the loops and nodes "stand" at fixed points, the energy is of ac composition, hence all amplitudes of voltage and current repeatedly build up and collapse.

Figure 12-3B shows a line of the same length, but closed at the end farthest from the generator. The shorted condition creates a current loop at the end, with zero voltage. Thus, the impedance is zero and, again, no matching load resistance is present, producing the standing wave condition shown. If a load resistance were used instead of a short, the ratio of loop amplitude to node amplitude would change to a degree, depending on whether the value of the load resistance approaches that of the generator impedance. The ratio of voltage loops and nodes (or current loops and nodes) is known as the *standing-wave ratio*, and is found by dividing the maximum value of voltage along the line by the minimum voltage value. A standing-wave ratio thus indicates the degree of mismatch between the load resistance and the impedance of the generator.

When a complete match exists between load and generator, the standing-wave ratio is equal to one, since loops and nodes no longer exist for either voltages or currents. Line reflections, however, cause standing waves and indicate mismatching. Consider the case in which the standing wave of current attains a value of 0.4 A, and the minimum standing wave of current is 0.04 A—the ratio is 10. This ratio indicates that the generator impedance is either 10 times larger than the load resistance, or one-tenth the value of the load resistance. Under these particular conditions, the standing-wave ratio of the voltage would, of course, also be 10.

Transmission-line sections that are a full wavelength long are shown in Fig. 12-3C and D. The open and closed terminations establish the same voltage and current relationships as the lines in A and B. The impedance at the generator is high in C, the same as at the end, while for D, a low impedance prevails both at the generator and the termination; the same conditions prevail in A and B. Thus, half-wavelength sections, or multiples thereof, can be used as one-to-one transformers because of their identical input and output impedances. (Practical applications will be shown later in this chapter.)

For the line sections in Fig. 12-3E and F, quarter wavelengths are shown. For the open line in E, a voltage loop is present, hence the impedance here is higher than at the generator. Consequently, such a length of line can be used as an impedance step-up device to match a low-impedance generator to a higher impedance load resistance unit. In Fig. 12-3F the closed termination drops voltage to zero, but raises current. At the generator, however, voltage is high, hence impedance is high. Thus, such a line section is useful as an impedance step-down transformer.

12-5. RESONANT AND REACTIVE SECTIONS

Because the transmission-line sections have characteristics of series inductance and shunt capacitance, resonance must prevail for a specific frequency, as is the case with any inductor-capacitor combination. Consequently, when the inductive- and capacitive-reactance values are equal (and opposite), resonance is achieved. It will be found, however, that the line is exactly *one-quarter wavelength* long for the frequency at which resonance is obtained.

For the quarter-wavelength line in Fig. 12-3E the generator sees a series-resonant circuit because the impedance of the line at the point where it connects to the generator has a minimum of impedance, just as in a series-resonant circuit. For the quarter-wavelength resonant section in F, however, the generator connects to a high-impedance section, hence the transmission line section has all the characteristics of a parallel-resonant circuit. As will be shown later in this chapter, such sections replace conventional capacitor-inductor combinations for higher frequency operations.

The series-resonance of the quarter-wave, open-line resonant section is destroyed if the line is either slightly shortened or slightly lengthened. If for instance, the line were shortened to less than a quarter wavelength, both the inductance and capacitance values would decrease. Thus, the inductive reactance would drop, but capacitive reactance would rise. Since the quarter-wavelength open line is equivalent to a series circuit, the rise in capacitive reactance cancels the decreased inductive reactance, causing a predominance of capacitive reactance and, hence, capacitance. Therefore, the shortened quarter-wave section behaves as a pure capacitance (assuming negligible resistance in the wires).

If the quarter-wave section of open line were made longer than a quarter wavelength (but not to a half wavelength), both inductance and capacitance would increase. Now the series opposition would be primarily inductive reactance and form a section equivalent to inductance. Since the closed quarter-wavelength lines have impedance characteristics opposite to those of the open lines, an inductance is formed for a line decreased in length, and a capacitance is obtained when the line length is increased over the quarter wavelength (but kept at less than a half wavelength). When the line is shortened, the lower inductance reactance in the parallel-resonant circuit carries most of the signal current, causing the current to have inductive characteristics. As open or closed sections of lines are increased in length beyond the quarter-wavelength, reactive characteristics invert, as shown in Fig. 12-4.

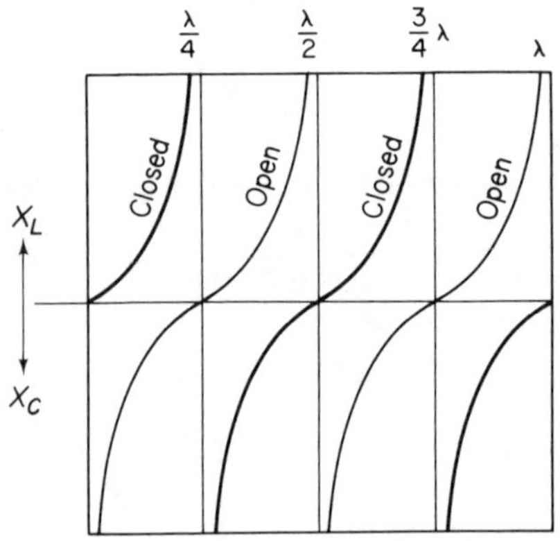

FIGURE 12-4. Reactance changes for line length.

12-6. LINE STUBS

Stub is the term applied to a short length of transmission line used for obtaining characteristics of inductance, capacitance, or resonance at high-frequency operation. The use of stubs for forming filters is shown in Fig. 12-5. Figure 12-5A shows a typical constant-*k* low-pass filter section, while B is its ultrahigh-frequency counterpart. Here, a closed-line section is placed in series with one leg of the transmission line. Such a stub is cut for a length less than a quarter wavelength and, hence, behaves like an inductance and performs the same reactive function as its physical counterpart in A.

To form the shunt capacitor at the output of the filter, an open section of line (less than a quarter wavelength long) is placed across the two wires of the transmission line as shown in Fig. 12-5B thus providing the necessary capacitance. Similarly, open and shorted stub sections also form the low-pass filter, as shown in C (low-frequency version) and D (the high-frequency counterpart). The open stub, less than a quarter wavelength, is again used as a capacitance, except that now it is placed in series

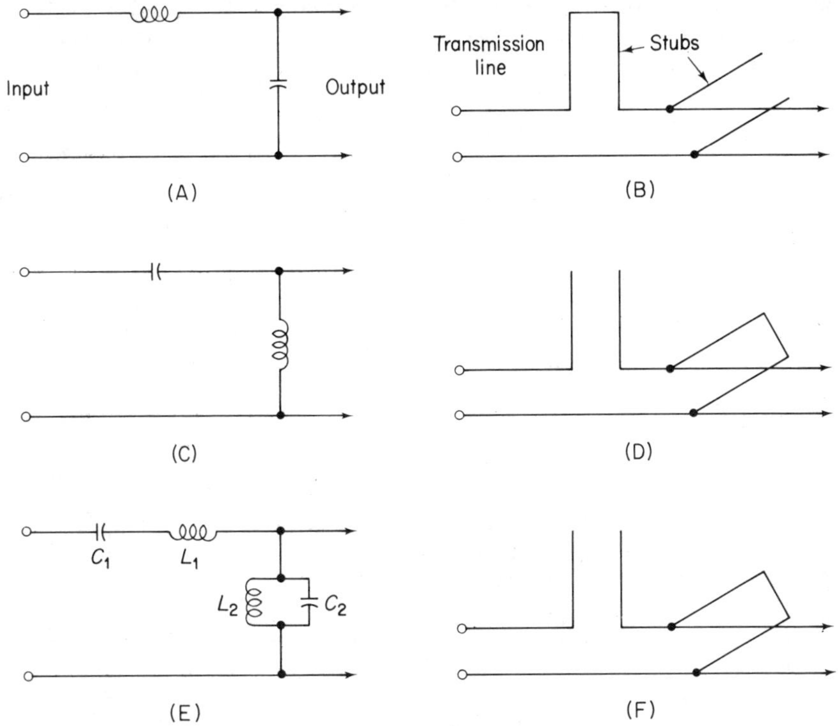

FIGURE 12-5. Filter sections.

with one line. The closed stub, acting as an inductance, is placed across the line to simulate the shunt inductance at the output of the high-pass filter.

If the stubs in Fig. 12-5B and D were made exactly a quarter wavelength long, resonant filters would be obtained. For Fig. 12-5B the closed quarter-wave section in series with one line acts as a parallel-resonant circuit and, hence, offers a high impedance to a band of frequencies clustered around the resonant frequency. The open quarter-wave section across the line, however, acts as a series-resonant circuit, shunting signals at or near the resonant frequency. Thus, for Fig. 12-5B, resonant stub sections form a band-stop filter with characteristics similar to those of the lower-frequency spectrum version.

Quarter-wave sections for the stubs in Fig. 12-5D would form a bandpass filter similar to the types shown earlier in Fig. 4-18. As shown in Fig. 12-5E and F, the open stub would act as a series-resonant circuit, passing signals with frequencies at or near the resonant one. The closed stub would behave as a parallel-resonant circuit.

Instead of using two-wire lines to form stubs, filter sections can be formed from stubs using coaxial-line segments. Coaxial lines have the same characteristics as two-wire lines with respect to quarter-wavelength resonance, and reactive quantities above and below the frequency of resonance. The only difference between the two-wire line and the coaxial line is that the latter is basically unbalanced with respect to ground since the

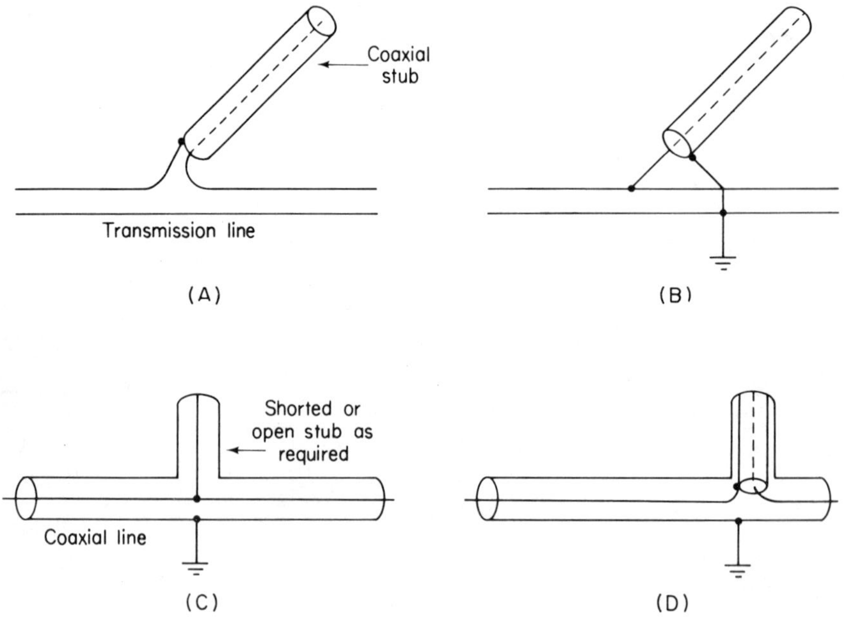

FIGURE 12-6. Coaxial-line stubs.

outer conductor (the *shield*) is usually placed at ground potential and, hence, the inner conductor is above ground.

As shown in Fig. 12-6, coaxial-line stubs can be used with two-wire lines or with coaxial transmission lines to form resonant or reactive sections. Figure 12-6A shows a coaxial stub in series with one wire of a two-wire line. If the stub is a quarter wavelength long and open, it will act as a series resonant circuit. (The transmission line must always be considered as the signal source, hence it is the generator with respect to a stub, whether the latter is in series or parallel to the line.)

In Fig. 12-6B, a coaxial stub parallels a two-wire line, and the length of the stub (and whether the stub is open or closed) again determines its characteristic. With coaxial stubs, the closed type is preferred since it minimizes losses at the open end. In Fig. 12-6C, both the stub and line are coaxial, with the stub section in parallel to the line. Thus, the stub in C can be used to form a shunt reactance or a shunt-resonant circuit. Figure 12-6D shows a coaxial stub in series with the inner conductor of a coaxial transmission line. Note the use of the double outer-conductor section, with both at ground potential.

12-7. RESONANT UHF OSCILLATOR STUBS

Figure 12-7 shows how two-wire line or coaxial sections form resonant circuitry in UHF oscillators. (Such sections are used for resonant circuits in RF amplifiers.) For the UHF oscillator in Fig. 12-7A, the collector is connected to one wire of the parallel-resonant line, while the other wire of the line couples to the base input circuit. This oscillator can be compared to the Hartley oscillator type (see Chap. 6) though it is sometimes called an *ultra-audion* type. The collector line section can be considered to be the collector inductance, while the resonant-line section at the base forms the base inductance. The reverse bias for the collector (positive for an *npn* transistor) is applied to the movable shorting bar (which tunes to resonance). Capacitor C_1 places the bar at *signal* ground, making it the same potential as the emitter. Thus, the emitter taps the inductance in a fashion similar to that of the Hartley oscillator.

The output from the oscillator is tapped by using a single-loop inductance, as shown by the broken-line section in Fig. 12-7A. Such a single-loop inductance is often called a *hairpin loop*, and the closeness (degree) of coupling determines the amount of signal energy transferred; the amount of coupled load applied to the oscillator; and the resultant circuit Q.

For the oscillator in Fig. 12-7B, a coaxial-cable section is used for resonant circuit purposes, and an FET unit replaces the transistor for illustrating the variations possible in such circuitry. Function is virtually

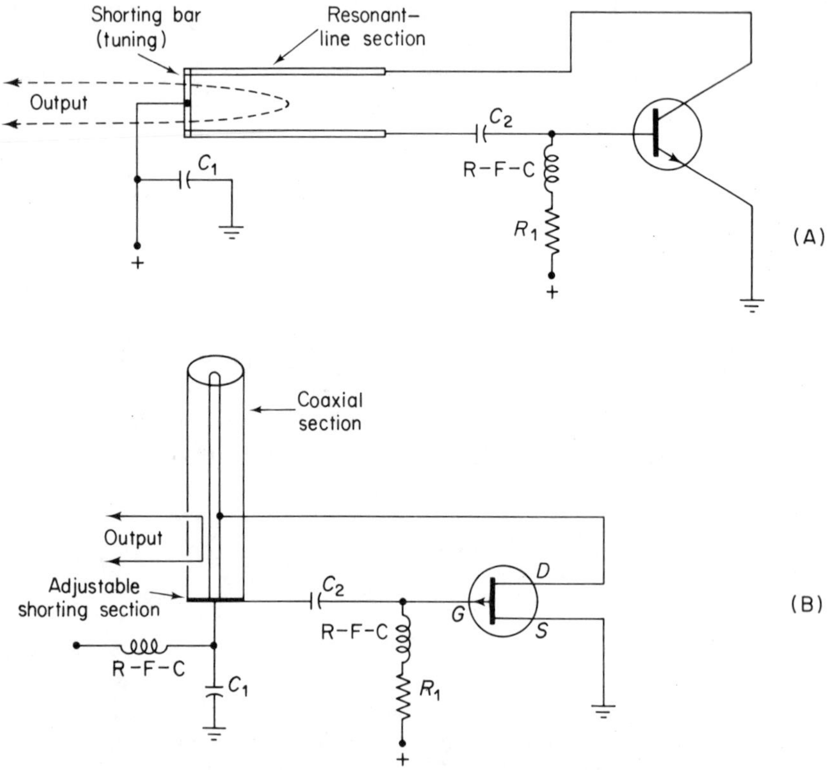

FIGURE 12-7. UHF oscillators using parallel lines.

the same as for the oscillator of Fig. 12-7A. The inner conductor of the coaxial cable is used for the drain element of the FET (or collector of a transistor). The outer conductor is not at direct (dc) ground, but rather is placed at signal ground by capacitor C_1. Output RF is obtained from a hairpin-loop system inserted in the coaxial element through small holes in the outer conductor as shown. For both oscillators, RF chokes prevent signal energy loss to ground or to the power-supply sections, and the capacitor C_2 blocks the dc potentials of the input circuits from that applied to the output.

The adjustable shorting bar often consists of a metal washer-type assembly mounted on a threaded rod connected to the tuning knob. RF energy is confined to the inside of the coaxial-cable section and does not penetrate through or leak to the outside of the tuning section. Because of the phenomenon known as the *skin effect* (defined below), RF signal energy flows on the outside of the inner conductor of a coaxial cable and on the inside of the outer conductor.

This characteristic of RF signal-energy conduction can be more readily understood by reference to Fig. 12-8, which shows a magnified cross-section of a single wire carrying electric current. Current flow creates a series of magnetic lines and such fields are distributed not only within the wire core, but around the perimeter as shown.

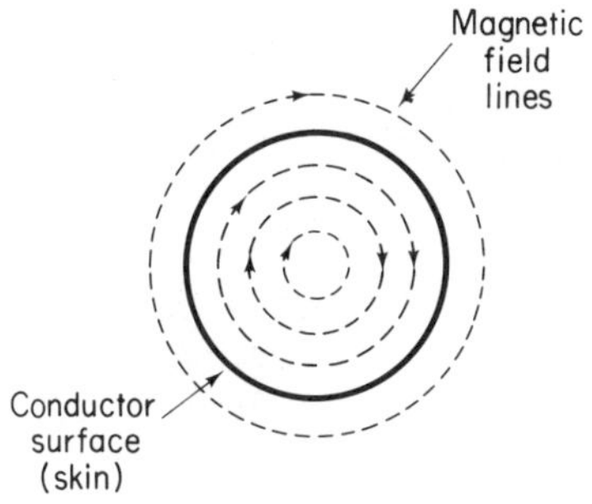

FIGURE 12-8. Skin effect.

These magnetic-field lines represent the inductive factor along the length of the wire and, hence, have reactive characteristics and oppose RF current flow. Since inductive reactance rises with higher-frequency signals, the opposition to ac within the wire rises as the frequency of the signal is increased. Consequently currents for high-frequency signals find it more difficult to flow through the inside of the wire than is normally the case with very low-frequency signals. However, since the first magnetic line on the outside of the wire is spaced a short (but definite) distance from the surface, the current flow established by the pressure of the voltage tends to be on the outside of the wire where it meets with less opposition.

This "surface path" for the current at high frequencies is likened to the skin of the wire, and hence is called *skin effect*. To provide the least opposition, wire diameters are increased to provide more surface (skin) area at high and ultrahigh frequencies. In transmitting use, copper tubing is often employed, since the inner solid copper interior of the wire is no longer useful for current-carrying purposes and can be dispensed with. For receiver applications it is more practical to use heavy copper wire (size AWG 18 or larger) for the coils, particularly since voltage and current levels are very much lower.

When coil diameters are increased to account for skin effect, there is a corresponding rise in the distributed capacitance of the inductor. The larger-diameter turns thus increase the shunting effect of the capacitance between turns and can also affect the true resonance of tuning circuitry. For this reason, the coils are usually designed with adequate spacing between turns to minimize the increase in capacitance effects. Fortunately, at higher frequency operation, the number of coil turns are fewer and hence capacitance effects do not become too large despite the larger-diameter wire and spacings.

Eventually, still higher frequency operation entails usage of the line sections for resonant circuitry. If still higher-frequency operation is necessary, a special microwave gear is employed.

12-8. MEASUREMENT, MATCHING, AND DELAY

When a section of transmission line is coupled to the resonant circuit of an RF amplifier or oscillator as shown in Fig. 12-9A, wavelength measurements can be made. Since an open or closed line does not

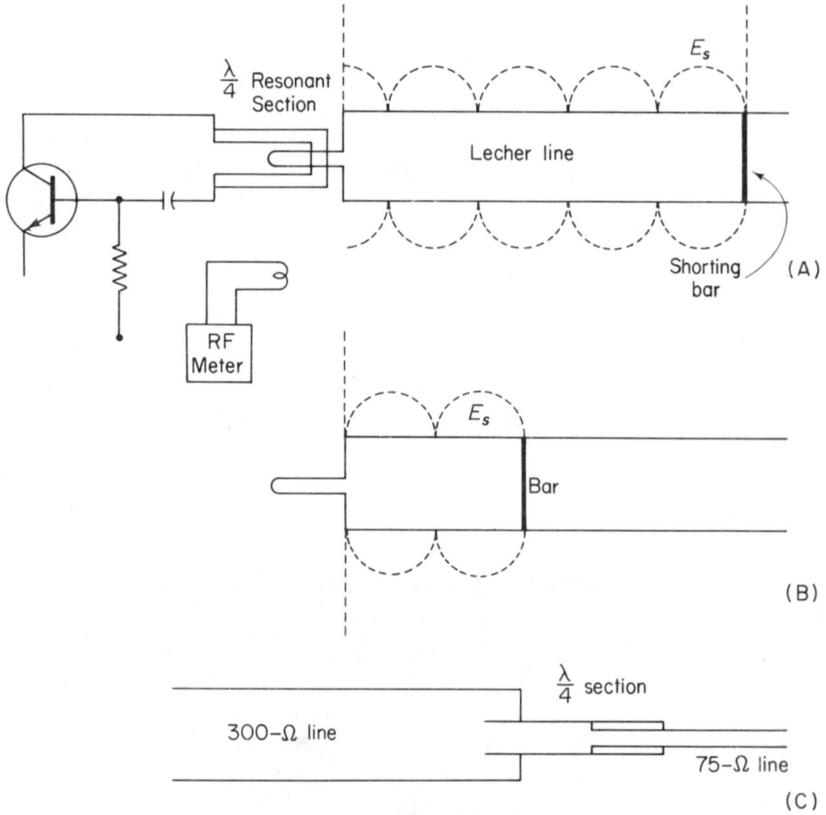

FIGURE 12-9. Line measurement and matching.

consume the signal energy picked up by the coupling loop, standing waves occur as previously mentioned. Thus, an RF-indicating meter can be used to seek out standing wave loops for measurement purposes. Such a measurement line is often referred to as a *Lecher line.*

Instead of moving the indicating device along the line, a shorting bar can be used as shown in Fig. 12-9B. At the shorting bar, the standing wave of voltage will always be zero and the current standing wave will be at its maximum. Either voltage or current loops can be used for measurement purposes by keeping the indicating meter stationary at the RF source end. Thus, as the shorting bar is moved, the loops of voltage and current change, and the distance the bar is moved between two loops (or two nodes) spans *one-half wavelength.*

When the distance between two loops is measured, the value so obtained can be inserted into either of the following equations for ascertaining the frequency of the signal generated by the RF oscillator (or amplified by the RF stage involved). For UHF, the measurement may be in inches, hence we can use the following equation, with $2d$ representing the distance in inches *between two loops* for obtaining the frequency in MHz.

$$\text{frequency (in MHz)} = \frac{11{,}808}{2d} \qquad (12\text{-}4)$$

Thus, if we were to measure 24.5 inches between two voltage loops, we would expect the frequency to be:

$$\frac{11{,}808}{59} = 200 \text{ MHz}$$

If the distance is measured in meters (d_m), we can use Eq. 12-5:

$$\text{frequency (in kHz)} = \frac{300{,}000}{2d_m} \qquad (12\text{-}5)$$

As shown in Fig. 12-9C, a closed-line section can be used for impedance matching. Here, a quarter-wavelength section of Lecher line acts as a step-down transformer because the impedance is high at the open end and zero at the closed end. Thus, by tapping off certain points, a high-impedance line can be matched to a low-impedance one as shown in the figure. The Lecher line can be reversed for impedance step-up purposes. An impedance match is obtained when a maximum amount of signal energy is transferred between generator and load, and standing waves are at a minimum.

12-9. DELAY LINE

Sections of series inductance and shunt capacitance are used for signal-delay purposes. As shown in Fig. 12-10, the line is tapped off at appropriate intervals in order to obtain the required signal delay. The line is terminated in a load resistor (R_L) equal in value to the characteristic impedance (Z_o) to reduce line reflections by absorbing the energy arriving at the end of the line.

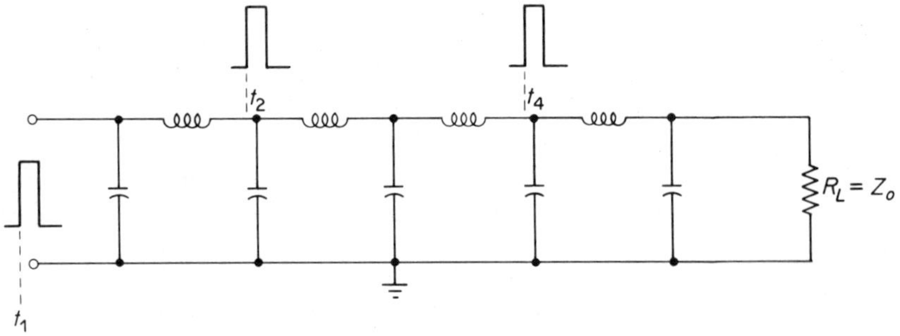

FIGURE 12-10. Delay lines.

The time in seconds for signal energy to travel a section of line is found by:

$$t = \sqrt{LC} \tag{12-6}$$

Thus, if we wish to find the delay for a section of line having a total inductance of 49 mH and a total capacitance of 0.001 μF, we obtain:

$$t = \sqrt{0.49 \times 10^{-3} \times 10^{-9}}$$
$$= 0.7 \times 10^{-6} \text{ s } (0.7\ \mu\text{s})$$

For multiples of the section calculated, the value obtained (0.7 μs in this instance) is multiplied by the number of sections involved. Thus, for two sections, each of 50 feet, we obtain $2 \times 0.7 = 1.4\ \mu$s.

12-10. ANTENNA RECIPROCITY

Antennas have the dual characteristic of serving as either the signal interceptor for a receiver or as the load resistance of a transmitter. This dual function is known as *antenna reciprocity* because the receiving functions of an antenna utilize identical characteristics of wavelengths, fields, and impedances, as the transmitting functions. Hence, in many low-power applications, particularly in portable transmitter-receiver combinations (*transceivers*), the same antenna is used for both transmitting and receiving.

The maximum signal power transferred from the transmitter to the antenna depends on the impedance-matching factors relating to transmission lines, as does the transfer of maximum signal power from antenna to receiver.

As a transmitting device, the antenna must convert the signal components of voltage and current to a composite electric and magnetic field structure, which will propagate through space. Similarly, during reception, the antenna must intercept the electric and magnetic fields making up the transmitted signal energy, and reconvert that energy into equivalent values of voltage and current for amplification and demodulation purposes. Thus, the material in the following sections of this chapter relates, for the most part, to both receiving as well as transmitting antennas.

12-11. ANTENNA PATTERNS AND FIELDS

A quarter-wavelength open section of line was shown in Fig. 12-3E. If such a section of line is fully opened, the opposite-polarity fields of the two wires no longer cancel to reduce radiation losses, and an antenna structure is formed like the one shown in Fig. 12-11A. (The generator has been omitted to simplify the illustration, though signal-feed methods will be covered later in this chapter.)

Since the line section was a quarter-wavelength long, the opened section now spans one-half wavelength and the voltage and current distribution is as shown. Thus, each end still has a voltage maximum, with current reaching its peak value at the center. Such an antenna span is the shortest length possible for a straight element representative of a resonant circuit for the signal frequency to be handled.

Such a simple antenna is often opened at the center for attaching the transmission line, in which case it is known as a *dipole antenna* or *Hertz antenna*, after Heinrich R. Hertz (1857–1894), the German physicist and researcher. The half-wave antenna transmits or receives signals at right angles to its length, as shown in Fig. 12-11B. The individual sections of the radiation pattern are known as *lobes* and show the relative intensity of signal transmission or reception for various directions.

The directional pattern shown in Fig. 12-11C represents a cross-sectional view, since the same pattern would be evident if observed from any side parallel to the antenna length. This is evident from C, since there

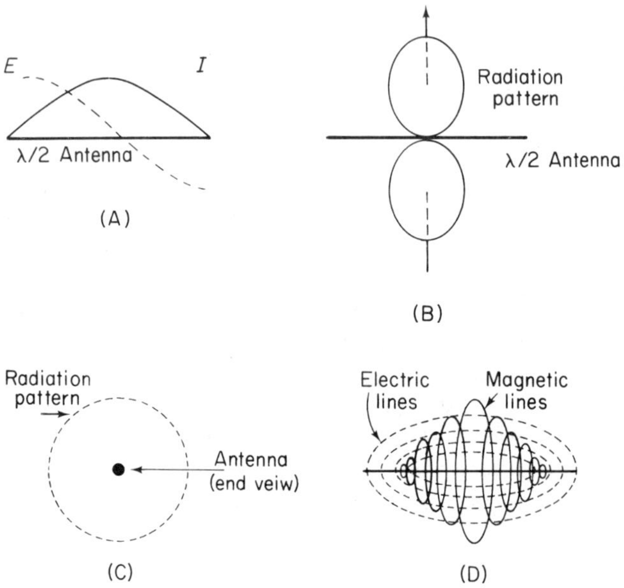

FIGURE 12-11. Half-wave antenna pattern.

the pattern is viewed from the antenna end and is shown as completely encircling the antenna. Such an antenna is capable of operating for signals coming from directions at right-angles to the antenna length.

When a transmitter feeds signal power into the antenna, electric and magnetic fields are built up around the antenna, as shown in Fig. 12-11D. The electric lines parallel the antenna length as shown, while the magnetic lines encircle the antenna, with highest amplitudes at the center. Since the signals are ac in nature, they build up with a specific polarity, collapse, and then build up again with an opposite polarity.

During the time the ac signal drops to zero between alternations we might expect the fields to collapse into the antenna. Because of the rapid change of polarity for high-frequency signals, however, new fields of opposite polarity emerge from the antenna before the existing ones can collapse back into the antenna. Hence, fields are forced beyond the influence of the antenna structure and propagate into space at the speed of light.

12-12 ANTENNA POLARIZATION

The composite fields, which make up the signal in free space, consist of expanding magnetic and electric lines as shown in Fig. 12-12. When the receiving or transmitting antenna is in a horizontal position with

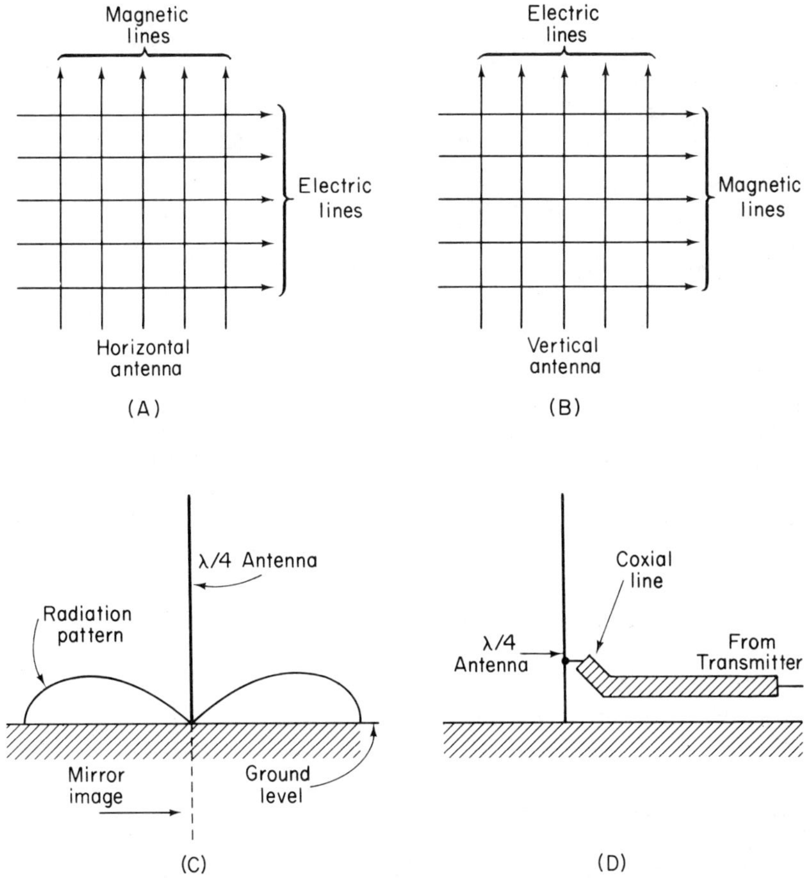

FIGURE 12-12. Polarization and Marconi antennas.

respect to earth, the propagated wave is *horizontally polarized*, with the electric lines also in a horizontal plane, as shown in Fig. 12-12A. When the antenna is in a vertical position, the wavefront of signal energy now has its electric lines in a vertical position, and hence is known as *vertical polarization*, as shown in B. For a maximum transfer of signal energy between transmitting and receiving antennas, identical polarization must exist between the two antennas. Other important factors are antenna height, proper positioning with respect to the radiation pattern, angle of radiation, and atmospheric conditions.

Most television signals are horizontally polarized, though at the receiver some vertical polarization may be present in the signals because of reflections and inversions during propagation between antennas. When signals are transmitted to or received at ground levels, the horizontally polarized antenna structure suffers shunt reactive losses because of the capacitance set up between the antenna and ground. Hence, vertical polarization is preferred at low-terrain levels.

When transmitting with vertically polarized antenna systems, such as in standard AM transmitting, a single quarter-wavelength vertical antenna is used, as shown in Fig. 12-12C. The bottom of the antenna is grounded, thus eliminating the need for a half wavelength to achieve resonance for the frequency of the signal to be transmitted. When the vertical antenna is grounded as shown, the system simulates the characteristics of a half-wave antenna because of the *mirror-image* effect. It is as though the earth had presented an extension of the quarter-wave section as shown in C, and the figure-eight radiation pattern shown in B of Fig. 12-11 still prevailed, though half is the theoretical mirror image as shown. Thus, such an antenna propagates in all directions along a horizontal plane. Such an antenna is referred to as *Marconi antenna*, after Marchese Guglielmo Marconi (1874–1937), the Italian physicist, who contributed much to early electronic knowledge.

Signal feed to the Marconi antenna can be illustrated as in Fig. 12-12D, using a coaxial cable for an unbalanced coupling (one end of the antenna and outer conductor of the coaxial line both grounded). Since the impedance of the vertical antenna is zero at ground, the impedance rises along its height. Thus, the inner conductor of the coaxial line is attached at a place where an impedance match is obtained.

12-13. ANTENNA LENGTH

The half-wavelength antenna in Fig. 12-11 is designed for a signal having a frequency related to the antenna length. Hence, if lower-frequency signals are used, antenna efficiency and effectiveness drop sharply. This is not to say that such an operation is impossible since virtually any metallic object will pick up transmitted signals to a degree, depending on the strength of the signals in the area. Similarly, a horizontal receiving antenna could be used for vertically polarized waves if the arriving signals are sufficiently strong to permit normal demodulation and amplification. For low-power transmission or distant reception, however, factors relating to length, height, orientation (pointing the receptive angle of the antenna into the desired direction), and polarization are important.

Where multiple-frequency signals are involved (such as in antennas for television reception), the radiation pattern changes sharply for signals higher than those at the half wavelength. If, for instance, a half-wave antenna receives signals of twice the fundamental frequency, the antenna may be considered to consist of two half-wave antennas of the higher-frequency signals joined to form a single length as shown in Fig. 12-13A. Thus, the unit now represents a full-wave antenna for the signal frequency used.

As shown in Fig. 12-13A, voltage and current distributions are now out of phase for each half wavelength. As shown in Fig. 12-13B, the individual halves of the antenna would have a figure-eight pattern, if it were not for the influence of the respective polarities. As also shown, out-of-phase conditions are present in both the true vertical and the true horizontal planes, and the 180° phase difference results in signal cancellation in these directions, both for a receiving antenna as well as for a transmitting antenna.

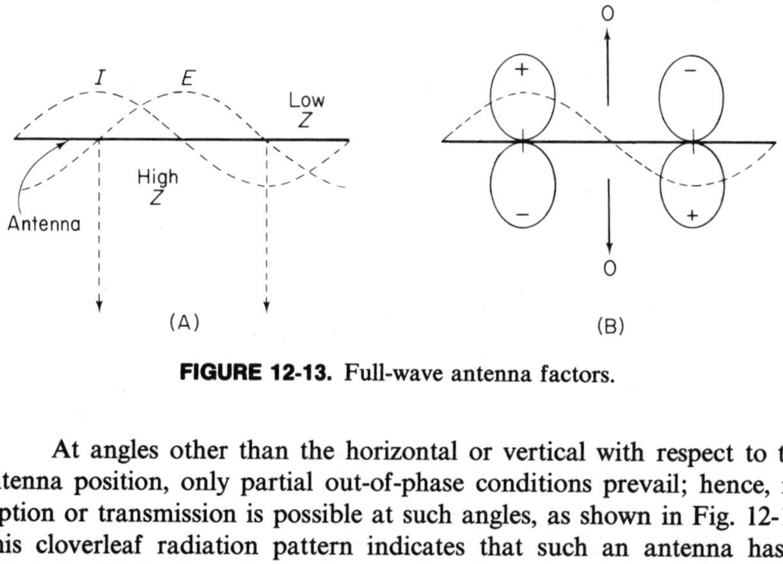

FIGURE 12-13. Full-wave antenna factors.

At angles other than the horizontal or vertical with respect to the antenna position, only partial out-of-phase conditions prevail; hence, reception or transmission is possible at such angles, as shown in Fig. 12-14. This cloverleaf radiation pattern indicates that such an antenna has a pickup sensitivity from four separate directions, with each lobe at a 54° angle with respect to the antenna plane. Similarly, a transmitting antenna a full wavelength long would also exhibit such a cloverleaf transmission characteristic.

If the same antenna is used for signals three times the fundamental frequency, it behaves as an antenna one and one-half wavelengths long, and the cloverleaf lobes again appear, though with a 42° angle. At higher frequencies, secondary lobes of low sensitivity also appear, clustered around the junction of the major lobes. Thus, multiple-directional results are obtained. While this may have some advantages for signals arriving from various angles, it, nevertheless, increases interference problems.

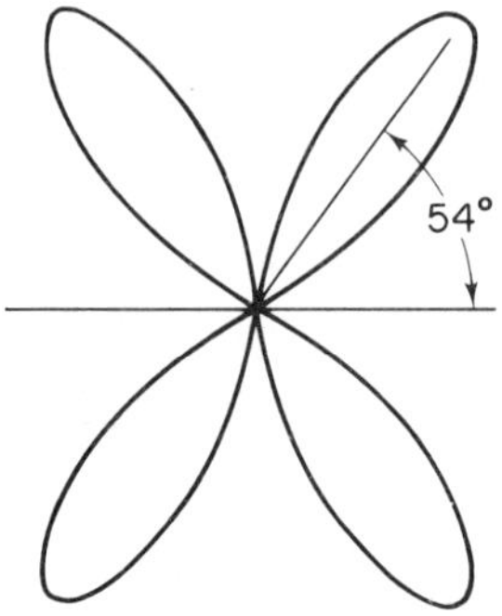

FIGURE 12-14. Full-wave antenna pattern.

Half wavelengths for specific frequencies can be found by using the following equations:

$$\frac{\lambda}{2} \text{ in meters} = \frac{15 \times 10^7}{f(\text{Hz})} \tag{12-7}$$

$$\frac{\lambda}{2} = \frac{150}{f(\text{MHz})} \tag{12-8}$$

Because of the effects of the wave traveling along a wire (instead of free space) and because of the *end effect*, which results from capacitance at the ends of the antenna, a correction factor is necessary, particularly for signals having frequencies above 30 MHz. Multiplication by 0.94 will give a close approximation of the required *electric length*, rather than the physical length. Thus, for a frequency of 60 MHz, a half-wave antenna would have a length derived as follows:

$$\frac{150 \times 0.94}{60} = 2.35 \text{ m}$$

The following formulas are also useful:

$$\frac{\lambda}{2} \text{ in feet} = \frac{492 \times 0.94}{f(\text{MHz})} = \frac{462.5}{f(\text{MHz})} \tag{12-9}$$

$$\frac{\lambda}{2} \text{ in inches} = \frac{5550}{f(\text{MHz})} \tag{12-10}$$

Thus, using the 60 MHz frequency again as an example, we have:

$$\frac{462.5}{60} = 7.7 \text{ ft}$$

For proof we can multiply the number of feet by 0.3048 to obtain the same length in meters: $7.7 \times 0.3048 = 2.3469$ m.

12-14. ANTENNA COUPLINGS

Transmission lines can be coupled to antennas at the end (high-impedance point) or at the center (low-impedance point), depending on requirements. For FM and TV reception the transmission lines are low-impedance types, hence the coupling methods shown in Fig. 12-15 may be employed. In Fig. 12-15A the dipole is formed by opening the half-wave antenna rod, and the twin-lead type transmission line is attached thereto.

Though in theory the impedance at the opened point should be zero, some capacitance is created between the open ends and thus some

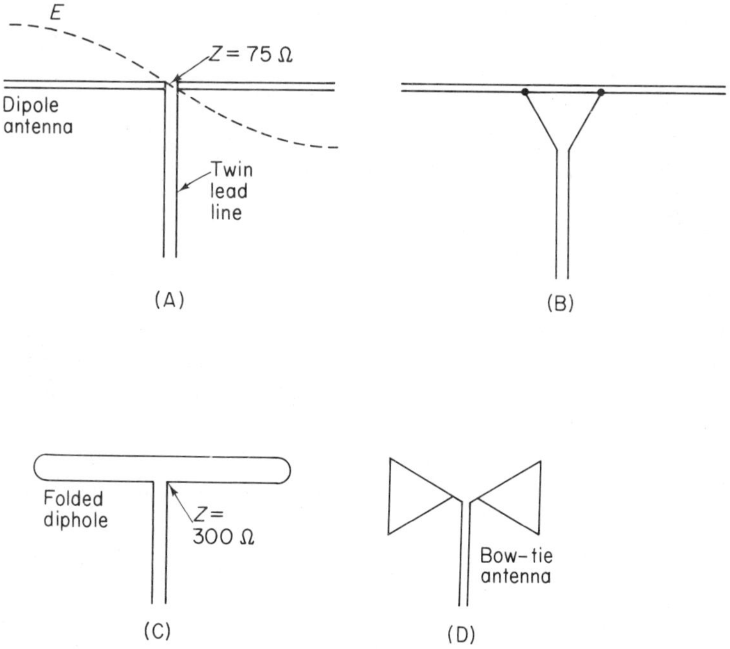

FIGURE 12-15. Line attachment.

reactive effect occurs. Also, depending on antenna diameter, some skin-effect opposition may be present. These factors contribute to a total impedance of approximately 75 Ω as shown. Thus, if a 300-Ω transmission line is used, a mismatch will occur, resulting in a reduction of the maximum possible transfer of signal between the antenna and receiver.

The current loop in an antenna is used as the reference for determining the *radiation resistance* in either a transmitting or a receiving antenna. In a transmitting system, signal power is fed to an antenna, and voltage and current measurements would indicate that power is consumed. Yet, the antenna itself does not consume this power, but only converts it to a type of energy that can be propagated. The equivalent resistance, which consumes such power, is therefore called *radiation resistance*.

For the receiving antenna, the radiation resistance can be defined as the ratio of power picked up by the antenna to the square of the effective current existing at the selected reference point on the antenna. Thus, for the dipole antenna, the current loop reference point makes the input impedance of the antenna equal to the radiation resistance. If the feed line were attached at the ends, however, the input impedance would no longer equal the radiation resistance, but rather would be determined by the ratio of E/I at the feed point.

Instead of forming a dipole, the half wavelength can be left intact as shown in Fig. 12-15B, and the wires from the transmission line fanned out and attached at points where an impedance match is obtained. This is possible because the impedance rises toward the right and left ends of the half-wave section, and spreading of the wires for a short distance is all that is required. This method is sometimes called a *delta match* because of its resemblance to the Greek letter (Δ).

A folded-dipole type antenna can be used as shown in Fig. 12-15C. This double-rod antenna provides for a 300-Ω impedance at the opened section of the lower rod, thus forming a perfect match for the standard 300-Ω twin lead. (Most tuners of TV and FM receivers have balanced-line inputs for 300-Ω transmission lines such as the twin-lead type so a match is provided between the line and the 300-Ω input impedance of the tuner.)

The so-called *bow-tie antenna*, sometimes used for UHF television, is shown in Fig. 12-15D. Again the line connects to the center where an approximate impedance match is obtained. Where a minimum of signal pickup by the line is intended, coaxial cables could also be used, with the outer (shield) conductor connected to one of the dipole rods and the inner conductor to the other. Since 75-Ω coaxial cables are common, an impedance match is readily obtained with the basic dipole-type antenna fed at the center. Losses, however, are greater for the coaxial cables used in television reception.

12-15. YAGI ANTENNA

If an additional rod is placed in parallel to the antenna, but a short distance away, the new rod intercepts some signal energy and reradiates it, thus (in effect) reflecting it back to the antenna. Such a rod is termed a *reflector* and causes an increase in signal pickup (or transmission) for the direction perpendicular to the antenna side not having the reflector. The reflector rod is approximately five percent longer than the antenna.

The addition of one or more rods is also possible ahead of the antenna structure as shown in Fig. 12-16 to form a structure known as the *Yagi antenna*, after the Japanese inventor and physicist, Hidetsugu Yagi. The Yagi construction not only increases antenna gain and sensitivity, but confines the radiation pattern to only one direction as shown by the dashed outline. The sharpness of the lobe also minimizes reception of undesired signals or signal reflection from objects near the signal path.

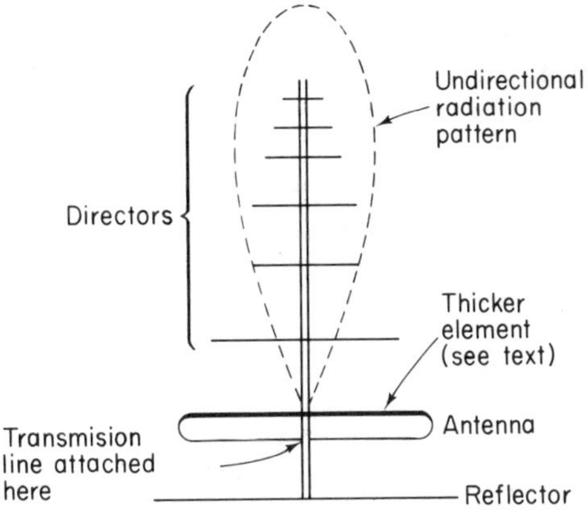

FIGURE 12-16. Yagi antenna.

As shown in Fig. 12-16, the forward rods are called *directors*; they aid in directing some of the propagated signal energy toward the antenna for increased gain. The directors or reflectors are called *parasitic elements* to distinguish them from the antenna proper to which the transmission line is attached. The antenna section itself is called the *driven element*.

As also shown in Fig. 12-16, all elements may be connected directly to the supporting metal rod, since their center areas are voltage-node points and have a minimum of impedance. The directors are often made progressively shorter for added sections to provide for increased bandwidth. Increasing response to various frequencies is often necessary with the Yagi because its configuration increases Q. If all elements are designed around a single frequency, the bandwidth becomes extremely narrow.

For Yagi structures, the reflectors are again usually made about five percent longer than the antenna element, thus bringing the reflector to the approximate physical length rather than the electric length mentioned earlier for the antenna. Directors are made about four percent shorter than the antenna for operation at or near the frequency for which the antenna operation is desired. For a broader band, however, successive directors should be progressively shorter as shown. Spacings often are 0.15 wavelength between the antenna rod and the reflector, and 0.1 wavelength between the director and antenna or between successive directors.

Gain increases rapidly for the Yagi as a reflector (or directors) are added. When a parasitic element is added to the driven element, the gain increases by about 5.5 dB over that of a single dipole (assuming a matched system). A four-element Yagi with proper design can achieve a gain of 9 dB over a single dipole. The addition of parasitic elements to the antenna system results in a decrease in the impedance at the feed point. However, the impedance can be increased again through use of a larger diameter, unbroken rod of the folded dipole. For a four-element Yagi, a 300-Ω impedance is achieved by making the diameter ratio between the unbroken rod and the broken rod (where the line is attached) four to one. Thus, if the unbroken rod element is a 1-inch diameter tubing, the section to which the line is attached should be $\frac{1}{4}$-inch tubing.

12-16. ANTENNA-STACKING FACTORS

Antennas of any type can be stacked one above the other, using a single common transmission-line feed. When proper matching and phasing precautions are taken, the stacking of two or more antennas in the vertical plane increases signal sensitivity and also alters the radiation pattern from that obtained by use of a single dipole. With stacking, signal sensitivity can be minimized in the vertical plane, for instance, and increased in the horizontal plane, thus increasing the direction-selectivity of the antenna. The primary disadvantage is the increased space occupied by the system. However, this is a factor that becomes less bothersome as the signal frequencies are raised.

To obtain a horizontal directivity pattern, it is necessary to stack the antennas one-half wavelength apart as shown in Fig. 12-17. Two interconnecting rods or transmission-line sections are used, and in one method the feed line is connected at the center, as in Fig. 12-17A. As shown in Fig. 12-17B, the feed line can also be attached to the lower end of the stacked

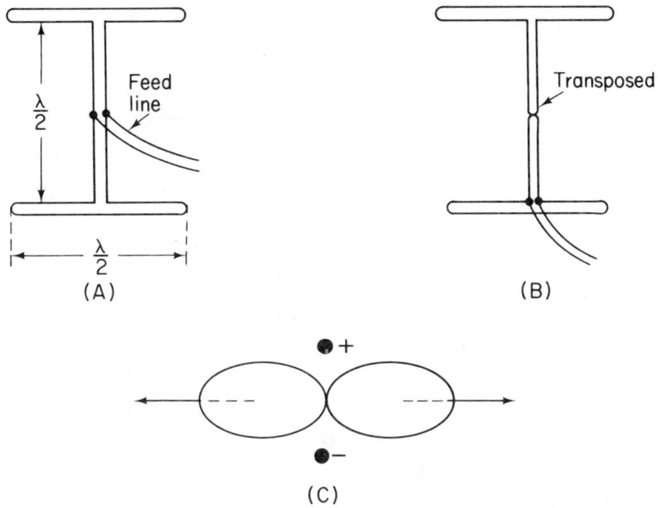

FIGURE 12-17. Antenna stacking.

array, provided that the section between the two antennas is transposed (as in the figure).

With either of the methods shown in Fig. 12-17A or B, the phase relationships for signals are identical for each antenna as shown in C. Thus, the in-phase conditions prevailing along the horizontal plane increase the radiation pattern. There is minimum sensitivity in the vertical plane because the signal energy of a particular polarity alters for a half wavelength. Thus, if the signal wavefront leaving the lower antenna is positive and travels upward, by the time it has spanned one-half wavelength, the signal emanating from the upper antenna will have a negative polarity and cancellation will occur. Similarly, even though at any instant the signals for each antenna are in phase, when the energy of the upper antenna propagates toward the lower, the time interval is sufficient for the lower antenna's signal to undergo a polarity change, thus creating opposing signal conditions when upper- and lower-antenna signals meet.

The stacking, in essence, parallels impedances of the two antennas, resulting in a decreased total impedance presented to the transmission line. Also, since the spacings are based on one-half wavelength, a change of signal frequency alters the radiation characteristics of the array.

The pattern type shown in Fig. 12-17C is called a *broadside pattern* because it is at right-angles to the plane of the stacked antennas. Additional antennas could have been stacked in the vertical plane to increase the horizontal directivity of the array. With half-wavelength spacings between antennas, however, bulk increases rapidly for lower-frequency systems.

If the interconnecting line sections in Fig. 12-17B were not transposed, the signal polarities at any instant would be opposite for the upper and lower antennas. Consequently, out-of-phase conditions would exist for horizontal directions. For vertical directions, however, the signal traveling from one antenna to the other element spans a half wavelength, hence by the time the signals arrive, the phases of the signals coincide. If, for instance, the signal were of negative polarity at the lower end and were propagated upward, its polarity would not change, but the signal leaving the upper antenna at the time the lower signal arrived would also have been of negative polarity, and hence no cancellation would have occurred.

When no wire transposition is used, for the antenna system in Fig. 12-17B, the radiation pattern in C would be in a vertical plane and would be called *end fire*, since it emanates from the ends of the stacked array. Again, more than two antennas could have been used for increasing gain in a narrower path.

12-17. REFLECTORS AND FLARED WAVEGUIDES

In microwave practices a parabolic reflector is used with an antenna system for both transmitting and receiving signals in a straight-line path with a minimum of wavefront expansion during propagation. The result is a high degree of efficiency because of minimum signal loss and pin-point type orientation, which is highly suitable for direction-finding purposes.

Since microwave signals have frequencies approaching those of light waves, the two behave in similar fashion in terms of reflection. Thus a metallic parabolic reflector has the ability to direct microwaves in one direction just as a mirrored reflector is used for light beam formation. For the microwave parabolic reflector, the antenna radiator must be placed at the focal point and the radiation from the antenna directed toward the bowl of the parabola, which then reflects the energy forward. As shown in Fig. 12-18A, a dipole element can be used, though often a metal shield is placed close to the antenna to aid in directing the signal energy toward the parabola.

As shown in Fig. 12-18B, the ends of a waveguide can be flared into a horn shape for propagating energy delivered via a unidirectional path. Though such a flared horn-type structure guides the energy in one direction, dispersion occurs as the signals travel outward; the narrow-path beam obtained from the parabolic structure is not attained with the flared-end radiator.

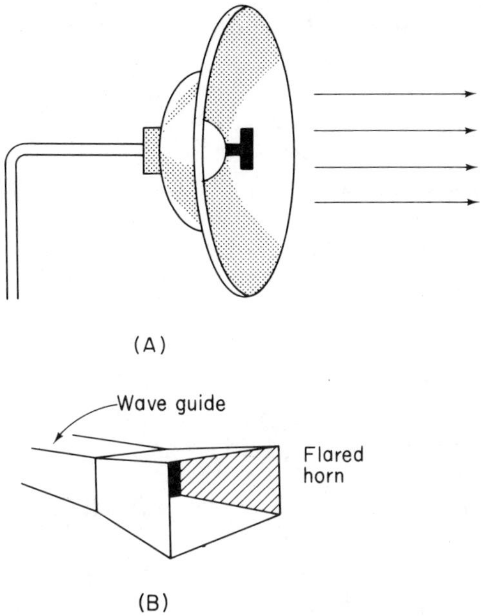

FIGURE 12-18. Parabolic and horn types.

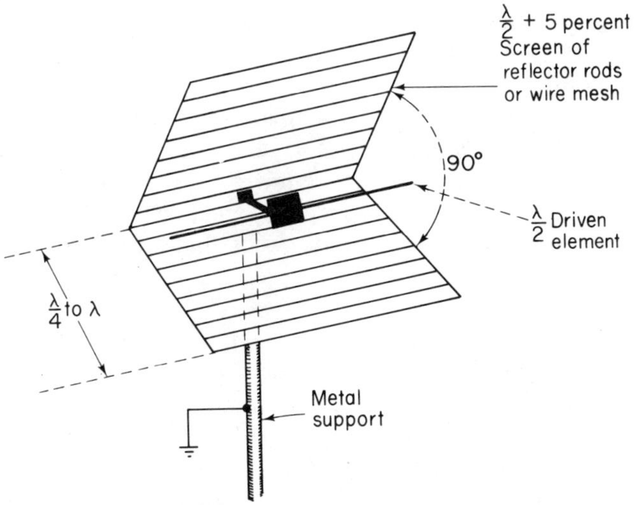

FIGURE 12-19. Corner reflector.

Rectangular metal shields can also be placed behind an antenna to act as large-scale reflector elements for increasing forward gain for both transmission and reception. Sometimes right-angle sections (*corner reflectors*) are used for minimizing sensitivity toward the rear. As shown in Fig. 12-19, rods or wire mesh are used to decrease wind resistance. Such reflectors are placed at ground potential since they are parasitic elements just as are the reflectors and directors discussed earlier in Sec. 12-15. As with the parabolic reflector, the corner reflectors are not driven elements, but must be used in conjunction with an antenna element.

12-18. FIELD INTENSITY

Stacked antenna arrays and multi-element units, such as the Yagi, are often considered to have voltage or power gain. Actually, any antenna does not radiate all the power that is supplied by the transmitter and fed to it through the transmission line, since line losses and antenna efficiency are limiting factors. However, complex antennas can, by directing propagated energy in specific directions, produce signal intensities at a given area which would be equivalent to an increase in power supplied to the antenna. This becomes evident when we compare the radiation pattern of the single antenna in Fig. 12-11C with those showing increased gain in specific directions, such as the Yagi in Fig. 12-16 and the stacked array in Fig. 12-17.

Thus, directive antennas can send the propagated wave in the direction of prescribed horizontal or vertical angles and increase signal strength in desired directions by utilizing radiated energy normally transmitted at undesirable angles. This is accomplished without an increase of the average power output of the antenna system. Hence, the reference to the *input power* of the final Class C amplifier stage of a transmitter becomes less valid at VHF, UHF, or microwave frequencies, since directive antennas are used in those cases. The signal delivered to a certain area may vary considerably in amplitude from that transmitted by another station, even though the two may have identical input powers to their final RF amplifier.

A factor in VHF-UHF communications is antenna height above ground; an increase raises the amplitude signal received in remote areas (line of sight transmission). Thus, the commonly used reference to transmitter power for TV and FM at the VHF-UHF areas is *effective radiated power*—the value obtained by taking the signal-power output of the transmitter's final RF stage, subtracting power loss in the transmission line, and multiplying the result by the power gain of the particular antenna system in use. Thus, a station might use 50 kW to the antenna, but, because the antenna produces a gain of 3, the station would have an effective radiated power of 150 kW.

Still another consideration is the signal attenuation, which tends to increase as the transmitted signal frequency is raised. Thus, where a lower-band (Channels 2 to 6) television station may obtain an effective radiated power rating of 100 kW from the FCC, stations in the Channel 7 to 13 range would obtain a rating allocation of over 300 kW. For UHF stations, a still higher effective radiated power rating would be issued by the FCC, with powers to 5 MW.

Since antenna height has a bearing on power radiated, the FCC must limit antenna height to meet certain conditions. Thus, a 1000-foot limit might be imposed for a certain effective radiated power, and if a higher antenna is to be used, the effective radiated power may have to be reduced accordingly. Specific restrictions depend on the geographical location of the station in terms of terrain, the number of other stations in the area, and other related factors.

The *field intensity* or *field strength* at a given distance from the transmitter is usually specified in *microvolts per meter*. This term refers to the number of RF-signal microvolts that are intercepted by a length of

TABLE 12-1. Antenna Gain and *Z* Factors

Antenna Type	dB Gain over Dipole	*Z* of Antenna
Straight $\lambda/2$ dipole	0	72 Ω
Folded dipole ($\lambda/2$)	0	300 Ω
Driven element (antenna) plus director 4% shorter, spaced:		
$\lambda/4$	3.5	0.75 *R**
0.1λ	5.5	0.2 *R*
Driven element (antenna) plus reflector 5% longer, spaced:		
$\lambda/4$	4.5	0.83 *R*
0.15λ	5.5	0.35 *R*
Driven element with director and reflector ($\lambda/4$ spacing)	6	0.35 *R*
Four-element Yagi	10	0.1 *R*
Corner reflector		
Driven element $\lambda/2$ from apex—reflectors λ long at 90°	10	2 *R*

**R* = Resistance of driven element (antenna) if no parasitic elements (directors and reflectors) are present.

wire exactly one meter long, properly oriented for the signal being received, and polarized correctly with respect to the transmitting antenna. Thus, the microvolts per meter expression relates to the voltage obtained at the particular height at which the measurement is taken. Obviously, a higher reading would be obtained if the wire were raised (conceding factors such as horizontal polarization, etc.), but the intent is to specify the reading at a selected height.

Field gain refers to the amount of signal increase at a selected point some distance from the transmitter antenna for a change of input power, antenna directivity, antenna location, etc. Thus, if a simple transmitting antenna system produces a reading of 250 microvolts on a field-strength meter, and a multi-element array increases this reading to 500 microvolts, there is a field gain of 2 for the larger unit. Since the values are expressed in terms of voltage, the decibel difference is 6. For field power measurements (or for effective radiated power measurements at the transmitter), a doubling of power would indicate a 3-dB change ($10 \log P_1/P_2$) in contrast to voltage (or current) doubling, where a 6-dB change occurs ($20 \log V_1/V_2$).

13

Vectors and Phase Relationships

13-1. ANGULAR VELOCITY AND RADIANS

A sinewave of ac has trigonometric relationships as shown in Fig. 13-1. In part A, the circle shows the aspects of radius compared with the circumference. When the length of the radius is laid along a part of the circumference, the angle for its arc is 57.3°. If the radius length were repeated around the circumference it would fit 2π or 6.28 times. The angle established by placing the radius length over the circumference is known as a *radian* (57.3°). Thus, since one radian is formed each time the radius is laid around the circumference, there are 6.28 radians to a circle.

The relationship between the radius and the velocity factor of an ac signal is shown in Fig. 13-1B. Assume the circle is a wheel rotating clockwise. If the radius is now made to revolve counterclockwise, there will develop a relationship between the rotating radius line and the rotating circle. When the wheel rotates clockwise through 360°, the radius line will also make a complete revolution (but in the counterclockwise direction). Now, if the point of the radius line which touches the circle were able to trace a pencil line as it moves, it would draw a sinewave as it moves through one complete rotation.

For the operations of Fig. 13-1 the term *vector* is sometimes used, and the radius is often called a *vector arm*. (For a discussion of the differences between the terms *phasor* and *vector*, see Sec. 13-2.) Once the radius arm has rotated from the horizontal to the vertical position, it will

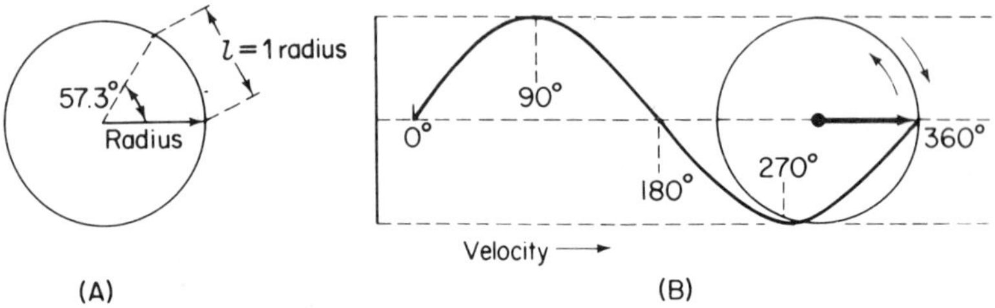

FIGURE 13-1. Radians versus angular velocity.

have made an angular change of 90° and at the same time the stylus at its point will have drawn one-half of an ac *alternation* (90° of the sinewave). As the radius arm rotates, it indicates progressive instantaneous values of the sinewave for positions other than the vertical. In the vertical position it indicates the peak amplitude of the sinewave signal (either for voltage or current).

Because the radius arm indicates the continuous changing of the angle as well as the instantaneous amplitude, it is an indication of the velocity of the sinewave. Hence, the expression $2\pi f$ ($6.28\, f$) is known as the *angular velocity*. The symbol for angular velocity is ω, the lower-case Greek letter omega.

As shown below, 2π radians = 360° since each radian is 57.3°. The relationships between these factors are as listed below:

Circumference = 2π times radius = 2π times arc of 1 radian
360° = 2π radians
1 radian = 57.3° (57° 17′ 44.8″ approx.)
180° = π radian
90° = $\frac{1}{2}\pi$ radian
1° = 0.01745 radian

13-2. PHASORS, VECTORS, AND SCALARS

The terms *vector* and *phasor* are often used synonymously, though there are basic differences between them. Strictly speaking, vector quantities are those having both *magnitude* and *direction*. Essentially, a vector quantity is represented by a straight-line segment in a particular direction (based on some reference system) to which the word *vector* then applies. For such a vector, the length is proportional to magnitude (to voltage or current in electric or electronic representations). The vector may have an arrowhead at the point where it reaches maximum amplitude to indicate direction.

The angle represented in a phasor diagram represents a *timing* difference, not a directional one, and in this respect differs from the vector. Both vectors and *scalars* are normally represented on phasor diagrams. A scalar can be defined as a quantity (i.e., length, mass, temperature, time, etc.) exactly specified numerically on an appropriate scale.

Sometimes reference is made to a *vector product*, wherein the product vector has a magnitude proportional to the product of the magnitudes of two related vectors, as will be illustrated later in this chapter. Another name for a vector product is *cross product*. A *scalar product* is the product of the lengths of two related vectors, multiplied by the cosine of the angle between the two. Other terms for the scalar product are *inner product* and *dot product*.

13-3. ADDITION OF SINUSOIDAL WAVEFORMS

On many occasions two or more waveforms of current or voltage are present simultaneously in circuits. In audio signal amplifiers, for instance, there may be a number of signals present, varying in amplitude, frequency, and waveshape. Also, such signals may be out-of-phase with each other; that is, each signal may start its positive alternation at a time that differs from that of the other signals. The net result in a circuit is usually the formation of a *composite* signal formed by the point-by-point addition of the instantaneous values of the waveforms. In some circuitry (such as the poly-phase types discussed later in this chapter), several waveforms may have the same amplitude and frequency, but may possess different phase relationships. However, there are instances where several waveforms may have the same frequency and phase, and differ only in amplitude.

When several sinewaves are of the same frequency and phase, their combination in a circuit results in a single sinewave of the same frequency, but with an amplitude that is equal to the sum of the original waveforms. Thus, if two in-phase voltages are present, each having a value of 100 V, their combination will produce a single sinewave of 200 V. Similarly, if one current waveform is 0.03 A and another is 0.02 A, the resultant composite would have a value of 0.05 A, provided the two were of the same phase and frequency. This combining process is shown in Fig. 13-2 where one waveform has a value of 100 V and the other 125 V. The composite resultant of 225 V is shown by the dashed outline.

The values shown in part A are peak values, though the rms values can also be used to obtain a total value. Thus, the two sinewaves of 100 V and 125 V have root mean square values of 70 V and 88.4 V, respectively,

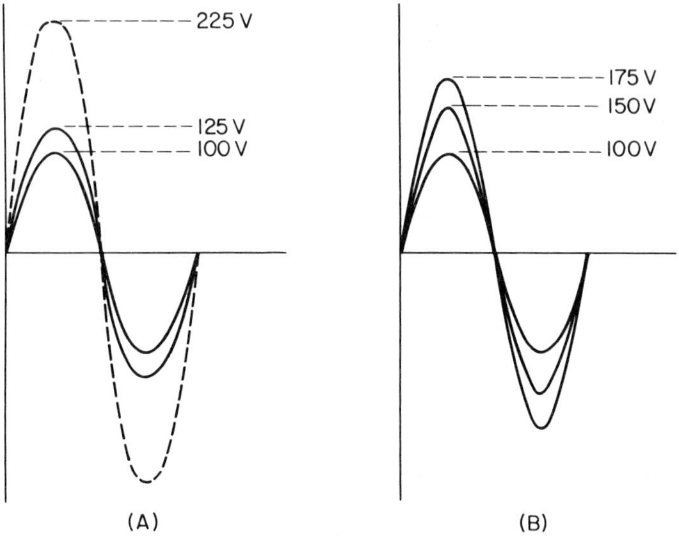

FIGURE 13-2. In-phase voltages having differing amplitudes.

and the total value of the composite waveform is approximately 158.4 V root mean square. Similarly, current waveforms can be calculated in terms of peak currents or in root mean square values.

Sinewaves of the same phase and frequency occur across resistors in ac circuits, and such resistors have voltage drops and current relationships conforming to the basic Ohm's law theory. Thus, parallel resistors have the same voltage across them, as for dc circuits. Similarly, series resistors have voltage drops which vary in amplitude in proportion to the current flow and resistance value. Assume for instance, that three resistors are in series and their values are 1400 Ω, 1200 Ω, and 800 Ω. Current is 0.125 A and the impressed voltage is 425 V. The individual voltages, therefore, are

$$E_1 = 0.125 \times 1400 = 175 \text{ V}$$

$$E_2 = 0.125 \times 1200 = 150 \text{ V}$$

$$E_3 = 0.125 \times 800 = 100 \text{ V}$$

Thus, each resistor has across it a sinewave of voltage different in amplitude from the others, but of the same phase and frequency as shown in Fig. 13-2B.

13-4. OUT-OF-PHASE WAVEFORMS

When several waveforms have the same frequency, but are out of phase with each other, we can no longer employ simple addition of the peak values to find the total amplitude of the composite wave produced. With out-of-phase waveforms, the peaks of voltage (or current) do not occur at the same time. A point-by-point summation of the waveforms will produce a peak value that is always less than the arithmetical sum of the individual peak values. The peak value of the composite waveform grows smaller as the phase difference becomes greater. For instance, two equal-amplitude voltages that are exactly 180° out of phase will produce a zero resultant.

The graphical and vector representations of two out-of-phase voltages are shown in Fig. 13-3. As shown in part A, each waveform has a peak value of 100 V, and the voltage E_2 lags voltage E_1 by 90° because E_2 starts its positive alternation 90 electrical degrees later than voltage E_1. The vector diagram for the two is shown in part B where E_2 is drawn along the horizontal X-axis, and E_1 is drawn along the vertical Y-axis of the graph. The lengths of the lines for E_1 and E_2 are equal, indicating the respective voltages are similarly equal. In constructing this graph, we can assign any length necessary to keep proportions within reasonable area limits. We could, for instance, assign the E_1 and E_2 lines lengths of 1 inch to represent 100 V. Next, we would find the resultant by drawing in the dashed lines on the diagram to form a square. The length of the diagonal line then gives us the resultant voltage—approximately 1.4 inches = 140 V. Note that the resultant diagonal line is displaced exactly 45° from both E_1 and from E_2. Correspondingly, note that the peak value of the composite waveform occurs at the center intersection of the E_1 and E_2 waveforms in A of

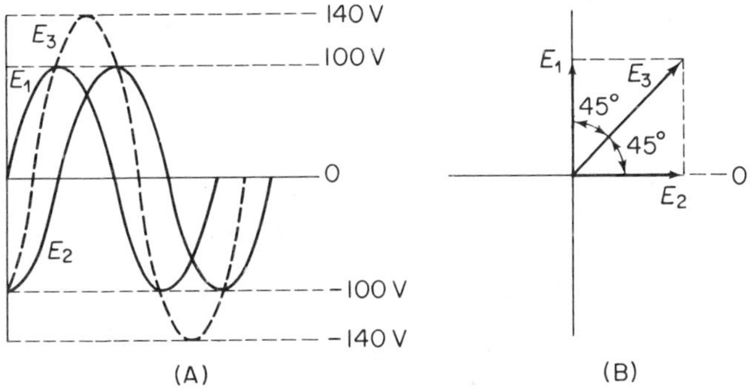

FIGURE 13-3. Two voltages 90° out of phase.

Fig. 13-3. Thus, the resultant can be considered to be the sum of the $E\sin\theta$ values of each waveform. The sin of 45° is 0.707 = (approximately) 70 V + 70 V = 140 V. Thus, the value is less than the arithmetical sum of 100 V + 100 V = 200 V. Note, also, that the composite wave has shifted in phase with respect to the original waveforms since it lags E_1 by 45° and leads E_2 by the same amount. Had these waveforms been representative of current rather than voltage, the same composite waveform would have resulted, with identical proportionate values. (If the two waveforms were each 100 mA, for instance, the total current would have been 140-mA peak value.)

When two or more waveforms have differences in their amplitudes as well as in their phases, a vector diagram can again be constructed for finding the relative phase angle of the composite wave formed by the combination, as well as its amplitude. Two sinewaves of this type are shown in Fig. 13-4. Here, voltage E_1 has a value of 100 V, and E_2 has a value of 150 V. The phase difference between the two is 90°. Again, E_2 can be represented along the X-axis as shown in part B, with its length proportional to the voltage. If the E_1 line is 1 inch long, the length of the E_2 line will be 1.5 inches long to correspond to the 150-V value for E_2. Now, instead of a square, we form a parallelogram because of the unequal lengths of the E_1 and E_2 lines. Our composite waveform E_3 now has an amplitude of approximately 180 V and is displaced by 34° with respect to E_2 and 56° with respect to E_1.

In Figs. 13-3 and 13-4, voltage E_1 was the reference voltage. This could also have been the generator voltage, with E_2 consisting of some signal having a phase deviation from that of the generator. Actually, however, the diagrams in B of Figs. 13-3 and 13-4 represent peak values at

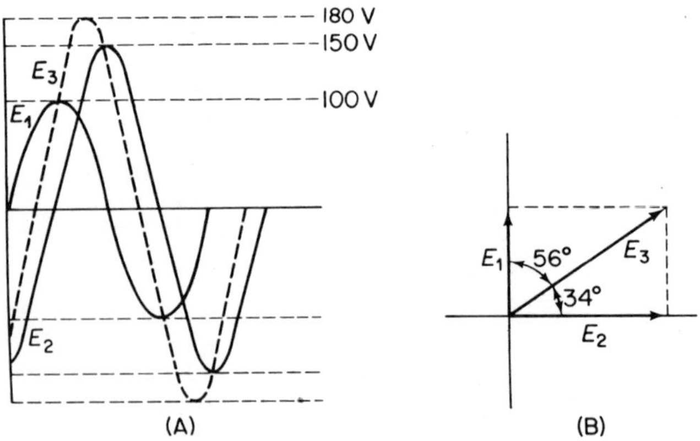

FIGURE 13-4. Out-of-phase voltages having differing amplitudes.

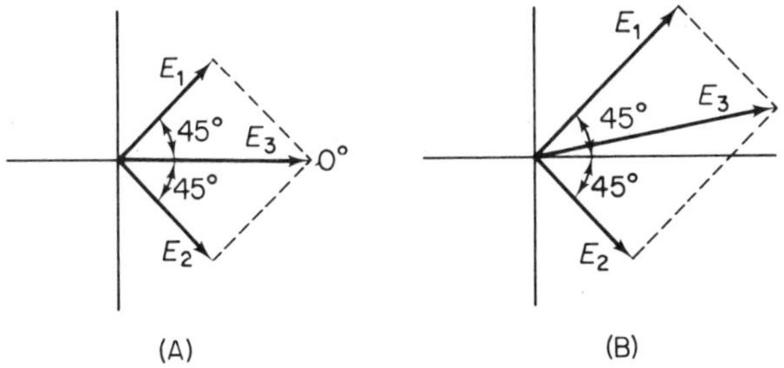

FIGURE 13-5. Vector diagrams of leading and lagging voltages.

a particular instant in time. With ac, peak values do not remain at their levels, but decline and build at a periodic rate related to the frequency of the signal. Thus, the entire vector diagram can be considered to be rotating, and such diagrams would be just as valid when representing some instant in time other than those previously shown. For the two examples previously given, for instance, we can construct diagrams at the instant in time when the E_2 values are negative, as shown in A and B of Fig. 13-5. The resultant values of the composite signal vectors will be the same as before.

13-5. POWER IN AC CIRCUITS

When effective values of ac pass through a resistor, the amount of electric energy consumed in watts is the same as it would be for a similar dc value. It would seem, therefore, that the standard power formula, $P = EI$, would apply. This, however, is not the case; for with ac, there are many occasions in electricity and electronics where current and voltage *are not in phase*. Sometimes the current will lag the voltage, as shown in Fig. 13-6A where the positive current build-up lags that of the voltage. The degree of such lag may be from a fractional degree to 180°. Also the voltage may lag the current, as shown in part B, again from a fractional degree to 180°. (Relative amplitudes of current and voltage are not a factor here. In part A, the current could have been higher than the voltage waveform, had the numerical unit values been reversed.) When voltage and current are not in phase, the amount of power is reduced because the peak values of current and voltage no longer coincide. Thus, the formula, $P = EI$, yields what is termed the *apparent power*. [We are assuming root mean square values without denoting the subscript "eff" since the effective (root mean square) value is most commonly measured by general test equipment.] The apparent power is not the *true power* when there is a

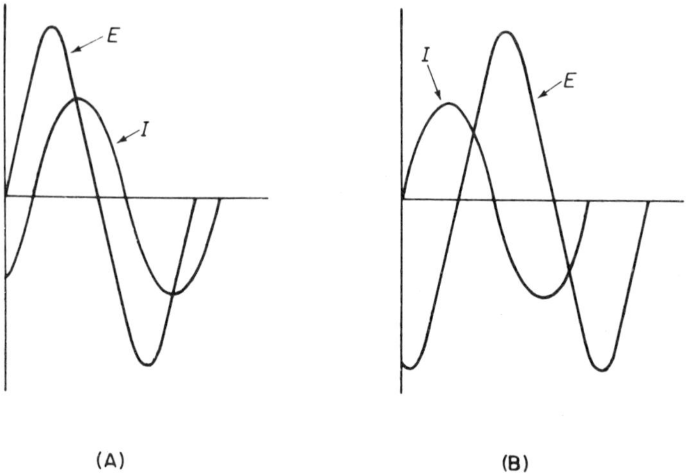

FIGURE 13-6. Leading and lagging voltages.

phase angle between current and voltage, but does become the true power in the absence of the phase angle. To make sure, however, that we are always solving for the true power, we must add to the original formula the *power factor*, which is the cosine of the phase angle. Thus, the equation for true power (in root mean square values) must be solved by using Eq. 3-16: $P = EI\cos\theta$.

When current and voltage are in phase, the angle $= 0°$, and the cosine $= 1$; hence, the apparent power is equal to the true power. When there is a phase difference, however, the resultant angle will have a cosine which is less than 1 and which will reduce the apparent power proportionately.

13-6. THREE-PHASE AC

Because the three-phase ac is the most widely used polyphase power in industry, our discussions in this chapter will be confined primarily to it. Two-phase systems are rarely used, except for special electrical or electronic applications where they can be employed for control purposes. They lend themselves to such specific usage because their operation can be affected by an error-control voltage. Where distribution systems from power companies are three-phase, and a single phase must be branched from them, the voltage is taken from across two of the three wires. Use of appropriate transformers connected to the three-phase system can be used, and the voltage stepped down to the value needed.

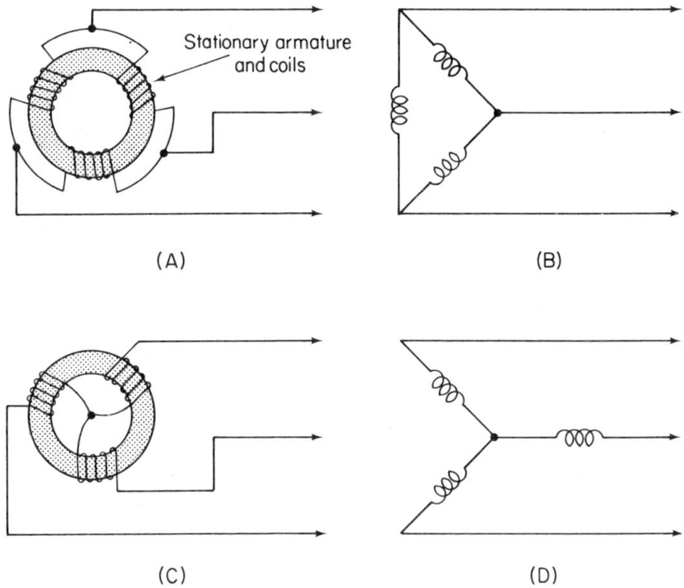

FIGURE 13-7. Three-phase ac delta and star connections.

Two wiring practices for producing three-phase ac from a generator are shown in Fig. 13-7. In part A the coil sections within the armature slots are series connected, forming three individual coils. The output wires are obtained from the interconnections of these three coils. This system is known as the *delta wiring method* because, when the inductor arrangement shown in part B is turned on its side, it resembles the Greek letter delta (Δ).

Another generator armature winding method is shown in Fig. 12-7C. Here, one terminal of each coil is joined to the other to form a common center terminal, and three new terminals are brought out as shown. This is known as the *star* or *Y* (sometimes spelled *wye*) connection because of the configuration indicated by the schematic shown in part D.

The armature coils, regardless of their number, are grouped into three sets and so arranged that each coil picks up a voltage, which differs from that of the other coils by *one-third* of a cycle, or 120°, as shown in Fig. 13-8A. Thus, the second phase is displaced from the first by 120°, and the third phase is displaced from the first by 240°. This is indicated by the vector diagram in Fig. 13-8B. The third phase, however, is displaced by only 120° from the second phase. Current, at one instant, flows out of one wire and returns through the other two. At another instant, current flows from the generator through two of the three wires and returns through the other one. All equipment used with the three-phase ac must be of the

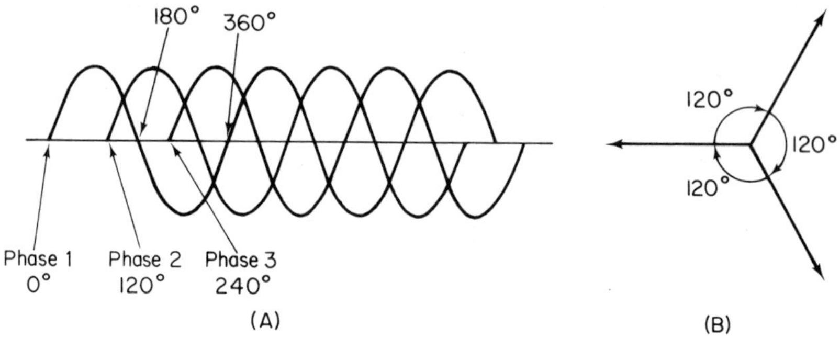

FIGURE 13-8. Phase relationships of three-phase ac.

three-terminal type, specifically designed for this polyphase ac. Three-phase loads could be independent and different, where each load draws current from one section of the winding in proportions at variance with the others. A balanced load, however, is preferred for more efficient and practical operation. With a balanced load system, each polyphase section sees the same load impedance (resistance) and has the same relative phase angle. Thus, the same *I* and *E* values prevail, but with the 120° phase angle for the three-phase system.

13-7. FOUR-WIRE, THREE-PHASE SYSTEMS

A neutral ground wire is often used in three-phase ac power distribution systems in industrial applications. When such a wire is connected to the junction of the *Y* system as shown in Fig. 13-9, the arrangement is called a *four-wire, three-phase* system. If the three inductors have identical characteristics and are working into a balanced load, the

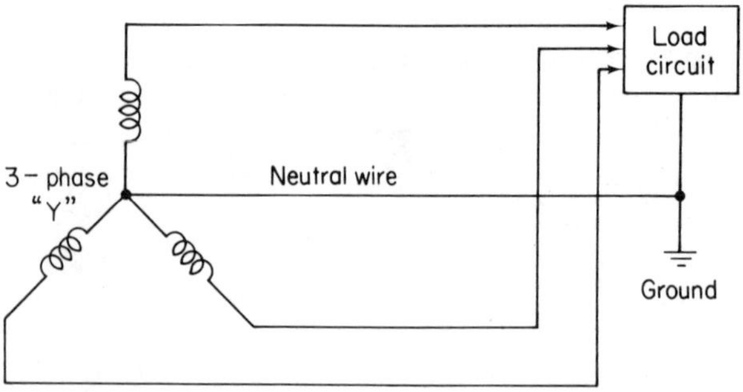

FIGURE 13-9. Neutral wire in a three-phase ac system.

voltage on the ground wire will be zero. With some mismatch, however, the unbalanced condition will cause some circulating currents to appear in the neutral wire. The balanced load is not essential, but is preferable because it reduces power loss in the neutral ground wire.

In the four-wire, three-phase system, the generator can supply three independent single-phase loads instead of the standard three-phase load. The generator could also supply both a single-phase load and a three phase at one time, as required. Without the neutral wire, however, the load can only be a three-phase type.

Several load connections to a four-wire, three-phase system are shown in Fig. 13-10. Here, a three-phase motor connects to the three terminals of the generator (or power line transformer secondary windings) as shown. Single-phase motors are connected across the neutral wire and one of the three-phase wires, thus furnishing the necessary single-phase ac. Lamps and small appliances also requiring single-phase ac are also connected between one of the three-phase wires and the ground (neutral) wire as illustrated. As will be explained later, the three-phase load has 208 V impressed on it, while each of the single phase load circuits has 120 V across it.

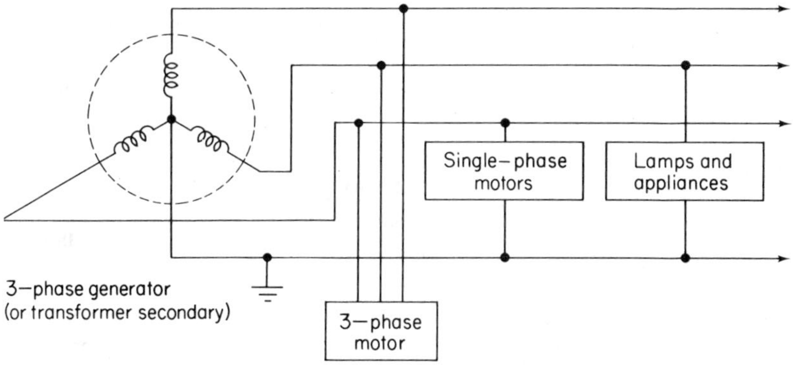

FIGURE 13-10. Various loads across a four-wire ac system.

13-8. THREE-PHASE NOTATION

In order to trace the interconnected windings of a three-phase system and also to simplify analysis of vector quantities of voltages, currents, and powers, a type of symbol notation must be used to provide quick identification. Arrows or single-subscript notations are inadequate for maintaining identification of the voltages or currents involved in polyphase systems. Hence, a type of notation has been generally adopted that uses two subscripts. This double-subscript notation is shown in

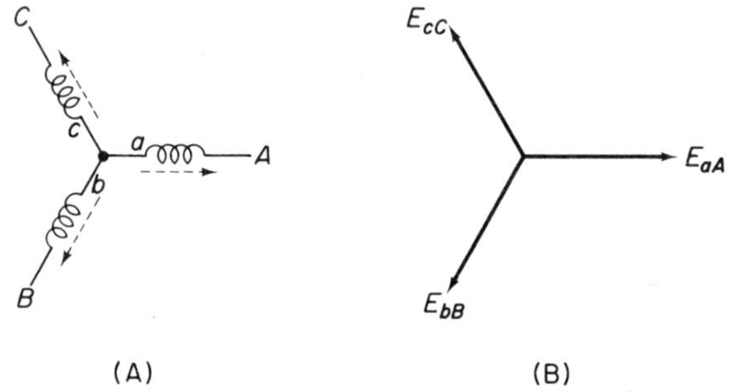

FIGURE 13-11. Double subscript notation for E (or I).

Fig. 13-11, where both upper and lower-case letter symbols are employed. This notation permits the tracing of circuit loops for the three-phase system as was done for the resistive circuits, using Kirchhoff's laws (Sec. 4-2).

In Fig. 13-11A, the *Y*-type circuit is shown with the common center connections of the coils marked *a*, *b*, and *c*. At the other end of each coil we have the upper-case counterparts of these letters: *A*, *B*, and *C*. If we traced a voltage loop from the center point from the *a* to *A* in the direction shown by the arrow, we would write this as E_{aA}. This notation then indicates that the tracing loop entered the coil at the place marked *a* and left at *A*. Similarly, E_{bB} identifies the direction in coil *B* as starting at *b* and leaving at *B*. The vector diagram with the accompanying notation is shown in Fig. 13-11B.

The first subscript identifies the loop entrance to the inductor; the second subscript shows where the tracing loop leaves. With interconnected three-phase windings we may find it necessary to trace a winding in the opposite direction, from *A* to *a*. In such an instance the notation becomes E_{Aa} indicating that the loop entered *A*. Thus, we use the first subscript for identifying the loop entrance to the coil or circuit, and the second subscript for the place where the tracing loop leaves. The arrows indicated in Fig. 13-11 do not indicate current flow since current direction constantly changes. Instead, the arrows merely depict the direction of the tracing loop in terms of energy from generator to load. In tracing, the general practice is to have the direction originate at the generator (also called an *alternator*) and then progress toward the load circuit. With the *Y* circuit, a neutral wire connection is often indicated as *n*, hence the center common terminal in Fig. 13-11A (or Figs. 13-9 and 13-10) can be designated as *n* or 0 (for zero) in double-subscript notation.

A vector diagram of a four-wire, three-phase *Y* system is shown in Fig. 13-12. Here, double-subscript notation is used, with the *n* subscript indicating the common junction of the three coils to which the neutral wire

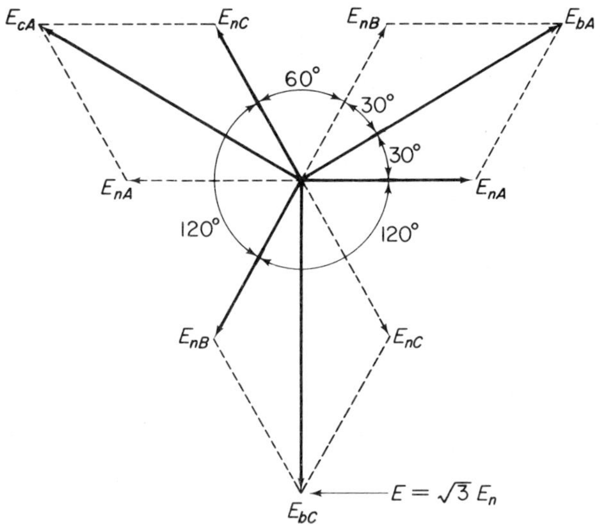

FIGURE 13-12. Vector diagram of four-wire, three-phase *Y* ac system.

is connected. (With a balanced load there would be no need for the neutral wire.) Under conditions of a balanced load the three individual line currents I_L have identical amplitudes and differ in phase by 120° as is the case with the voltages. If the alternator is generating a 120 V rms for each phase, we have

$$E_{nA} = 120\ \text{V}\underline{/0^\circ}$$

$$E_{nB} = 120\ \text{V}\underline{/-120^\circ}$$

$$E_{nC} = 120\ \text{V}\underline{/120^\circ}$$

From the foregoing, and as illustrated in Fig. 13-12, we have the typical three-phase balanced system, with the individual voltages equal in value and phase displacement. Hence, the three-wire *line voltage* (the total voltage applied to the balanced three-phase load) is also made up of voltages that are equal and have a 120° phase relationship to each other. Thus, the line voltage will be greater than the voltage of each individual phase. Note in Fig. 13-12 that the isosceles triangle that has E_{bA} as its base and E_{nA} as one of its sides, has base angles of 30°. Thus, the voltage E_{bA} is:

$$E_{bA} = \sqrt{3}\ E_{nA} \tag{13-1}$$

Thus, if the phase voltage is 120 volts, we have

$$E_{bA} = \sqrt{3} \times 120$$
$$= 1.73 \times 120 = 208 \text{ V}$$

The power consumed by the load is the sum of the wattages for each of the phases, and in a balanced load system they are equal.

$$P_T = 3E_{nA} I_A \cos\theta \qquad (13\text{-}2)$$

It is customary to refer to the wattages with respect to the *line voltage* (between two of the three lines), and since E_{bA} (Eq. 13-1) involves the square root of 3, we have:

$$P_T = \sqrt{3}\, E_L I_L \cos\theta \qquad (13\text{-}3)$$

The line current (I_L) can be found by the following equation:

$$I_L = \frac{P}{\sqrt{3}\, E_L \cos\theta} \qquad (13\text{-}4)$$

If the total power, line voltage, and line current are known, the following equation solves the power factor:

$$\text{power factor} = \frac{P}{1.73 E_L I_L} \qquad (13\text{-}5)$$

The following equations solve for the power and current of each phase. With a balanced load, the power will be evenly distributed and will be one-third of the total power consumed.

$$I_{nA} = \frac{I_L}{1.73} \qquad (13\text{-}6)$$

$$P_{nA} = \frac{P_T}{3} = E_{nA} \times I_{nA} \times \cos\theta \qquad (13\text{-}7)$$

13-9. DELTA AND WYE INTERCONNECTIONS

Figure 13-13A shows the *Y generator* feeding a *Y* load. Since this is a balanced load (with each section of the *Y* load presumed to have the same impedance) the neutral wire is not necessary. However, where

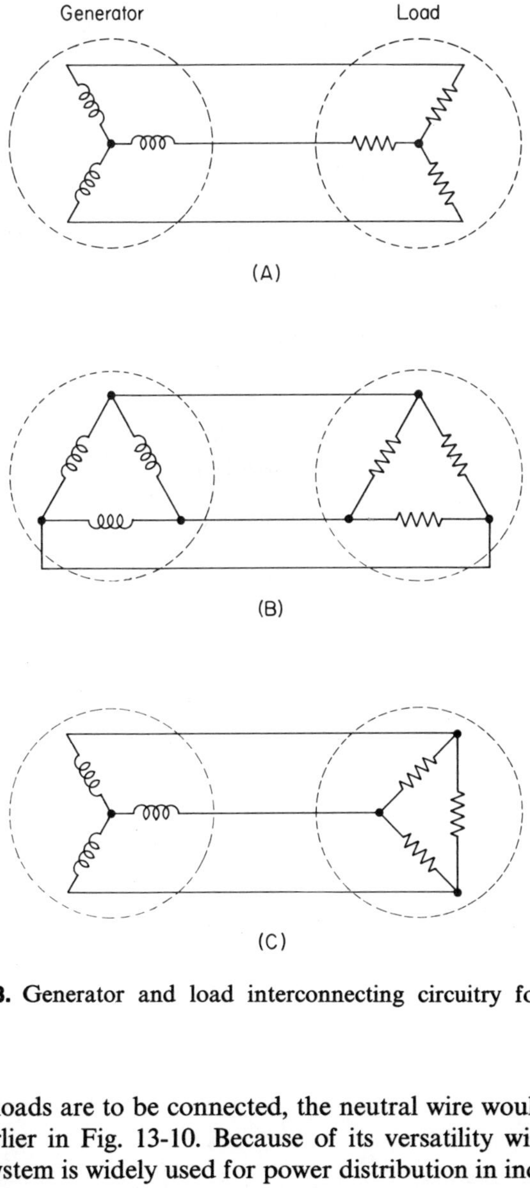

FIGURE 13-13. Generator and load interconnecting circuitry for *Y* and delta systems.

single-phase loads are to be connected, the neutral wire would be included as shown earlier in Fig. 13-10. Because of its versatility with the neutral wire, the *Y* system is widely used for power distribution in industry.

The delta system is not as extensively used as the *Y* because the common center junction is not present, and a lack of the neutral ground wire prevents use of the single-phase loads as with the four-wire system. In part B the delta generator is shown connected to a delta-wire load system. Again a balanced system is presumed, and the same power formula used earlier for the *Y* system also applies here (Eq. 13-3).

A *Y generator* can also feed a delta load, as shown in Fig. 13-13C. Similarly, a delta generator could feed a *Y* load, using the interconnections shown in C.

13-10. THREE-PHASE TRANSFORMERS

In three-phase distribution systems (as in single phase), transformers are used for changing the power main voltages to those desired at the load. With transformers, the primary and secondary windings can both be delta or *Y*, or the two can be interchanged as in the generator vs. load systems just discussed.

Figure 13-14 shows a transformer with a delta primary and a *Y* secondary winding. The turns ratio determines the voltages obtained from the secondary windings. It was mentioned earlier that the voltages measured between the lines are referred to as the line voltages, as opposed to the four-wire system where one voltage is measured with reference to the neutral or ground wire.

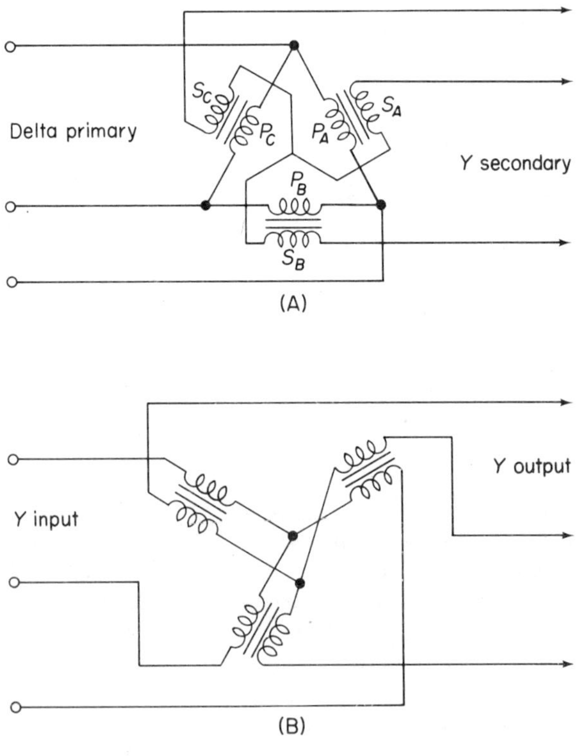

FIGURE 13-14. Three-phase ac transformers.

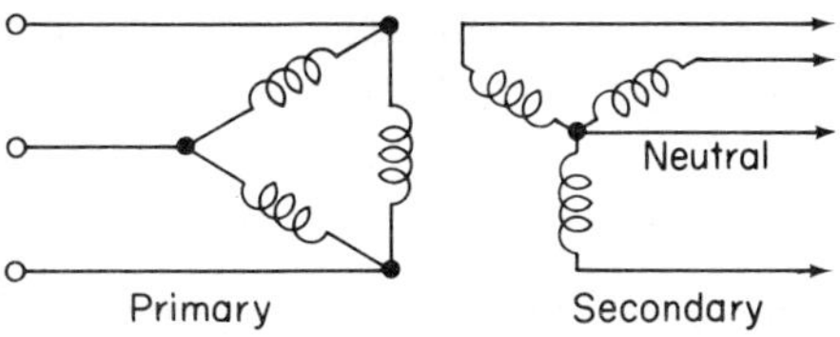

FIGURE 13-15. Delta transformer primary to four-wire *Y* secondary.

The transformer shown in part B has a *Y* winding for the primary as well as for the secondary. Both the illustrations in parts A and B are awkward representations of the three-phase transformer system, and often the transformer resembles the one shown in Fig. 13-15. Here, the core material is assumed to be part of the transformer, and the drawings simply indicate the type of windings in the primary and secondary. For 13-15, we again have a delta primary. With the delta primary, we can still have a four-wire system by connecting the secondary to a *Y winding* and attaching the neutral wire as shown. The turns ratio of each primary vs. secondary winding again establishes the voltage at the secondary.

Example

A three-phase transformer has a turns ratio of 60 to 1 for each phase winding. If the primary voltage per phase is 13,200 V, what is the secondary voltage per phase, and the line voltage for a *Y* secondary?

Solution

Turns ratio = 60 to 1

$$\frac{13{,}200}{60} = 220 \text{ V per phase}$$

$$E_L = 1.73 \times 220 \text{ V} = 380.6 \text{ V}$$

13-11. PEAK, AVERAGE, AND EFFECTIVE VALUES

The peak of one alternation of a sinewave is of only momentary duration, though that value represents the maximum voltage or current value attained periodically. By dividing the sinewave alternation into a number of ordinates and averaging them, we obtain what is known as the *average value* of alternating current or voltage.

$$E_{\text{average}} = 0.637 \times E_{\text{peak}} \qquad (13\text{-}8)$$

Equation 13-8 also applies to the average current. For finding the peak value when the average is known, the following equation applies:

$$E_{\text{peak}} = 1.57 \times E_{\text{average}} \tag{13-9}$$

The *effective value* of voltage or current is that which is equivalent to the dc value. That is, a 120-V electric light bulb will give as much light when used on 120-V dc as it will for 120-$V_{\text{effective}}$ ac. The effective value is obtained by taking a number of instantaneous values, squaring them, adding the squared values, and then finding the average value. The square root of the average value produces the *effective* value. This is also termed the *rms value* (*root mean square*). The following equations apply:

$$E_{\text{effective}} = 0.707 \times E_{\text{peak}} \tag{13-10}$$

$$E_{\text{peak}} = 1/0.707 = 1.414 \times E_{\text{eff}} \tag{13-11}$$

Again, Eqs. 13-10 and 13-11 also apply to currents. For these equations the 0.707 = one-half of the square root of 2, while 1.414 equals the square root of 2.

14

Miscellaneous Tables and Related Information

14-1. LIST OF TABLES IN OTHER CHAPTERS

In addition to the tables given in this chapter, a number of others also appear in this text where appropriate to the particular topics discussed. The following listing gives the section numbers where the additional tables may be found, as well as the table number and title.

Section Number	Table Number	Title
2-1	2-1	Miscellaneous Abbreviations and Symbols
	2-2	Bipolar Parameter Symbols
	2-3	Miscellaneous FET Symbols
2-3	2-4	Resistance in Ohms (Ω)
2-4	2-5	Ceramic Types
	2-6	Mica Types
3-1	3-1	SI Units and Symbols
3-2	3-2	Comparison Between *mks* and *cgs*
3-3	3-3	Decibel Comparisons of E, I, and P
3-5	3-4	Standard Prefixes and Letter Symbols
	3-5	System Differences
3-12	3-6	Time Constants
	3-7	Exponential Functions
7-1	7-1	VHF Television Station Allocations (U.S.)
	7-2	UHF Television Station Allocations (U.S.)

Section Number	Table Number	Title
7-4	7-3	CB Listings
	7-4	Amateur Listings
7-5		General Frequency Designations
7-6		Military Frequency Designations
7-7		The International Morse Code
9-3	9-1	OR Logic (A+B+C)
	9-2	OR Logic (0+1)
	9-3	AND Logic (ABC)
15-9	15-1	Conversion Factors Involving Length
	15-2	Conversion Factors Involving Velocity or Speed
15-13	15-3	Greek Alphabet

14-2. LOGARITHMS

Common or natural logarithms can be read on scientific calculators or obtained from tables. The basic factors relating to both types are discussed in this section, and appropriate examples are included. Initially the common logarithm factors are covered and referenced to Table 14-1. Natural (Napierian) logarithms are given at the end of this section.

In Chapter 3, Sec. 3-5, Powers and Prefixes, it was shown that powers of 10 could be expressed as 10^1, 100 as 10^2, and 1,000 as 10^3, etc. Obviously, intermediate power values for numbers between 10 and 100, or between 100 and 1,000, also exist. Similarly, powers for numbers below 10 are also in existence and can be represented by 10 to some fractional power. Inasmuch as 10^0 is equal to 1 and 10^1 is equal to 10, the exponent of a number between 1 and 10 would be a fractional exponent, since it must be less than 1. A *logarithm table* shows the powers for the intermediate numbers mentioned above. A logarithm (abbreviated "log") is the exponent of the intermediate number, without the base written in. The left-hand vertical column of numbers in Table 14-1 represents the intermediate numbers for which the logarithm is to be found, and the succeeding vertical columns show the logarithm or exponent without the base. For instance, the logarithm of the number 3 is 0.4771. This means that, instead of expressing 3 as 10 to the 0.4771 power, the 0.4771 is written without the base 10, and hence is known as the logarithm or log of 3. Since the base is 10, the log of 30 or 300 or 3,000 would contain the same digits as for log 3, except for the decimal point. When 10 is expressed as 10^1, and 100 is expressed as 10^2, it is obvious that the exponent of numbers between 10 and 100 must fall between 1 and 2. For the same reason then, the logarithm of a number between 10 and 100 must be between 1 and 2. Hence, to express the log of 30, the original number 0.4771 is employed, but it must be added to the original exponent in 10^1 and, therefore, would equal 1.4771. Since the power of 10 for the number 100 is 10^2, the power of 10 for 300 would be $10^{2.4771}$. Hence, the logarithm of 300 is 2.4771. Therefore, the logarithm to the right of a decimal point does not change when additional zeros are added to the original number. The number to the left of the decimal point, however, does increase by a numerical value of 1 each time the original number is multiplied by 10. The fractional portion of the logarithm (to the right of the decimal point) is known as the *mantissa* and is always *positive*. The whole number to the left of the decimal point is known as the *characteristic*, and may be positive or negative. (It is impossible to take the log of a negative number or of zero.)

TABLE 14-1. Common Logarithms

N	0	1	2	3	4	5	6	7	8	9
10	0000	0043	0086	0128	0170	0212	0253	0294	0334	0374
11	0414	0453	0492	0531	0569	0607	0645	0682	0719	0755
12	0792	0828	0864	0899	0934	0969	1004	1038	1072	1106
13	1139	1173	1206	1239	1271	1303	1335	1367	1399	1430
14	1461	1492	1523	1553	1584	1614	1644	1673	1703	1732
15	1761	1790	1818	1847	1875	1903	1931	1959	1987	2014
16	2041	2068	2095	2122	2148	2175	2201	2227	2253	2279
17	2304	2330	2355	2380	2405	2430	2455	2480	2504	2529
18	2553	2577	2601	2625	2648	2672	2695	2718	2742	2765
19	2788	2810	2833	2856	2878	2900	2923	2945	2967	2989
20	3010	3032	3054	3075	3096	3118	3139	3160	3181	3201
21	3222	3243	3263	3284	3304	3324	3345	3365	3385	3404
22	3424	3444	3464	3483	3502	3522	3541	3560	3579	3598
23	3617	3636	3655	3674	3692	3711	3729	3747	3766	3784
24	3802	3820	3838	3856	3874	3892	3909	3927	3945	3962
25	3979	3997	4014	4031	4048	4065	4082	4099	4116	4133
26	4150	4166	4183	4200	4216	4232	4249	4265	4281	4298
27	4314	4330	4346	4362	4378	4393	4409	4425	4440	4456
28	4472	4487	4502	4518	4533	4548	4564	4579	4594	4609
29	4624	4639	4654	4669	4683	4698	4713	4728	4742	4757
30	4771	4786	4800	4814	4829	4843	4857	4871	4886	4900
31	4914	4928	4942	4955	4969	4983	4997	5011	5024	5038
32	5051	5065	5079	5092	5105	5119	5132	5145	5159	5172
33	5185	5198	5211	5224	5237	5250	5263	5276	5289	5302
34	5315	5328	5340	5353	5366	5378	5391	5403	5416	5428

TABLE 14-1. (*Continued*)

N	0	1	2	3	4	5	6	7	8	9
35	5441	5453	5465	5478	5490	5502	5514	5527	5539	5551
36	5563	5575	5587	5599	5611	5623	5635	5647	5658	5670
37	5682	5694	5705	5717	5729	5740	5752	5763	5775	5786
38	5798	5809	5821	5832	5843	5855	5866	5877	5888	5899
39	5911	5922	5933	5944	5955	5966	5977	5988	5999	6010
40	6021	6031	6042	6053	6064	6075	6085	6096	6107	6117
41	6128	6138	6149	6160	6170	6180	6191	6201	6212	6222
42	6232	6243	6253	6263	6274	6284	6294	6304	6314	6325
43	6335	6345	6355	6365	6375	6385	6395	6405	6415	6425
44	6435	6444	6454	6464	6474	6484	6493	6503	6513	6522
45	6532	6542	6551	6561	6571	6580	6590	6599	6609	6618
46	6628	6637	6646	6656	6665	6675	6684	6693	6702	6712
47	6721	6730	6739	6749	6758	6767	6776	6785	6794	6803
48	6812	6821	6830	6839	6848	6857	6866	6875	6884	6893
49	6902	6911	6920	6928	6937	6946	6955	6964	6972	6981
50	6990	6998	7007	7016	7024	7033	7042	7050	7059	7067
51	7076	7084	7093	7101	7110	7118	7126	7135	7143	7152
52	7160	7168	7177	7185	7193	7202	7210	7218	7226	7235
53	7243	7251	7259	7267	7275	7284	7292	7300	7308	7316
54	7324	7332	7340	7348	7356	7364	7372	7380	7388	7396
55	7404	7412	7419	7427	7435	7443	7451	7459	7466	7474
56	7482	7490	7497	7505	7513	7520	7528	7536	7543	7551
57	7559	7566	7574	7582	7589	7597	7604	7612	7619	7627
58	7634	7642	7649	7657	7664	7672	7679	7686	7694	7701
59	7709	7716	7723	7731	7738	7745	7752	7760	7767	7774
60	7782	7789	7796	7803	7810	7818	7825	7832	7839	7846
61	7853	7860	7868	7875	7882	7889	7896	7903	7910	7917
62	7924	7931	7938	7945	7952	7959	7966	7973	7980	7987
63	7993	8000	8007	8014	8021	8028	8035	8041	8048	8055
64	8062	8069	8075	8082	8089	8096	8102	8109	8116	8122
65	8129	8136	8142	8149	8156	8162	8169	8176	8182	8189
66	8195	8202	8209	8215	8222	8228	8235	8241	8248	8254
67	8261	8267	8274	8280	8287	8293	8299	8306	8312	8319
68	8325	8331	8338	8344	8351	8357	8363	8370	8376	8382
69	8388	8395	8401	8407	8414	8420	8426	8432	8439	8445
70	8451	8457	8463	8470	8476	8482	8488	8494	8500	8506
71	8513	8519	8525	8531	8537	8543	8549	8555	8561	8567
72	8573	8579	8585	8591	8597	8603	8609	8615	8621	8627
73	8633	8639	8645	8651	8657	8663	8669	8675	8681	8686
74	8692	8698	8704	8710	8716	8722	8727	8733	8739	8745

TABLE 14-1. (*Continued*)

N	0	1	2	3	4	5	6	7	8	9
75	8751	8756	8762	8768	8774	8779	8785	8791	8797	8802
76	8808	8814	8820	8825	8831	8837	8842	8848	8854	8859
77	8865	8871	8876	8882	8887	8893	8899	8904	8910	8915
78	8921	8927	8932	8938	8943	8949	8954	8960	8965	8971
79	8976	8982	8987	8993	8998	9004	9009	9015	9020	9025
80	9031	9036	9042	9047	9053	9058	9063	9069	9074	9079
81	9085	9090	9096	9101	9106	9112	9117	9122	9128	9133
82	9138	9143	9149	9154	9159	9165	9170	9175	9180	9186
83	9191	9196	9201	9206	9212	9217	9222	9227	9232	9238
84	9243	9248	9253	9258	9263	9269	9274	9279	9284	9289
85	9294	9299	9304	9309	9315	9320	9325	9330	9335	9340
86	9345	9350	9355	9360	9365	9370	9375	9380	9385	9390
87	9395	9400	9405	9410	9415	9420	9425	9430	9435	9440
88	9445	9450	9455	9460	9465	9469	9474	9479	9484	9489
89	9494	9499	9504	9509	9513	9518	9523	9528	9533	9538
90	9542	9547	9552	9557	9562	9566	9571	9576	9581	9586
91	9590	9595	9600	9605	9609	9614	9619	9624	9628	9633
92	9638	9643	9647	9652	9657	9661	9666	9671	9675	9680
93	9685	9689	9694	9699	9703	9708	9713	9717	9722	9727
94	9731	9736	9741	9745	9750	9754	9759	9763	9768	9773
95	9777	9782	9786	9791	9795	9800	9805	9809	9814	9818
96	9823	9827	9832	9836	9841	9845	9850	9854	9859	9863
97	9868	9872	9877	9881	9886	9890	9894	9899	9903	9908
98	9912	9917	9921	9926	9930	9934	9939	9943	9948	9952
99	9956	9961	9965	9969	9974	9978	9983	9987	9991	9996

Numbers may not be simply single digits followed by zeros. For instance, to find the logarithm of 2,720, the number 27 is located in the left-hand column of the table. Along the horizontal row of columns, the logarithm under 2 is now found in order to complete the logarithm of 272. This is found to be 4346. To place the decimal point, the decimal point in the original number is moved to the left until the remaining number lies between 1 and 10. Thus, the decimal point is placed in the original number so that the latter is 2.720. Since the decimal place was moved three places, this number forms the characteristic of 3. Hence, the logarithm of 2,720 is 3.4346. As another example, to find the logarithm of 60,000, locate the number 60 in the left-hand column. Since the original number has no additional digits, read the number 7782 in the zero column next to the original number 60. Point off the original number to the left until only one digit (between 1 and 10) remains. This requires the pointing off of 4 places. Hence, the characteristic is 4, and the log of 60,000 is 4.7782.

The logarithm of fractional powers can also be ascertained. As an illustration, assume that the logarithm of the number 0.0015 is to be found. The number 15 is located in the left-hand column and, since there are no additional digits following this number, the initial logarithm obtained is 1761. This is expressed as 0.1761, and the decimal place in the original number is moved to the right until a single digit remains to the left of the decimal number. Thus, the decimal number is moved to the right three places in the original number, indicating that the characteristic is 3. Hence, the log of 0.0015 is $-3+0.1761$. The latter number can also be expressed as $\bar{3}.1761$, with the overbar at 3 indicating that the characteristic alone is negative. It would be incorrect to write the number as -3.1761, since this would imply that both the characteristic and mantissa are negative. The number $\bar{3}.1761$ can also be written as 7.1761 minus 10.

If the logarithm for a given number is known, the original number can be ascertained from the log table. This process yields the *antilogarithm* and, in such a procedure, the original number, which produced the logarithm, is known as the *antilog*. For instance, to find the antilog of 2.6599, the .6599 portion of the number is located in the logarithm table. This provides the number 457. The latter number must be assumed to be a number between 1 and 10 and, hence, it is considered to be 4.57. Since the characteristic of the number for which the antilog is to be found is 2, the decimal place is moved over 2 points to give 457 for the antilog.

Earlier in Chapter 3, Secs. 3-12 and 3-15 (Equations 3-24 and 3-39), examples of the applications of log functions to capacitors and inductors were given. Exponential functions were given in Table 3-7 for determining values of ϵ^{-x} where ϵ is 2.71828... (base of Napierian or natural logs). On occasion the $\log\epsilon$ is given as L_ϵ though often in scientific calculators it is given as L_N to represent natural logs.

The L_ϵ of a number is approximately 2.3026 times the common log (L_{10}) of the same number. The L_{10} of a number is 0.4343 times the L_ϵ of the same number (or L_{10} is L_ϵ of the number divided by 2.30259). Thus, using the same number 2,720 as the example given earlier, the L_ϵ of this number is 7.9083. When 7.9083 is multiplied by 0.4343, we obtain 3.4345746, or 3.4346 obtained earlier for the common log. To find L_ϵ when L_{10} is given, we have 3.4346 multiplied by $2.3026 = 7.7085$ which is off slightly because the 2.3026 multiplier yields only a close approximation.

The natural logs are also useful for performing other mathematical tasks. As an example, to find $28^{3.2}$ using the scientific calculator keys, we would enter 28 and depress the L_N key, then multiply the results by 3.2 to get 10.66272. Now punching the ϵ^x key gives us the answer of 42,732. Similarly we can find cube roots or larger roots easily. Thus, to solve for $\sqrt[3]{34{,}012{,}224}$ we enter 34012224 and depress the L_N key and divide by 3 to obtain 5.7806666. Now the ϵ^x key is depressed to obtain the answer of

323.97 or 324. Similarly, to find $\sqrt[5]{17,210,368}$ we enter the 17210368 and depress L_N and divide by the root identification 5 to obtain 3.3322. Now depressing the ϵ^x key gives the answer of 27.999=28.

If the ϵ^x of a number is given, the number can be found by taking L_N. Thus, if $\epsilon^x=8103$, this number is entered and the L_N key depressed to yield 9. On the other hand if $L_N=2.1972$, the ϵ^x gives 9 as the original number.

14-3. TRIGONOMETRIC RELATIONSHIPS

Trigonometry is the study of various angles and the mathematical relationships among them. That branch of trigonometry relating to *right angle triangles* is reviewed here. As shown in Fig. 14-1A, the sides of a triangle are assigned specific names *using the angle as the reference*. Thus, if we are calculating for the angle at the lower right of the triangle in Fig. 14-1A, the horizontal line extending from this angle is designated as the *side adjacent* to the angle. The vertical line opposite the angle is called the *side opposite*, and the diagonal line from the side opposite to the angle is known as the *hypotenuse*. The angle is the reference point and, as shown in Fig. 14-1B, the designations follow a pattern similar to that of Fig. 14-1A.

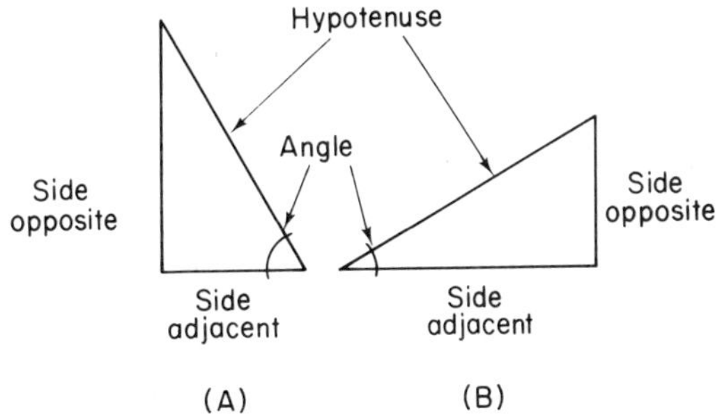

FIGURE 14-1. Triangle terms.

In electronic work, the angles involved in ac are often important in circuit analysis and design, since the opposition to ac offered by capacitors and inductors must be calculated on the basis of simple trigonometry.

A useful form of trigonometry consists in solving for unknown lengths of a triangle by employing the known angle in conjunction with the length of one of the sides. The relationships of the sides can also be employed to ascertain the angles. For instance, the ratio of the length of the side opposite to the length of the hypotenuse determines the angle.

Relationships also hold for the ratio of the opposite side to the adjacent side, etc. When such ratios are set down in table form (see Table 14-2, which follows), the various angles of triangles can be ascertained by calculating the ratio of lengths of the sides. The following are some of the most frequently used ratios:

$$\frac{\text{Opposite side}}{\text{Hypotenuse}} = \sin\theta \text{ (sine of the angle)} \qquad (14\text{-}1)$$

$$\frac{\text{Opposite}}{\text{Adjacent}} = \tan\theta \text{ (tangent of the angle)} \qquad (14\text{-}2)$$

$$\frac{\text{Adjacent}}{\text{Hypotenuse}} = \cos\theta \text{ (cosine of an angle)} \qquad (14\text{-}3)$$

TABLE 14-2. Trigonometric Ratios

Degrees	(opp)/(hyp) Sin	(adj)/(hyp) Cos	(opp)/(adj) Tan	Degrees	(opp)/(hyp) Sin	(adj)/(hyp) Cos	(opp)/(adj) Tan
0	0.0000	1.0000	0.0000	20	0.3420	0.9397	0.3640
1	.0175	.9998	.0175	21	.3584	.9336	.3839
2	.0349	.9994	.0349	22	.3746	.9272	.4040
3	.0523	.9986	.0524	23	.3907	.9205	.4245
4	.0698	.9976	.0699	24	.4067	.9135	.4452
5	.0872	.9962	.0875	25	.4226	.9063	.4663
6	.1045	.9945	.1051	26	.4384	.8988	.4877
7	.1219	.9925	.1228	27	.4540	.8910	.5095
8	.1392	.9903	.1405	28	.4695	.8829	.5317
9	.1564	.9877	.1584	29	.4848	.8746	.5543
10	.1736	.9848	.1763	30	.5000	.8660	.5774
11	.1908	.9816	.1944	31	.5150	.8572	.6009
12	.2079	.9781	.2126	32	.5299	.8480	.6249
13	.2250	.9744	.2309	33	.5446	.8387	.6494
14	.2419	.9703	.2493	34	.5592	.8290	.6745
15	.2588	.9659	.2679	35	.5736	.8192	.7002
16	.2756	.9613	.2867	36	.5878	.8090	.7265
17	.2924	.9563	.3057	37	.6018	.7986	.7536
18	.3090	.9511	.3249	38	.6157	.7880	.7813
19	.3256	.9455	.3443	39	.6293	.7771	.8098

TABLE 14-2. (*Continued*)

Degrees	(opp)/(hyp) Sin	(adj)/(hyp) Cos	(opp)/(adj) Tan	Degrees	(opp)/(hyp) Sin	(adj)/(hyp) Cos	(opp)/(adj) Tan
40	.6428	.7660	.8391	65	.9063	.4226	2.1445
41	.6561	.7547	.8693	66	.9135	.4067	2.2460
42	.6691	.7431	.9004	67	.9205	.3907	2.3559
43	.6820	.7314	.9325	68	.9272	.3746	2.4751
44	.6947	.7193	.9657	69	.9336	.3584	2.6051
45	.7071	.7071	1.0000	70	.9397	.3420	2.7475
46	.7193	.6947	1.0355	71	.9455	.3256	2.9042
47	.7314	.6820	1.0724	72	.9511	.3090	3.0777
48	.7431	.6691	1.1106	73	.9563	.2924	3.2709
49	.7547	.6561	1.1504	74	.9613	.2756	3.4874
50	.7660	.6428	1.1918	75	.9659	.2588	3.7321
51	.7771	.6293	1.2349	76	.9703	.2419	4.0108
52	.7880	.6157	1.2799	77	.9744	.2250	4.3315
53	.7986	.6018	1.3270	78	.9781	.2079	4.7046
54	.8090	.5878	1.3764	79	.9816	.1908	5.1446
55	.8192	.5736	1.4281	80	.9848	.1736	5.6713
56	.8290	.5592	1.4826	81	.9877	.1564	6.3138
57	.8387	.5446	1.5399	82	.9903	.1392	7.1154
58	.8480	.5299	1.6003	83	.9925	.1219	8.1443
59	.8572	.5150	1.6643	84	.9945	.1045	9.5144
60	.8660	.5000	1.7321	85	.9962	.0872	11.4301
61	.8746	.4848	1.8040	86	.9976	.0698	14.3007
62	.8829	.4695	1.8807	87	.9986	.0523	19.0811
63	.8910	.4540	1.9626	88	.9994	.0349	28.6363
64	.8988	.4384	2.0503	89	.9998	.0175	57.2900
				90	1.0000	.0000	......

Tables such as 14-2 are accurate only to the degree of the number of places shown. Thus, a four-place number may have been a five or six place one originally and was rounded off. Thus for 70° in the table the sine is .9397, but a scientific calculator may display 0.93969. For the scientific calculators the inverse trigonometric functions are useful for relating the angle to any of the trigonometric functions. Thus, if the tangent is given as 0.26795, we enter this on the keyboard and depress $\tan^{-1}$ to obtain 15°.

Similarly, if the cosine is 0.91355 depressing the $\cos^{-1}$ key gives us the angle (24°).

The degree/radian switch on scientific calculators is also useful for converting to either mode as needed. Thus, to solve for $(\tan\pi/4)$ we enter the $\pi/4$ and set the switch to RAD, then depress the tangent key to read 1.

Another basic equation that holds for the right angle triangles is the *Pythagorean theorem*, which states that the sum of the squares of the side adjacent and the side opposite of a right triangle is equal to the square of the hypotenuse. This theory was formulated by the Greek scholar Pythagoras (about 500 B.C.) and the formula related to this theorem may be stated as follows:

$$a^2+b^2=c^2 \tag{14-4}$$

In the foregoing formula, a represents the side opposite, b the side adjacent, and c the hypotenuse. Thus, by mathematical rearrangement of the symbols and powers shown above, the hypotenuse can be ascertained

TABLE 14-3. Standard Resistor Values

Ω	Ω	Ω	Ω	Ω	Ω	MΩ	MΩ	MΩ
—	1.0	10	100	1,000	10,000	0.1	1.0	10
—	1.1	11	110	1,100	11,000	0.11	1.1	11
—	1.2	12	120	1,200	12,000	0.12	1.2	12
—	1.3	13	130	1,300	13,000	0.13	1.3	13
—	1.5	15	150	1,500	15,000	0.15	1.5	15
—	1.6	16	160	1,600	16,000	0.16	1.6	16
—	1.8	18	180	1,800	18,000	0.18	1.8	18
—	2.0	20	200	2,000	20,000	0.20	2.0	20
—	2.2	22	220	2,200	22,000	0.22	2.2	22
0.24	2.4	24	240	2,400	24,000	0.24	2.4	—
0.27	2.7	27	270	2,700	27,000	0.27	2.7	—
0.30	3.0	30	300	3,000	30,000	0.30	3.0	—
0.33	3.3	33	330	3,300	33,000	0.33	3.3	—
0.36	3.6	36	360	3,600	36,000	0.36	3.6	—
0.39	3.9	39	390	3,900	39,000	0.39	3.9	—
0.43	4.3	43	430	4,300	43,000	0.43	4.3	—
0.47	4.7	47	470	4,700	47,000	0.47	4.7	—
0.51	5.1	51	510	5,100	51,000	0.51	5.1	—
0.56	5.6	56	560	5,600	56,000	0.56	5.6	—
0.62	6.2	62	620	6,200	62,000	0.62	6.2	—
0.68	6.8	68	680	6,800	68,000	0.68	6.8	—
0.75	7.5	75	750	7,500	75,000	0.75	7.5	—
0.82	8.2	82	820	8,200	82,000	0.82	8.2	—
0.91	9.1	91	910	9,100	91,000	0.91	9.1	—

from the following formula:

$$c = \sqrt{a^2 + b^2} \tag{14-5}$$

This equation, except for the substitution of electronic symbols instead of the a, b, and c symbols, is used extensively.

TABLE 14-4. Resonant Frequency or Wavelength for a Given *LC* Product

Wavelength (meters)	Frequency in kHz	$L \times C$ ($L = \mu$H) ($C = \mu$F)	Wavelength (meters)	Frequency in kHz	$L \times C$ ($L = \mu$H) ($C = \mu$F)
1	300,000	0.0000003	220	1,364	0.01362
2	150,000	0.0000111	230	1,304	0.01489
3	100,000	0.0000018	240	1,250	0.01621
4	75,000	0.0000045	250	1,200	0.01759
5	60,000	0.0000057	260	1,154	0.01903
6	50,000	0.0000101	270	1,111	0.0205
7	42,900	0.0000138	280	1,071	0.0221
8	37,500	0.0000180	290	1,034	0.0237
9	33,333	0.0000228	300	1,000	0.0253
10	30,000	0.0000282	310	968	0.0270
20	15,000	0.0001129	320	938	0.0288
30	10,000	0.0002530	330	909	0.0306
40	7,500	0.0004500	340	883	0.0325
50	6,000	0.0007040	350	857	0.0345
60	5,000	0.0010140	360	834	0.0365
70	4,290	0.0013780	370	811	0.0385
80	3,750	0.0018010	380	790	0.0406
90	3,333	0.0022800	390	769	0.0428
100	3,000	0.00282	400	750	0.0450
110	2,727	0.00341	410	732	0.0473
120	2,500	0.00405	420	715	0.0496
130	2,308	0.00476	430	698	0.0520
140	2,143	0.00552	440	682	0.0545
150	2,000	0.00633	450	667	0.0570
160	1,875	0.00721	460	652	0.0596
170	1,764	0.00813	470	639	0.0622
180	1,667	0.00912	480	625	0.0649
190	1,579	0.01015	490	612	0.0676
200	1,500	0.01126	500	600	0.0704
210	1,429	0.01241	505	594	0.0718

TABLE 14-4. (*Continued*)

Wavelength (meters)	Frequency in kHz	$L \times C$ ($L = \mu$H) ($C = \mu$F)	Wavelength (meters)	Frequency in kHz	$L \times C$ ($L = \mu$H) ($C = \mu$F)
510	588	0.0732	685	438	0.1321
515	583	0.0747	690	435	0.1340
520	577	0.0761	695	432	0.1360
525	572	0.0776	700	429	0.1379
530	566	0.0791	705	426	0.1399
535	561	0.0806	710	423	0.1419
540	556	0.0821	715	420	0.1439
545	551	0.0836	720	417	0.1459
550	546	0.0852	725	414	0.1479
555	541	0.0867	730	411	0.1500
560	536	0.0883	735	408	0.1521
565	531	0.0899	740	405	0.1541
570	527	0.0915	745	403	0.1562
575	522	0.0931	750	400	0.1583
580	517	0.0947	755	397	0.1604
585	513	0.0963	760	395	0.1626
590	509	0.0980	765	392	0.1647
595	504	0.0996	770	390	0.1669
600	500	0.1013	775	387	0.1690
605	496	0.1030	780	385	0.1712
610	492	0.1047	785	382	0.1734
615	488	0.1065	790	380	0.1756
620	484	0.1082	795	377	0.1779
625	480	0.1100	800	375	0.1801
630	476	0.1117	805	373	0.1824
635	472	0.1135	810	370	0.1847
640	469	0.1153	815	368	0.1870
645	465	0.1171	820	366	0.1893
650	462	0.1189	825	364	0.1916
655	458	0.1208	830	361	0.1939
660	455	0.1226	835	359	0.1962
665	451	0.1245	840	357	0.1986
670	448	0.1264	845	355	0.201
675	444	0.1283	850	353	0.203
680	441	0.1302	855	351	0.206

TABLE 14-4. (*Continued*)

Wavelength (meters)	Frequency in kHz	$L \times C$ ($L = \mu$H) ($C = \mu$F)	Wavelength (meters)	Frequency in kHz	$L \times C$ ($L = \mu$H) ($C = \mu$F)
860	349	0.208	935	321	0.246
865	347	0.211	940	319	0.249
870	345	0.213	945	317	0.251
875	343	0.216	950	316	0.254
880	341	0.218	955	314	0.257
885	339	0.220	960	313	0.259
890	337	0.223	965	311	0.262
895	335	0.225	970	309	0.265
900	333	0.228	975	308	0.268
905	331	0.231	980	306	0.270
910	330	0.233	985	305	0.273
915	328	0.236	990	303	0.276
920	326	0.238	995	302	0.279
925	324	0.241	1000	300	0.282
930	323	0.243			

TABLE 14-5. Conversion Table: Kilohertz to Meters (or Meters to Kilohertz)

kHz (meters)	meters kHz	kHz or m	m or kHz	kHz or m	m or kHz
10	29,982.0	360	832.8	710	422.3
20	14,991.0	370	810.3	720	416.4
30	9,994.0	380	789.0	730	410.7
40	7,496.0	390	768.8	740	405.2
50	5,996.0	400	749.6	750	399.8
60	4,997.0	410	731.3	760	394.5
70	4,283.0	420	713.9	770	389.4
80	3,748.0	430	697.3	780	384.4
90	3,331.0	440	681.4	790	379.5
100	2,998.0	450	666.3	800	374.8
110	2,726.0	460	651.8	810	370.2
120	2,499.0	470	637.9	820	365.6
130	2,306.0	480	624.6	830	361.2
140	2,142.0	490	611.9	840	356.9
150	1,999.0	500	599.6	850	352.7

TABLE 14-5. (*Continued*)

kHz (meters)	meters kHz	kHz or m	m or kHz	kHz or m	m or kHz
160	1,874.0	510	587.9	860	348.6
170	1,764.0	520	576.6	870	344.6
180	1,666.0	530	565.7	880	340.7
190	1,578.0	540	555.2	890	336.9
200	1,499.0	550	545.1	900	333.1
210	1,428.0	560	535.4	910	329.5
220	1,363.0	570	526.0	920	325.9
230	1,304.0	580	516.9	930	322.4
240	1,249.0	590	508.2	940	319.0
250	1,199.0	600	499.7	950	315.6
260	1,153.0	610	491.5	960	312.3
270	1,110.0	620	483.6	970	309.1
280	1,071.0	630	475.9	980	303.9
290	1,034.0	640	468.5	990	302.8
300	999.4	650	461.3	1000	299.8
310	967.2	660	454.3		
320	967.9	670	447.5		
330	908.6	680	440.9		
340	881.8	690	434.5		
350	856.6	700	428.3		

Note: Higher values can be obtained by shifting the decimal point. For every zero added to the first column, the decimal place in the second column is moved one place to the *left*. Thus, where 190 kHz = 1,578 m, for instance, 1900 kHz would be 157 m, or 19000 kHz = 15.78 m. Similarly, 10,000 kHz = 29.98 m.

TABLE 14-6. International Atomic Weights

Element	Symbol	Atomic Number	Atomic Weight
Actinium	Ac	89	227
Aluminum	Al	13	26.98
Americium	Am	95	*243
Antimony	Sb	51	121.76
Argon	A	18	39.944
Arsenic	As	33	74.91
Astatine	At	85	*210
Barium	Ba	56	137.36
Berkelium	Bk	97	*249
Beryllium	Be	4	9.013
Bismuth	Bi	83	209.00
Boron	B	5	10.82
Bromine	Br	35	79.916
Cadmium	Cd	48	112.41
Calcium	Ca	20	40.08

TABLE 14-6. (*Continued*)

Element	Symbol	Atomic Number	Atomic Weight
Californium	Cf	98	*249
Carbon	C	6	12.011
Cerium	Ce	58	140.13
Cesium	Cs	55	132.91
Chlorine	Cl	17	35.457
Chromium	Cr	24	52.01
Cobalt	Co	27	58.94
Copper	Cu	29	63.54
Curium	Cm	96	*245
Dysprosium	Dy	66	162.51
Einsteinium	Es	99	*255
Erbium	Er	68	167.27
Europium	Eu	63	152.0
Fermium	Fm	100	*255
Fluorine	F	9	19.00
Francium	Fr	87	*223
Gadolinium	Gd	64	157.26
Gallium	Ga	31	69.72
Germanium	Ge	32	72.60
Gold	Au	79	197.0
Hafnium	Hf	72	178.50
Helium	He	2	4.003
Holmium	Ho	67	164.94
Hydrogen	H	1	1.0080
Indium	In	49	114.82
Iodine	I	53	126.91
Iridium	Ir	77	192.2
Iron	Fe	26	55.85
Krypton	Kr	36	83.80
Lanthanum	La	57	138.92
Lawrencium	Lw	103	*257
Lead	Pb	82	207.21
Lithium	Li	3	6.940
Lutetium	Lu	71	174.99
Magnesium	Mg	12	24.32
Manganese	Mn	25	54.94
Mendelevium	Md	101	*256
Mercury	Hg	80	200.61
Molybdenum	Mo	42	95.95
Neodymium	Nd	60	144.27
Neon	Ne	10	20.183
Neptunium	Np	93	*237
Nickel	Ni	28	58.71
Niobium	Nb	41	92.91
Nitrogen	N	7	14.008

TABLE 14-6. (*Continued*)

Element	Symbol	Atomic Number	Atomic Weight
Nobelium	No	102	*253
Osmium	Os	76	190.2
Oxygen	O	8	16.000
Palladium	Pd	46	106.4
Phosphorus	P	15	30.975
Platinum	Pt	78	195.09
Plutonium	Pu	94	*242
Polonium	Po	84	210
Potassium	K	19	39.100
Praseodymium	Pr	59	140.92
Promethium	Pm	61	*145
Protactinium	Pa	91	231
Radium	Ra	88	226.05
Radon	Rn	86	222
Rhenium	Re	75	186.22
Rhodium	Rh	45	102.91
Rubidium	Rb	37	85.48
Ruthenium	Ru	44	101.1
Samarium	Sm	62	150.35
Scandium	Sc	21	44.96
Selenium	Se	34	78.96
Silicon	Si	14	28.09
Silver	Ag	47	107.880
Sodium	Na	11	22.991
Strontium	Sr	38	87.63
Sulfur	S	16	32.066
Tantalum	Ta	73	180.95
Technetium	Tc	43	*99
Tellurium	Te	52	127.61
Terbium	Tb	65	158.93
Thallium	Tl	81	204.39
Thorium	Th	90	232.05
Thulium	Tm	69	168.94
Tin	Sn	50	118.70
Titanium	Ti	22	47.90
Tungsten	W	74	183.86
Uranium	U	92	238.07
Vanadium	V	23	50.95
Xenon	Xe	54	131.30
Ytterbium	Yb	70	173.04
Yttrium	Y	39	88.92
Zinc	Zn	30	65.38
Zirconium	Zr	40	91.22

* Denotes isotope weight value for most stable type.

TABLE 14-7. Bessel Functions

Modulation Index	Carrier Amplitude	Relative Amplitude of Sidebands								
(m)	$J_0(x)$	$J_1(x)$	$J_2(x)$	$J_3(x)$	$J_4(x)$	$J_5(x)$	$J_6(x)$	$J_7(x)$	$J_8(x)$	$J_9(x)$
0	1.000									
0.01	1.000	0.005								
0.02	0.999	0.010								
0.05	0.999	0.025								
0.1	0.998	0.050								
0.2	0.990	0.100								
0.5	0.938	0.242	0.310							
1.0	0.765	0.440	0.115	0.003						
2.0	0.224	0.577	0.353	0.129	0.034					
3.0	−0.260	0.339	0.486	0.309	0.132	0.043	0.012			
4.0	−0.397	−0.066	0.364	0.430	0.281	0.132	0.049	0.015		
5.0	−0.178	−0.328	0.047	0.365	0.391	0.261	0.131	0.053	0.018	
6.0	0.151	−0.277	−0.243	0.115	0.358	0.362	0.246	0.130	0.057	0.021

Note: The table relates the number of significant sidebands to the modulation index in FM, where the modulation index m is obtained by dividing the frequency deviation of the carrier by the frequency of the modulating signal. Blank sections in the table represent sideband amplitudes that have been omitted because of insignificance. For an unmodulated wave the carrier amplitude is 1.0, though the algebraic addition of carriers and sidebands for the various values of modulation index does not produce 1.0 because ac waveforms are involved and vector addition is necessary.

TABLE 14-8. Properties of Copper Wire Conductors (American Wire Gauge)

Size (gauge no.)	Diam in mils at 20°C, 68°F	Area circular in mils	Ohms per 1,000 ft 25°C, 77°F
1	289.3	83690	0.1264
2	257.6	66370	0.1593
3	229.4	52640	0.2009
4	204.3	41740	0.2533
5	181.9	33100	0.3195
6	162.0	26250	0.4028
7	144.3	20820	0.5080
8	128.5	16510	0.6405
9	114.4	13090	0.8077
10	101.9	10380	1.018
11	90.74	8234	1.284
12	80.81	6530	1.619
13	71.96	5178	2.042
14	64.08	4107	2.575
15	57.07	3257	3.247
16	50.82	2583	4.094
17	45.26	2048	5.163
18	40.30	1624	6.510
19	35.89	1288	8.210
20	31.96	1022	10.35
21	28.46	810.1	13.05
22	25.35	642.4	16.46
23	22.57	509.5	20.76
24	20.10	404.0	26.17
25	17.90	320.4	33.00
26	15.94	254.1	41.62
27	14.20	201.5	52.48
28	12.64	159.8	66.17
29	11.26	126.7	83.44
30	10.03	100.5	105.2
31	8.928	79.70	132.7
32	7.950	63.21	167.3
33	7.080	50.13	211.0
34	6.305	39.75	266.0
35	5.615	31.52	335.0
36	5.000	25.00	423.0
37	4.453	19.83	533.4
38	3.965	15.72	672.6
39	3.531	12.47	848.1
40	3.145	9.88	1069.0

TABLE 14-9. Conversion of Inches to Millimeters

Inches	Millimeters	Inches	Millimeters	Inches	Millimeters
0.001	0.025	0.290	7.37	0.660	16.76
0.002	0.051	0.300	7.62	0.670	17.02
0.003	0.076	0.310	7.87	0.680	17.27
0.004	0.102	0.320	8.13	0.690	17.53
0.005	0.127	0.330	8.38	0.700	17.78
0.006	0.152	0.340	8.64	0.710	18.03
0.007	0.178	0.350	8.89	0.720	18.29
0.008	0.203	0.360	9.14	0.730	18.54
0.009	0.229	0.370	9.40	0.740	18.80
0.010	0.254	0.380	9.65	0.750	19.05
0.020	0.508	0.390	9.91	0.760	19.30
0.030	0.762	0.400	10.16	0.770	19.56
0.040	1.016	0.410	10.41	0.780	19.81
0.050	1.270	0.420	10.67	0.790	20.07
0.060	1.524	0.430	10.92	0.800	20.32
0.070	1.778	0.440	11.18	0.810	20.57
0.080	2.032	0.450	11.43	0.820	20.83
0.090	2.286	0.460	11.68	0.830	21.08
0.100	2.540	0.470	11.94	0.840	21.34
0.110	2.794	0.480	12.19	0.850	21.59
0.120	3.048	0.490	12.45	0.860	21.84
0.130	3.302	0.500	12.70	0.870	22.10
0.140	3.56	0.510	12.95	0.880	22.35
0.150	3.81	0.520	13.21	0.890	22.61
0.160	4.06	0.530	13.46	0.900	22.86
0.170	4.32	0.540	13.72	0.910	23.11
0.180	4.57	0.550	13.97	0.920	23.37
0.190	4.83	0.560	14.22	0.930	23.62
0.200	5.08	0.570	14.48	0.940	23.88
0.210	5.33	0.580	14.73	0.950	24.13
0.220	5.59	0.590	14.99	0.960	24.38
0.230	5.84	0.600	15.24	0.970	24.64
0.240	6.10	0.610	15.49	0.980	24.89
0.250	6.35	0.620	15.75	0.990	25.15
0.260	6.60	0.630	16.00	1.000	25.40
0.270	6.86	0.640	16.26	......	......
0.280	7.11	0.650	16.51	......	......

TABLE 14-10. Conversion of Millimeters to Inches

Millimeters	Inches	Millimeters	Inches	Millimeters	Inches
0.01	0.0004	0.35	0.0138	0.68	0.0268
0.02	0.0008	0.36	0.0142	0.69	0.0272
0.03	0.0012	0.37	0.0146	0.70	0.0276
0.04	0.0016	0.38	0.0150	0.71	0.0280
0.05	0.0020	0.39	0.0154	0.72	0.0283
0.06	0.0024	0.40	0.0157	0.73	0.0287
0.07	0.0028	0.41	0.0161	0.74	0.0291
0.08	0.0031	0.42	0.0165	0.75	0.0295
0.09	0.0035	0.43	0.0169	0.76	0.0299
0.10	0.0039	0.44	0.0173	0.77	0.0303
0.11	0.0043	0.45	0.0177	0.78	0.0307
0.12	0.0047	0.46	0.0181	0.79	0.0311
0.13	0.0051	0.47	0.0185	0.80	0.0315
0.14	0.0055	0.48	0.0189	0.81	0.0319
0.15	0.0059	0.49	0.0193	0.82	0.0323
0.16	0.0063	0.50	0.0197	0.83	0.0327
0.17	0.0067	0.51	0.0201	0.84	0.0331
0.18	0.0071	0.52	0.0205	0.85	0.0335
0.19	0.0075	0.53	0.0209	0.86	0.0339
0.20	0.0079	0.54	0.0213	0.87	0.0343
0.21	0.0083	0.55	0.0217	0.88	0.0346
0.22	0.0087	0.56	0.0220	0.89	0.0350
0.23	0.0091	0.57	0.0224	0.90	0.0354
0.24	0.0094	0.58	0.0228	0.91	0.0358
0.25	0.0098	0.59	0.0232	0.92	0.0362
0.26	0.0102	0.60	0.0236	0.93	0.0366
0.27	0.0106	0.61	0.0240	0.94	0.0370
0.28	0.0110	0.62	0.0244	0.95	0.0374
0.29	0.0114	0.63	0.0248	0.96	0.0378
0.30	0.0118	0.64	0.0252	0.97	0.0382
0.31	0.0122	0.65	0.0256	0.98	0.0386
0.32	0.0126	0.66	0.0260	0.99	0.0390
0.33	0.0130	0.67	0.0264	1.00	0.0394
0.34	0.0134	....	......	....	......

TABLE 14-11. Frequencies of Musical Tones (in Hz)

	C	C#	D	D#	E	F
Progressive Octaves	0032.703	0034.648	0036.708	0038.891	0041.203	0043.654
	0065.406	0069.296	0073.416	0077.782	0082.407	0087.307
	0130.813	0138.591	0146.832	0155.563	0164.814	0174.614
	0261.626	0277.183	0293.665	0311.127	0329.628	0349.228
	0523.251	0554.365	0587.330	0622.254	0659.255	0698.456
	1046.502	1108.731	1174.659	1244.508	1318.510	1396.913
	2093.005	2217.461	2349.318	2489.016	2637.021	2793.826
	4186.009	4434.922	4698.636	4978.032	5274.042	5587.652
	F#	**G**	**G#**	**A**	**A#**	**B**
	0046.249	0048.999	0051.913	0055.000	0058.270	0061.735
	0092.499	0097.999	0103.830	0110.000	0116.540	0123.470
	0184.997	0195.998	0207.652	0220.000	0233.082	0246.942
	0369.994	0391.955	0415.305	0440.000	0466.164	0493.883
	0739.989	0783.991	0830.609	0880.000	0932.328	0987.767
	1479.978	1567.982	1661.219	1760.000	1864.655	1975.533
	2959.955	3135.964	3322.438	3520.000	3729.310	3951.066
	5919.910	6271.928	6644.876	7040.000	7458.620	7902.132

TABLE 14-12. Binary Notation vs. Base 10

Binary Number	Base 10	Binary Number	Base 10
00000	0	01111	15
00001	1	10000	16
00010	2	10001	17
00011	3	10010	18
00100	4	10011	19
00101	5	10100	20
00110	6	10101	21
00111	7	10110	22
01000	8	10111	23
01001	9	11000	24
01010	10	11001	25
01011	11	11010	26
01100	12	11011	27
01101	13	11100	28
01110	14	11101	29

TABLE 14-12. (*Continued*)

Binary Number	Base 10	Binary Number	Base 10
11110	30	101001	41
11111	31	101010	42
100000	32	101011	43
100001	33	101100	44
100010	34	101101	45
100011	35		
100100	36		
100101	37		
100110	38		
100111	39		
101000	40		

Note: This table can be extended by following the pattern indicated. Thus, the rightmost column continues with alternate 0's and 1's. The second from right continues with dual 1's and 0's; the third from right with sets of four 1's and 0's; the fourth with sets of eight 1's and 0's, etc.

TABLE 14-13. Powers of 2

n	2^n	n	2^n
1	2	21	2097152
2	4	22	4194304
3	8	23	8388608
4	16	24	16777216
5	32	25	33554432
6	64	26	67108864
7	128	27	134217728
8	256	28	268435456
9	512	29	536870912
10	1024	30	1073741824
11	2048	31	2147483648
12	4096	32	4294967296
13	8192	33	8589934592
14	16384	34	17179869184
15	32768	35	34359738368
16	65536	36	68719476736
17	131072	37	137438953472
18	262144	38	274877906944
19	524288	39	549755813888
20	1048576	40	1099511627776

Note: Powers of 2 represent successive doubling of numerical values and indicate the progression of place values for binary numbers (see Table 14-12). Thus, a binary representation of 001 = 1 (since first place values are equal for binary and base-ten notation), but 010 represents 2, because the binary 10 represents a double of the 001 value. Similarly, 100 = 4, a doubling of the 010 value, etc. The following shows relative values and powers:

etc.	8	7	6	5	4	3	2	1	← Place
	2^7	2^6	2^5	2^4	2^3	2^2	2^1	2^0	← Power
	128	64	32	16	8	4	2	1	← Place

TABLE 14-14. Base 10, Octal and Binary Comparisons

Base 10	Octal	Binary	Base 10	Octal	Binary
0	00	000 000	21	25	010 101
1	01	000 001	22	26	010 110
2	02	000 010	23	27	010 111
3	03	000 011	24	30	011 000
4	04	000 100	25	31	011 001
5	05	000 101	26	32	011 010
6	06	000 110	27	33	011 011
7	07	000 111	28	34	011 100
8	10	001 000	29	35	011 101
9	11	001 001	30	36	011 110
10	12	001 010	31	37	011 111
11	13	001 011	32	40	100 000
12	14	001 100	33	41	100 001
13	15	001 101	34	42	100 010
14	16	001 110	35	43	100 011
15	17	001 111	36	44	100 100
16	20	010 000	37	45	100 101
17	21	010 001	38	46	100 110
18	22	010 010	39	47	100 111
19	23	010 011	40	50	101 000
20	24	010 100	41	51	101 001

Note: In octal notation, a binary number of any length is broken into sets of three bits each. The octal system has a radix (base) of eight and each three-bit binary group from right to left increases by a power of eight.

						Triad Group	
etc.	000	000	000	000	000	000	← Place
	8^5	8^4	8^3	8^2	8^1	8^0	← Power
	32,768	4096	512	64	8	1	← Value

Thus, each group of three increases in value by a factor of 8 times the numerical value of the previous group.

TABLE 14-15. Gray Code, Base 10, and Binary Comparisons

Gray Code	Binary	Base 10
0000	0000	0
0001	0001	1
0011	0010	2
0010	0011	3
0110	0100	4
0111	0101	5
0101	0110	6
0100	0111	7
1100	1000	8
1101	1001	9
1111	1010	10
1110	1011	11
1010	1100	12
1011	1101	13
1001	1110	14
1000	1111	15

The *Gray code* is a special computer code often used to code variables. It minimizes errors because only one digit changes when progressing from a given number to the next highest number. This is not the case with the binary code given in Table 14-12 (going from 7 to 8, for instance, changes four digits: 0111 to 1000). The Gray code is sometimes called the *cyclic code*, the *minimum-error code*, or the *reflected binary code*. To convert a binary number into its Gray code equivalent, the binary number is added to itself without carry, but the added number is indexed (moved over) to the right by one place, dropping the digit that would extend beyond the original number.

The following examples illustrate the conversion:

```
  1101  (binary 13)
 +1101  (binary 13 indexed to right)
 -----
  1011  (Gray code representation of 13)

 10000  (binary 16)
+10000  (indexed)
 -----
 11000  (Gray code for 16)
```

TABLE 14-16. Binary-Coded Decimal Notation

Base 10	Binary Coded		
01	0001		
02	0010		
03	0011		
04	0100		
05	0101		
etc.			
10	0001	0000	
11	0001	0001	
12	0001	0010	
etc.			
20	0010	0000	
21	0010	0001	
22	0010	0010	
etc.			
346	0011	0100	0110
758	0111	0101	1000

In binary-coded decimal notation, groups of four binary bits are used to identify the base-ten number, as shown in Table 14-16. Thus, the number 16,205 is represented as 0001 0110 0010 0000 0101.

TABLE 14-17. Squares, Cubes, and Roots

n	n^2	$\sqrt{n}$	n^3	$\sqrt[3]{n}$
1	1	1.000000	1	1.000000
2	4	1.414214	8	1.259921
3	9	1.732051	27	1.442250
4	16	2.000000	64	1.587401
5	25	2.236068	125	1.709976
6	36	2.449490	216	1.817121
7	49	2.645751	343	1.912931
8	64	2.828427	512	2.000000
9	81	3.000000	729	2.080084
10	100	3.162278	1,000	2.154435
11	121	3.316625	1,331	2.223980
12	144	3.464102	1,728	2.289428
13	169	3.605551	2,197	2.351335
14	196	3.741657	2,744	2.410142
15	225	3.872983	3,375	2.466212
16	256	4.000000	4,096	2.519842
17	289	4.123106	4,913	2.571282
18	324	4.242641	5,832	2.620741
19	361	4.358899	6,859	2.668402
20	400	4.472136	8,000	2.714418
21	441	4.582576	9,261	2.758924
22	484	4.690416	10,648	2.802039
23	529	4.795832	12,167	2.843867
24	576	4.898979	13,824	2.884499
25	625	5.000000	15,625	2.924018
26	676	5.099020	17,576	2.962496
27	729	5.196152	19,683	3.000000
28	784	5.291503	21,952	3.036589
29	841	5.385165	24,389	3.072317
30	900	5.477226	27,000	3.107233
31	961	5.567764	29,791	3.141381
32	1,024	5.656854	32,768	3.174802
33	1,089	5.744563	35,937	3.207534
34	1,156	5.830952	39,304	3.239612
35	1,225	5.916080	42,875	3.271066
36	1,296	6.000000	46,656	3.301927
37	1,369	6.082763	50,653	3.332222
38	1,444	6.164414	54,872	3.361975
39	1,521	6.244998	59,319	3.391211
40	1,600	6.324555	64,000	3.419952

TABLE 14-17. (*Continued*)

n	n^2	$\sqrt{n}$	n^3	$\sqrt[3]{n}$
41	1,681	6.403124	68,921	3.448217
42	1,764	6.480741	74,088	3.476027
43	1,849	6.557439	79,507	3.503398
44	1,936	6.633250	85,184	3.530348
45	2,025	6.708204	91,125	3.556893
46	2,116	6.782330	97,336	3.583048
47	2,209	6.855655	103,823	3.608826
48	2,304	6.928203	110,592	3.634241
49	2,401	7.000000	117,649	3.659306
50	2,500	7.071068	125,000	3.684031
51	2,601	7.141428	132,651	3.708430
52	2,704	7.211103	140,608	3.732511
53	2,809	7.280110	148,877	3.765286
54	2,916	7.348469	157,464	3.779763
55	3,025	7.416198	166,375	3.802952
56	3,136	7.483315	175,616	3.825862
57	3,249	7.549834	185,193	3.848501
58	3,364	7.615773	195,112	3.870877
59	3,481	7.681146	205,379	3.892996
60	3,600	7.745967	216,000	3.914868
61	3,721	7.810250	226,981	3.936497
62	3,844	7.874008	238,328	3.957892
63	3,969	7.937254	250,047	3.979057
64	4,096	8.000000	262,144	4.000000
65	4,225	8.062258	274,625	4.020726
66	4,356	8.124038	287,496	4.041240
67	4,489	8.185353	300,763	4.061548
68	4,624	8.246211	314,432	4.081655
69	4,761	8.306624	328,509	4.101566
70	4,900	8.366600	343,000	4.121285
71	5,041	8.426150	357,911	4.140818
72	5,184	8.485281	373,248	4.160168
73	5,329	8.544004	389,017	4.179339
74	5,476	8.602325	405,224	4.198336
75	5,625	8.660254	421,875	4.217163
76	5,776	8.717798	438,976	4.235824
77	5,929	8.774964	456,533	4.254321
78	6,084	8.831761	474,552	4.272659
79	6,241	8.888194	493,039	4.290840
80	6,400	8.944272	512,000	4.308869

TABLE 14-17. (*Continued*)

n	n^2	$\sqrt{n}$	n^3	$\sqrt[3]{n}$
81	6,561	9.000000	531,441	4.326749
82	6,724	9.055385	551,368	4.344481
83	6,889	9.110434	571,787	4.362071
84	7,056	9.165151	592,704	4.379519
85	7,225	9.219544	614,125	4.396830
86	7,396	9.273618	636,056	4.414005
87	7,569	9.327379	658,503	4.431048
88	7,744	9.380832	681,472	4.447960
89	7,921	9.433981	704,969	4.464745
90	8,100	9.486833	729,000	4.481405
91	8,281	9.539392	753,571	4.497941
92	8,464	9.591663	778,688	4.514357
93	8,649	9.643651	804,357	4.530655
94	8,836	9.695360	830,584	4.546836
95	9,025	9.746794	857,375	4.562903
96	9,216	9.797959	884,736	4.578857
97	9,409	9.848858	912,673	4.594701
98	9,604	9.899495	941,192	4.610436
99	9,801	9.949874	970,299	4.626065
100	10,000	10.000000	1,000,000	4.641589

15 Miscellaneous Information and Data

15-1. HIGH-FIDELITY TERMS

Stereo receivers, amplifiers, phonograph cartridges, and record player devices are rated in terms of how well the units perform. Such ratings involve clarity of sound reproduction, audio power output, RF signal pickup, and other such characteristics. Manufacturers have adopted acceptable standards as the basis for evaluating published ratings. Uniform standards among manufacturers, however, have been difficult to obtain because design engineers often employ different testing procedures. Though a number of general standards are used, there are instances where manufacturers upgrade the ratings of their equipment and devices. The most common performance terms are given in this section, and these have been widely used by all manufacturers and publications.

AM Suppression (or Rejection). This phrase refers to an FM receiver's ability to reject amplitude modulation (AM). Ratings are in dB, with the higher decibel rating indicating greater rejection ability. Hence, a 45-dB rating is superior to a 35-dB rating.

Capture Ratio. This term refers to how well the receiver tuner can pull in (*capture*) one station while rejecting another of nearly the same frequency. Hence the capture ratio represents the tuner's characteristic rejection of undesired signals that have a specific dB relationship to that of the desired station. Thus, a 1.5-dB capture-ratio rating means that the tuner will not pass a station's signal if it is 1.5 dB lower in signal strength than the one to which the radio is tuned. Hence, the lower dB rating is the preferred one. A capture ratio of 1 dB provides a rejection system superior to that of another receiver rated at 2 or 3 dB.

Damping Factor. A term relating to the ability of amplifier and loudspeaker to rapidly suppress the motion of the cone once the actuating signal has abruptly dropped to zero. A damping factor of 45 is superior, for instance, to one of 15 or 20. A good damping characteristic reduces the *hangover* effect in the sound output where tones tend to die off slowly or hang over beyond where they should.

Fifty-dB Quieting. This term refers to the standard that is generally accepted to indicate the degree of noise suppression required to obtain high-fidelity performance. With such noise suppression, the reception is sufficiently noise free for enjoyable listening. More signal strength is required for stereo reception than for mono reception to achieve the 50-dB quieting.

Frequency Response. This term relates to how uniform the reproduction remains for signals of different frequencies. A substantially flat response over an extended frequency range is desirable (as from 20 Hz to 15 kHz). If the variations in uniform amplitude are only a dB or less the response is considered to be excellent. The 15 kHz is often the upper limit of some records as well as general FM broadcasting. Many amplifiers, however, have a substantially flat response well over 20 kHz. As discussed in Section 3-3, ratings in decibels are comparisons; thus a doubling of signal *power* represents a change of 3 dB, while a halving of signal power is a change of −3 dB. A signal *voltage* doubling represents 6 dB, while a drop by half in signal voltage is expressed as −6 dB. Many manufacturers consider a frequency response substantially flat if it has only a 1- or 2-dB change.

Harmonic and IM Distortion. As discussed in Section 1-3, signal distortion consists of waveshape deviation of the output signal of an amplifier as compared with the input signal. Undesired changes in signal waveshape (in amplitude or phase, etc.) result in poor-quality signal output. *Harmonic distortion* involves spurious signals harmonically related to the original signal, while *intermodulation distortion* is created by the mixing (heterodyning) of two primary signals. Harmonic distortion (HD) and intermodulation distortion (IM) are given in percentages related to the total signal amplitude. Harmonic distortion is tested by comparing the waveshape of the output signal with that of the input signal, with the latter set at 1 mV. Often manufacturers rate both the harmonic and intermodulation distortion as total harmonic distortion (THD) and may give the percentage for several signal frequencies or for the total frequency span of the receiver (such as 0.2 percent for 20 Hz to 20 kHz). In most modern good-quality receivers the distortion is kept well below the point where even an experienced listener can detect it.

When making comparisons of distortion ratings, the lower figure denotes the preferred rating. Thus, a rating of 0.2 percent at 1 kHz is preferred over 0.5 percent. Total harmonic distortion ratings should be based on the full frequency response of the amplifier because there is a tendency for distortion to increase at the extremes of the frequency-response span (that is, both at the low and high ends).

IHF Sensitivity. This rating refers to the characteristics of the tuner of a radio receiver and it indicates the μV required at the input of the tuner to produce an output signal of less than 3 percent distortion and noise. The *IHF* refers to the *Institute of High Fidelity*.

The IHF sensitivity for an FM tuner is superior for lower figures. Thus, a 1.8-μV sensitivity is superior to a 1.9-μV or a 2-μV rating, and both of these are much better than a 2.3-μV rating. Stereo sensitivity is poorer than mono because of the comparatively greater signal strength needed to produce equivalent noise-free reception.

Image Rejection. This phrase refers to the ability of a receiver tuner to reject image-frequency signals (produced by the heterodyning of the signal produced by the tuner's oscillator with that of the undesired signal). Other undesired signals are also included in this rating; for example, any spurious signals entering the system. The higher the dB rating, the better the rejection characteristics. A rating of 100 dB is thus superior to a rating of 90 dB.

Power Output. This term rates the signal power available from an amplifier. The signal-power output level is established by the amplitude of the input signal and the ability of the amplifier's circuitry to raise such signals to those levels needed to produce a specific signal-power output.

Power output ratings for amplifiers have been given in rms EIA and IHF. (These letters refer to *Electronic Industries Association* and *Institute of High Fidelity*.) The rms (root-mean-square) values are the effective values of voltage, current, or power obtained by multiplying the peak value of an ac signal by 0.707. The effective ac power is the equivalent to the dc value required to perform the same work. In testing for this signal-power output from amplifiers, a single-frequency signal input is used, and the output is measured for rms voltage across a given value of load resistance ($P = E^2/R$).

Power rating for stereo amplifiers usually refers to the signal power (wattage) available per channel. Thus, a rating of 60-W rms per channel provides a total power output of 120 W for a constant-E input signal with controls set for maximum output. Speaker ohmic values of 4- or 8-Ω load conditions are usually specified by the manufacturer for a given power output rating.

Selectivity. This term relates to the ability of a tuning circuit to reject undesired signals having a frequency higher or lower than the desired signal. Thus, selectivity relates to the bandpass characteristics of a circuit. The higher the rating for selectivity in a receiver, the better the bandpass and the ability to reject unwanted signals. Hence, a selectivity rating of 80 dB, for instance, is much better than a rating of 40 or 50 dB.

Signal-to-noise Ratio (S/N). This term indicates the degree to which a receiver can raise the signal amplitude of the desired station above the general residual noise level. The higher the S/N ratio, the better. Hence, a 70-dB rating is superior to one of 60 dB.

Stereo Separation. This term refers to the ability of a stereo receiver, amplifier, or phonograph cartridge to minimize the spillover of signals between stereo channels. Generally, a 20-dB rating provides adequate stereo separation. The manufacturer's specifications are usually based on a test performed with a 1-kHz signal, and the rating is expressed in decibels (dB). The higher the dB rating, the better the separation. Hence, a 30-dB rating indicates a superior characteristic to one having a 15- or 20-dB rating.

15-2. PHONOGRAPH TERMS

The better-quality phonograph turntables generally operate at uniform speeds and have a minimum of motor noises or rumbles. The latter noises are often transferred to the phono cartridge via the tone arm. After a phono player has had prolonged use, lack of lubrication may produce variations in speed or erratic performance. Ratings, however, are furnished to represent the average characteristics of a system at the time of purchase. Hence manufacturers furnish listings regarding the percentages of speed variations and the degree of the so-called wow and flutter, or rumble transfer to the phono tone arm. The wow and flutter ratings are expressed as being "less than 0.03 percent" or "less than 0.1 percent" etc.

Antiskate. This term refers to the balancing out of the lateral force applied to a phono needle (and thus the cartridge and tone arm) as the record grooves apply pressure to the needle. As the record turns, the tone arm assembly is gradually pushed toward the record center. An antiskate device consists of a mechanical arrangement that provides a counterforce adjustable for the particular tracking force used. The antiskate device minimizes skating (sliding) of the needle over the record's surface. Proper turntable level (both for its width and depth) is essential in minimizing needle skating.

Compliance. The inherent mobility of a phonograph needle and cartridge during play is called compliance. Thus it is the ability of the phonograph needle to *comply* with the variations within the record grooves that produces the sound. The greater the compliance, the better the reproduction of various frequency signals. Compliance can be considered as the ability of the needle to move freely from side to side within the record groove. A cartridge rating of 35×10^{-6} has excellent compliance and one of 15×10^{-6} is good, while any lower rating usually is found in the lower-priced units.

Tracking Force. This term defines the grams of pressure exerted by a phonograph needle on the record during play. A lower-tracking force produces less record wear; hence a needle exerting 1-gram pressure is much more desirable than a needle having a tracking force of 3 grams. For a tracking force of less than 1.5 grams, however, the tone arm and balance mechanism must be mechanically designed for free movement vertically and horizontally and preferably must have an *antiskate device* (discussed earlier). Also, the cartridge must have good *compliance* (discussed earlier in this section) for the lower-tracking force operation.

15-3. TAPE CASSETTE, CARTRIDGE, AND REEL SPEEDS

Open-reel tape recorders operate at standard speeds of $3\frac{3}{4}$ and $7\frac{1}{2}$ inches per second (ips), though some machines may have even slower speeds for special recording techniques. Cartridge tapes are $\frac{1}{4}$-inch wide, and their speed is $3\frac{3}{4}$ inches per second. The cassette tape has a width slightly greater than $\frac{1}{8}$ (0.146) inch as compared to the open-reel tape, whose width is slightly less than $\frac{1}{4}$ (0.246) inch in width. Cassette tape speed is $1\frac{7}{8}$ inches per second. Cassette and cartridge tapes are enclosed in a housing and wound on spools (cassettes measure $\frac{1}{2}\times2\frac{1}{2}\times4$ inches). The devices require no tape threading or handling. Like the open reel, the cassette unit can be wound fast in forward or reverse. The cartridge units are continuous-operation types with the tape forming a continuous loop within the housing.

The cassette's narrow tape requires that the stereo tracks be reduced to 0.024 inch each, with an 0.012-inch separation between the left and right

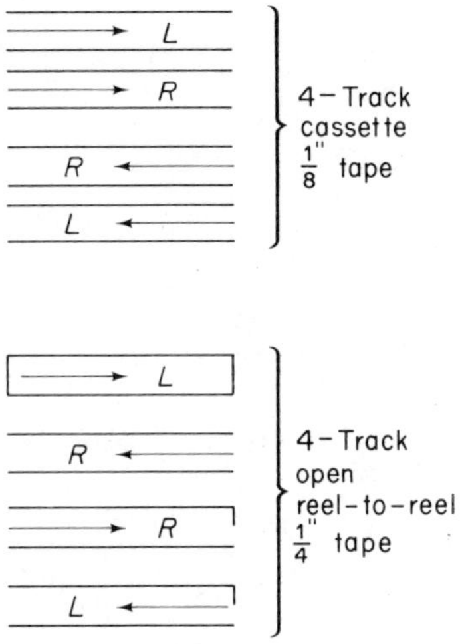

FIGURE 15-1. Tape track comparisons.

channels of a particular pair, and an 0.026-inch separation between stereo pairs. Cassettes record and play a stereo section of dual tracks side by side, thus permitting playback on a mono machine. This indicates that the cassettes are compatible, and stereo or mono units can be played on either a stereo or mono machine. Reel-to-reel tapes are not compatible, since in the latter case, stereo pairs are interlaced between the pair of the second track in four-track operation and can't be played on a mono machine. (See Fig. 15-1.)

15-4. FREQUENCY SPECTRUM

The *frequency spectrum* span from audible ranges up to the gamma ray region is shown in Fig. 15-2. Designations are in kilohertz (kHz), megahertz (MHz), and angstroms (Å). (See also Secs. 3-1 and 3-6.) One angstrom unit (also known as the "tenth-meter") has a length of 10^{-10} meters. It is included in Table 15-1 in the listing of conversion factors involving length.

The *audible-frequency spectrum* ranges from approximately 15 Hz to 20 kHz. Below 15 Hz vibrations are felt rather than heard, and above 10 kHz, the degree of hearing depends heavily on the age of the listener. *Overtones* (harmonics) of musical sounds extend beyond the range of fundamental tones and are related to the fundamental tone—they are even or odd multiples of the fundamental frequency. Harmonics or overtones

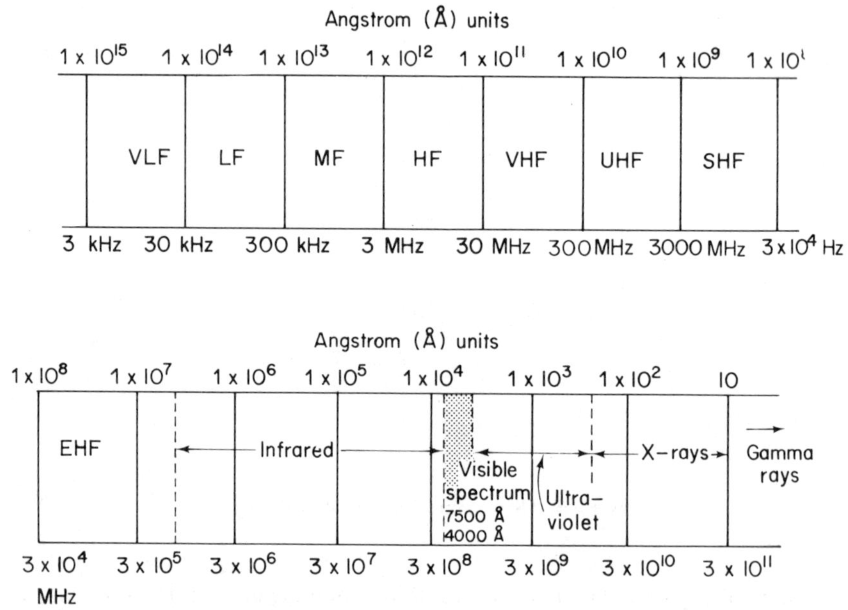

FIGURE 15-2. Frequency spectrum.

have progressively lower amplitudes for frequencies above the fundamental one.

As shown in Fig. 15-2, the *visible spectrum* ranges from about 4000 Å to 7500 Å. The infrared region is at the low-frequency end of the visible spectrum; the ultraviolet is at the high-frequency end. In the *intermediate frequencies*, i.e., those between the audible and visible regions, lie the various communication systems—public-service broadcasting, amateur, aircraft, entertainment TV, FM and AM, ship-to-shore, etc.

15-5. LASER AND MASER DATA

The terms *laser* and *maser* are acronyms; that is, the words are formed from the initial letters of the words in the phrase describing the system. Thus, laser stems from the phrase *Light Amplification by Stimulated Emission of Radiation*. Maser stems from the phrase *Microwave Amplification by Stimulated Emission of Radiation*. A low energy level of light or microwave signals can be amplified to a marked degree by these processes.

Of importance to the concept of laser and maser functions is *Planck's constant*, formulated by the German physicist Max Planck (1858–1947) in 1900 in relation to his quantum theory. In equation form, it is given as $E=hf$; where E is energy, h is Planck's constant, and f is frequency. Planck's constant thus relates to the energy relationship with respect to the frequency of the initiating signal; E is the product of the amount of radiant energy produced by signal frequency f and the constant h. This formula thus equates the difference in energy (dE) between two levels. Planck's constant is applicable to various aspects of fluorescence, lasers, masers, secondary-emission, and the quantum physics of photons.

Planck's constant can be expressed in terms of joules or electron volts as:

$$6.624 \times 10^{-27} \text{ erg-seconds} \quad \text{or}$$
$$4.13 \times 10^{-15} \text{ electron-volt second}$$

Photon and emission factors for laser operation show behavior in their baisc aspects similar to that of a fluorescent lamp. Operation of the latter depends on the ability of phosphor materials to absorb radiant energy of one frequency and release it at another frequency. (This frequency difference accounts for the characteristic colors of neon lamps, etc., with the color produced dependent on the type of gas used.)

All electrons of an atom can exist on different energy levels, but normally any particular electron is in its so-called *ground state* (its normal energy level), as shown in Fig. 15-3. When an electron absorbs energy from external excitation, it is elevated to a higher energy level. The high energy level, however, is unstable and within a few microseconds the elevated electron (or electrons) falls back to the normal energy level. As it falls back, however, each electron releases the energy that it absorbed during the elevation. The energy is released in the form of light. The after-glow in fluorescence, however, indicates that not all the electrons have resumed their lower levels at the same time.

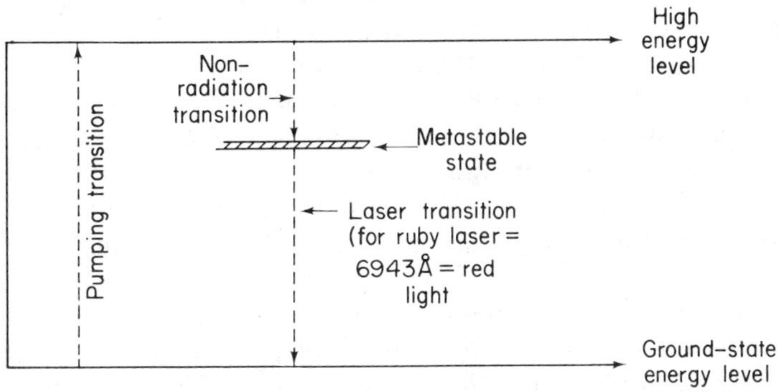

FIGURE 15-3. Laser energy-level factor.

Lasers may be formed by gases, certain plastic materials, or solid-state synthetic gems such as rubies (formed of aluminum oxide, with some doping of chromium atoms as well as oxygen atoms). Certain excitation orbits in chromium atoms are *metastable*; that is, electrons in the orbits have the ability of remaining at higher energy levels briefly before dropping back. When they drop back, there is a minimum of delay among the electrons, assuring virtual coincidental release of energy in the form of light by all electrons.

The ruby laser, gas laser, or other type laser is subjected to a burst of light. This process is *pumping* from a light source (which can be likened to a flashbulb type device). For the maser, pumping is performed by a microwave oscillator, which generates the required signal.

The light used to pump the laser is termed *incoherent*, since it contains frequencies ranging throughout the light spectrum. As the laser is pumped, electrons are elevated and absorb considerable energy. When the first drop-back occurs for any electron that had momentarily been resting at the metastable level, that electron emits a photon (a red-light photon for the ruby laser). The energy thus released results in the triggering of all other metastable-level electrons. This sudden dumping of all the elevated electrons causes an extremely high-amplitude release of photon energy with the light waves of the emitted photons being *coherent* (in-phase) and unidirectional. This sudden release of a single monochromatic-frequency signal establishes the laser (or maser) as the remarkable device that it is.

Laser light intensity can reach millions of times the intensity of the light of the sun on a *relative bandwidth basis*. The sun has an apparent temperature of 6000°K. Within the bandwidth comparable to that of the ruby laser, the sun emits $\frac{1}{20}$ watt of light energy per square centimeter. Lasers, on the other hand, can emit kilowatts of power per square centimeter. Also, the sun radiates its energy omni-directionally, while the laser's radiation is unidirectional.

The structure of the laser material (ruby, special plastic, etc.) determines how narrow the laser beam will be. Most of the coherent light that is emitted is radiated in the direction of the atomic alignment within the laser material. For the ruby laser, the alignment is in the direction of the chromium atom alignment within the crystal. Additional optical focusing can be employed where necessary.

Lasers have a variety of uses, among them are the cutting of metals, the formation of holograms and the observation of them (discussed in Sec. 15-6). Lasers also find widespread employment in communications, where the laser beam can be optically modulated. The advantages of laser modulation for communications are the pinpointing of the transmission, the great capacity for the amount of information that can be transmitted, and the lack of scattering, which aids in maintenance of privacy during communication. The maser has similar advantages in communications.

15-6. HOLOGRAPHY DATA

Holography relates to the practice of utilizing the coherent light from lasers (see Sec. 15-5) to produce a photographic image termed a *hologram*, which, when viewed, appears in three dimensions. The word stems from the Greek root *holos*, relating to the whole part or something complete in all aspects. The hologram is actually a two-dimensional photographic transparency, which, when inspected visually, appears as a film with multiple whirling lines in it.

The holographic process involves placing on a photographic film certain interference patterns that are created between two light waves; one obtained from a reference beam; the other reflected directly from the object being photographed. One basic process is shown in Fig. 15-4A. Here the laser is the source of coherent light. Its light output is directed to a *beam splitter* (a special mirror). There, some of the illuminating beam is diverted to a photographic plate. This diverted beam is usually called the *reference* beam. The major portion of the laser light is directed onto the object itself and from it is reflected toward the photographic plate, as

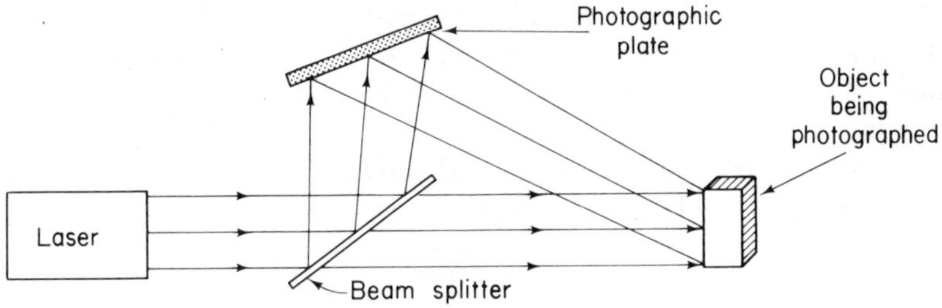

Formation of hologram

(A)

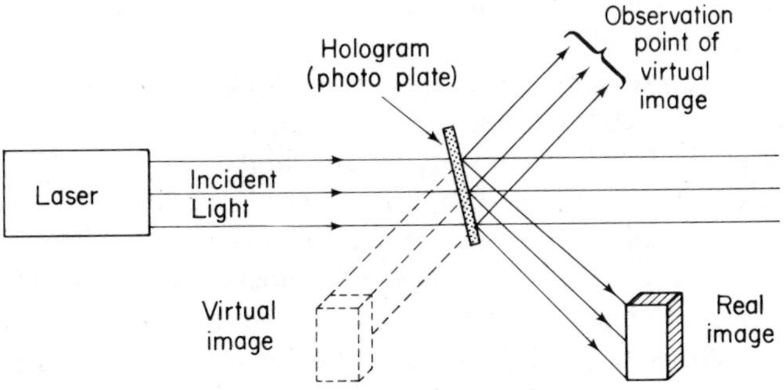

(B)

FIGURE 15-4. Basic holography.

shown in part A. Next, the reflected light from the object and the reference beam meet at the photographic plate, and interference patterns are produced. Each interference pattern can be considered equivalent to a circular diffraction grating. The result is a series of patterns containing complete informational recordings of the object being photographed.

When the completed hologram is illuminated by the light from a laser (as shown in Fig. 15-4B), the original object becomes visible and possesses *depth*, *perspective*, and *parallax* between far and near objects. The image appears suspended in air, but has the surprising characteristic of being able to be viewed as a three-dimensional representation of a real object, without the necessity for special viewing lens or so-called 3-D (three dimensional) eyeglasses. If the viewer moves around, the perspective of the viewed object also changes, permitting him to see more of one side than the other, or of another object in back of the original (if two were present during photography).

As shown in Fig. 15-4B, the reconstruction of the object is made visible by the light from the hologram; such types are called *transmission holograms*. Two images in the shape of the original one are formed—one is called the *virtual image*; and the other the *real image*. The virtual image is positioned at the place that was occupied by the original object (in relation to the hologram). The real image can be considered a complementary one positioned as shown in Fig. 15-4B. It is more difficult to observe than the virtual image.

Another hologram type is the *reflection hologram*, wherein the image can be seen from the reflected light of the hologram film.

15-7. CRYOGENIC DATA

Cryogenics is the science of supercold temperatures and deals with their effect on certain devices. Subjects under study include computer storage devices, super-strength magnets, and the superconductivity of electric current through cryogenic materials.

The word *cryogenic* stems from the Greek word *kryos* meaning *icy cold*, since the science utilizes temperatures below $-300°F$. Low temperatures are produced with special equipment similar, in basic principle, to a refrigerator or air conditioner. Compressed gas is fed into a chamber where the gas expands, absorbing heat from the material being cooled. The process can be repeated until the desired temperature is reached.

Cryogenic temperatures affect molecular movement, which at normal temperatures is very high in gases such as air (even when such gases appear without movement). In liquids, molecules are also in motion, though they can be considered to be gliding smoothly over one another. In solids, the molecular movement is not as perceptible, though it still exists in the form of a *vibratory motion*. At −459.72°F, even such slight vibratory motion ceases. (One must not confuse molecular movement with electron spin around the nucleus of its atom. The orbital electron spin still continues, since this relates to the basic construction of matter.)

Molecular movement ordinarily interferes with electric-current flow. Hence, metal becomes *super-conductive* at cryogenic temperatures. A current induced in a lead ring, for instance, would continue circulating for a long time without need of additional electric energy.

15-8. IONS AND PLASMA

In a normal atom, the total value of the positive charge of the atom's nucleus is equal to the total negative charge of the planetary electrons surrounding the nucleus. Since the nucleus has a positive value and the electrons have a negative value, they are equal though opposite in their charge relationship, and the atomic structure as a whole may be considered as having a *neutral* charge.

In various branches of electronics there are occasions where conditions are created that either remove or add electrons to the normal quota surrounding an atom's nucleus. To define this altered atomic characteristic, the word *ion* is applied to an atom that is no longer neutral, but has either gained or lost one or more electrons from its original quota. When an atom has acquired an additional amount of electrons, an unbalanced condition is created between the planetary electrons and the nucleus because the excessive electrons now cause the atom to be predominately negative. Hence, an atom having one or more electrons above its normal quota is a *negative ion*. Thus, when a number of atoms of this type are involved, they are simply referred to as *ions*.

Ions can also be formed by removal of one or more electrons from an atom, creating an electron deficiency. Hence, if an atom has less than the normal amount of electrons in its planetary system, the positive charge of the nucleus predominates and a *positive ion* is formed. Ions of both types are important in electronic applications using gas-filled tubes, cathode-ray tubes, transistors, and other devices.

The term *plasma* also applies to ionization, particularly to ionized gases forming a cloud of ions in a highly agitated state. As such, the plasma can be considered equivalent to an electric conducting fluid that can be acted on by magnetic fields. Because it is actually neither a true solid, gas, nor liquid, it has been referred to as the fourth state of matter.

The word plasma stems from the Greek word *plassein*, meaning *to form* or *to mold*. While plasma is usually produced by ionization of gases, it can also be formed within solid-state devices. Practical applications apply to all gas-filled electron tubes, thermonuclear processes, missile or space vehicle re-entry problems, industrial processes for application of refractory coatings to base metals, as well as some aspects of metal shaping and welding processes.

Plasma temperatures start at about 10,000°F, and gas ionization causes molecular structures to break up into individual atoms with a loss of normal charge neutrality. In industrial utilization and research, magnetic fields are employed as containers of the plasma, since solid materials disintegrate because of the extremely high temperatures.

15-9. WEIGHTS AND MEASURES

APOTHECARIES' WEIGHT

20 grains = 1 scruple
3 scruples = 1 dram = 60 grains
8 drams = 1 ounce = 24 scruples = 480 grains
12 ounces = 1 pound = 96 drams = 288 scruples = 5760 grains

AVOIRDUPOIS WEIGHT

$27\frac{11}{32}$ grains = 1 dram
16 drams = 1 ounce = $437\frac{1}{2}$ grains
16 ounces = 1 pound = 256 drams = 7000 grains
100 pounds = 1 hundredweight = 1600 ounces
20 hundredweight = 1 short ton = 2000 pounds
112 pounds = 1 long hundredweight
20 long hundredweight = 1 long ton = 2240 pounds

METRIC EQUIVALENTS

1 gram = 0.03527 ounce
1 ounce = 28.35 grams
1 kilogram = 2.2046 pounds
1 pound = 0.4536 kilogram
1 metric ton = 0.98421 English ton
1 English ton = 1.016 metric ton

TROY WEIGHT

(Used for gold, silver, and jewels)
24 grains = 1 pennyweight
20 pennyweights = 1 ounce = 480 grains
12 ounces = 1 pound = 240 pennyweights = 5760 grains

CIRCULAR MEASURE

60 seconds (″) = 1 minute (′)
60 minutes = 1 degree (°)
90 degrees = 1 quadrant
4 quadrants = 1 circle of circumference

CUBIC MEASURE

1728 cubic inches = 1 cubic foot
27 cubic feet = 1 cubic yard
128 cubic feet = 1 cord (wood)
40 cubic feet = 1 ton (shipping)
2150.42 cubic inches = 1 standard bushel
231 cubic inches = 1 standard gallon (U.S.)

DRY MEASURE

2 pints = 1 quart
8 quarts = 1 peck = 16 pints
4 pecks = 1 bushel = 32 quarts = 64 pints
105 quarts = 1 barrel = 7056 cubic inches

LINEAR MEASURE

12 inches = 1 foot
3 feet = 1 yard = 36 inches
$5\frac{1}{2}$ yards = 1 rod = $16\frac{1}{2}$ feet
40 rods = 1 furlong = 220 yards = 660 feet = $\frac{1}{8}$ mile
8 furlongs = 1 statute mile = 1760 yards = 5280 feet
3 miles = 1 league = 5280 yards = 15,840 feet

METRIC EQUIVALENTS

1 centimeter = 0.3937 inch
1 inch = 2.54 centimeters
1 decimeter = 3.937 inches = 0.328 foot
1 foot = 3.048 decimeters
1 meter = 39.37 inches = 1.0936 yards
1 yard = 0.9144 meter
1 dekameter = 1.9884 rods
1 rod = 0.5029 dekameter
1 kilometer = 0.62137 mile
1 mile = 1.6093 kilometers

LIQUID MEASURE

4 gills = 1 pint
2 pints = 1 quart = 8 gills
4 quarts = 1 gallon = 8 pints
$31\frac{1}{2}$ gallons = 1 barrel = 126 quarts
2 barrels = 1 hogshead = 63 gallons = 252 quarts

SQUARE MEASURE

144 square inches = 1 square foot
9 square feet = 1 square yard = 1296 square inches
$30\frac{1}{4}$ square yards = 1 square rod = $272\frac{1}{4}$ square feet
160 square rods = 1 acre = 4840 square yards
640 acres = 1 square mile = 3,097,600 square yards

METRIC EQUIVALENTS

1 square centimeter = 0.1550 square inch
1 square inch = 6.452 square centimeters
1 square decimeter = 0.1076 square foot
1 square foot = 9.2903 square decimeters
1 square meter = 1.196 square yards
1 square yard = 0.8361 square meter
1 acre = 4,047 square meters
1 square kilometer = 0.386 square mile
1 square mile = 2.59 square kilometers

TABLE 15-1. Conversion Factors Involving Length

Multiply Number of	by	To Obtain Number of
inches	2.540	centimeters
inches	0.02540	meters
feet	30.48	centimeters
feet	0.3048	meters
miles	5280.0	feet
miles	1.6093	kilometers
miles	1609.3	meters
centimeters	0.3937	inches
centimeters	0.01	meters
centimeters	10.0	millimeters
meters	100.0	centimeters
meters	3.2808	feet
meters	39.37	inches
meters	1000.0	kilometers
microns	10^{-6}	meters
microns	10^{-4}	centimeters
millimicrons	10^{-7}	centimeters
angstroms	10^{-10}	meters
angstroms	10^{-8}	centimeters

TABLE 15-2. Conversion Factors Involving Velocity or Speed

Multiply Number of	by	To Obtain Number of
feet/second	1.097	kilometers/hour
feet/second	0.6818	miles/hour
feet/second	0.01136	miles/minute
centimeters/second	1.969	feet/minute
centimeters/second	0.036	kilometers/hour
centimeters/second	0.02237	miles/hour
miles/hour	44.70	centimeters/second
miles/hour	88.0	feet/minute
miles/hour	1.467	feet/second
miles/hour	26.82	meters/minute

15-10. ROMAN NUMERALS

General rules for Roman numerals are: (1) When a symbol precedes one having greater value, it subtracts therefrom, as: IV=4; (2) When a symbol follows one of equal or greater value, it adds to the value of the number, as: II=2, and VI=6; (3) When a symbol is between two of higher value, it subtracts from the third, and adds the remainder to the first, as: CIX=109; (4) When a letter is repeated its value is also repeated, as: XX=20, CC=200, CCC=300, LXXX or XXC=80.

I=1	XXX=30
II=2	XL=40
III=3	L=50
IV=4	LX=60
V=5	LXX=70
VI=6	LXXX=80
VII=7	XC=90
VIII=8	C=100
IX=9	CC=200
X=10	CCC=300
XI=11	CD=400
XII=12	D=500
XIII=13	DC=600
XIV=14	DCC=700
XV=15	DCCC=800
XVI=16	CM=900
XVII=17	M=1000
XVIII=18	MM=2000
XIX=19	MMM=3000
XX=20	

15-11. DIELECTRIC CONSTANT (K)

The *dielectric constant* (k) for air is considered to be 1, and all other materials have a higher k. The term *constant* is misleading, however, since in some materials k varies with temperature, operating frequency, applied voltage, and other such factors. The following listing provides approximate values of k for a number of materials.

Air	1.0	Nylon	3.00
Aluminum silicate	5.3 to 5.5	Paper	1.5 to 3
Bakelite	3.7	Paraffin	2 to 3
Beeswax (yellow)	2.7	Polyethylene	2.2
Butyl Rubber	2.4	Polystyrene	2.5
Formica XX	4.00	Porcelain	5 to 7
Glass	4 to 10	Quartz	3.7 to 4.5
Gutta-percha	2.6	Steatite	5.3 to 6.5
Halowax oil	4.8	Teflon	2.1
Kel-F	2.6	Tenite	2.9 to 4.5
Lucite	2.8	Vaseline	2.16
Mica	4 to 8	Water (distilled)	76.7 to 78.2
Micarta 254	3.4 to 5.4	Wood	1.2 to 2.1

15-12. MATHEMATICAL SYMBOLS AND CONSTANTS

General mathematical symbols and basic constants are given below. Common practice is to use a, b, and c for known quantities, and x, y, and z for unknown values.

$\times$ or $\cdot$	Multiplied by
$\div$ or :	Divided by
$+$	Positive. Plus. Add
$-$	Negative. Minus. Subtract
$\pm$	Positive or negative. Plus or minus
$\mp$	Negative or positive. Minus or plus
$=$ or ::	Equals
$\equiv$	Identity
$\cong$	Is approximately equal to
$\neq$	Does not equal
$>$	Greater than
$\gg$	Is much greater than
$<$	Less than
$\ll$	Is much less than
$\geqslant$	Greater than or equal to
$\leqslant$	Less than or equal to
$\therefore$	Therefore

$\angle$	Angle
Δ	Increment or Decrement
$\perp$	Perpendicular to
$\parallel$	Parallel to
$\|n\|$	Absolute value of *n*
$\sqrt{\ }$	Square root
$\sqrt[3]{\ }$	Cube root

$\pi = 3.14$
$2\pi = 6.28$
$(2\pi)^2 = 39.5$ (All are rounded off)
$4\pi = 12.6$
$\pi^2 = 9.87$
$\frac{\pi}{2} = 1.57$
$\frac{1}{\pi} = 0.318$
$\frac{1}{2\pi} = 0.159$
$\frac{1}{\pi^2} = 0.101$
$\frac{1}{\sqrt{\pi}} = 0.564$
$\sqrt{\pi} = 1.77$

$\sqrt{\frac{\pi}{2}} = 1.25$
$\sqrt{2} = 1.41$
$\sqrt{3} = 1.73$
$\frac{1}{\sqrt{2}} = 0.707$
$\frac{1}{\sqrt{3}} = 0.577$
$\log\pi = 0.497$
$\log\frac{\pi}{2} = 0.196$
$\log\pi^2 = 0.994$
$\log\sqrt{\pi} = 0.248$
Base of natural logs s = 2.718
1 radian = $180°/\pi = 57.3°$
$360° = 2\pi$ radians

15-13. GREEK ALPHABET

Various Greek letters, both capital and lower-case, are used extensively in electric and electronic terminology, as well as in mathematics. Thus, μF denotes microfarads, Ω indicates ohms, $\pi = 3.1416$, etc. The following table lists the complete alphabet:

TABLE 15-3.

Greek Capital Letter	Greek Lowercase Letter	Greek Name
Α	α	Alpha
Β	β	Beta
Γ	γ	Gamma
Δ	δ	Delta
Ε	ϵ	Epsilon
Ζ	ζ	Zeta
Η	η	Eta
Θ	θ	Theta

TABLE 15-3. (*Continued*)

Greek Capital Letter	Greek Lowercase Letter	Greek Name
I	ι	Iota
K	κ	Kappa
Λ	λ	Lambda
M	μ	Mu
N	ν	Nu
Ξ	ξ	Xi
O	o	Omicron
Π	π	Pi
P	ρ	Rho
Σ	σ	Sigma
T	τ	Tau
Υ	υ	Upsilon
Φ	φ	Phi
X	χ	Chi
Ψ	ψ	Psi
Ω	ω	Omega

15-14. TYPICAL FREQUENCY RANGE OF VARIOUS SOUNDS

Type of Sound	Approximate Frequency Span (in Hz)
Desirable range for good speech intelligibility	300 to 4,000
Audibility range (normal hearing, young person)	16 to 20,000
Piano	26 to 4,000
Baritone	100 to 375
Tenor	125 to 475
Soprano	225 to 675
Cello	64 to 650
Violin	192 to 3,000
Piccolo	512 to 4,600
Harmonics of sound	32 to 20,000

15-15. APPROXIMATE SOUND LEVELS

The following listing gives approximate levels of sound by decibel (dB) comparsons. (See Sec. 3-3 for a discussion of decibels and nepers.)

Type of Sound	Relative Intensity in Decibels
Reference level	0
Threshold of average hearing	10
Soft whisper; faint rustle of leaves	20
Normal whisper; average sound in home	30
Faint speech; softly playing radio	40
Muted string instrument; softly spoken words (at a distance of 3 ft.)	50
Normal conversational level; radio at average loudness	60
Group conversation; orchestra slightly below average volume	70
Average orchestral volume; very loud radio	80
Loud orchestra volume; brass band	90
Noise of low-flying airplane; noisy machine shop	100
Roar of overhead jet-propelled plane; loud brass band close by	110
Nearby airplane roar; beginning of hearing discomfort	120
Threshold of pain from abnormally loud sounds	130

15-16. COMPARISONS OF *RLC* CALCULATIONS

The following listings compare the calculations required for finding total values of resistance, inductance, capacitance, reactance, and impedance relating to series and parallel circuits.

TOTAL VALUE OBTAINED BY SIMPLE ADDITION

$$(n_1 + n_2 + n_3 + \cdots)$$

Resistance of resistors in series
Voltage of batteries or cells in series
Inductance of coils in series (not coupled)
Inductive reactance of coils in series (not coupled)
Capacitive reactance of capacitors in series
Capacitance of capacitors in parallel
Current of resistors in parallel

TOTAL VALUE FOUND BY RECIPROCAL EQUATION

$$\left[\frac{1}{\frac{1}{n_1}+\frac{1}{n_2}+\frac{1}{n_3}+\cdots}\right]$$

Resistance of resistors in parallel
Capacitance of capacitors in series
Capacitive reactance of capacitors in parallel
Inductive reactance of coils in parallel (not coupled)
Inductance of coils in parallel (not coupled)

TOTAL VALUE FOUND BY VECTOR EQUATION

$$\sqrt{a^2+(b-c)^2}$$

Impedance of inductance and resistance in series
Impedance of capacitance and resistance in series
Voltage across circuit composed of inductance and resistance in series
Voltage across circuit composed of capacitance and resistance in series
Current of a circuit composed of capacitance and resistance in parallel
Current of a circuit composed of inductance and resistance in parallel

15-17. EFFECTS OF FREQUENCY ON *L*, *C*, AND *R* CIRCUITRY

The effects of a change of frequency on circuitry containing *L*, *C*, and *R* (singly or in combination) are given in the following listings. Frequency changes alter the values of reactance or impedance (the combination of *R* and *X*).

Component	Effect of Frequency	
	Increase	Decrease
Resistance (*R*)	None	None
Capacitance (*C*)	None	None
Capacitive reactance (X_C)	Lowers X_C	Raises X_C
Inductance (*L*)	None	None
Inductive reactance (X_L)	Raises X_L	Lowers X_L
Series capacitor-resistor combination (*Z*)	Lowers *Z*	Raises *Z*
Series inductance-resistor combination (*Z*)	Raises *Z*	Lowers *Z*
Parallel capacitor-resistor combination (*Z*)	Lowers *Z*	Raises *Z*
Parallel inductance-resistor combination (*Z*)	Raises *Z*	Lowers *Z*
Series resonance (*Z*)	Raises *Z*	Raises *Z*
Parallel resonance (*Z*)	Lowers *Z*	Lowers *Z*

15-18. THERMAL UNITS

Celsius temperature units are based on a freezing point of water, represented by 0°C and a boiling point of 100°C, as opposed to the Fahrenheit scale, where water freezes at 32°F and boils at 212°F. The degree Kelvin is based on an *absolute zero*, equivalent to approximately −273.18°C. The following table indicates some equivalent temperatures in the different scales:

°C	°F	°K
5000	9032	5273
1000	1832	1273
500	932	773
250	482	523
100	212	373
0	32	273
−100	−148	173
−273.18	−459.72	0

To change degrees Fahrenheit to degrees Celsius:

$$°C = \tfrac{5}{9}(°F - 32)$$

To change degrees Celsius to degrees Fahrenheit:

$$°F = \left(\tfrac{9}{5} \times °C\right) + 32$$

To change degrees Celsius to degrees Kelvin:

$$°K = °C + 273°$$

To change degrees Kelvin to degrees Celsius:

$$°C = °K - 273°$$

15-19. RESISTIVITY VALUES OF VARIOUS MATERIALS

The *resistance* (electrical opposition) of a section of material is directly proportional to the material's length and inversely proportional to its cross-sectional area. The listing below gives the ohmic resistivity values of various materials in micro-ohms ($\mu\Omega$) per square centimeter, at a temperature of 18°C. For example, the resistivity value of 2.94 for aluminum means 2.94×10^{-6} ohms (Ω) per *square centimeter.*

Aluminum	2.94	Steel	16.00
Bismuth	119.00	Steel (hard)	45.00
Brass	6.6	Lead	20.80
Carbon	0.35	Mercury	95.60
Copper (drawn)	1.78	Platinum	11.00
Gold	2.42	Silver	1.66
Iron (cast)	74.40	Tin	11.30
Iron (wrought)	13.90	Zinc	6.10

15-20. CURRENT-READING RANGES

When a meter is used for current measurement, the current to be read must flow through the meter inductor. Thus, a current meter must be connected in *series* with the circuit in which the current is to be measured. For this reason, the *current-reading meter* must have a low dc resistance so that it offers little opposition to the circuit-current flow and does not upset circuit function by consuming any appreciable amount of electrical energy.

The magnitude of the current that can flow safely through a meter depends on the internal resistance of the meter and the shunting resistors used to bypass currents whose values would endanger the meter movement. In microampere (μA) meters, milliampere (mA) meters, and ammeters the needle (pointer) deflection will be proportional to the current flowing through the instrument up to the maximum needle deflection. Thus, if the maximum deflection is 1 mA, the meter reads that amount as a maximum, but is capable of reading fractional values of the maximum.

The range of the basic meter movement can be increased by placement of several shunting resistors in the circuit, as shown in Fig. 15-5A. For each such parallel resistor that can be selected by a switch, an additional scale must be provided on the meter dial to read the current flow within the range provided by the shunt resistor that is selected. (Current-reading meters are often combined with the voltmeters and ohmmeters described in the following sections.)

If the circuit in part A uses a 0 to 1 mA meter movement, the maximum possible current that can flow within the meter will be 1 mA. Higher currents can, of course, be read by shunting the excessive amounts. The ranges established by the shunting resistors are determined by the internal resistance of the meter. If a 0 to 1 mA meter had an internal resistance of 100 Ω, for instance, another 100-Ω resistor in shunt would

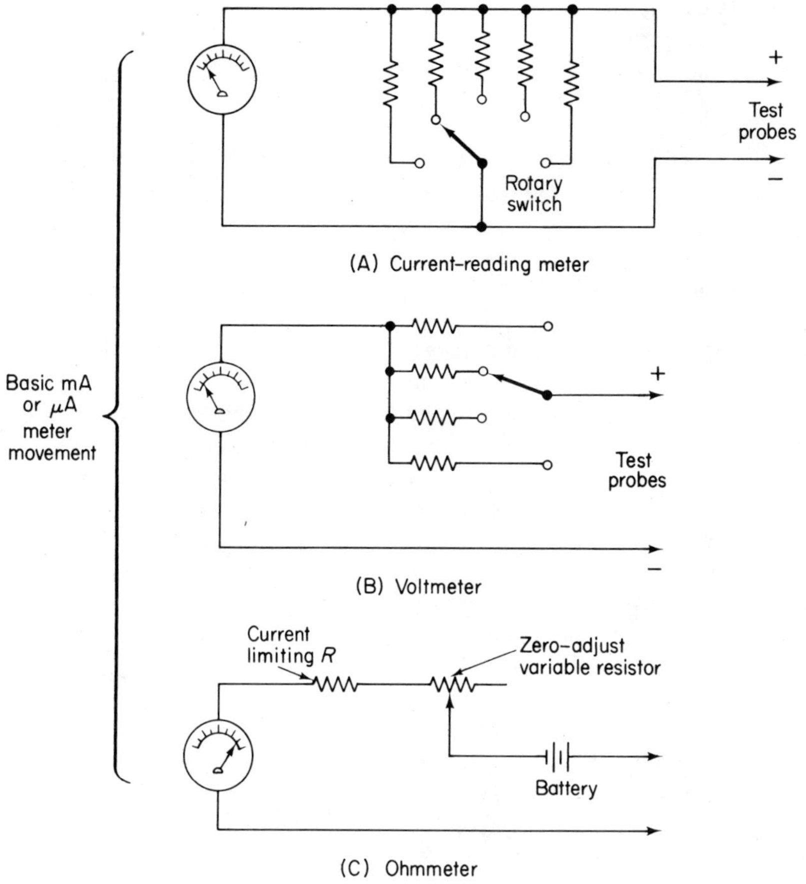

FIGURE 15-5. Basic instrument circuitry.

permit a reading of double the current. The following equation applies:

$$R_{Sh} = \frac{R_m}{(N-1)} \tag{15-1}$$

where R_{Sh} = the value of the shunt resistance in ohms
R_m = the meter resistance in ohms
N = the value of the number by which the meter scale is to be increased.

Thus, if we wished to obtain a maximum reading of 5 mA with the 0–1 mA movement (100-Ω resistance), the required shunting resistor (by

Eq. 15-1) would be:

$$R_{sh} = \frac{100}{5-1} = 25\ \Omega$$

Current-reading meters must, of course, be placed in series with the current flow. This necessitates opening the circuit for meter insertion.

15-21. VOLTMETER RANGES

A *voltmeter* is placed across a resistor or other device for ascertaining the voltage drop across that unit. Thus, in contrast to the current-reading meter, the voltmeter must have a high internal resistance so it does not act as a shunting device. If the voltmeter resistance is low, some of the current flowing in the circuit to be measured will branch into the voltmeter and thus upset true voltage readings and affect circuit performance as well.

Voltmeters are constructed by utilizing basic microampere meters, milliampere meters, or ammeters. The microampere movements are preferred since high-resistance meters are formed. As with the current-reading meter of Sec. 15-20, the maximum ratings must not be exceeded. Thus, if a 50-μA meter is used, the maximum current flow through the meter will be 50 μA, and external series resistors must be used so that the applied voltage will divide in a manner such that currents will not be higher than 50 μA. Consequently, the largest proportion of voltage drops across the external resistor in series as shown in Fig. 15-5B.

The following equation applies to the calculation of the ohmic value of the series resistor for the required voltage range:

$$R_s = R_m(N-1) \tag{15-2}$$

where R_s = the resistance value of the series resistor
R_m = the resistance of the meter inductor
N = the value of the number by which the meter scale is to be increased.

As an example, assume the meter is to read 5-V full scale. To apply Eq. 15-2, it is necessary to determine the value of N by dividing the desired full-scale reading by the voltage drop produced across the internal resistance of the meter for a full deflection current. If a 50-μA meter with an internal resistance of 2 kΩ is used, the voltage needed to deflect the meter fully is:

$$E = IR = 50\ \mu\text{A} \times 2000\ \Omega = 0.1\ \text{V}$$

Thus, 5 V divided by 0.1 equals 50, and this number is placed in Eq. 15-2 and employed in finding the required resistance for a full 5-V deflection:

$$R_s = 2000(50-1) = 98 \text{ k}\Omega$$

The ohmic value of the series resistor needed to obtain a specific voltage range can also be found by Ohm's law. In the foregoing example, for instance, 5 V was the required maximum deflection, and 50 μA was the maximum current that could flow in the series circuit composed of the resistor and meter. The *total* resistance, therefore, is:

$$R_T = \frac{5}{50 \times 10^{-6}} = 100 \text{ k}\Omega$$

Since we know the meter resistance is 2 kΩ, however, this value must be subtracted from the above 100 kΩ value in order to obtain the required series resistance of 98 kΩ.

The term *ohms-per-volt* refers to the required total resistance for a deflection of one volt maximum scale. For the 50-μA meter mentioned above, this resistance would be 1 V/50 μA = 20,000 Ω (20 kΩ), and this meter is referred to as a *20,000-Ω per volt meter*. For the 0–1 mA meter with 100-Ω internal resistance, one-volt full scale would require 900 Ω plus 100 Ω for the meter—a total of 1,000 Ω—making this a 1000-Ω per volt meter. The higher ohms-per-volt ratings have less loading effect on circuitry under test.

15-22. OHMMETER

An *ohmmeter* is a device that measures the ohmic value of resistors by employing a voltage source (such as a battery) and measuring the amount of current flow in the circuit formed by the resistance to be measured and the meter circuit. The basic ohmmeter circuit is shown in Fig. 15-5C. When the test probes are shorted together, the ohmmeter circuit is closed and battery current flows through the meter and the series resistors. The variable resistor is then adjusted to obtain full pointer deflection, indicating zero resistance at the test probes.

When the test probes are not touching, infinite resistance reading is indicated, and the meter pointer is then at the extreme left (the point of maximum resistance reading). When the probes are placed across a resistor, the amount of current flow is inversely proportional to the ohmic value of the resistor. Hence, a high ohmic value for the resistor does not permit so much current to flow as a low value. The meter scale is calibrated accordingly to show the particular resistance of the unit under test.

The range of such a device can be altered by increasing the potential of the battery. As the battery potential is raised, the current-limiting and zero-adjust resistor values are increased to permit adjustment at the "0" line. Higher-value resistors can then be read with appropriate scale calibration changes.

15-23. WATT-HOUR METER

The most practical unit of electric energy, where electric power consumption is calculated in terms of time, is the *kilowatt hour*. Thus, the product of power and time indicates electric energy measurement with respect to watt hours. In practical usage, the watt-hour meter shown in Fig. 15-6 provides a continuous indication of the amount of power consumed in terms of time. The four dials register the kilowatt hours of the energy used. They are read periodically and the information is recorded by trained personnel from the power company. The rate per kilowatt hour is then applied by the power company in billing the consumer for the energy used.

The meter constitutes an induction-type device based on the dynamometer principle because the current is induced into the moving system. The latter is an aluminum disk, which is supplied torque by the

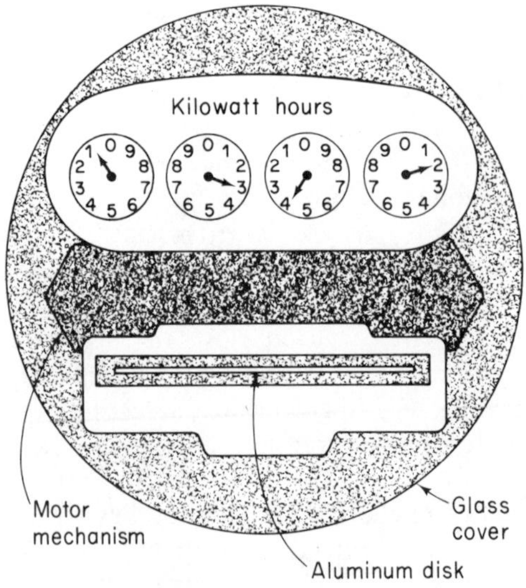

FIGURE 15-6. Watt-hour meter.

energy induced by two electromagnets. One of these, made of heavy wire (in series with the line), provides in-phase flux conditions. The other magnet is wound of fine wire and is connected across the line. This electromagnet, plus an additional coil for phase shifting, provides a 90° current lag. The coil combinations produce the necessary rotating field for turning the disk and hence the assembly resembles a basic motor. The torque in the rotating disk is proportional to the *power*. Permanent magnets are placed close to the disk so that their fields, when picked up by the disk, will produce magnetic currents (*called eddy currents*) in the disk, which in turn produce a torque opposed to the disk rotation. This retarding torque is directly proportional to the disk *speed*, and *the speed becomes proportional to the power consumed by the load*. Precise gears actuate a set of dials which indicate the number of revolutions directly. The amount of power used by the load system will be the difference in meter readings taken over a fixed period of time.

15-24. SPECIAL ELECTRONIC EFFECTS, TERMS, AND DESIGNATIONS

Contact Potential. This term identifies the voltage established by placing into contact two dissimilar metals.

Eccles-Jordan Trigger. A term relating to the circuit also known as the *flip-flop*. It is a bistable device that can be triggered into a logic 1 or a logic 0 state by the application of an input signal.

Edison Effect. The production of current flow between two vacuum-tube elements. Electrons from a heated cathode of negative potential flow to a positive-potential anode structure.

Flywheel Effect. A term designating the continuous interchange of electric energy between the storage capabilities of an inductor and capacitor in a parallel-resonant circuit.

Hall Effect. A term that refers to the voltage developed between the edges of a crystal slab (formed of indium arsenide, for instance) that is subjected to a magnetic field. The voltage develops when current is passed through the crystal structure, and the voltage forms at right angles to the direction of current flow. This developed potential is proportional to the product of the field (H) and the current (A).

Hangover Effect. A term relating to the inability of an audio amplifier-speaker system to reproduce a sharp cut-off tonal characteristic. Instead, the tone's amplitude decays sufficiently to create a hangover beyond its proper termination.

Heterodyne Process. The electronic mixing of two signals of different frequencies in a nonlinear circuit to produce a third signal having a frequency equal to the difference between the original signals. The new signal is also termed the intermediate-frequency (IF) signal.

Hole Flow. Current carriers in semiconductor devices. Hole flow occurs below the conduction band, and the direction of flow is opposite to that of electron flow.

Ionosphere. Ionized layers above the earth's surface that affect high-frequency communications (both reception and transmission). The earlier term was *Kennelly-Heaviside* layer.

Magnetoresistive Effect. This refers to Hall-effect devices wherein the resistive characteristic is altered by the application of a magnetic field.

Magnetostrictive Effect. This term relates to the change in length that occurs when certain metals are magnetized.

Peltier Effect. This refers to a temperature change phenomenon that occurs when current is passed through the junction of a *p-n* semiconductor.

Photoelectric Effect. This designation has reference to the effect of incident light on photo-sensitive materials such as germanium, cesium, and certain semiconductor junctions. For the photoconductive devices a change of light intensity causes a resistance change in the unit. For the photovoltaic types, a potential is generated in proportion to the intensity of the light impinging on it.

Piezoelectric Effect. A term relating to crystals used as transducers that generate a voltage between the crystal faces when placed under physical stress (e.g., when twisted slightly), or vibrate at a specific frequency when electric potentials are applied.

Planck's Constant. This refers to the constant 6.624×10^{-27} that relates energy to the frequency of the initiating signal. In the equation $E = hf$, the amount of E (radiant energy) produced by a signal frequency f multiplied by Planck's constant (h) expresses the difference between two energy levels. Planck's constant thus relates to such phenomena as lasers, masers, fluorescence, and other aspects of quantum physics involving photons.

Resonance. A condition achieved when a system is tuned to a frequency that causes circuit X_L to have an identical ohmic value to circuit X_C. The result is a cancellation of X characteristic effects; and consequently, only R is the predominate circuit factor. Resonance permits tuning to a specific signal frequency and the rejection of undesired signals having frequencies other than that of resonance.

Seebeck Principle. This term relates to the production of a voltage with the heating of the junction of dissimilar metal wires such as constantan and iron wires.

Skin Effect. The tendency for current to flow on the outer surface (skin) of a wire at very high frequency operation. The higher frequency raises the rate of change of the wires' current and magnetic fields, increasing internal inductive reactance.

Standing Waves. The phenomenon that occurs at very high signal frequencies where reflections of signal energy occur along transmission lines, resulting in the formation of loops and nodes of voltage and current at specific places along the line.

Tunnel Effect. This term relates to the solid-state unit known as the tunnel diode. In the tunnel diode the current carriers have the effect of passing through the potential barrier of the semiconductor material with virtually the speed of light—as though they were tunneling beneath the barrier to overcome its transfer-delay characteristics.

Zener Region. A term that has reference to the point reached in a silicon-crystal diode when the reverse voltage reaches an amplitude causing high conduction. During this high-conduction period there is a significant stability of voltage that permits use of the zener diode as a voltage-regulation device.

16

Modulation Data

16-1. AMPLITUDE MODULATION

As was discussed in Chapter 6, Sec. 6-6, a modulator output in series with the dc feed line to a Class C amplifier will produce amplitude modulation of the RF carrier. The rise and fall of the amplitude of the modulated carrier creates a form of sinewave RF signal distortion; hence, signals of other frequencies are generated. (See Sec. 1-3, Chapter 1.) The generated signals are termed *sidebands* and these have frequencies related to the modulating signal. Thus, if the broadcast station carrier frequency is 900 kHz, for instance, and the modulating frequency is 5 kHz, two sidebands are created; one at 905 kHz and the other at 895 kHz. Consequently this particular station would require a bandwidth of 10 kHz to transmit the 5-kHz audio signal. For a 3-kHz modulating signal, the sidebands would consist of an upper one having a frequency of 903 kHz, and a lower one of 897 kHz. If both the 5-kHz and 3-kHz modulating signals are applied simultaneously, there would be four sidebands plus the carrier signal transmitted.

Since the audio-modulating signal does not travel along with the modulated carrier, it is necessary to sense the envelope contour of the modulated signal during detection as discussed in Chapter 6 and illustrated in Fig. 6-10. In amplitude modulation the modulated carrier appears as shown in Fig. 16-1. Part A shows the modulating signal (a sinewave in this instance), and the modulated carrier is shown at B. This amplitude-changing waveshape represents the carrier plus the sidebands. If the individual

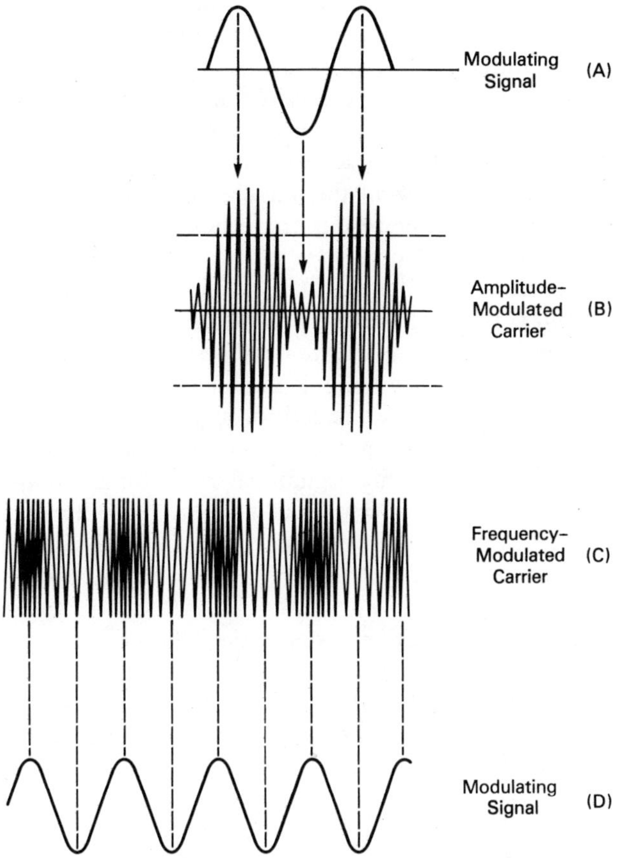

FIGURE 16-1. AM and FM modulated carriers.

sidebands were filtered out of this carrier composite signal, the carrier remaining would be a single-frequency constant-amplitude waveform.

In television broadcasting the picture (video) information is transmitted by the amplitude-modulation process as in public entertainment AM radios and in citizens' band (CB) transmitting/receiving. (See Chapter 7, Sec. 7-1 for public entertainment broadcast listings, and Secs. 7-2 and 7-4.)

16-2. FREQUENCY AND PHASE MODULATION

In the frequency modulation system, the audio-modulating signal causes the carrier to change frequency in relation to the characteristics of the modulating signal. Thus, for one alternation of an ac-modulating signal the RF carrier will shift higher in frequency, while for the next alternation of the modulating signal the carrier shifts to a lower frequency. The rate at which the carrier shifts above and below its normal or resting frequency depends on the frequency of the modulating signal. Thus, if a 4-kHz modulating signal is employed, the RF carrier will shift above and below its resting frequency 4,000 times a second. The *extent* of the RF carrier shift depends on the *amplitude* of the modulating signal. Thus, if a carrier shifts 1.5 kHz each side of the resting frequency for a particular modulating signal, it would shift 2 or 3 kHz each side for an increase in the amplitude of the modulating signal. The relationships between the modulating signal and carrier are shown in parts C and D of Fig. 16-1.

During the frequency-modulation process there are also sidebands generated as was the case for amplitude modulation discussed in Sec. 16-1. In AM, only two sidebands are created for any one modulating signal of single frequency. In FM, however, there is an infinite number of sidebands created for a given modulating signal having a single frequency. An infinite number of sidebands would take up a prohibitive amount of spectrum space. Fortunately, however, only a few of the sidebands generated have sufficient amplitude and energy to be of significance, as shown later in this section.

For frequency modulation systems, the ratio of the frequency shift (also termed *deviation*) of the RF carrier to the frequency of the modulating signal causing such carrier deviation is called the *modulation index*. Another term, the *deviation ratio*, relates to maximum values. In equation form, the modulation index is:

$$m_f = \frac{df_c}{f_m} \tag{16-1}$$

where m_f = modulation index for FM
df_c = frequency deviation of carrier
f_m = frequency of modulating signal.

The deviation ratio relates the maximum deviation of the RF carrier frequency to the highest-frequency modulating signal:

$$\begin{matrix}\text{deviation}\\ \text{ratio}\end{matrix} = \frac{\text{maximum freq. deviation of carrier}}{\text{highest freq. of modulating signal}} \tag{16-2}$$

Equation 16-2 represents the limits of the spectrum span occupied by the carrier shift relative to the highest-frequency audio signal to be used to initiate such a carrier shift. This, then, is a maximum-condition evaluation and is rarely encountered in actual practice because both the frequency and amplitude of the audio modulating signals vary from moment to moment during standard FM broadcasting.

The significant amount of sidebands generated are related to the modulation index. With a modulation index of 5, for instance, there are eight sidebands generated that are of significance during transmitting and reception. Thus, if a musical tone of 4,000 Hz were used to modulate the carrier, there would be 16 sidebands produced (eight above and eight below the resting frequency). Each sideband would be spaced from the adjacent one by 4 kHz (the modulating-signal frequency). The number of significant sidebands for a particular modulation index can be ascertained by using the Bessel functions table shown earlier in Chapter 14 (see Table 14-7).

In addition to public entertainment FM (See Chapter 7), the sound portion of television is also transmitted as FM. A special detector must be used to demodulate the FM carrier as was shown earlier in Chapter 6 (Fig. 6-10). The advantages of FM over AM include a reduction of noise interference and less interference from adjacent stations in the same general broadcasting area. (Because of the high-frequency transmission, distant stations cannot be received under normal conditions.)

There are several ways in which a carrier can be frequency modulated. One system is based on the similarity between AM and FM when the latter has a very low modulation index. As shown by the Bessel function table, at low deviation there are only two sidebands produced, as is the case for AM when a single-frequency modulating signal is used. The difference, however, is that the two sidebands produced in FM during low modulating levels are displaced 90° in relation to the RF carrier. For AM, the two sidebands are in phase relationships to the carrier. Thus, the AM can be converted to FM by displacing the two AM sidebands by 90° in relation to the carrier. This system is referred to as *indirect* FM because the RF carrier is not caused to shift directly by the modulating audio signal. The deviation can be increased by successive stages of frequency multiplication. A simple series resistor-shunt capacitor (termed a predistorter) compensates for the inherent tendency in phase modulation for the carrier to shift to a greater degree for louder signals. (The carrier should only shift to a greater degree for an increase in modulating signal amplitude.) The sidebands can be removed and inserted again by using the balanced modulator-type circuitry covered in Sec. 16-5. (This modulator is also useful for single-sideband production or for subcarrier suppression as must be done for the color subcarrier in television and the multiplexing subcarrier in stereo FM.)

A *direct* system of FM production is shown in Fig. 16-2. Such a system must be capable of permitting the carrier to be shifted by the modulating signal, while at the same time maintaining a stable-frequency

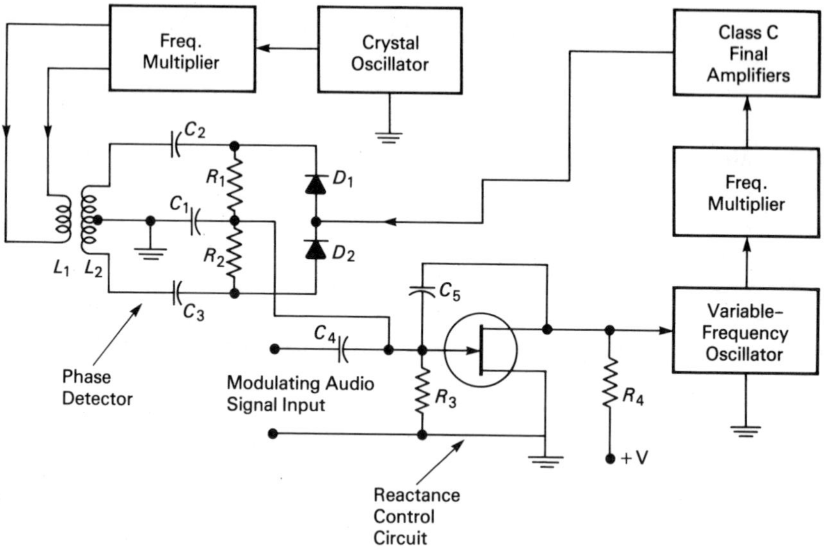

FIGURE 16-2. Production of FM.

carrier at the resting frequency. To do this, both a variable-frequency oscillator and a crystal oscillator are used as shown. The crystal oscillator is a stable fixed-frequency type with its output applied to a frequency multiplier circuit to bring the frequency to that needed for the resting frequency of the carrier. The output from the frequency multiplier is applied to a phase detector system as shown. The phase detector also connects to a reactance-control circuit having the ability to change its reactive characteristics, as was described in Chapter 11 (see Sec. 11-7 and Fig. 11-6). The modulating signal is also applied to the input of the reactance circuit, and the output of this transistor is applied to the variable-frequency oscillator. The reactance transistor circuit forms part of the resonant circuit of the variable-frequency oscillator. Hence, any signal input (whether from the modulator or the phase detector) alters the frequency of the variable-frequency oscillator by changing the resonance. Thus, sound input to the reactance circuit causes the necessary frequency deviations of the RF carrier generated by the variable-frequency oscillator. The output from the latter, in turn, is applied to frequency multipliers and to the final Class C output-amplifier stages as shown.

A sample of the signal is obtained from the output and applied to the phase detector diode junction (D_1 and D_2) as shown. Thus, if the frequency established by the variable-frequency oscillator coincides with that of the crystal oscillator, the phase detector circuit is balanced, just as in the case of a bridge circuit. If the carrier frequency drifts off center, however, it no longer coincides with the frequency of the crystal oscillator, and a correction potential is produced and fed to the reactance circuitry. Thus, the latter alters its reactance (either capacitive or inductive, depending on design) and corrects the frequency shift of the variable-frequency oscillator.

In an actual application, the signal from the output RF amplifiers to the phase detector is filtered to eliminate the rapid deviations caused by the audio modulating signals. Thus, only the slow drift off frequency is sensed by the phase detector. If the rapidly shifting carrier were applied directly to the phase detector, it would nullify the FM production. Capacitor C_4 isolates the dc in the phase detector from the input circuitry of the modulator. Capacitor C_5 and resistor R_3 establish the degree of reactance as was detailed earlier in Chapter 11.

Public-entertainment FM systems utilize a noise reduction process involving the use of a *pre-emphasis* circuit at the transmitter and a *de-emphasis* network at the receiver as shown in Fig. 16-3. Interelement transistor noises as well as circuit noises by other components are usually generated at a fixed level in a given FM system. Hence, the signal-to-noise ratio can be increased by raising the level of the signal over the constant-level noise signals. Because the noise signals generated increase their amplitude with higher-frequency audio signals, the level of the audio-frequency signals is raised at an increasing rate for higher-frequency signals (pre-emphasis) in the circuit of Fig. 16-3A.

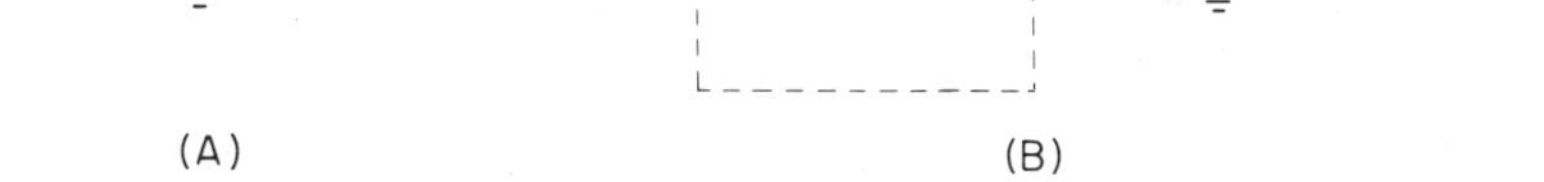

FIGURE 16-3. Pre-emphasis and de-emphasis.

The Federal Communications Commission (FCC) has set the rate of incline for the pre-emphasis process. The rise in the amplitude above the normal value for the audio signals begins at about 400 Hz and rises gradually: at 1,000 Hz the increase is 1 dB; at 1.5 kHz the increase is almost 2 dB. At 2 kHz the amplitude rise is approximately 3 dB; and at 2.5 kHz there is almost a 4-dB increase. From this point on, the increase is virtually linear, reaching 8 dB for a 5-kHz audio signal and 17 dB for a

15-kHz signal. The time constant for the RC pre-emphasis network is 75 microseconds (μs); that is, $RC = 75 \times 10^{-6}$s. This produces optimum results without excessive increase of frequency deviation because of the increase of signal amplitude at the higher-frequency signals.

At the receiver it is necessary to de-emphasize the rise of the amplitude of the higher-frequency signals to prevent shrill and harsh high-frequency audio response. A simple series resistor and a shunting capacitor is used, as shown in Fig. 16-3B, with the same time constant, i.e., 75 μs, provides for an increasingly lower reactance in the shunt capacitor for higher-frequency signals. This effectively decreases the amplitude of the signals.

A later pre-emphasis system that has also been included in FM broadcasting is one using the Dolby noise-reduction principle. Its adoption was brought about because of the widely used Dolby-B noise-reduction system in stereo cassette tape recorders and tape decks. For such tape systems the Dolby circuitry is usually encapsulated within an IC and thus becomes an integral part of the tape circuitry. During the recording process the high-frequency, low-amplitude music signal levels are altered by successive boosting to a degree related to amplitude. Essentially, the system thus lifts the noise-prone higher-frequency signals above the constant-level noise signals. Upon playback, a decoding circuit within the Dolby IC reverses the signal amplitude rise process and thus decreases the signals to their normal levels. By this procedure, the usual tape background noises such as high-frequency hiss are reduced—often by as much as 10 dB.

With the standard pre-emphasis process used in FM broadcasting, there is a tendency for the bandwidth to increase because of the greater carrier deviation when the high-frequency signals are raised in amplitude. In Europe the pre-emphasis process uses a less objectionable 50-μs time constant. For high-fidelity transmission, however, the wide band audio-frequency response desired still poses some problems. Hence, stations often utilize compression circuitry or employ automatic peak-limiting devices to prevent excessive bandwidths. With the addition of the Dolby system, the selected pre-emphasis and de-emphasis was reduced to 25 μs. This was found to be suitable for the noise reduction broadcast system, but it requires a special decoder within the receiver for obtaining best results in noise reduction. If a receiver is tuned to a station using the Dolby system, but the receiver does not have the necessary decoder system, the high tones of the reproduced music will be altered noticeably. For receivers properly equipped with the decoding network, a switch is available for selection of either the 75-μs or the 25-μs de-emphasis system decoded by the built-in Dolby circuitry.

16-3. PULSE MODULATION SYSTEMS

There are several systems utilizing pulses and modifying their amplitude, width, or position in accordance with the waveform of the modulating signal. One system is known as *pulse-amplitude modulation* (PAM). In this system, the amplitude of a series of pulses is raised or lowered in accordance with the modulating signal, as shown in Fig. 16-4. For the modulating signal shown in Fig. 16-4A, two pulse amplitude systems can be employed. In that shown in part B, both positive and negative pulses are used, with a positive pulse peak being reached at the peak of the positive alternation of the modulating signal, and the negative peak reached for the second alternation of the modulating signal, as shown. In the second system shown in Fig. 16-4C, maximum pulse height is reached for the positive peak of the modulating signal, while the lowest pulse amplitude occurs at the negative peak of the second alternation of the modulating signal.

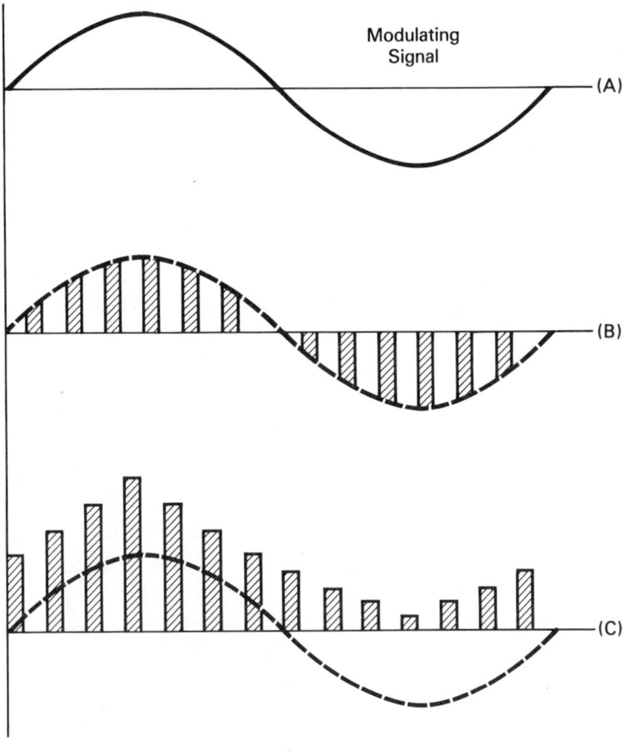

FIGURE 16-4. Pulse amplitude modulation types.

The system known as *pulse position modulation* (PPM) is shown in Fig. 16-5. This has also been referred to as *pulse time modulation* (PTM) because changes in the amplitude of the modulating signal cause a change in the pulses' position in time. The time change can relate to the time interval between pulses or to the time a pulse occurs in relation to a fixed marker pulse position. For the latter, one of each pair of pulses shown in Fig. 16-5 would be in a fixed position, such as directly below the dashed vertical position lines shown.

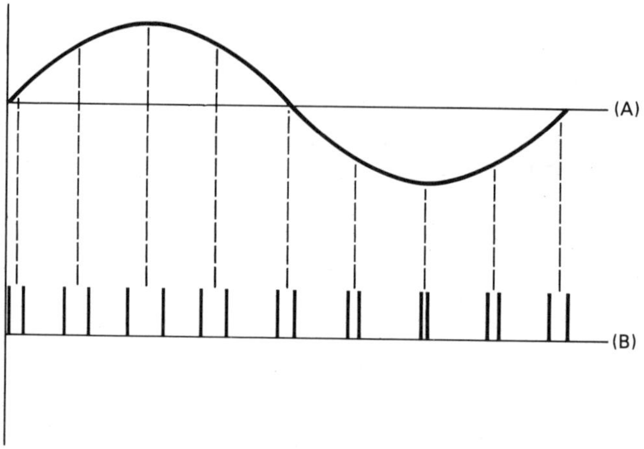

FIGURE 16-5. Pulse position modulation.

The *pulse-duration modulation* (PDM) system is shown in Fig. 16-6. This system is also known as the *pulse-width modulation* (PWM) system because the width of each pulse is progressively altered to conform to the amplitude of the modulating signal (as shown in Fig. 16-6A and B). Because the pulses have a fixed amplitude, any noise signals that accompany the transmitted energy can be removed by amplitude limiters or clippers at the receiver. As with other pulse-modulation systems the employment of narrow pulses of very short duration permits the inclusion of additional pulse transmissions by insertion of the second pulses between the original ones. This increases the number of information channels and aids in reducing spectrum space. For the pulses shown in part B of Fig. 16-6, wider than normal pulses are shown for convenience in illustrating the method. Also, in actual systems, many more pulses would be utilized per modulating cycle than illustrated.

For the pulse-width systems, the modulation can vary either the leading edge (initial edge) of the pulse, or the trailing edge. When the train of pulses shown in Fig. 16-6B is applied to an integrator circuit, the

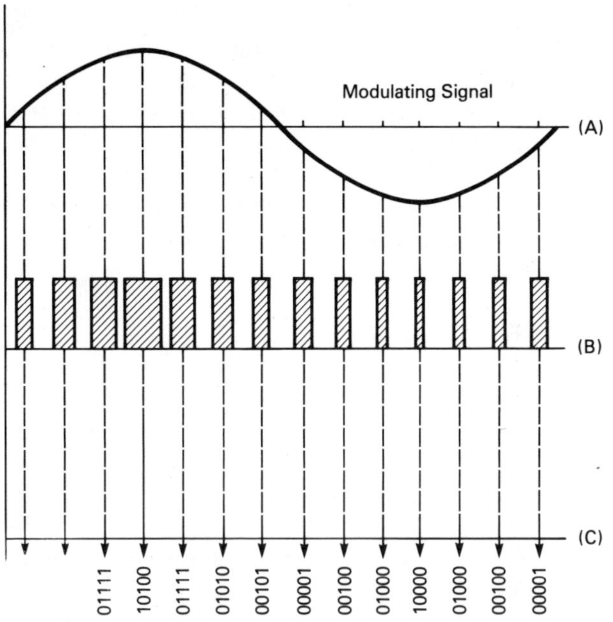

FIGURE 16-6. Pulse width and pulse code modulation.

demodulation process occurs. This was illustrated earlier in Fig. 6-11C and D, where the pulse amplitude modulation system was illustrated regarding the discussion of Class D amplification in Sec. 6-8.

The *pulse-code modulation* (PCM) system is illustrated in Fig. 16-6C, where amplitude variations in the modulating signal are converted to a set of pulses that, in binary form, represents a specific amplitude. The binary numbers shown beneath the vertical dashed lines represent the particular pulse positions present to form the binary number needed. Thus, the number 01010 represents only two pulses (since the 1's only indicate pulses). This modulation process requires several sequential operations, including the sampling of the modulating signal at a predetermined rate. Because of the amplitude changes of the modulating signal, the train of pulses also has variations in height.

The pulses obtained by the process have their amplitude compared to a selected scale of discrete levels, and each pulse is assigned a value that corresponds to the closest found by the comparison process. This procedure is termed *quantizing* and the values that are thus obtained are translated into a pulse code. The usual code selected is the *binary* (base 2) used extensively in digital electronics. This feature, as well as the minimum influence of noise or signal attenuation encountered with this method of pulse modulation, has made this a practical and widely used system.

In pulse-code modulation the number of amplitude levels that can be sampled for a single alternation of the modulating signal depends on the maximum number of pulses used in the code group. With a three-pulse maximum only 7 amplitude variations can be referenced, unless 000 is also used, in which case 8 are available. For a code group of four pulses, 16 levels can be sampled (from 0 to 15 or, in binary form, from 0000 to 1111). Binary vs. base-ten listings will be found in Table 14-12.

16-4. TELEMETRY, FDM, AND TDM

In modern electronic practices, telemetering utilizes several special modulating systems for the transmission of information. Essentially the gathering of data is achieved by the measurement and sensing of data by transducers such as pressure-sensitive devices, speed indicators, temperature-reading units, and light-sensitive components. The changes sensed are basically analog functions and are converted into a representative quantity for use in the modulation process.

Telemetry utilizes multiplexing, and the system permits the transmission of various data (including voice transmissions) in industrial-control applications, space exploration devices, and other similar services. One system is known as *frequency-division multiplexing* (FDM). This procedure uses several frequency bands to transmit two or more modulating signals. In addition to a primary RF carrier, separate subcarriers are used and these, in turn, modulate the primary carrier. (This procedure is used in stereo FM, where a subcarrier is used in a multiplexing process and then suppressed. At the receiver a special signal generator must form the subcarrier before demodulation can be obtained. Color television also utilizes a color subcarrier to form the color signals, and again the subcarrier is suppressed. At the receiver, the subcarrier must be reformed. This subject is discussed more fully in Sec. 16-6.)

The frequency-division multiplexing system has been used extensively for increasing the capacity of cable or radio-link devices in international telephone applications. Some problems are often encountered with this system in areas of intermodulation and the presence of undesired noise signals. Hence, the pulse modulation systems described earlier in this chapter are often preferred.

Time division multiplexing (TDM) is a system that is capable of transmitting two or more signals by allocating each a finite time interval. Instantaneous amplitudes of the various signals are sampled and transmitted in a time sequence and repeated after the last signal has been sampled. Any of the pulse modulation types previously described in this chapter can be used. If the sampling rate is high (such as 8000/*s*), only negligible signal information is lost, even for voice waveforms. Each channel transmission is subsequently decoded separately to provide the original signal data used for the original modulation process.

16-5. BALANCED MODULATOR

Balanced modulators are useful for generating certain signal components, while suppressing others. Thus, the balanced modulator is of value in communication systems for modulating the carrier to produce sidebands, then suppressing the carrier itself. As a result, only the sideband signals are obtained from the output of the balanced modulators. In single-sideband transmissions, a filter follows the balanced modulator to remove one of the two sidebands. In stereo FM and in color television, the sidebands that are produced are utilized, but the carrier is no longer needed and hence is suppressed because of spectrum space requirements. Actually, the stereo sidebands in FM and the color sidebands are generated by modulating a *subcarrier*. During the demodulation process the receiver must generate the missing carrier so the sidebands can be rejoined with the carrier for proper detection.

A typical balanced modulator is shown in Fig. 16-7, and two *pnp* transistors are used. The *npn* types can be used if accompanied by reversal of supply potentials. Note that the RF carrier signal is injected in series with both the supply potential and the center tap of the input transformer L_2. Thus, the RF input signal is applied in phase to both base elements of Q_1 and Q_2. Hence, for a single RF signal alternation across L_3, both base elements undergo the same forward-bias change. Consequently, if the voltage across L_3 opposes the negative forward bias, the resultant decrease in bias also will cause a decrease in the current in both collector-emitter

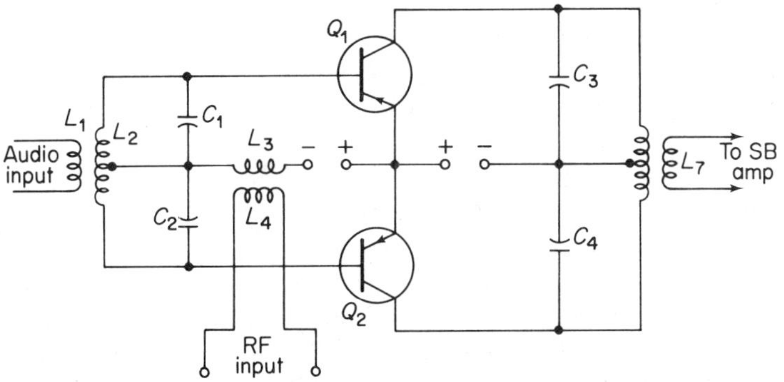

FIGURE 16-7. Balanced modulator.

circuits. Since the collectors are connected for push-pull operation, current changes in L_5 and L_6 will be equal, but will have opposing polarities. Thus, cancellation occurs for such current changes representative of the RF signal. (A balanced circuit, with matched characteristics for Q_1 and Q_2, is essential.)

The audio signals that develop across L_2 appear at the base inputs of Q_1 and Q_2 out of phase by 180° because of the split secondary winding. Thus, at the input the signals have voltage relationships as follows for the carrier (E_c) and the modulating voltage (E_m) respectively:

$$E(\text{base of } Q_1) = E_c \cos \omega t + E_m \cos \omega t \tag{16-3}$$

$$E(\text{base of } Q_2) = E_c \cos \omega t - E_m \cos \omega t \tag{16-4}$$

Because the audio signals cause changes in collector-current flow, the carrier-frequency currents within each transistor undergo modulation. Thus, sidebands are produced, which find resonant circuits in the output (C_3 and L_5 for Q_1; C_4 and L_6 for Q_2). These resonant circuits offer a low impedance for audio signals and thus minimize their appearance at the output. Since the carrier has been suppressed, only sideband signal energy is obtained from the balanced modulation system.

Capacitors C_1 and C_2 at the input have a low reactance for the RF signal energy and thus provide coupling to the transistor base inputs. For the audio signal appearing across L_2, however, these capacitors have a very high reactance and hence offer virtually no shunting effect.

16-6. PLL SUBCARRIER GENERATOR

As mentioned in earlier sections of this chapter, in multiplexing modulation practices a subcarrier is used to generate necessary signals (such as in stereo FM or color TV), but to conserve spectrum space, the subcarrier is not transmitted. Instead, it is suppressed at the transmitter by circuits such as the balanced modulator shown in Fig. 16-7. The sidebands that are produced by modulation of the subcarrier are transmitted, but cannot be demodulated unless the missing subcarrier is recombined with them. Consequently, at the receiver, it is necessary to generate a signal having the same frequency as the original subcarrier. The new subcarrier is then rejoined with the sidebands and demodulated.

A typical subcarrier signal generator system is shown in Fig. 16-8, and this is the type used in color television receivers. The subcarrier for color television is 3.58 MHz (actually 3.579545 as indicated in Chapter 7, Sec. 7-3), and a crystal oscillator is used as shown. Since true color

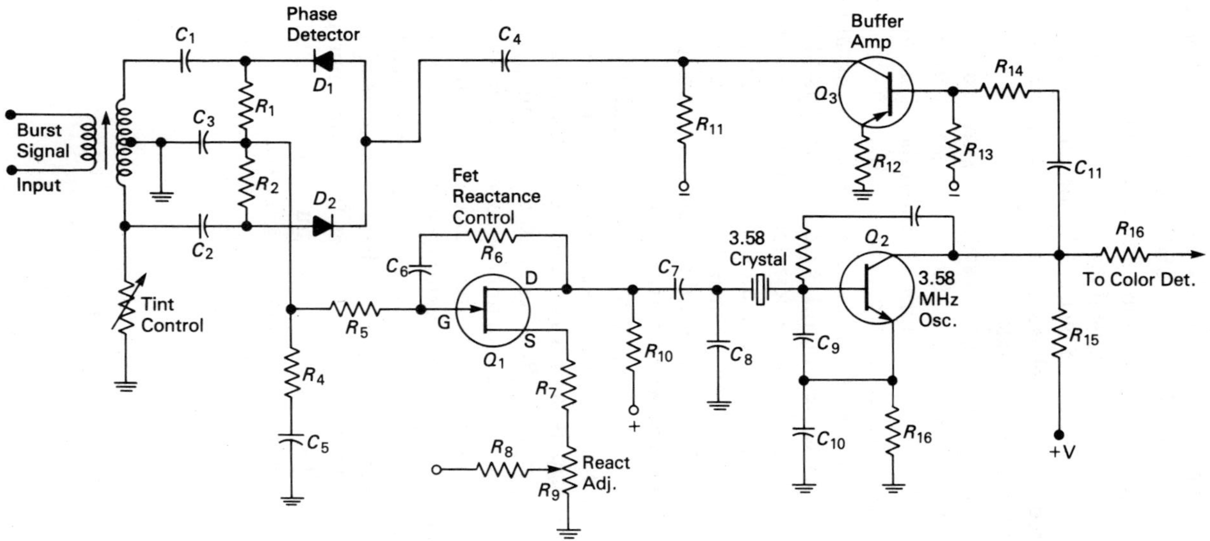

FIGURE 16-8. PLL Subcarrier generator.

rendition requires careful phase relationships between the signals, a crystal oscillator alone is inadequate, even though it maintains precise control over drift. To assure exact frequency and phase control, the transmitter sends out a synchronizing signal consisting of approximately eight cycles (termed a *burst*) mounted on the blanking pulses that are also transmitted. This burst signal is applied to the phase detector network, as shown in Fig. 16-8, where its frequency and phase are compared to the signal generated by the 3.58-MHz subcarrier oscillator.

Note that the output from the oscillator is sent to the color detectors, but capacitor C_{11} also couples the output signal to the input of a buffer amplifier, and the latter, in turn, channels the signal to the junction of the phase detector diodes. If the two signals coincide in phase and frequency, a static condition prevails and no correction signal is felt at the gate input of the reactance control FET. If the 3.58-MHz subcarrier oscillator drifts, however, the phase detector applies a correction potential to the input of the reactance control, and the change of reactance is felt at the input of the crystal oscillator. Since the reactance change at the input of this oscillator alters the resonance, the frequency is changed to synchronize with the incoming 3.58-MHz burst signal.

The circuit shown in Fig. 16-8 closely resembles the FM-transmitting circuitry shown earlier in Fig. 16-2. In both circuits, a comparison is made between two signals, and a reactance circuit is used for frequency and phase control purposes. Both circuits are essentially phase locked loops (PLL), since there is a continuous circuit loop from the phase detector around the system via the reactance control and the controlled oscillator, with the output from the latter going back to the phase detector. For the system shown in Fig. 16-8, the variable controls relate to the color system. Thus, a variable resistor in the phase detector section alters phase relationships sufficiently to affect color tint for control purposes. A variable resistor in the FET source circuit adjusts the characteristics of the reactance circuit for optimum center-range characteristics.

Index

A

Admittance, 65
Allocations (broadcast), 145
Alternating current, 1
  effective, 245
  peak, 245
  phase, 230
  power, 235
  three-phase, 236
Alternation, 1
Amateur radio, 154
Amplifiers,
  classes, 130, 142
  complementary-symmetry, 135
  D type, 142
  intermediate frequency, 136
  load lines, 123
  power, 126
  push-pull, 132
  R-F, 136
  stereo, 180
  video, 138
Amplitude modulation, 139
AND gate, 166
Angular velocity, 47
Antennas, 196
  coupling, 219
  field intensity, 226

Antennas *(Contd.)*
  gain and Z, 227
  horn type, 224
  length, 216
  line, 219
  parabolic, 224
  patterns, 213
  polarization, 214
  reciprocity, 212
  reflectors, 224
  stacking, 222
  waveguide, 224
  Yagi, 221
Antiskate, 277
Atomic weights, 260
Attenuators, 82
Average values, 245

B

Bessel functions, 263
Binary, 157
  coded decimal, 270
  comparisons, 269
  complement, 160
  powers, 268
  table, 267
Bridge circuits, 98
Broadcast allocations, 145

C

Capacitance, 42
  reactance, 47
Capacitor
  codes, 21
  series-parallel, 73
  unit, 42
Capture ratio, 274
Cartridge, 278
Cassette, 278
Charge, 36
Citizens band, 153
Coaxial cable, 197, 206
Coil (*see* Inductance)
Color codes, 20
Complementary symmetry, 135
Compliance, 278
Composite signal, 231
Concentric line, 197
Conductance, 37
Constant power dissipation, 124
Contact potential, 301
Conversion table, 259, 265, 288
Converter, 190
Copper wire table, 264
Coulomb, 36, 43
Coupling
  coefficient, 75
  coils, 75
  transformer, 58, 60
Cryogenic data, 284
Current, 36
  meter ranges, 296

D

Damping factor, 275
Decibels, 28
Deemphasis, 309
Delay line, 212
Delta wiring, 237
Detectors (demodulator), 140, 181
Deviation ratio, 306
Diamagnetic, 41
Dielectric constants, 290
Differentiation, 81
Digital
  circuits, 163, 169
Digital *(Contd.)*
  gates, 166
  logic, 154, 166
Distortion, 1
  harmonic, 275
  types, 5
Dual trace, 9
Dyne, 31

E

Eccles-Jordan, 301
Edison effect, 301
Effective values, 245
Electromotive force (emf), 36
Exclusive OR, 170
Exponential functions, 44, 46

F

Farad, 43
Ferromagnetic, 41
Field effect transistors, 108, 136, 175, 187, 192
Fifty dB quieting, 275
Filters, 89, 205
Flip flop, 163, 171, 301
Flux, 39
Flywheel effect, 301
Forward current ratio, 105, 107
Frequency, 34
  effects on LCR, 294
  modulation, 304
  ranges, 292
  response, 275
  spectrum, 279
  table of tones, 267
Full wave, 9, 185

G

Generator, 233
Gilbert, 58
Greek alphabet, 291

H

Half-power frequencies, 78
Half wave, 8, 184
Hall effect, 301

Harmonics, 4
  distortion, 275
Henry, 51
Hertz, 1, 34
Heterodyne, 302
High fidelity terms, 274
  hangover effect, 301
  phonograph, 277
  tape, 278
High voltage, 194
Holography data, 283

I

IF amplifier, 136
IHF sensitivity, 276
Image rejection, 276
Impedance, 38, 48, 54, 56
  antenna, 227
  characteristic *Z*, 198
  matching, 210
Inductor
  mutual, 75
  reactance, 54
  reactor, 58
  series-parallel, 74
  unit, 50
Integrated circuits, 172
  fabrication, 174
  symbols, 178
Integration, 79
International System units, 25
Ion data, 285
  ionsphere, 302

J

j operator, 62
JFET, 109
joule, 38, 43

K

Kirchhoff's laws, 71

L

Lasar data, 280
Linear circuits, 130
Load line, 123
Logarithms, 248

M

m-derived, 91
Magnetism, 39
Magnetomotive force, 58
Magnetoresistive, 302
Magnetostrictive, 302
Marconi antenna, 215
Maser data, 280
Mathematics
  constants, 290
  RCL calculations, 293
  symbols, 290
Mixer, 190
Modulation, 139, 304
  balanced, 315
  index, 306
  pulse, 311
  subcarrier, 316
Morse code, 155
MOSFET, 110

N

NAND gates, 167
Nepers, 28
Neutralization, 136, 139
NOR gates, 167
Norton's theorem, 73
Number systems, 162

O

Octal table, 269
Ohm
  law, 37
  meter, 299
OR gate, 166
Oscillator, 187
  crystal, 187
  relaxation, 188
  UHF type, 207
  variable, 188
Oscilloscope, 8

P

Pads, 82
Parabolic antenna, 224
Paramagnetic, 41
Parameters, 115, 119
Peak values, 245
Peltier effect, 302
Permeability, 40
Phase, 1
  color TV, 152
  inversion, 134
  modulation, 304
  notation, 239
  relationships, 229
Phasors, 230
Phonograph
  terms, 277
Photoelectric effect, 302
Piezoelectric, 302
Planck's constant, 280, 302
Plasma data, 285
Power, 32
  amplifiers, 126
  binary, 268
  dissipation, 124
  factor, 38
  in ac circuits, 238
  output rating, 276
  supplies, 184, 194
Preemphasis, 309
Prefixes, 32
Push pull, 132

R

Radian, 229
Radio frequency (RF), 34
  amplifiers, 136
  lines, 196
  modulation, 304
  neutralization, 136, 139
Reactance
  capacitive, 47
  inductive, 54
  L-C, 67
  lines, 203
  varactor, 191
Rectangular notation, 62
Reactor (*see* Inductor)
Reflectors, 224
Regulation, 186
Relaxation oscillator, 188
Reluctance, 40
Resistance, 37
  of metals, 295
  (*see also* Resistor)
Resistor
  codes, 20
  series and parallel, 69
  standard values, 256
  unit, 37
Resonance, 66
  effect, 302
  frequency table, 257
  lines, 207
Roman numerals, 289

S

Scalars, 230
Seebeck principle, 302
Selectivity, 77, 277
SI (International System), 25
Sidebands, 304
Signals 1,
  composite, 231
  data, 150
  noise ratio, 277
  scope patterns, 8
  variations, 6
  waveform addition, 231
Sinewave, 1
  addition of waveforms, 231
  wavelength, 35
Skin effect, 208, 303
Sound levels, 293
Squares, cubes, and roots, 271
Standing waves, 201, 303
  measurement, 210
Stereo
  separation, 277
Subcarrier, 316
Susceptance, 65
Symbols, 11
  diode, 17
  IGFET, 18

Symbols *(Contd.)*
letter, 33
miscellaneous, 18
transistor, 17

T

Tables, 250
listings, 247
Tape factors, 278
Telementry, 314
Television
allocations, 145
circuitry, 182
color factors, 151
signal data, 150
video amplifiers, 138
Terms, 25
Thevenin's theorem, 72
Time constants, 42, 50
Tone control, 83
Tracking force, 278
Transconductance, 114
Transformers, 58
mutual inductance, 75
three-phase, 244
turns ration, 60
Transistors, 104, 175
FET, 108, 175
hole flow, 302
load line, 123
parameters, 115, 119
power dissipation, 124
transfer characteristics, 113
Transmission lines, 196
Trigonometric factors, 253
ratios, 254
Truth tables, 167
Tunnel effect, 303
Turns ratio, 60

U

Unilateralization, 136
Units,
admittance, 65
capacitance, 42
cgs, 27

Units *(Contd.)*
charge, 36
conductance, 37
conversion table, 259, 265
current, 36
farad, 43
flux, 40
gilbert, 58
henry, 51
impedance, 38
joule, 38, 43
magnetism, 39, 58
mks, 27
permeability, 40, 51
power, 32
resistance, 37
SI, 25
susceptance, 65
thermal, 295
voltage, 36

V

Varactor, 191
tuning system, 193
Vectors, 229
Velocity, 34
Video amplifiers, 138
Voltage, 36
meter ranges, 298
VU (volume units), 31

W

Watt
meter, 300
second, 38
Waveguides, 224
Wavelength, 34
Weights and measures, 286
Wire table, 264
Wye connections, 237

Y

Yagi antenna, 221

Z

Zener region, 303

$$e = \frac{it}{c}$$